RUSSELL M.
NELSON

RUSSELL M. NELSON

FATHER · SURGEON · APOSTLE

SPENCER J. CONDIE

DESERET
BOOK

SALT LAKE CITY, UTAH

Library of Congress Cataloging-in-Publication Data

Condie, Spencer J.
    Russell M. Nelson : father, surgeon, apostle / Spencer J. Condie.
    p.   cm.
    Includes bibliographical references and index.
    ISBN 1-57008-947-7 (hardbound : alk. paper)
    1. Nelson, Russell Marion.   2. Surgeons—Utah—Biography.   3. Mormons—Biography.   I. Title.

BX8695.N42C66 2003
289.3'092—dc21   2003000160

Printed in the United States of America   54459-6986
Malloy Lithographing Incorporated, Ann Arbor, MI

10   9   8   7   6   5   4   3   2   1

To Dantzel
Elder Russell M. Nelson's
wonderful wife
caring confidante
courageous companion
faithful friend

CONTENTS

PREFACE

EIGHTEEN YEARS AFTER HE "left his net" as a surgeon to become an Apostle of the Lord Jesus Christ, Elder Russell M. Nelson was honored by the American Heart Association with its 2002 Gold Heart Award for his many achievements and contributions.[1] All three members of the First Presidency attended the April 2002 ceremonies to honor their esteemed associate.

President Gordon B. Hinckley, in his inimitable, eloquent way, paid the following tribute to Elder Nelson:

"You are a man of tremendous energy. I have traveled with you. You have not spared yourself in following where a sense of duty led you.

"You are a man of great learning, recognized over the world for your medical skills. You have literally given life to thousands of people who must forever be grateful to you.

"Your achievements in medicine are so very many, and your contributions have been so remarkable that we cannot possibly enumerate them.

"You are a pioneer, a member of the first team in performing open-heart surgery at the University of Minnesota in 1951. You were the first to perform this surgery in the state of Utah in 1955.

"You are a man of remarkable skills, a great teacher and a great practitioner. You have gone across the earth imparting your skills to surgeons in many lands. Not content with demonstrating procedures to others, you have learned their languages. You speak French, Russian, Spanish, and Chinese. I have listened to you and have been amazed with your fluency.

"You are a man of great faith. I have heard you pray. I have heard you give the wisdom of scripture. I have seen you speak to large congregations who have hungered for your words. Through faith you have moved ever forward and upward in the remarkable course of your life.

"You are a man of humility. You have recognized a power beyond your own. You have looked to the Almighty for help, for understanding, for direction. You have been a magnificent witness of the Lord Jesus Christ, whom you serve with such devotion.

"You are a husband to a remarkable woman. Your beloved Dantzel has been the polar star of your life. What a treasure she is. You are the father of a wonderful family where love and appreciation reign.

"You are, Russell, a dear friend whom we cherish, whom we respect, whom we honor, whom we love.

"May God bless you as you now are honored, and may He bless you in all the years to come."[2]

In March 2001, when I received the invitation to write Elder Nelson's biography, I was stunned. I immediately questioned whether it was possible for a sparrow who has spent most of his life perched on the rafters of a barn to adequately capture the life of an eagle who has soared to the lofty heights of his profession, his apostolic ministry, and his most important calling, that of father.

As I began sifting through stacks of daily records, speeches, and transcripts of interviews, I began to sense the imperative nature of the task. The urgency of this undertaking was not just in writing of Elder Nelson's *life* but also in presenting to a needy world the lessons from his and Dantzel's *way of life*.

The Lord revealed, "I will give unto you a *pattern in all things,* that ye may not be deceived" (D&C 52:14; emphasis added). The world has all but lost the pattern—the pattern of families living "after the manner of happiness" (2 Nephi 5:27). What were once unthinkable thoughts and unspeakable deeds a generation ago have become common topics of discussion and frequent objects of legislation that undermine the sanctity of the traditional family.

The First Presidency and the Quorum of the Twelve Apostles have sought to rescue and reestablish this pattern by, among other things, publishing *The Family: A Proclamation to the World.* The heart of the family pattern is the great plan of happiness, and at the heart of one great family are a heart surgeon and his eternal companion. That is why, as this project progressed, it became less of a biography in the strictest sense and more of a handbook for happiness.

The importance and eternal nature of the family was emphasized on the evening of September 21, 1823, when the angel Moroni appeared to the young Joseph Smith. Moroni informed him that the prophet Elijah would return to earth to "plant in the hearts of the children the promises made to the fathers, and the hearts of the children shall turn to their fathers." Without this, "the whole earth would be utterly wasted" (D&C 2:2–3).

Elder Nelson has testified, "Grand as it is, planet Earth is part of something even grander—that great plan of God. Simply summarized, the earth was created that families might be. Scripture explains that a husband and wife 'shall be one flesh, and all this that the earth might answer the end of its creation.'"[3] Elder and Sister Nelson understand well Nephi's declaration: "Behold, the Lord hath created the earth that it should be inhabited; and he hath created his children that they should possess it" (1 Nephi 17:36).

Few men live lives that reflect a greater appreciation for and a better understanding of the great plan of happiness than does Elder Nelson. As a devoted husband to his beloved Dantzel, as a loving father of nine daughters and one son, and as a doting grandfather of fifty-four grandchildren and eight great-grandchildren (with more coming), he has enjoyed the rich rewards of living after the manner of happiness. He has reaped a bounteous harvest indeed!

Elder Nelson gave his heart to Dantzel White half a century ago. Their hearts, in the intervening years, have been captured by their children and grandchildren. How perfectly natural it is that such a man as Russell M. Nelson would become a heart surgeon who spent his days repairing and strengthening diseased and defective hearts, and an Apostle who spends his ministry blessing and healing bruised and broken hearts.

As I interviewed President James E. Faust for this biography, he counseled, "Make Russell the great human being he is, not just a great scholar-surgeon. You must capture his great soul and great heart."[4]

This I have humbly tried to do. In order to observe Elder and Sister Nelson in their home environment, one Monday evening in May 2001 my wife and I were invited to participate in the monthly Nelson extended family home evening and birthday party. The monthly venue rotates among the homes of the married children, all of whom reside in the Salt Lake Valley. This Monday evening's activities were held at the Irion home in Murray. Dr. Richard Irion is married to the Nelsons' daughter Gloria, and they have seven children.

When we arrived, the good doctor was draped in a large chef's apron rather than in an obstetrical gown, notwithstanding that he had delivered two babies earlier in the day and would soon be delivering a third. Rich was busily barbecuing, and the cousins and their parents were enjoying themselves either playing volleyball in the backyard, swimming in the pool, or seeing how many grandchildren could fit in the hot tub.

It was not surprising to see Elder Nelson give each of his daughters a gentle kiss as they arrived, but one would not have anticipated that his sons-in-law would also receive a kiss from the family patriarch. Indeed, from the love expressed in this family, it is difficult to discern who are the biological offspring and who are the in-laws.

At last the time arrived for bringing out the monthly birthday cake. The large 1½-by-2-foot rectangular cake was adorned with beautiful frosting, the left side decorated in a yellow congratulatory message recognizing various wedding anniversaries that month. The right side of the cake was scrolled in scrumptious red writing extending birthday wishes to all those born in May. As the cue was given, everyone sang the family's happy birthday/anniversary song, the final phrase punctuated by a deep breath in order to finish with "happy birthday dear Brad, Spencer, Dick, Matthew, Ricky, and Aunt Enid. Happy birthday to you."

During the course of the evening, Elder Nelson took photos of the cake and of those celebrating birthdays and anniversaries. Later, he and Dantzel distributed those photos to each family for their records.

While driving home, we couldn't help but think of the words from Proverbs 17:6: "Children's children are the crown of old men; and the glory of children are their fathers."

ACKNOWLEDGMENTS

IT IS IMPOSSIBLE TO THANK everyone who has significantly contributed to this biography, but I do wish to thank the Brethren, family members, friends, and professional colleagues who generously granted their time for interviews and for sharing helpful insights along the way.

The Apostle John concluded his gospel with this disclaimer: "And there are also many other things which Jesus did, the which, if they should be written every one, I suppose that even the world itself could not contain the books that should be written" (John 21:25). An insightful student of the scriptures has asserted that one reason John made this statement is that the Savior's life history contains not only an account of the creation of "worlds without number" (Moses 1:33) but also the history of each of *our* lives, which are touched and changed as we come unto Him.[1] In a similar vein, though it would be desirable to discuss all the individuals and events involved in Elder Nelson's family life, medical career, and ministry in great detail, wisdom dictates that several significant persons and inspiring experiences be glossed over for the sake of brevity.

Sister Kathleen Moultrie deserves special thanks for her patience in making revisions to numerous drafts of this biography. I am also grateful for her candid comments and encouragement. After typing the chapter titled "Living after the Manner of Happiness," she said,

"Every young married couple ought to read that chapter." On another occasion, I returned to my office to see Kathleen in tears. When I asked if I could help alleviate her distress, she said, "No, I'm just finishing the chapter on 'The Refiner's Fire.'" Elder Nelson's secretary, Bonnie Marchant, has also been extremely helpful in providing any information I requested.

Jennifer St. Clair and Carol Johnson of the Church History Library deserve special thanks for their assistance in locating various original sources and in verifying references. John L. Hart of the *Church News* kindly provided several articles and photographs, and Bruce Pearson of the Church's Visual Resources Library generously obtained additional photographs. Jed Clark deserves thanks for improving the clarity of certain photographs.

I am grateful to Sheri Dew, president of Deseret Book, for her encouragement from beginning to end. I also appreciate the quiet reassurance of Cory Maxwell throughout the project, and I wish to thank Michael Morris for his editing and helpful suggestions.

I express my gratitude to Elder Russell M. Nelson for his patience during our regular interviews over the course of the past two years. Most of the significant biographical events prior to his calling as an Apostle were documented in his autobiography, *From Heart to Heart.* I have borrowed generously from that source to describe events prior to 1979. With Elder Nelson's permission, I have made minor editorial modifications to that original source to facilitate brevity and a smooth transition to the present time. Chapters 35, 38, and 39, based on published teachings by Elder Nelson, have also undergone slight modification as appropriate for a different audience.

I also express generous gratitude to my eternal companion, Dorothea, for her patience with this project.

CHAPTER 1

GATHERING TO EPHRAIM

THE SUMMER OF 2000 PROVIDED a double honor for Elder Russell M. Nelson and his wife, Dantzel. Their first honor was an invitation by the Saints in Sweden and Denmark to participate in the sesquicentennial commemoration of the introduction of the gospel to Scandinavia by Elder Erastus Snow in June 1850. The second honor was an invitation for Elder Nelson to represent the United States as the main speaker at the annual Rebild Festival, held in northern Denmark near Ålborg.

The Rebild Festival is the largest celebration of American independence outside the United States.[1] The festival, held each Fourth of July, features elaborate festivities, during which a distinguished American citizen delivers the keynote address. The program also includes rousing instrumental music performed by an American military band and the singing of "The Star Spangled Banner," "America the Beautiful," and "God Bless America."

As part of the festivities, Elder Nelson presided at the unveiling of a large statue, *Family*, representing a Danish family preparing to immigrate to America and symbolizing the eighteen thousand Danes who left their native land between 1850 and 1900.[2] Then, speaking from a podium centrally located among the lush green hills surrounding Rebild, Elder Nelson addressed an appreciative audience of about fifteen thousand Danes who had an obvious affection

1

Elder and Sister Nelson in the churchyard in Gørding, Ribe County, Denmark. Russell's great-grandmother Margrethe Christensen Nielsen was christened in this church.

for America and Americans. In his values-oriented address, he stressed the importance of striving to do good and of reaching one's potential.[3]

The day preceding the Rebild Festival was an uncommonly warm Scandinavian summer day drenched in Danish sunshine. Russell and Dantzel had strolled slowly through the well-manicured churchyard cemetery in the village of Gørding, Vejrup, in Ribe County. The old, immaculate, white church with the red tiled roof and bell tower was where Elder Nelson's great-grandmother, Margrethe Christensen, was christened following her birth on January 11, 1830.[4]

Gørding, Vejrup, is a small village with few commercial establishments, readily bringing to mind fragments of Thomas Gray's "Elegy Written in a Country Church Yard," a reverie regarding residents laid to rest beneath sacred soil:

> *Beneath those rugged elms, that yew-tree's shade,*
> *Where heaves the turf in many a mould'ring heap,*

Each in his narrow cell for ever laid,
The rude forefathers of the hamlet sleep.

Far from the madding crowd's ignoble strife,
Their sober wishes never learned to stray;
Along the cool sequestered vale of life
They kept the noiseless tenor of their way.[5]

Upon arriving in Denmark in June 1850, Elder Erastus Snow began teaching the inhabitants of Denmark of the Book of Mormon and of a newly restored Church with a foundation of prophets and Apostles. Though Elder Snow's knowledge of Danish was at first limited, through interpreters and the influence of the Spirit, he and his companion, Peter Hansen, softened the hearts of many of their listeners. As a result, many of their converts' "sober wishes" *did* stray to thoughts of leaving the verdant rolling hills of Denmark to gather in the desert land of Zion.[6]

The Prophet Joseph Smith explained that the purpose of gathering to Zion "was to build unto the Lord a house whereby He could reveal unto His people the ordinances of His house and the glories of His kingdom, and teach the people the way of salvation."[7]

Just two years after missionary work was introduced in Scandinavia, the First Presidency issued a formal, open letter to the world, stating: "The invitation is to all, of every nation, kindred and tongue, who will believe, repent, be baptized, and receive the Gift of the Holy Ghost, by the laying on of hands, come home; come to the land of Joseph, to the valleys of Ephraim."[8] One great-great-grandfather and all eight of Russell Nelson's great-grandparents literally gathered to Ephraim—Ephraim, Utah—between 1855 and 1863. Many of them lived in Fort Ephraim, which was completed in 1855 and covered about seventeen acres.[9]

By mid-March 1860, residents of Fort Ephraim were constructing homes on city lots surrounding the fort.[10] As the Saints began to extend their farms and ranches beyond the protection of the fort, they became more vulnerable to occasional raids by Ute Indians, who viewed the settlers as intruders. On April 9, 1865, in a fit of pique, one settler from nearby Manti pulled a young Indian brave off his horse. With tensions already high between the Utes and the Saints, this act precipitated the outbreak of the Black Hawk War.[11]

The pressure of starvation had caused the Utes to take desperate measures for survival, raiding an estimated five thousand head of cattle and killing as many as ninety settlers between 1865 and 1867.[12] In 1867, Chief Black Hawk sued for peace, and the war eventually drew to a close.[13] Three years later, Black Hawk visited several Latter-day Saint congregations throughout central and southern Utah, soliciting the understanding and forgiveness of the Saints and explaining that his motives in waging war had merely been to prevent the starvation of his people.[14]

It was during this challenging era of clearing the land, establishing new settlements, and negotiating peace with their Native American neighbors that Elder Nelson's ancestors arrived in Ephraim. This arid land would take some getting used to by all faithful immigrants who were not accustomed to a sun-baked land of sagebrush and rattlesnakes, but their initial burdens were lightened because they knew in their hearts that this land was their land of promise. Here they would help build a temple to their God and accomplish the purposes for which they had gathered to Zion.

It may be helpful to refer to the pedigree chart as various ancestors are mentioned. The numbers in parentheses following each name below correspond to the respective individuals in the pedigree chart.

NIELS CHRISTENSEN (16)

The oldest of the Nelson ancestors to arrive in Ephraim was Niels Christensen, who would become one of Russell's great-great-grandfathers. Niels responded to the message of the missionaries in April 1856, joining the Church in Støre Brondum, near the Rebild

16 Niels Christensen
1788–?

8 Mads Peter Nielsen
1833–1891

9 Margrethe Christensen
1830–1914

10 Johan Andreas Jensen
1795–1882

11 Petra Andrea Amundsen
1828–1909

12 Nils Kristian Andersson
1835–1913

13 Ingeborg Poulsen
1823–1908

14 Stephen Williams
1816–1897

15 Emma Jane Hillard
1826–1897

4 Andrew Clarence (A. C.) Nelson
1864–1913

5 Amanda Jensen
1863–1945

6 Andrew Charles Anderson
1860–1943

7 Sarah Elizabeth Williams
1864–1945

2 Marion Clavar Nelson
1897–1990

3 Floss Edna Anderson
1893–1983

1 **Russell Marion Nelson**
9 September 1924

hills of Jutland in northern Denmark. Five years later, at age seventy-three, he immigrated to America, leaving behind his wife and eight children.[15] When he boarded the *Monarch of the Sea* in Liverpool, England, he had ten dollars in his pocket to finance his journey. Seven months after Niels's departure, his wife died in Denmark.

MADS PETER NIELSEN (8)

For many years in Scandinavia, it was the patronymic custom for children to acquire their family name from the first name of their father. Thus, when Mads Peter was born to Niels and Bodil Christensen on August 3, 1833, he did not assume the last name of Christensen but was given the family name of Nielsen, signifying that he was the son of Niels.

A year after his father left Denmark for Zion, young Mads immigrated to America at age twenty-eight. With only fourteen dollars to his name, he sailed on the *Franklin*, which left the Hamburg, Germany, harbor on April 15, 1862, and arrived in New York City six weeks later, on May 29.[16] The following year he met and married Margrethe Christensen in Ephraim. Their first child, Andrew, was born on January 20, 1864. Little did they know that he would become the grandfather of an Apostle of the Lord.[17]

MARGRETHE (GRETHE) CHRISTENSEN (9)

Margrethe Christensen, as a single woman of twenty-five, boarded the ship *Charles Buck* in Liverpool on January 17, 1855, traversed the icy Atlantic Ocean, and arrived in New Orleans three months later, on March 14.[18] She crossed the plains to the Salt Lake Valley and went on to Ephraim, where she married Mads P. Nielsen and eventually became the mother of Russell's grandfather Andrew C. Nelson.[19]

A. C. AND AMANDA J. NELSON (4, 5)

At some undocumented point in the Nielsen family history, the family began spelling their name "Nelson." In 1878, Grandfather

Russell's paternal grandparents: Andrew Clarence Nelson and Amanda Jensen Nelson.

Andrew C. Nelson, generally known as "A. C.," moved at age fourteen with his family from Ephraim to Redmond, Utah. At age twenty, he decided to become a teacher and began attending Brigham Young Academy in Provo. On August 5, 1885, he married Amanda Jensen in Manti, Utah, and they moved to Koosharem, Utah, remaining there for three years. In pursuit of further education, they moved to Provo in 1889, where A. C. returned to Brigham Young Academy. After graduating, he was called by Dr. Karl G. Maeser to supervise the seminary in Manti and was set apart as a teacher in the Church schools by Elder Anthon H. Lund. It was while the couple was living in Manti that Russell's father, Marion C. Nelson, was born.[20]

A. C. Nelson's intellectual and spiritual growth at Brigham Young Academy is reflected in an eloquent poetic tribute to Dr. Maeser. Written in December 1900, "My Teacher" honors Brother Maeser for his profound influence as an administrator and teacher at a struggling institution that would one day become Brigham Young University:

When I was an obscure boy,
Unnoticed as a summer fallen leaf;
When the dark clouds of suspicion and despondency
Had wrapt my soul in their black folds
And rocked it in their cradle of poverty and want;
When overwhelmed by the chilling blasts of seclusion;
There came, like a gentle zephyr,
The sweet breath of consolation,
Issuing from the heart of one who had entered
Within the portals of the holy sanctuary,
The inspiration, a voice, which bade me look up
And dispel these delusive obstructions
And be guided by the constellation of hope,
Determination, and virtuous ambition.
Blessings to the name of this holy man.[21]

A. C. Nelson had a great love and admiration for his parents and for their faithful devotion to the Church that had caused them to gather to Zion. On one occasion, while he was attending an education convention in Washington, D.C., a prominent educator from another region of the country began to malign A. C.'s religious beliefs. Instantly, A. C. revealed the depth of his religious commitment by publicly responding with unmistakable clarity: "My mother walked across the plains from Omaha to Salt Lake City, drawing a handcart for many weary miles. She made that journey for the sake of that faith, and I will permit no man to speak disparagingly of it."[22]

On November 6, 1900, A. C. was elected superintendent of public instruction for the state of Utah, succeeding the late Dr. John R. Park. His renomination four years later on the Republican ticket came by acclamation. He served so well that he was elected to four successive terms, requiring his family to move to Salt Lake City, where he and Amanda reared ten children. An eleventh child, Everett, died before he was three months old. Brokenhearted, A. C. wrote in his journal: "Feb. 24, 1901, death snatched from me the sweetest flower in the garden of my family. Little Everett Y. was plucked from us by that grim gatherer of roses who has no respect for feelings. His coming brought us joy; his departure left us broken-hearted. Yet we say blessings to the memory of the sweet little angel."[23]

A. C. kept a modest journal, and one of his most inspiring entries was the record of a visitation from his father, Mads Peter Nielsen, who had recently died. This experience, included verbatim below, has blessed the Nelson family:

"On the night of April 6, 1891, I had a strange dream or vision in which I saw and conversed with my father, who died January 27, 1891. I felt so impressed after it that I desired to write it for my own benefit and the benefit of my family and friends.

"Though some may scorn and laugh at the idea of such a visitation, yet I feel assured that it was real, and it has been and I hope always will be a source of much pleasure and satisfaction to me. To corroborate my testimony of the possibility of such a visitation I quote the following: 'Spirits can appear to men when permitted; but not having a fleshy tabernacle can not hide their glory.'[24] I was in bed when father came in or entered the room; he came and sat on the side of the bed. I could plainly see my wife and children in bed too.

"When father came to the bed, he first said: 'Well, my son, being you were not there (at Redmond) when I died, so that I did not get to see you, and as I had a few spare minutes. . . .' 'I am very glad to see you, father. How do you do?' 'I am feeling well my son, and have had very much to do since I died.'

"'What have you been doing since you died, father? Have you seen (here I mentioned the names of some of our dead friends)?'

"This question he did not answer but looked at me and smiled.

"'My son, I have been traveling together with Apostle Erastus Snow ever since I died; that is, since three days after I died; then I received my commission to preach the Gospel. You can not imagine, my son, how many spirits there are in the Spirit world that have not yet received the Gospel; but many are receiving it, and a great work is being accomplished. Many are anxiously looking forth to their friends, who are still living, to administer for them in the Temples. I have been very busy in preaching the Gospel of Jesus Christ.'

"'Will all the spirits believe you, father, when you teach them the Gospel?' 'No, they will not.'

"'How are you and mother, the boys, Emillie and the girls getting along?' 'I am well, father, and when I last heard from Redmond the folks there were well.'

"'Father, can you see us at all times, and do you know what we are doing?' 'No, my son, I can not. I have something else to do. I can not go when and where I please. There is just as much, and much more, order here in the Spirit world than in the other world. I have been assigned work and that must be performed.'

"'We intend to go to the Temple and get sealed to you as soon as my school is closed. I have talked with the girls about it and they want to be sealed to you.' 'That, my son, is partly what I came to see you about. We will yet make a family and live throughout Eternity.'

"'How do you feel at all times, father?' 'I feel splendid, and enjoy my labors; still, I must admit that at times I get a little lonesome to see my family; but it is only a short time till we will again see each other.'

"'O, father, how glad I am that you died in full faith in the Gospel, and in full fellowship in the Church.' 'Well, my son, your father always did know since he joined the Church that the Gospel was true, and you know that I always taught it to you, when you were a small boy. I got a little stubborn, but who is there of us that has not been a little cross and naughty at times. The short time that I was cross does not amount to 15 minutes in comparison to Eternity. I was punished for it. But it is all right. My son, you take care that you do not get that way.'

"'Father, is it natural to die? Or does it seem natural? Was there not a time when your spirit was in such a pain that it could not realize what was going on or taking place?' 'No, my son, there was not such a time. It is just as natural to die, as it is to be born, or for you to pass out of that door (here he pointed at the door). When I had told the folks that I could not last long, it turned dark and I could not see anything for a few minutes. Then, the first thing I could see was a number of spirits in the Spirit world. Then, I told the folks that I must go. The paper you gave me, my son, is dated wrong, but it makes no particular difference; correct records are kept here.'

"'Father, is the principle and doctrine of the Resurrection as taught us true?' 'True. Yes, my son, as true as can be. You can not avoid being Resurrected. It is just as natural for all to be Resurrected as it is to be born and die again. No one can avoid being Resurrected. There are many spirits in the Spirit world who would to God that there would be no Resurrection.'

"'Father, is the Gospel as taught by this Church true?' 'My son, do you see that picture' (pointing to a picture of the First Presidency of the Church hanging on the wall)? 'Yes, I see it.' 'Well, just as sure as you see that picture, just so sure is the Gospel true. The Gospel of Jesus Christ has within it the power of saving every man and woman that will obey it, and in no other way can they ever obtain a salvation in the Kingdom of God. My son, always cling to the Gospel. Be humble, be prayerful, be submissive to the Priesthood, be true, be faithful to the covenants you have made with God. Never do anything that will displease God. O, what a blessing is the Gospel! My son, be a good boy.'

"'Good bye.'

"I then saw him leave the room. He was neatly dressed in a suit of light gray clothes, which I had never seen him wear when alive."[25]

A. C. Nelson's record of this visitation has had a profound impact upon his grandchildren, and, on occasion, Elder Nelson has quoted excerpts at funerals of various family members.

A. C.'s friends described him as a man of great optimism, with the ability to always focus on the brighter side of life. His cheerful philosophy is reflected in the following verses that he penned:

> *I heard a bird sing*
> *In the dark of December*
> *A magical thing*
> *And sweet to remember.*
>
> *We're nearer to Spring*
> *Than we were in September;*
> *I heard a bird sing*
> *In the dark of December.*[26]

Russell never knew his famous Grandfather Nelson. He died of cancer just a month short of his fiftieth birthday, on December 26, 1913. He endured multiple operations and intense pain because of his illness, yet his journal makes no mention of this.[27]

Following A. C.'s death, his widow, Amanda, lived for an additional thirty-two years. Russell remembers his grandmother as always cheerful even though a widowed mother of ten children must have had her times of discouragement, and he recalls her ebullient buoyancy and example of selflessly serving others. She taught her children and grandchildren to love one another as she diligently served others all the days of her life. Russell remembers the aroma and taste of her delicious baked desserts, and whenever he went to visit her, he thought that each batch of raisin-filled sugar cookies had been baked just for him. She was the only grandparent to live long enough to participate in Russell and Dantzel's wedding festivities. She died less than two months later, on October 22, 1945.[28]

JOHAN ANDREAS JENSEN (10)

Perhaps the most dramatic conversion of any of Russell's great-grandparents was that of Johan Andreas Jensen, who was born November 16, 1795, near Frederikstad, Norway. Johan's father died when the boy was but eight years old, compelling the young lad to go to sea at a tender age. His determination and love for the ocean eventually qualified him to become a ship's captain, and he navigated his way through many fascinating parts of the world. In 1849, he became intensely interested in religion and was so deeply impressed by the Christian doctrines he had learned that he distributed most of his worldly goods among the poor. He also felt a compelling need to call the residents of Norway to repentance, including King Oscar of Sweden-Norway. Johan's zeal eventually cost him his freedom.[29]

In the spring of 1852, three days after publishing a letter about his religious convictions in a Frederikstad newspaper, the *Christianposten*, Johan was taken before a judge to defend his letter, in which he decried the moral laxity of King Oscar. When confronted by the judge, Johan described King Oscar as "the biggest liar of all the liars in our Country." For his written words and actions, Johan was sentenced to a year in prison.[30]

Six weeks later, as punishment for preaching the restored gospel in Norway, Elders Christian J. Larsen and Svend Larsen were coincidentally consigned to the same jail as Johan and his friend, a Mr. Jacobsen. The jail was actually more of an apartment than a prison, and Johan and the elders shared the same apartment from mid-June through the fall of 1852. The jailer, Mr. Fjeldstad, treated the inmates kindly, and though their reading materials were initially removed, they were soon restored in response to Elder Svend Larsen's earnest pleas.[31]

The elders invested their time in singing, praying, and reading the scriptures. On Sunday morning, April 24, 1853, when the jailer and his son paid a visit to the elders, Johan Jensen joined in their lengthy conversation about religion. The Spirit of the Lord was evident during their discussion as Johan suddenly began to weep and declared that the message the missionaries had brought to Norway was, indeed, true. The elders later recorded that Johan's face shone with joy.[32] After he was released from prison, Johan was baptized in the nearby Glåma River, on February 25, 1854.

PETRA AMUNDSEN (11)

Johan, his wife, Petra Amundsen, and their children left their native Norway and immigrated to the United States on the ship *Antarctic*, which sailed from Liverpool on May 28, 1863.[33] When their journey began, their family included six children, two of whom were infant twin daughters born March 28, 1863. The ship docked in New York City on July 10, 1863, and although the twins were tiny, the family made the long journey across the United States with their meager belongings, eventually settling in Ephraim. One of the twin baby daughters, Julia, died July 18, 1863, en route somewhere in Nebraska, but the other twin, Amanda, survived. She later became Russell's Grandmother Nelson. She married A. C. Nelson in 1885, and they later moved from Ephraim to Salt Lake City.[34]

NILS KRISTIAN ANDERSSON (12)

Nils Kristian Andersson, another great-grandfather, was born November 26, 1835, near Lund, Sweden. He joined The Church of Jesus Christ of Latter-day Saints at age eighteen[35] and came to America on the *John J. Boyd*, leaving Liverpool on December 12, 1855, and arriving in New York City on February 15, 1856.[36] From there, he was called to Iowa on a mission. At the conclusion of his mission, he came to Utah, crossing the plains in Capt. Mathias Cowley's seventh handcart company,[37] composed of 334 Saints who left Iowa on July 3, 1857.

The company had considerable difficulty crossing the stream at Loup Fork, Nebraska, but they were graciously assisted by Indians. They went three weeks without meat after their rations diminished, but they resisted shooting buffalo for fear of causing a stampede. Miraculously, some army officers approached the handcart camp and offered them an ox that was suffering from a crushed foot. The

In June 2000, the Nelsons visited the building where the Saints in Malmö, Sweden, met during the time Elder Nelson's great-grandfather Nils K. Andersson served as the Skåne District president (1873–75). Left to right: Elder Spencer J. Condie, Sister Dorothea S. Condie, Sister Dantzel W. Nelson, Elder Russell M. Nelson, Sister Shirley S. Clarke, and President Allan T. Clarke of the Sweden Stockholm Mission.

Saints mercifully killed the animal and rejoiced in their feast.[38] A few years after arriving in Ephraim, Nils became an active participant in the Black Hawk War.[39]

During the summer of 2000, in conjunction with sesquicentennial activities commemorating the arrival of the first Latter-day Saint missionaries in Scandinavia in 1850, Russell and Dantzel met with the Swedish Saints at firesides in Stockholm, Göteborg, and Malmö. Ever conscious of his apostolic responsibility for missionary work, Elder Nelson also spoke to all of the full-time missionaries laboring in Sweden.

Local Church leaders were pleased to take the Nelsons to the place where Nils K. Andersson had served a mission as an adult, and they presented the Nelsons with a copy of a newly published history of the Church in Sweden. It gave Elder Nelson great satisfaction to find on the list of past district presidents the name of his great-grandfather, who had presided over the Skåne District from 1873 to 1875.[40]

Upon returning home from his mission to Sweden, Nils became a worker in the Manti Utah Temple after it had been dedicated in May 1888.[41] Nils died June 11, 1913, in Ephraim.

INGEBORG POULSEN (13)

Great-grandfather Andersson's wife, Ingeborg Poulsen, was born April 9, 1823, in Dypvag, Aust-Agder, Norway. Coincidentally, she sailed to America on the same ship, the *John J. Boyd*, as her future husband, Nils.[42] She too was a handcart pioneer, traveling from St. Paul, Minnesota, to Utah. Their son, Andrew C. Anderson, was born October 1, 1860, in Ephraim. He became Russell's other grandfather. Ingeborg died February 25, 1908, in Ephraim.

STEPHEN WILLIAMS AND EMMA HILLARD (14, 15)

Across the North Sea from Scandinavia, in Hartford, Devonshire, England, Stephen Williams was born May 31, 1816. In 1840 he married Anna Rendal, who passed away three years later. In June 1844 Stephen married Emma Jane Hillard, a member of the Church from Ditcheat, Somersetshire, England. In February 1848, after being deeply moved by the message of the Restoration, Stephen joined the Church.

Because of their membership in the Church, Stephen and Emma became subject to persecution and ridicule, eventually emigrating from England on the sailing vessel *Windermere* with 477 other Latter-day Saint emigrants.[43] They departed from Liverpool on February 12, 1854, notwithstanding that Emma Jane was five months pregnant. After fifteen days at sea, her understandable anxiety increased as an outbreak of smallpox afflicted thirty-nine passengers. To her great relief, the epidemic was "suddenly checked in answer to prayer."[44]

They arrived in New Orleans on April 23, 1854, and set out for Utah, traveling with the Darian Richardson company of forty-two wagons. They reached Salt Lake City on Sunday, September 30, 1854. Like many other faithful pioneers who experienced the refiner's fire, their little two-year-old son, Joseph Alma, died en route and was buried in an unknown grave somewhere in Missouri or Nebraska. Another son, Samuel Moroni, was born en route near Council Bluffs, Iowa, on August 11, 1854.[45]

Stephen was a tanner by trade, and Emma Jane was a popular vocalist. After President Brigham Young called the couple to make Ephraim their home, Emma Jane became the community's first Primary president. Stephen and Emma Jane had eight children before the birth of Sarah Elizabeth Williams, born February 13, 1864. She would become Russell's Grandmother Anderson. Four of the eight children preceding Sarah were born in England, two of whom died in childhood. The names of Sarah's older brothers— Thomas, Stephen, Joseph Alma, Moroni, and Nephi—indicate the influence the scriptures had in the life of this family. Ultimately, Stephen and Emma Jane had twelve children. Besides rearing her own family, Emma Jane also cared for three of her sister's sons.[46] Stephen passed away on January 8, 1897, in Emery, Utah. His beloved Emma Jane followed him in death only six months later, on June 27, 1897.

ANDREW AND SARAH ANDERSON (6, 7)

The Anderson grandparents, Andrew C. and Sarah E. Williams, were married in Ephraim on April 28, 1881, and remained there to welcome ten children into their family. A serious diphtheria epidemic claimed the lives of two of their daughters within a period of four weeks. Their home was quarantined, so when the children died,

*Russell's maternal grand-
parents: Andrew C.
Anderson and Sarah
Williams Anderson.*

it was impossible to obtain outside assistance for their burial. Andrew applied his skills as a carpenter to make two small coffins, one for five-year-old Clarissa and another for tiny Elizabeth, who was nearly two years old. Sarah sewed burial clothes for the children, and Andrew dug their graves. He then took the coffins by horse and wagon to the old Ephraim Cemetery, where the girls, surrounded only by immediate family members, were laid to rest.

For the eight children who survived, Andrew and Sarah strongly encouraged education. One son became a medical doctor, and two others became dentists. The daughters, who were also encouraged to develop talents and skills, all became teachers. Elder Nelson's mother, Edna Anderson, was the sixth child, born May 17, 1893.[47]

Elder Nelson remembers Grandmother and Grandfather Anderson with great fondness. His grandfather was a carpenter and a craftsman, building the cabinets for the food storage room in the

Nelson home at 974 South 1300 East in Salt Lake City. Young Russell took great delight in helping Grandfather Anderson, who not only taught Russell how to miter corners but also emphasized principles of exactness. He taught Russell to "measure twice and cut once." Many years later, when Russell became Dr. Nelson, he found his grandfather's wise counsel to be excellent advice in the operating room.[48]

Russell recalls the fun of swinging on the front porch swing with his grandfather, and he has warm memories of good visits together. As his grandparents grew older, they especially enjoyed riding in an automobile with Russell's family. The children cherished those fleeting moments. Russell's grandfather died December 28, 1943, in his eighty-fourth year, and his grandmother passed away April 13, 1945, in her eighty-second year. Russell is grateful to them for many things, but especially for providing him with such an angel mother.[49]

Reflecting upon his heritage, Elder Nelson said, "It seems remarkable that eight great-grandparents from four populous nations in Europe should all have come to the tiny town of Ephraim, Utah, so remote and different from anything they had previously known. Although I never knew my great-grandparents, I frequently wonder how they would feel about what Dantzel and I are doing now with the legacy they left to us. Their lineage and legacy are part of an inheritance that I treasure, and for which I hope to be worthy, at least in part."[50]

CHAPTER 2

HONOR THY FATHER
AND THY MOTHER

R USSELL'S FATHER, MARION C. Nelson, was born January 11, 1897, in Manti, Utah, the sixth of eleven children of Andrew C. and Amanda Jensen Nelson. When A. C. became the superintendent of public instruction for the state of Utah, the family was required to move to Salt Lake City.[1] At an early age, Marion exhibited many of his father's leadership abilities. While attending West High School in 1912, young Marion was elected president of the sophomore class. The following year, he began attending the newly constructed East High School, where he was subsequently elected student body president. He simultaneously served as editor of the *Red and Black*, the joint monthly publication of West High and East High Schools.[2]

During his junior year in high school, the day after Christmas 1913, Marion lost his father to cancer. He immediately missed his father's dynamic presence and spiritual influence. With ten other children in the family, Marion had to go to work to assist his widowed mother in supporting his five younger siblings who were still living at home.[3]

Like many youngsters his age, Marion was engaged in a variety of odd jobs, but his experience in high school journalism sparked a great interest in the newspaper business. He started out as a newspaper carrier for the *Deseret News* but soon worked his way up to

Russell's parents: Marion C. Nelson and Edna Anderson Nelson.

become a writer for the paper. While Marion was attending the University of Utah, President John A. Widtsoe, who would later be called to be an Apostle, arranged to have Marion be the campus reporter. The Salt Lake City newspapers paid him by the column inch for every article accepted for publication.[4]

With the advent of World War I, many of the nation's colleges and universities, including the University of Utah, were closed. With four older brothers called into military service, Marion found that his widowed mother's need for help became even more urgent. So he left school and returned to full-time employment at the *Deseret News,* becoming both the sports editor and the automotive editor.[5]

Marion enjoyed covering athletic events and the exciting new developments in automobiles, but occasionally he was assigned to cover other stories. One of these assignments required him to cover a forthcoming concert of the Mormon Tabernacle Choir. To a young man with sports and cars foremost on his mind, the task of covering a concert seemed a bit onerous. Nevertheless, the family needed

food for the table, so he swallowed his pride and went to the concert with notepad in hand.[6]

The guest soloist that evening had an impressive reputation as a
coloratura soprano with a very pleasing voice. The minute she began
to sing, Marion Nelson was grateful that sports editors could cover
concerts. Edna Anderson so charmed him with her grace, natural
beauty, and sonorous sounds of song that he was absolutely smitten.
After the concert, journalism had a competing challenge for
Marion's heart.[7]

Edna Anderson, who would become Russell Nelson's mother,
was born May 17, 1893, in Ephraim, the sixth of ten children. She
spent all her school days in Ephraim, including two years at Snow
Academy (now Snow College), from which she graduated in 1913.
Following graduation, she moved to Salt Lake City, where she
became director of the Lafayette School's music department. She
sang with various musical groups and especially welcomed opportunities of soloing with the Mormon Tabernacle Choir.[8] When the
newly constructed Utah State Capitol building was dedicated
October 16, 1916, Edna sang *Cara Nome* as part of the dedicatory
services.[9]

That first evening she sang in front of Marion Nelson was always
a fond memory, and she confessed that when they were first introduced, she was just as eager as he was to see their friendship grow.
Friendship blossomed into love, leading to their marriage on August
25, 1919. Their bishop, Elias S. Woodruff, who coincidentally served
as publisher of the *Deseret News,* performed the marriage.

During the following year, the couple's first child, Marjory, was
born. Four years later, on September 9, 1924, Edna Nelson gave
birth to a nine-pound, eleven-ounce baby boy. It was miraculous
that such a petite five-foot-three mother could bear such a large
baby. They named him Russell Marion Nelson.[10] Three weeks after
Russell's birth, radio station KSL broadcast the proceedings of general conference to Latter-day Saints in Utah for the first time. That

same year, George Gershwin's symphony *Rhapsody in Blue* was first performed.[11]

Marion's employment at the *Deseret News* brought him into contact with the Gillham Advertising Agency, which later offered him employment.[12] His drive and executive skills eventually propelled him to the top of the company, and he became its president and general manager in 1930. With his wife's constant devotion and encouragement, Marion also became an influential leader of the business community, serving over the years as president of the Salt Lake Advertising Club, the Salt Lake Chamber of Commerce, the Rotary Club, and the Bonneville Knife and Fork Club, and as a member of the Honorary Colonels Corps of the Utah National Guard.[13]

Russell's mother was also active in community affairs. In addition to her musical fame, she served as president of the Douglas School Parent Teacher Association and of the Mothers Clubs for the Delta Delta Delta and Sigma Chi groups at the University of Utah.[14]

Notwithstanding their commitment to the community, Marion and Edna always placed their family first in their lives. Their fidelity and love for one another strengthened their family and engendered a deep sense of security and belonging in the hearts of each of their children. Russell's childhood was pleasant and his family life rich largely because his parents built family solidarity on a few dependable traditions.

Elder Nelson recalled, "They made love the prevailing influence in their home. Completely absent were expressions of anger, criticism, and denigration of others. Our parents led, guided, and provided; but they were not possessive, and they did not unduly interfere in the lives of their children. The important decisions in life—choice of career, selection of a marital partner, and all other opportunities—were to be made individually, after parental counsel.

"They were always available. Never did the Nelson children feel the insecurity which may come from absentee parents. The only

Russell's parents, Edna and Marion, exchange
endearing glances.

exception was when our parents went on a trip together; but when
that occurred, we were well tended by other members of their
extended family.

"Quality time together as a family was always provided. Not
only was there an annual vacation together, but just about every
night was family home evening as well. We read together, sang
together, played together, and worked together. In the early years the
economic struggle was very real; yet they seemed to have everything
in life that money could not buy. Eventually, our father's hard work
was rewarded by greater financial stability, but most of that came
after the formative years had passed and the children were launched
on their respective ways.

"In the Nelson home education was highly valued. Early in our lives, Father and Mother assured us that they would assist us in achieving as much education as we could obtain. They were willing to make whatever sacrifices would be required to help us children to achieve that which we wished to make of ourselves. No words of mine can adequately express the gratitude I feel for this commitment to excellence in education and this level of support. Without their encouragement and absolute assurance of the validity of education and service, my life as it exists could never have been."[15]

The major adolescent anxiety that plagued young Russell Nelson was his parents' indifference to the Church during his formative years. Notwithstanding the legacy of their rich pioneer heritage, their lack of religious devotion demonstrated that the Church is always just one generation away from a loss of commitment. Russell's father told him of the day when he, as a young lad in Manti, and other young people were suddenly rounded up and put on a school bus. Marion asked, "Where are we going?" One of the adult leaders responded, "We're driving up to the Manti Temple, where you will all be baptized." For some reason, this way of doing things without his foreknowledge or consent rubbed young Marion the wrong way, and he asked to get off the bus.[16]

It was not long afterward that the family moved to Salt Lake City, where, with a busy and often absent father and a mother shepherding ten other children, Marion Nelson began to lose his commitment to the Church. Thus, he and Edna were not married in the temple, and though they were pleased with Russell and Dantzel's activity in the Church, they continued to remain rather indifferent to things of the Spirit.

Notwithstanding Marion's spotty church attendance, he was a man of great honesty and integrity. In 1967, Elder Thomas S. Monson was given the assignment to serve as chairman of the newly established Church Leadership Committee. Brother Wendell J. Ashton and Brother Neal A. Maxwell were also called to serve on that committee, later to be joined by Brothers James E. Faust and Hugh W. Pinnock. During the course of their labors together, the

Three generations of Nelsons—Marion C., Russell, and Russell Jr.—in October 1984 following the priesthood session of general conference.

committee oversaw the production of a leadership training film. One scene featured a milk truck with the logo of a well-known local dairy. Brother Ashton happened to be vice president of the same advertising agency of which Marion Nelson was president. After previewing the film, Wendell indicated that the name on the side of the milk truck would have to be changed, because that particular company was one of his advertising agency's clients. Brother Ashton strenuously declared that Marion Nelson would never approve of such a self-promotion, which was against the agency's high ethical standards.[17]

With Russell's gentle, patient prodding and the persistent prayers of his siblings and children, on February 6, 1977, a month after Marion's eightieth birthday, Russell ordained his father an elder in the Melchizedek Priesthood. The following month, on March 26, Marion and Edna were sealed in the Provo Utah Temple.[18] In reminiscing about favorite Christmases, Russell said unequivocally that the best Christmas of all was in 1977. "We realized then that Mother and Daddy had given us the finest gift they could ever give, as they took upon themselves the covenant of celestial marriage that year, thereby sealing us and their posterity to them for time and all eternity. It is the only gift we ever really wanted from our dear parents. To receive that from them was the most memorable gift of all."[19]

President Thomas S. Monson, who knew Russell's father, observed, "Marion loved the Church and was a very talented man." Then, as an afterthought, he added, "All of Russell's brains didn't just fall on him accidentally." President Monson recounted, "One of the nicest scenes I ever saw was following a session of general priesthood meeting, which had been held in the Tabernacle. Walking in front of me happened to be three persons: Marion C. Nelson, Russell, and Russell Jr. I thought, 'Talk about linking families together for eternity!'"[20]

This scene from the mid-1980s described by President Monson had, for nearly half a century, been but an elusive dream for Russell. As he attended church without his parents and as his fledgling testimony grew during his teen years, Russell had a concomitant concern that perhaps they would never be sealed in the temple. These anxieties persisted until his parents claimed the blessings of eternal marriage and had their children sealed to them.

Russell has immense empathy for those struggling to find their way in life. Through personal experience with his parents, he gained great appreciation for the Savior's counsel: "Unto such shall ye continue to minister; for ye know not but what they will return and repent, and come unto me with full purpose of heart, and I shall heal them; and ye shall be the means of bringing salvation unto them" (3 Nephi 18:32).

CHAPTER 3

THE FORMATIVE YEARS

N OTWITHSTANDING THE CONVERGING influence of his eight
faithful great-grandparents, Russell's own parents were, as previously mentioned, more involved in community affairs than in
Church activities. However, the Nelson home was always a happy
one, filled with excitement and love, and Russell bristles at any dis-
paraging comments about his parents' early lack of faith. They did
not hold formal family home evenings, but nearly every evening was
a home evening of sorts in which they sang and read together and
discussed the day's activities.[1]

Russell fondly remembers spending many pleasant hours in the
backyard, building miniature highways around the flowers and rocks
of his mother's garden to accommodate his little Tootsie Toy automobile. Toys and recreation were luxury items during those formative years of the Great Depression. Between 1929 and 1933, the
annual per capita income plummeted from $527 to $300, and
unemployment in Utah reached 36 percent, compared to the
national rate of 25 percent.[2] Still vivid in Russell's memory is the
Christmas Day, during the depths of the Depression, that he
received a black Iver Johnson bicycle. He was just barely tall enough
to reach the pedals, so his daddy helped to balance him.[3] Russell still
has that bicycle, a symbol of parental love when times were tough.
He keeps it at the family's getaway home in Midway, Utah, for the

grandchildren to ride. As a matter of fact, many of the Brethren, including President Gordon B. Hinckley, have taken a spin around the block on the venerable bike during one of their visits to Midway.[4]

Russell's sister Marjory was four years older than he, and his sister Enid was less than two years younger, so Russell can never remember life without his sisters. In retrospect, having sisters was good preparation for becoming the father of nine daughters. Russell's younger brother, Robert, was born March 26, 1931, when Russell was six and a half. He remembers his feelings of joy when his father came home and announced to the children that they had a new little brother. Russell felt especially blessed to have a brother of his own.[5]

Not long after Robert's birth, the family moved to a home at 974 South 1300 East, next door to Paul Nelson, a family cousin. The boys spent countless hours together playing football in their driveway and passing the football back and forth over rooftops.[6]

When Paul was seven and Russell was eight, their uncle, J. Clifford Nelson, who was active in the military reserve, pinned honorary lieutenant bars on each of them during a ceremony at Camp Williams, southwest of Salt Lake City. Afterward, the young lads were honored guests at a dinner and at boxing matches that followed. This was the first time Russell had ever witnessed a boxing match, and he still remembers "how completely repugnant this was to me to see grown men intentionally striving to injure each other. It tainted the luster of all the uplifting activities that had preceded the fights, so that in spite of the great honor given to us, including pictures in the newspaper, the memory remains of the seeming brutality of men fighting one another."[7]

At that tender age, Russell already seemed to have an inherent respect for the human body as the temple of the spirit. Thus, as a young lad, he invariably tried to protect his body from harm and noxious substances—like beef liver! The Nelson home was only two and a half blocks from Douglas Elementary School, so Russell went home for lunch every day. Once a week his mother felt obliged to feed him liver, which, long before the discovery of cholesterol, was viewed by many to be an almost perfect food rich in iron and vitamins. Russell could abide neither the taste nor the texture of liver, and it required some creativity on his part to clandestinely dispose of this least-favorite lunch. His most successful solution was to watch carefully for a moment when his mother was distracted and then to quickly shove the liver into his trouser pocket. As he walked back to school, he would pull the liver out of his pocket and throw it into a vacant lot. He sheepishly concedes, "This maneuver was a little hard on pockets, but it was, nevertheless, very successful."[8]

Russell's daddy had a ritual each morning of coming into the children's rooms and boisterously singing to them, "Up, up, the sun is up, the dew is on the grass." Even when they were not too pleased about leaving their warm beds, it was always comforting to hear their father's cheerful greeting to each new day.[9] Whether through genetic endowment or repetitive training, Russell readily emulates his father's example by beginning each day in a pleasant, cheerful mode.

While at Douglas School, Russell was appointed to be one of the school's bell ringers. That weighty responsibility required that he go to school early so he could ring the bell to summon students to class. Later, he played a bugle in the school bugle corps, which performed each day during the raising and lowering of the American flag. Russell did not play as well as others, but what he lacked in skill he compensated for in volume as he felt a patriotic surge of pleasure by participating in that daily ritual.[10]

As a precocious youngster with an inquisitive mind, Russell was advanced from the fourth grade to the sixth grade. Having a birthday in September, he was already one of the youngest in his class, so jumping over the fifth grade made him more than a year younger than most of his classmates. The jump did not really seem to make much difference for him academically, except perhaps to leave him a little deficient in working fractions.[11]

During the seventh grade, Russell and other Salt Lake City school children were honored by being listed in a new commemorative monument on the west side of the City County Building in downtown Salt Lake City. The children were asked to sign their names and express their ambitions in life on a document encased in the monument. Russell remembers clearly writing down two goals: to be self-employed and to go around the world.[12]

Russell M. Nelson at about age two.

Russell's recollections of Douglas School are pleasant ones because he loved learning and he loved his teachers. He does not recall missing a single day of school, and to the date of this writing, he has never missed a day of work because of injury or illness.[13]

One of the Nelsons' notable neighbors was Elder Joseph Fielding Smith. Russell's acquaintance with him dated back many years. When Russell was a young boy growing up in the family home at 974 South 1300 East, Elder Smith lived but half a block away at 998 Douglas Street. Two of his sons, Douglas A. Smith and Milton E. Smith, were among Russell's close friends and classmates, and Russell used to play marbles with them at Douglas School. Russell would often play at their home, where he became acquainted with Elder Smith. Although the Nelson home was harmonious and free of contention, young Russell felt a different kind of spirit in the Smiths' home, and he welcomed every opportunity to sit at the Apostle's feet and partake of his remarkable wisdom and kindness.[14]

The Nelsons' extended family members were close to each other, and they frequently got together for picnics. As a young man, Russell was delighted to play horseshoes with his uncles.[15]

For Russell, the tenderest times of all were those with his mother and father. He remembers well how beautifully his mother sang to him whenever he was weary or not feeling well. She would cuddle him while singing "Carry Me Back to Old Virginny" in her soothing soprano voice. The feeling was so

Russell M. Nelson at age twelve.

comforting and reassuring that, on occasion, he may even have feigned illness in order to have her sing to him so lovingly. To this day, Russell says, "I can hardly sing that song without getting a lump in my throat because of its special significance."[16]

It was his mother who taught him how to pray, and she would patiently listen to his prayers at night before he would retire. And though his parents were indifferent to Church activities, he remembers how they would send him to Sunday School and how dutifully he went. However, Russell recalled, "My boyish mind was unimpressed with the feelings I had while there, occasioned primarily by the rowdiness of my classmates and the ridicule to which I was subjected when I did attend, for I was not a regular attender."[17]

He added, "I had the feeling that whatever it was we were to learn in Sunday School must not be very important if we were never given any examinations on the subject matter. I often felt that all that was accomplished in my Sunday School class was a feeling of antagonism between students and the teacher."[18]

On occasion, he would leave home in his Sunday clothes, acting as if he were going to Sunday School, but then he would go to

Harvard Park and play football with other Sunday delinquents. He recalled, "We carefully noted the time, knowing we could get together shortly after ten o'clock and play until about 11:30 A.M., the time for Sunday School to end."[19] The boys would then tuck in their shirts, straighten their hair, and walk home as if they had all been to Sunday School. Russell's parents may often have wondered why he came home somewhat disheveled and sweaty from Sunday School, but they never voiced their suspicions.[20]

Ministering angels come in many different shapes and sizes, and one of these was a faithful home teacher named Jonas Ryser. He gently and persistently intervened in Russell's life when he was sixteen years of age by successfully convincing his parents that their four children should be baptized. As a result, Russell was baptized November 30, 1940, by his good friend Foley C. Richards, confirmed the following day by Brother Ryser, and warmly welcomed by his wonderful bishop, Sterling W. Sill, who subsequently would be called to be an Assistant to the Twelve.[21] Fifty-four years later, Elder Nelson, as an Apostle, would speak at his former bishop's funeral.[22]

Bishop Sill was spearheading the building of a chapel for the newly created Garden Park Ward at 1150 Yale Avenue, and Russell and his priests quorum played an active role in developing the pond that now exists on the grounds. They dug the channel and laid a cement foundation that has stood the test of time. Russell's most influential teacher in the Garden Park Ward was Hoyt W. Brewster, a young returned missionary who had served in Holland and who sincerely cared about Latter-day Saint youth. He taught the priests quorum with the Spirit, and he entertained the young men with songs he had learned on his mission. More important, he inspired them with faith, and he generated inner stirrings of testimony that Russell had not felt from any previous teacher.[23]

Sunday School, taught by Junius S. Romney, also became a valuable experience. Brother Romney was always thoughtful and kind, and Russell began to realize that the gospel and its teachings were becoming increasingly important in his life. Bishop Sill ordained

Russell a priest on November 9, 1941, and Bishop Joseph W. Bambrough ordained him an elder on April 30, 1944.[24]

It became a source of increasing concern to Russell to be reared in a family where the daily application of the gospel was not a high priority. He remembers the day he was looking through the home's storage room and found some bottles of alcoholic beverage. In righteous indignation, and perhaps as an indicator of his growing testimony, Russell smashed the bottles on the cement floor of the laundry room, pouring their contents down the drain. When his father found out about this raid by a one-man temperance union, his first reaction was one of "understandable vexation." But he controlled himself and never scolded Russell. "As a matter of fact," Russell recalled, "I have no memory of receiving a scolding or any significant punishment from either of my parents, who were always understanding, compassionate, and kind. Their first priority was always the family."

Russell's younger sister, Enid, concurred with her brother's assessment of their parents. "Our parents lived for their children, but religion was not a priority in their lives," Enid said. She relishes the recollection of the undivided devotion her doting father gave to his children.

The end of the streetcar line was 900 South and 1300 East, a stone's throw from the Nelson home. Not infrequently, in the late afternoon, the children would catch the streetcar headed downtown, where they would meet their daddy at his office. From there, they would go to Alex's Café, Keeley's, or Sutton's Café for a bite to eat and then top off the evening at the movies.[25]

During the hot summer months, the family would converge at Colville Ice Cream, where the "Vanilla Lady" would satisfy their desires for some cool refreshments to stave off the summer heat. The popcorn stand close to the east side of the City and County Building was also a favorite place to meet to partake of hot buttered popcorn. Marion Nelson may not have spent much time in priesthood meeting, but he did spend countless hours with his children. He loved baseball, and it was important to him to transmit this

Family portrait taken in 1935: seated: Enid, Russell, Robert; standing: Marion, Marjory, Edna.

affinity to his children. They frequently found themselves at Liberty Park, where their father never tired of hitting flies and grounders to them.[26]

Marion was not much of a fisherman, but he felt that all young children should have the experience of fishing, so, on occasion, they would drive to the fish hatchery up Ogden Canyon, where they were all guaranteed to catch fish—for a price.[27]

"Growing up during the years of the Great Depression, things were financially tight in the family, but Daddy was always committed to seeing that we had enough to eat," Russell recalled. "Nourishing foods were always provided, yet I was trained to ask permission from my mother before eating a banana or an apple."[28] These scarce commodities were always a welcome treat, and candy was virtually unknown to the Nelson children. In later years, when Marion and Edna became grandparents, they continued to treat their grandchildren with fresh fruit rather than candy.[29]

When the Nelson children were quite young, Russell's father would borrow money to pay for family vacations. There was never a summer that the Nelson family did not have "a significant experience vacationing together." They enjoyed many wonderful vacations, going to the seashore in California, Rocky Mountain National Park in Colorado, Utah's colorful national parks, and Sun Valley, Idaho. Vacations together contributed greatly to cementing feelings of love within the family.[30] Russell recalled one trip in particular when he, his parents, and his three siblings traveled to Washington and Oregon and the national parks in western Canada.

"While driving in Jasper National Park, Daddy tried to shoo a bumblebee out of the car and ended up in the ditch, causing minor damage to the car in addition to creating an embarrassing inconvenience. Then, while hiking in Yoho National Park, my mother twisted her ankle and sustained a very bad sprain, which caused her ankle to swell a great deal, and she had to be assisted for the rest of the trip. Later on, I received a bad bee sting on my thigh, which began to swell so much that I could not walk. My parents had to call a doctor to make a personal call at their hotel in Portland, Oregon."[31]

On that same trip, as the family was walking along the bank of the Columbia River east of Portland, Russell's brother, Bob, fell down a steep embankment toward the river. He would have drowned had each family member not locked arms, forming a human chain to rescue him. With all of these complications coming within just a few days of each other, Russell's father firmly said, "Everybody get in the car. I'm locking all the doors. We're going straight home. We're not going to make any stops except for gas!" He then drove about seventeen hours straight to get the family home in one piece.[32]

Edna, an accomplished musician, was eager for each of her children to develop their musical abilities. Marjory became proficient at the piano and was conscientious in practicing, and Russell started taking piano lessons at his mother's insistence, performing in a few recitals at the home of their teacher, Mattie Reid Evans. As an enticement to practice, she would give Russell some beads, one bead for each high mark achieved at his lessons. He did not do badly, but his heart was not in it, and he strongly resisted encouragement to practice up to an hour a day when he would much rather be doing something else.[33]

Russell was further diverted from piano lessons by the opportunity to go to work at age ten as an errand boy for his father, who had become president of the Gillham Advertising Agency. Russell thrived on getting out and meeting the important and interesting people he encountered on his errands. He was never without a job afterward. His older sister, Marjory, recalled, "After Russell started making money as an errand boy, he gave his mother a gift on *his* birthday with a note: 'Thanks for having me!' He never lost this love and appreciation for his mother, and he extends similar reverence and devotion to the mother of his own children and the mothers of his grandchildren."[34]

Upon graduating from Douglas School, Russell spent the next two years at Roosevelt Junior High School. At the end of his first year there, he successfully ran for student body vice president. His responsibilities as vice president included public safety at school, where he opened and closed the padlock on the room where students parked their bicycles. He thoroughly enjoyed junior high school, participating in the school play *Penrod and Sam* and in the glee club, under the direction of George H. Durham, father of Elder G. Homer Durham. It was George H. who taught the young men, "Don't waste time, boys. It's the stuff life's made of."[35]

After his experience working as an errand boy for his father at Gillham Advertising Agency, Russell thought it would be challenging to strike out on his own. So he got a job as a bank messenger at Tracy Loan and Trust Company. He filled the pens on Saturday morning (that was before the days of the ballpoint pen), and he eventually worked his way up the organizational hierarchy to become a part-time teller and posting clerk while he was still in school. He was even encouraged to take shorthand and typing and to do stenographic work for bank vice president Newell B. Dayton, who was always kind to his young employee. Russell's salary of sixty dollars a month was regarded at the time as a high wage for someone in part-time employment.[36]

While working for Tracy Loan and Trust, Russell developed an avid interest in photography, even writing a research paper on the chemistry of photography for his high school chemistry class. He took his research paper to Pete Ecker of Ecker's Studio to see if he thought the material was impressive enough to offer Russell employment. Mr. Ecker said he would be glad to employ him, but given Russell's inexperience, he felt Russell's services should initially be offered for free. Russell started out working for nothing but eventually was able to earn enough money to buy photoflood reflectors and lamps—for his father for Christmas. Though Marion seemed grateful at the time, he never used the items, so Russell used them instead as he pursued his hobby of photography.[37]

Russell's parents allowed him to build a darkroom, featuring a photographic enlarger, in the attic of their home. He even put a sign on the darkroom door that read "975," distinguishing it from the house address of 974. His hobby provided Russell with a wonderful hideaway, where he could process pictures and feel the satisfaction of personal accomplishment.[38]

"To supplement my income further," Russell said, "I worked at Christmastime as a mail sorter for the U. S. Post Office. For the first week or so, learning the names of the streets of the city was an interesting challenge." His interest soon began to wane, however, and he became a clock-watcher. When this job came to an end, Russell was grateful for faithful post office veterans who were so reliable. He resolved to prepare himself for employment that would allow him to lose himself in his work.[39]

It was about this time in his young life that he began to seriously entertain pursuing a medical career. He later recalled, "The decision to go into medicine was forged by two realizations: One was that was where my talents lay. I had a great desire to do research, to go into the unknown. The other was that I liked people. I wanted to serve them. I reasoned that the finest career that would be available to a human being would be that of mother. Inasmuch as that was out of the question for me, I reasoned that the second occupation would be medicine. There I could help people every day and teach them."[40]

Russell entered East High School in 1938 at age fourteen and engaged in many extracurricular activities, "the most memorable of which were the East High A Cappella Choir, under the direction of Miss Lisle Bradford, and the debate team, under the direction of Mr. Valois Zarr."[41] Russell sang in two high school operettas under Miss Bradford's direction: *Rose Marie* during his first year and *Maryland, My Maryland* during his last year.

When the a cappella choir performed at assemblies in other high schools and at various concerts throughout the valley, Miss Bradford put Russell "on display" to demonstrate his perfect pitch. She would place Russell at the stage's front and center and randomly call two or three people out of the audience to serve as witnesses. They would observe which note was played on the piano, after which Russell would be asked to identify the note for the audience. Everyone was amazed that he could accurately name the notes, but doing so seemed perfectly logical for Russell. It was not until Miss Bradford "made something of it" that he realized that not everyone possessed this gift of perfect pitch.[42]

Later, at the University of Utah, professor Thomas Giles would call on Russell to give the pitch for the university a cappella choir. This occasionally generated a small problem because Russell took choir during his lunch hour. Not infrequently, he would sneak a bite of sandwich during class only to hear Professor Giles say, "Nelson, give us our pitch!" Russell found that the gift of perfect pitch can sometimes even be annoying, such as when sopranos and certain musical instruments are out of tune.[43]

In addition to singing in the choir, Russell worked on the East

High School yearbook and participated in many other extracurricular activities, including debate.[44] His debate team partner was Glendon E. Johnson, whom Russell describes as "a very remarkable young man who was very intelligent, quick, and kind." Russell and Glendon became fast friends and together won many trophies. Upon graduating, they became debate partners for the University of Utah debate team.

During his freshman year in high school, Russell stood five-foot-four and weighed only 120 pounds. Undaunted by his diminutive stature, however, he tried out for and made the "C" football squad. The following year he didn't go out for football at all. At that time, students had to attend East High School for only two years, which meant Russell would have graduated at age fifteen—still five-foot-four and 120 pounds. His parents thought he would look a little peculiar going to college looking so young, so they decided that he should take another year at East High School to allow him time to literally grow up. And grow he did. During that third year, he reached six feet tall and 172 pounds, prompting him to try out for the "A" football team, which he made.[45]

But Russell never competed favorably with the other players in football. One of the reasons was that he always felt protective of his hands, fearing someone might step on them with their cleated shoes. "I think it was this awareness of my wanting to protect my hands that caused Coach W. McKinley Oswald to keep me on the bench during most of the games," Russell surmised. These were the same hands that would operate on Coach Oswald nearly forty years later![46]

Russell's sister Enid was grateful for his mature example as her older brother, and she has always considered him to be her best friend. She confessed to feeling some pressure following in Russell's footsteps in high school. For instance, the choir director, apparently wondering why she did not have perfect pitch, asked, "You're Russell's sister? What happened to you?" Enid later spent several years singing in the Mormon Tabernacle Choir.

Enid appreciated Russell's occasional intervention when her

parents thought it best that she stay home on a given evening. Russell would gently proffer his opinion that he thought it okay for Enid to go out provided she returned home at an appropriate hour. She recalled, "My parents sought and respected Russell's opinion."[47]

Looking back, Enid said, "I didn't know until 1984 how special Russell was." She then concluded, "I can see the hand of the Lord in preparing him. Choice men have been foreordained for positions of leadership, and their early lives are a period of preparation."[48]

During his years on the high school debate team, Russell and his partner would enter debate tournaments not knowing beforehand whether they would be taking the pro or the con side of a given issue. Such early training put him "at ease" in speaking extemporaneously, including during press conferences.[49] So it is that "out of small things proceedeth that which is great" (D&C 64:33).

CHAPTER 4

LOVE BLOSSOMS
IN A PEA PATCH

A FTER GRADUATING IN 1941 AS the East High School valedictorian, Russell had numerous opportunities for a college education outside of Salt Lake City, but he chose the University of Utah. "I really wanted to be there because I loved home more than any place else," he said. Three months after enrolling, on December 7, 1941, Pearl Harbor was attacked. Afterward, Russell's private world would never be the same.[1]

The outset of World War II caused many young men and women to think about the things that matter most in life, and it was about this time that Russell seriously reflected on the direction his life should take. His self-inventory of interests revealed a sincere desire to serve other people, and he responded well to courses requiring precision, such as chemistry, biology, and mathematics. Thus, his previous inclination toward a medical career was solidified. His parents seemed somewhat disappointed at Russell's preference for medicine because they had fostered a dream of passing on the successful advertising business to their sons. Nevertheless, they willingly supported him in his academic aspirations.[2]

Because of the war, Russell compressed four years of premedical preparation into only three years, and though his academic load was challenging and time-consuming, he still took time out for family events, dating, and other social activities. The first year at

the university, he had the leading role in the play *Excursion*, a part
he enjoyed playing very much.[3]

One day in 1942, Gail Plummer, of the University of Utah
theater staff, approached Russell, urging him to participate in the
play *Hayfoot, Strawfoot*. Because of the demands of his premedical
courses, Russell courteously declined the invitation. Later, for some
reason, Mr. Plummer returned with a persistent plea for Russell's
help in the production. "So with great reluctance, I finally agreed,"
Russell said.[4]

As he and Mr. Plummer entered Kingsbury Hall on April 16,
1942, Russell was suddenly overwhelmed by the soprano voice of a
beautiful brunette on stage. Russell asked Mr. Plummer, "Who is
that beautiful girl singing up there?" Mr. Plummer replied, "That's
Dantzel White. She's the one with whom you will be performing in
this play."[5]

At that moment, Russell sensed that this extraordinarily beautiful young woman might someday become his wife. He had dated
several girls, but at age seventeen, he was much more concerned
about pursuing a medical career than getting married. But after
meeting obligations for dates he had already arranged, Russell never
dated anyone but Dantzel. She had won his heart![6]

Dantzel was more than a year younger than Russell, so their
romance was largely confined to a companionship as friends. Two
months after their first meeting, Dantzel returned home to Perry,
Utah, for a three-month summer vacation. Upon arriving, she
announced to her parents that she had met "the perfect man."
Dantzel and Russell feel that they each received an independent confirmation by the Spirit that they would become eternal companions.[7]

Russell had a rich and successful experience as a university student. During his freshman year, he was elected to the honorary
scholastic fraternity, Phi Eta Sigma, in recognition for receiving
straight A's. He was subsequently elected to several other honorary
scholastic societies, including Skull and Bones, Owl and Key, the
Beehive Honorary Society, Phi Kappa Phi, and Phi Beta Kappa. In

*Dantzel and Russell at the
University of Utah in
1942.*

addition, he was elected president of Sigma Chi. Russell received his
bachelor's degree in June 1945; Dantzel received her degree the following year.[8]

Russell was admitted to the fourth class to enter the new
University of Utah four-year college of medicine, beginning his program in September 1944. The arduous demands of medical school
provided a great time of testing for medical students, both married
and unmarried. Dantzel and Russell often met on the lawn to eat
their sack lunches together, frequently in the company of their
friends Marjorie Taylor and Howard C. Sharp. After Russell and
Howard would spend an entire morning working in the anatomy
lab, they would meet their girlfriends for lunch "with the smell of
formaldehyde" reeking from their skin and clothes.[9]

By the summer of 1944, Russell and Dantzel's relationship had
become more serious, and Russell felt uneasy unless he could be
with her on a daily basis during the summer months. Located about

fifty miles north of Salt Lake City, Perry was considered to be a substantial distance from the capital, but Russell rode the Bamberger
train to see Dantzel as often as he could.[10]

Russell recalled that special summer of 1944: "As I would frequently ride the Bamberger train from Salt Lake City to Perry, my
feeling of deep love and affection became more firmly entrenched,
and the warm acceptance that I received from her wonderful parents, brothers, and sisters made me feel a love for the White family
that reinforced the impression that this union would be a highly
desirable one."[11]

One day, while Russell was visiting the White family home,
Dantzel's mother asked her and Russell to harvest a few fresh peas
for dinner. Many poets have written of romantic settings like laven-
der fields and meadows punctuated with clover in bloom, but for
Russell and Dantzel, love blossomed in a pea patch.[12]

As they walked through the pea patch on a beautiful new summer's day, there seemed to Russell to be no better spot to pop the
question. As he and the young woman whom he considered to be
the most beautiful in the world began picking peas, he slowly
reached over and held her hand, looked deeply into her dark, radiant
eyes, and asked, "Dantzel, will you please marry me?" The question
was not much of a surprise to her, but the unromantic setting of the
pea patch was a little unexpected. Nevertheless, she accepted his proposal on the spot. Russell recalled, "It didn't seem to be a very official
proposal, certainly not in a very romantic setting, but it was a ver-
balization of an unspoken agreement that we would marry when we
could."[13]

Inasmuch as both of them were students with no visible means
of support, Dantzel received no engagement ring. In fact, the ring
she now wears was a Christmas gift after she had been married
twelve years.[14]

In the summer of 1945, Russell's application to the Naval
Reserve was accepted. He would continue his medical education as
an apprentice seaman, and the navy would provide for his tuition

Wedding portrait taken at Russell and Dantzel's reception in the Jade Room of the Hotel Utah on August 31, 1945.

and books and pay him a whopping salary of $125 a month—
enough to enable the couple to marry.[15]

In his younger years, Russell had resisted his mother's attempts to
have him become a proficient pianist, but her efforts blossomed
many years later in the summer of 1945 when he took keyboard har-
mony and piano lessons from Professor William O. Peterson. As a
gifted musician herself, Dantzel was pleased with Russell's progress.[16]
In later years, he learned to play the organ, which has been a blessing to the Brethren since 1984, when he began accompanying the
hymns sung in their Thursday morning temple meetings.

On August 31, 1945, Russell and Dantzel were sealed to each
other in the Salt Lake Temple by Nicholas G. Smith. Russell
remembers the joy of seeing Dantzel in the temple and how angelic
she looked dressed in white. He was also pleased to see her mother
and father and other members of her family who were present.[17] But
the happiness of this occasion was diminished by the fact that
Russell's parents could not attend the sealing ceremony, and the only
members of his family to witness the wedding were his sister
Marjory and her husband, Bob Rohlfing. Russell's parents were,
however, supportive of his temple marriage, and they hosted a wedding breakfast in the Hotel Utah. That evening the Whites provided
a wedding reception in the Jade Room of the Hotel Utah, where
hundreds of friends and relatives extended their best wishes.[18]

Because Russell and Dantzel were married during a school break,
their honeymoon had to be brief. Russell's parents allowed them to
use their 1944 Dodge to tour Zion National Park and Bryce
Canyon, which are especially scenic in late summer. Their time
alone together was a wonderful experience, marred only by the fact
that Dantzel became quite ill after eating some nuts left over from
the wedding reception. As they arrived home and Russell's parents
discovered that Dantzel had been sick during her honeymoon,
"Their thoughts turned in a direction that required a little reassurance on our part," Russell recalls with a distinct twinkle in his eye.[19]

CHAPTER 5

DANTZEL: ANGELIC COMPANION, MOTHER OF TEN

DANTZEL'S GREAT-GRANDPARENTS, Elizabeth and Israel Justus Clark, married in New York and eventually joined the Saints in Nauvoo, where they were endowed and sealed January 30, 1846, in the Nauvoo Temple. Like many other faithful Saints, they were soon tested by the travails of severe persecution for their beliefs. The Clarks were not in the vanguard of pioneer Saints that left Nauvoo in February 1846, but in September 1846, a violent mob drove them and most of the remaining members of the Church out of Nauvoo. At age twenty-five, Elizabeth crossed the Mississippi River to Lee County, Iowa, where, on September 13, 1846, she gave birth to a baby boy under the protective cover of a wagon.

Elizabeth's husband, Israel, had remained behind in Nauvoo, providing assistance to others in crossing the vast Mississippi. During her delivery, Elizabeth was alarmed to hear the sound of gunshots across the river in Nauvoo. Fortunately, her husband soon safely joined her, and their little family began the trek westward. They named their baby Cyrus Edward Clark, and he would eventually become Dantzel's grandfather.[1]

Dantzel was born of saintly parents, Maude Clark and LeRoy Davis White, in Perry, Utah, on February 17, 1926. She has many pleasant memories of a happy home life as the fifth of seven children. Dantzel claims that her mother was much more energetic than

Dantzel's parents: LeRoy D. White and Maude C. White.

she, but her mother's family was smaller, and the children were spaced further apart.[2]

Dantzel's father was a prominent citizen in the community, serving as a bishop for eleven years and in the Utah House of Representatives for Box Elder County for several years. In addition to operating his farm, he was involved in banking and real estate, and he served for a time as the mayor of Perry.[3]

Dantzel was five when she entered kindergarten. About this same time, her sister Marjorie, eleven years her senior, contracted rheumatic fever and was bedridden for an extended period. Dantzel remembers sitting on her big sister's bed while Marjorie taught her how to sing. After Marjorie recovered, she took little Dantzel with her to high school, where Dantzel performed favorite Shirley Temple songs, such as "The Good Ship Lollipop," with the high school choir.[4] This experience helped Dantzel develop poise and self-confidence at a very tender age.

As the White sisters shared their dreams of the future, Dantzel's sister Beth always expressed her desires to marry a traveling man so she could see the world. By contrast, Dantzel aspired to marry a farmer so she could stay at home. She loved everything about the farm, including its sounds and smells. She enjoyed playing in the barn and dancing on top of the chicken coop, and she had a great affinity for farm animals. She loved to sit atop the family's large draft horse, which pulled the plow as her father guided it up and down the furrows of the field. She also rode the derrick horse, which pulled the rope attached to the "jack-fork" as hay was transported from the hay wagon to the top of the haystack.[5]

As she reached high school age, Dantzel became good friends with two young men who would eventually become General Authorities. One of them was a young lad named Boyd K. Packer from Brigham City; the other was Malcolm S. Jeppson from Mantua. In those days, it was usually the athletes who gained the attention and admiration of their peers, but Dantzel remembers that, although neither Boyd nor Malcolm played on the athletic teams, both were widely admired and respected student leaders.[6]

Boyd Packer was artistic and was generally in charge of the decorations for the school proms. He also painted the scenery for school plays and musicals, such as *Seven Brides for Seven Brothers*, in which Dantzel played the part of one of the older daughters. Every Christmas, Boyd would paint a beautiful winter scene on the windows of his father's garage and car dealership.[7]

Malcolm Jeppson was the senior class president, and his ready wit endeared him to all his friends. He and Dantzel had a mutual friend who died an untimely death from cancer during their teens, and both Malcolm and Dantzel spoke at her funeral. This event sensitized the youth of Box Elder High School to a realization of their own mortality and of their need to take life seriously and to prepare for the eternities.[8]

Toward the end of her senior year, Dantzel was surprised to see her parents, in the middle of the school day, attending the school's last program prior to graduation. Her father was a member of the school board, so it was not unusual to have him come to the stand.

But Dantzel was completely surprised when he presented her with the American Legion Medal for the Outstanding High School Student. The medal was inscribed with the words "Courage, Character, Service, Companionship, and Scholarship."[9]

Dantzel's mother was eager to have all her children gain an appreciation for good music, so they took piano lessons from Aunt Gladys White in nearby Willard. Dantzel also sang in the high school glee club and served in the color guard for the marching band. As her beautiful singing voice began to mature, her parents provided her with lessons from professor Richard P. Condie of the music faculty at the University of Utah, who was also assistant conductor of the Mormon Tabernacle Choir. Dantzel would catch the Bamberger train from Perry to Salt Lake City and walk up the avenues to the old McCune Mansion for her voice lessons.[10]

After Dantzel enrolled at the University of Utah, she continued her lessons and often performed recitals in the McCune Mansion. While she participated in student teaching at East High School, the musical director, Miss Lisle Bradford, would invite Richard Condie and Dantzel to sing duets for her students. They also sang duets during performances of the a cappella choir at the University of Utah. Years later, Brother Condie sang "The Lord's Prayer" at the funeral for Dantzel's father.[11]

After meeting Dantzel in the musical production *Hayfoot, Strawfoot*, Russell enthusiastically recalled, "My attention for her was so immediate and so compelling, I find it very easy to believe that my affinity for her may have been established in a holier pre-mortal sphere." From that moment on, he "loved to be with her and loathed being apart from her."[12]

The love Russell felt for Dantzel soon expanded to all members of her family as they warmly welcomed Russell's visits to their home. Russell said, "Her parents were so dear and kind to me. When I finally asked for her hand in marriage, they were so understanding and supportive. Father White's handling of that situation proved to

Russell and Dantzel shortly before announcing their engagement in the summer of 1945.

be a worthy model for me when I was in the same circumstance many years later."[13]

After Russell and Dantzel's marriage, he occasionally joined Dantzel's brothers in fishing and golfing, and White family reunions became cherished associations for Russell and Dantzel and their children as cousins developed a genuine love for each other throughout the years.[14] Dantzel's father was a good husband and father, and he became an admired friend to Russell. Of Dantzel's mother, Russell said, "She was an influence for good, and I revere her for rearing a daughter who would bear and rear ten wonderful children. Dantzel's mother always went the extra mile and was available whenever she was needed, and Grandmother White became a very special person to each of the Nelson children."[15]

Russell humbly acknowledges that "having lived closely by the side of this angel, Dantzel, for these many years, I can truly say that I've never met a person more selfless and completely without guile. Some people have written eloquent poetry about loving one another, and others have expressed their love in song, but this precious woman's very life is a living answer to the questions: 'What can I do in my life to bless others? How can I be more righteous, more honest in my doings?'"[16]

Sometimes Dantzel's unflinching commitment to honesty has been a great source of family amusement. On one occasion, she and Russell boarded a flight from New York City to Salt Lake City. They had just transferred from a long and tiresome overnight flight from South America and had been assigned specific seat numbers on the flight. Only a handful of passengers were on the large plane, which had plenty of room for passengers to flip back their arm rests, enabling them to stretch out and take a good nap. When Russell suggested to Dantzel that one of them leave their assigned seat so they could stretch out and recline in a more comfortable fashion elsewhere on the plane, she was reluctant to do so. It was only after the flight attendant assured Dantzel that it would be all right to change seats that she yielded to Russell's persuasion to get the rest she so badly needed.[17]

Reflecting upon his pea patch proposal, Russell stands in awe at the faith Dantzel had in making marriage vows with a young, unproven, premedical student. In effect, she was casting her future with his, dedicating herself to motherhood so that her children might be fulfilled through her selfless efforts.

Dantzel had just been accepted for admission to the Julliard School of Music when the desire for marriage preempted her accepting that opportunity. Dantzel's mother was disappointed because she realized the great talent her daughter possessed. At the university, Dantzel had elicited shouts of approval from the audience after singing "Vissi d'arte," from *Tosca*, and "Ah, fors' e lui," from *La Traviata*. The power of her voice was inspiring.

"Yet, in making the decision to marry me," Russell said, "she ultimately exchanged a promising future in music for the privilege of singing lullabies to her little ones in a rocker and cradle."[18]

When they made their vows in the temple, Dantzel unequivocally said, "Yes." As Russell took her to Minnesota for his internship, she again said, "Yes." When Russell answered the call to military duty in Washington, D.C., which later took him to war in Korea, she willingly stayed behind in faraway Utah with their two children and their extended families. When Dr. Nelson said he would like to remain an additional year in Boston before returning to Minneapolis, Dantzel again agreed.

Russell recalled, "In the meantime, as we welcomed our third daughter and were getting ready to bring our fourth child into the world, never once did she murmur because some of her classmates had homes and furniture of their own after they had been married seven or eight years." The years went on and the debts piled up, Russell said, as "the Lord blessed us with a continuing increase as daughter after daughter was brought into the world through their saintly mother."[19]

With unvarnished pride in his eternal companion, Russell recalled those early years together: "Totally committed to the Lord and to His church, Dantzel cheerfully responded to all the calls that came to her. While living in Boston, she served as district Relief Society counselor, which took her to Maine, New Hampshire, and remote parts of Massachusetts. Whether her service was in Minneapolis, Washington, Boston, or Salt Lake City, she has always loved to teach young children, and she has felt ennobled by service and callings in the Primary." During Russell's service as stake president, Dantzel was called as the choir director of the Singing Mothers of the stake. The choir's outstanding concert performances reflected her musical expertise.[20]

Two years after returning to Salt Lake City, Dantzel was invited to join the Squeakers and Squawkers Club, a group of accomplished women musicians. Some group members were violinists with the Utah Symphony, while others were pianists or vocalists. They would rotate each month for lunch at the homes of the various members, during which one member would perform a composition for violin or piano, and another would sing a solo.[21] To encourage the development of their talents, they established a rule requiring that each member prepare and perform a composition that she had never previously performed.[22]

Obedient to Elder Kimball's counsel at the time Russell was called to be stake president, Dantzel postponed her participation in the Mormon Tabernacle Choir, despite persistent prodding from choir director Richard P. Condie, her former vocal teacher. Only after the children grew older did she agree to sing with the choir. Dantzel loved her twenty years of singing with the choir. Generally, whenever she went away on a choir tour, Russell stayed home to assume domestic responsibilities as "Mr. Mom."

Frequently, when the Mormon Tabernacle Choir was on tour, Dantzel and Russell's sister Enid would be hotel roommates. Enid observed firsthand Russell's deep and abiding love for Dantzel. Every day during a choir tour, Dantzel would discover a beautiful new love note lying in her sheet music or a heartfelt expression of affection tucked away in an article of clothing.[23]

For two weeks in June 1982, Elder Nelson accompanied Sister Nelson and other choir members on a concert tour of Norway, Sweden, Finland, Denmark, Holland, and England aboard the cruise ship *Oceanos*. This was the only time he accompanied Dantzel while she was a member of the choir.[24]

After the Nelsons had built their hideaway home in Midway, they would sometimes spend weekends there. Occasionally, Russell would stay in Midway for Sunday School and priesthood meeting while Dantzel would drive back to Salt Lake City to participate in the weekly broadcast of "Music and the Spoken Word." When asked where Sister Nelson was, Russell would respond, "She's in the Tabernacle Choir," adding, "I come first in her life, right after the Tabernacle Choir." He admitted, "She would not agree with that statement, but she did jealously guard her time so that she would be able to fulfill that duty."[25]

Russell gained greater appreciation for Dantzel one Saturday afternoon during her absence. When one of their daughters came home, she flew right past her father as though he didn't even exist and asked, "Where's Mom?"[26] It was always a wonderful feeling for the children to come home and find their mother there.

Russell recalls a discussion he and Dantzel had one summer in the northern woods of Minnesota before their first daughter, Marsha, was born, in which they gingerly discussed how large a family to have. Russell said, "We each timidly queried the other's attitude on that question, but after we had explored it a bit, we both came to the conclusion that an even dozen would do! I don't know how serious we were at that time; we were so young and naive. We didn't know what it was like to be the parents of one, let alone one dozen. How the Lord blessed us with those lovely children one by one!"[27]

One night as Dantzel and Russell were walking down Boylston Street in Boston, Dantzel pressed her nose against the windowpane of a furniture store and wistfully asked, "Do you think we'll ever be able to afford a lamp?" They had been married nine years by then, and Russell thought this was not an unreasonable request. They had become accustomed to looking at the things others had without really feeling much envy because they simply knew they could not afford them. That was the only time Russell ever heard Dantzel express a desire for any material possessions she did not have. "It seems amazing to me that a woman could genuinely be as selfless as she has been," he says, "for all she ever wanted was enough to provide for the children that were so near and dear to us."[28]

Russell has seen Dantzel suffer the agony of several operations and the pain of a herniated spinal disc, with its nerve root irritation. He has seen her endure the pain of heavy labor amplified by an intravenous drip of strong uterine stimulants that caused her blood pressure to soar and her body to develop hemorrhages as a result of associated strain.[29] Her five-year bout with lymphoma, requiring surgery and subsequent chemotherapy, with its unpleasant side effects, enhanced Russell's devotion to his eternal companion, who always bore her suffering with patience and faith.

Russell recalled: "I've seen her pick up her children after injury or amidst a convulsion resulting from a high fever, and she was never beyond control. She was always composed, calm, and in command, as if having been given a special dimension of strength when needed for the benefit and welfare of those depending on her. How grateful I am that not one of our beautiful children has ever been, even for a moment, disrespectful or disobedient to her. They, too, know of her saintly nature and sense almost continuously that their being is a result of her willingness and eagerness to give them life and quality of life."[30]

Someone once asked Dantzel how she managed to rear ten children with so little help from her busy surgeon-husband. She candidly replied, "When I married him, I didn't expect much, so I was never disappointed."[31] One of the Nelson daughters observed that when someone asked her mother how she dealt with all the stress of rearing such a large family, Dantzel calmly replied, "What stress?"[32]

Asked about growing up with parents like Russell and Dantzel, the Nelson children candidly replied, "Mother's perfect, and Daddy nearly is." The children, now with families and child-rearing challenges of their own, observe that "patience" is the characteristic that best describes their mother. Not one of them recalls ever having seen their mother become angry or raise her voice. The daughters do remember, however, on rare occasion, hearing their father late at night bellow in an authoritative voice from the top of the stairs, "Could you girls please keep it down; there are people whose lives depend upon your father getting a good night's sleep!"[33]

One day as Brenda dropped by to visit her mother, her two-year-old daughter accidentally broke one of Dantzel's beautiful, expensive Lladro figurines. The little granddaughter immediately sensed she was in deep trouble, and as she began to cry, her loving grandmother quickly enveloped her in her arms and said, "Mindy, don't worry about that. It's just a thing, and that's not important. You're the one who's important."[34]

On another occasion, Rosalie brought her infant son, Tally, to visit his grandmother. The baby had not been feeling well, so Rosalie had given him some red gelatin water in a bottle. Suddenly, Tally threw up, splattering the red mixture on Dantzel's light-colored carpet. The red coloring permanently discolored the carpet, and all attempts at removing the stains failed. Without the least degree of distress, Dantzel merely put a small area rug over the discolored section and never mentioned the incident afterward.[35] The Savior's words to His disciples describe Dantzel well: "In your patience possess ye your souls" (Luke 21:19).

Dantzel confessed to an occasion when she *nearly* lost her temper. She had inherited a family heirloom, a beautiful cut-glass bowl that had been given to her mother as a wedding gift, which she had placed on a table in the living room. As the grandchildren were playing upstairs on this occasion, a ball came rolling down, bouncing onto the table and smashing the bowl into countless shards of glass. After taking a deep breath, she said, "Well, it's my own fault. I should have known better than to put that beautiful cut-glass bowl on that table with little children around."[36]

Dantzel recalled a statement by her mother: "When the children come home and leave their dirty fingerprints on the windows, cupboards, and doors, I don't know whether I should wash them off or varnish them on."[37]

One year the members of the Yale Second Ward participated in a production of *Fiddler on the Roof*, with Dantzel playing the part of Golda, the Jewish-Russian mother. Some of the Nelson daughters took parts as Golda's daughters. In one scene, Golda was supposed to become upset with one of her daughters. Gloria was shocked to see her mother acting angry, but Brenda, smiling, admitted, "Mother really wasn't very convincing while acting as if she were angry."[38]

Dantzel loved caring for her newborn grandchildren just as she had enjoyed caring for her own infants. Brenda, after arriving home from the hospital with a new baby, learned a great lesson from her mother about the things that matter most. Instead of cleaning the house and doing the dishes, her mother would cuddle and read to the young siblings so that they felt loved and secure when the new competition arrived. Brenda recalled, "The house was not spotless when the new baby came home, but the younger children had been perfectly primed by their loving grandmother to anxiously await the arrival of their new little sibling with great love and anticipation."[39]

The Nelson daughters recalled how, when they were little girls, their mother would prepare them for their dad's arrival home from work by saying, "Okay, girls, let's pick up all your toys so the house will be clean when Daddy comes home. And when he walks through the door, let's all give him some hugs and kisses." Dantzel was, in many respects, the CEO of a challenging conjugal corporation, and she was efficient at giving her daughters different jobs. In the process, she showed them that it was fun to be a mother.

The daughters indicated that their mother taught domestic skills more by example than by systematic instruction. They helped their mother bake cookies and make candy, but Dantzel did not consciously prepare them for future marriage by having them master twenty recipes. Rather, she impressed her daughters with her cooking abilities and obvious pleasure in preparing meals, not only for the family but also for frequent guests in their home. For example, rather than serve halibut casserole on a plate, she would serve it in large individual seashells, thus teaching the importance of meal presentation.[40] Dantzel still receives several phone calls each week from her daughters, requesting consultation regarding how much salt to put in the stew or how long the rolls should rise before going into the oven.

The daughters are older now and lead their own lives, but they reciprocate their mother's support and assistance, especially when she entertains large groups in the Nelson home. When Elder Hans B. Ringger was granted emeritus status after having served as a Seventy for ten years, Russell and Dantzel wanted to honor Hans and his wife, Helen, for their faithful service in furthering the work of the kingdom in Europe. The Nelsons invited to their home all of the former mission presidents and wives who had worked with the Ringgers during his ten years in the area presidency in Europe. Notwithstanding the large numbers of guests, the Nelson sisters quietly and unobtrusively assisted with preparing and serving food, refilling drinks, and cleaning up. The sons-in-law cheerfully served as chauffeurs and parking valets. At the end of the evening, Dantzel had feelings of satisfaction rather than of being overwhelmed.

Dantzel has accompanied Russell to China on various occasions. On one trip, while he was instructing the Chinese physicians in the finer points of cardiovascular and thoracic surgery, she was asked to teach English to the medical students, who needed English language proficiency to go abroad for advanced training. On another trip, she was asked to teach English in an elementary school. When the time came to bid their friends farewell, Russell remarked, that the tears shed for Dantzel easily exceeded those shed for him.[41]

Marsha said of her mother, "She thrives in the background; she is not a limelight person. She loves to create fun and memories at all of the family gatherings." As the oldest daughter, Marsha still remembers some of the times her father faced the most pressures. "One of Mother's greatest gifts to us was the way she prepared us for the last-minute interruptions which prevented Daddy from attending one of our programs or recitals," she said. "Instead of letting it become a little crisis, Mother would say, 'Something very important has come up, so Daddy won't be able to make it, but we're going to have a great time anyway.'"[42]

Life has not always been easy for Dantzel. As she and Russell have traveled among people who believe that large families are the cause of the world's problems, she has not always been received warmly. Her reward is the knowledge that she has been obedient to the laws of God and to the commitments she and her husband made in the temple. Her testimony has fortified her against the wiles of the adversary and strengthened her for her trials.[43]

Dr. Conrad B. Jenson, Russell's professional colleague, associate,

*Dantzel W. Nelson is introduced to
members of the Jacksonville Florida
West Stake during stake conference
on January 19, 1997.*

and close friend for more than thirty years, said of Dantzel, "She is a queen among women."[44]

Elder Nelson's apostolic colleague, Elder Robert D. Hales, described his brother in the Quorum of the Twelve as a "great husband and father." He then added, "His wife is something! One thing you learn about this man is that he can do the things he has done because he has been married to an incredibly selfless caregiver."[45]

On one of his visits to the Nelsons' home in Midway, President Thomas S. Monson recalled watching Dantzel play basketball one-on-one with Russell Jr. "She could dribble and shoot as well as young Russell could," he said. President Monson observed, "With Russell and Dantzel, one plus one equals three, and Dantzel is a big part of the equation."[46]

As a tender tribute to his companion of fifty-seven years, Russell said of Dantzel, "I don't know how long she will live or whether I may precede her in death. It is well we don't know those things. But I do know that she loves God and He loves her. The most challenging task that I might have will be to be worthy of life with her, as promised through our temple covenants, in those eternities that lie ahead. If I can do this, I will be worthy of the love that she has so selflessly given to each of us. I love her and honor her as one of God's noble, special, and sacred creations with whom it has been my great privilege to live."[47]

The concluding verses in Proverbs characterize well this angelic mother of ten: "She openeth her mouth with wisdom; and in her tongue is the law of kindness. She looketh well to the ways of her household, and eateth not the bread of idleness. Her children arise up, and call her blessed; her husband also, and he praiseth her" (Proverbs 31:26–28).

CHAPTER 6

CHILDREN ARE AN
HERITAGE OF THE LORD

AFTER RUSSELL AND DANTZEL moved to Minneapolis, Dantzel often became extremely lonesome because Russell's internship consumed nearly all of his time. While he studied at the University of Utah Medical School, she at least had relatives and friends nearby. In Minnesota, Russell was required to remain at the hospital for several days at a stretch, and Dantzel often traveled the cold, snowy, icy streets of Minneapolis more than ten miles twice daily to teach school, only to return to an empty apartment.[1]

Russell remembers one night when Dantzel said over the phone somewhat tearfully, "I've got to have something *live* around the house." Russell said, "I recognized that this was a reasonable request—so I bought her a goldfish!" This event, along with nudges from other sources, caused them to realize that, despite their poverty, the time had come to begin their family. It was not long afterward that they were expecting their first child.[2]

MARSHA

Marsha arrived July 29, 1948, as Russell's internship year drew to a close. Dantzel shared hospital facilities with Muriel Humphrey, the wife of Hubert H. Humphrey, mayor of Minneapolis and subsequent senator from Minnesota. After Marsha's birth, Dantzel's mother came to Minneapolis to give her the benefit of her experience and wisdom as well as her love and service for those first few postpartum days. The Nelson parents provided a new crib, which was subsequently used for all ten of the Nelson children. It would be many, many years before Dantzel would again yearn for "something *live* around the house."[3]

"Marsha blessed our lives as only the first child can," Russell said. "She converted Dantzel's life from one of potential to one of purpose. We all seemed to grow together, for we were as new at parenthood as she was at childhood. Because we wanted several children, Dantzel and I reasoned that if our first child turned out well, that would be our best assurance the others would too. Marsha has repaid us many times for our efforts on her behalf."[4]

As the icebreaker, Marsha was blessed with all the attention the first child receives, but she also suffered from deprivations caused by the lengthy medical education her father had chosen. For many years, she slept in a sleeping bag on a cot in lieu of having her own canopy bed with a mattress, bedspread, and decorative pillows. She learned, however, to adapt to all the changes in the lives of her parents.

On one of those rare occasions when Russell had a free weekend, he and Dantzel took little Marsha for a boat ride on one of the many lakes near Minneapolis. After the minutes turned into hours, Marsha decided it was time to get out of the boat, and she would have stepped out into the water but for the persuasive restraint of her parents.

Years later, Russell would use this incident to illustrate the plan of eternal progression, urging the Saints to get on the boat and stay on it until they reached their heavenly harbor.[5]

Notwithstanding all the disruptions in her young life, moving from Minneapolis to Boston to Washington, D.C., to Minneapolis again, to Salt Lake City, Marsha contends that she had "a completely happy and wonderful childhood." She agrees with her mother that "when Dad was home he was completely available. When we were little, he gave us baths, and when we were older, he helped us with our homework." The only time she remembers her father watching television was on New Year's Day when he would spread out papers and review the family's annual financial condition while watching football games.[6]

Music became a high priority in Marsha's life. She learned to play the piano and violin well, and, like her mother, she learned to sing well. As she reached her teens, Russell recalled, "She worked in our professional office, assisting our secretary-receptionist, Mrs. Helen P. Kemp, and brightening the lives of all of us and our patients." In 1970, she married H. Christopher McKellar, himself an accomplished professional musician who is the principal violist in the Utah Symphony. Marsha and Chris became the parents of Nathan Christopher, Stephen Hugh, Laura, and Angela, providing Russell and Dantzel with their first grandchildren.[7]

WENDY

Born during the uncertainty of the Korean War, on April 5, 1951, in Washington, D.C., Wendy was a small baby by Nelson standards. Russell and Dantzel were concerned that little Wendy was susceptible to illness during her infancy, and they sometimes wondered if she would survive her first year on earth. Happily, through the tender care of her mother and the caring companionship of her older sister, Wendy's resistance to illness increased and she began to thrive.[8]

Like her mother and older sister, Wendy sings beautifully. She also plays the piano and guitar. In her younger years, she also had a natural affinity for ballet and modern dance. Her parents referred to her as "the peacemaker" in their home because she provided a calming influence within a household in which as many as five children shared one bedroom.[9] Wendy later confessed that she loved sleeping in the same room with her sisters.[10] In fact, her mother said that when the family moved from their home on 1300 East in Salt Lake City to their present, larger home on Normandie Circle, the first year all the girls still insisted on sleeping in the same bedroom.[11]

Wendy has always been outgoing and gregarious, enjoying many friends of both genders. Russell recalled, "We became adroit at handling the awkward situation in which more than one boyfriend was in our home at the same time."[12] Wendy recalls her mother waiting up for the girls after their dates so they could "just talk about things."[13]

Russell recalled, "Young Elder Norman A. Maxfield momentarily interrupted his missionary labors in Australia to make an important long-distance phone call to reinforce his relationship with Wendy at a crucial time in her life."[14] Two years after Elder Maxfield arrived home from an honorable mission, Norman and Wendy were married in the Salt Lake Temple. Their marriage has been blessed with seven children: Marissa, Blake Jeremy, Matthew Nelson, Brady Norman, Megan, Bryndy, and Makenzie. Norman is an orthodontist and has served as a bishop in the Church.

When Norm was in dental school and the couple lived far from their parents' homes, Wendy fondly remembers the weekly letters she received from her father.[15]

GLORIA

While Russell and Dantzel were living in Washington, D.C., their third daughter, Gloria, arrived amid prayerful circumstances. Dantzel's expected delivery date was Sunday, September 21, 1952. The next day, Russell had an assignment to go to New York City for a week. As Dantzel's due date approached with no apparent sign of labor, Russell became concerned about leaving her alone to deliver the baby and care for the other two children. On September 21, Russell and Dantzel attended the morning session of stake conference. Afterward, Russell said, "We supplicated the Lord in mighty prayer that the baby might come."[16]

Shortly thereafter, Dantzel began experiencing the onset of labor, and at 1:45 P.M. their lovely, healthy baby girl arrived—just before the beginning of the afternoon session of stake conference, during which news of the baby's arrival was announced. Russell recalled, "We were so overwhelmed and grateful, the only phrase we could think of was 'Glory to God in the highest.' So we named our daughter Gloria, that she and we might always remember our gratitude to a loving Heavenly Father who answered our prayers."[17]

Russell declared with some delight, "Gloria and Wendy were our two little bargain babies. Because I was in the army at the time, our out-of-pocket expenses for their deliveries were under $5 each." Gloria was a healthy and happy little lady who always seemed to be invincible amid the vicissitudes of life. Russell recalled a New England clambake that left the toddler covered with mosquito bites. "But she smiled so contagiously," he said, "everyone about her became happy too."[18]

Gloria described her father's efforts in assisting her mother to care for the young children, especially on Saturdays: "He was always a tender father. He didn't need to unwind in front of the TV, and he had no need to vent his emotions." She shared fond memories of how he would preside at Saturday night baths with a "four-in-a-tub-shampoo-train." Russell would pour water and a dab of shampoo on each little girl's head and then have them massage each other's scalps until he gave the command, "About face." Then, amid giggles of great glee, the girls would turn around in the tub and begin to shampoo the hair of the sister who had just been working on them. The shampoo train was an elementary lesson on the Golden Rule.[19]

Gloria had such an enthusiastic penchant for football, baseball, and tennis that she once informed her parents that she was their "boy." She also demonstrated athletic prowess as an expert swimmer and diver, which qualified her to work as a lifeguard and instructor at the Salt Lake Swimming and Tennis Club and also at the Deseret Gymnasium.[20]

Like her sisters, Gloria also has a lovely singing voice, and she plays the piano, violin, and accordion. Gloria, Wendy, Brenda, Sylvia, and Emily all enjoyed ballet, performing in *The Nutcracker* at the University of Utah.[21]

Several Latter-day Saint young men visited Gloria at the Nelson home, but her parents had some serious concerns when a young man of another faith began frequenting their residence. During several serious discussions about temple marriage and the eternal nature of families, Gloria sought to assuage her parents' anxieties by continually assuring them that Rich Irion was "just a friend." But with the passage of time, their friendship turned to love. After many prayers and several sleepless nights, and much to Dantzel and Russell's delight, Rich began studying the gospel. Though Gloria may have initiated Rich's interest in the Church, with assistance from an institute teacher named Jeffrey R. Holland, his conversion to The Church of Jesus Christ of Latter-day Saints was real, true, and lasting. Elder Holland recalled that when Rich walked into his first institute class, "I saw 'Latter-day Saint' written all over him."[22]

Gloria and Rich were married in the Salt Lake Temple on March 14, 1974. They are the parents of Elizabeth, Kathryn, Richard Nelson, Emily, Robert Alan, Lindsay, and Russell Thomas. Rich is an obstetrician and gynecologist and has served as a bishop.[23]

BRENDA

Russell and Dantzel's fourth-born was Brenda, who arrived February 3, 1954, while Dr. Nelson extended his medical training in Boston. Her birth was different from the birth of her siblings because the other children had been born in hospitals where their father was working, and he could be close at hand to encourage and sustain Dantzel in her labor. Because the Massachusetts General Hospital had no obstetrical patients, Dantzel went instead to the Richardson House at the Boston Lying-in Hospital, where all deliveries were done by appointment. Women were brought in the night before labor was to be induced and then scheduled for delivery, much as one would schedule an elective operation. Dr. Nelson's duties at the Massachusetts General Hospital were such that he could not be excused to be with his wife. So, on February 3, 1954, the head nurse announced the great moment to him as he was in the operating room. She entered and said, "Doctor Nelson?"

"Yes," he responded.

"We've just received word from the Richardson House that your wife has successfully delivered your new baby," she said.

"Yes," he replied, concentrating on the human life in his care at that moment.

"Would you like to know what it is?"

"Yes."

"It is your fourth baby girl!" she said. "She and your wife are doing well!"

Tears of joy drenched Dr. Nelson's surgical mask. He was extremely disappointed about not having been with Dantzel, but she felt that she had received better care at the Richardson House than in any other hospital. Russell said, "She commented on the lovely pink linens used for bed sheets in the hospital and the elegant service she received, and she did not seem to feel deprived at all."[24]

Dantzel's sister Marjorie W. Mecham and her daughter Patricia appeared as ministering angels shortly after Brenda's birth to care for Marsha, Wendy, and Gloria, as well as Dantzel. The Nelsons greatly enjoyed their visit and managed to find time to take them to the seashore and enjoy french-fried clams. They also bought some fresh lobsters, which Marsha used for lobster races on the linoleum floor of the kitchen. The lobsters were later cooked in baby Brenda's sparkling new diaper pail.[25]

Each of the Nelson children has unique talents and traits. Brenda established her unique niche through a special head of hair that stood out straight, as if she had just put her finger in a light socket. She was a cute, cuddly, and welcome addition to the growing Nelson clan.[26]

Brenda often complained of becoming carsick on family automobile trips, but quite miraculously her symptoms could be alleviated by ice cream cones. She became known as the "ice cream girl" because that particular panacea seemed to cure anything that went awry.

Brenda was a delightful traveling companion, frequently providing comic relief during long trips in close quarters. Like most young children, she was inquisitive, persevering until her curiosity was completely satisfied.[27]

Brenda's persistence was reflected in the way she practiced the flute until she became quite proficient. Today, it is reflected in her competency as a teacher and in her unmeasured patience, which elicits love and admiration from children.[28]

Brenda described her adolescent years as a lot of fun, "like living in a girls' dorm. We all got along fine, except for occasional disagreements regarding who got to wear which clothes." She recalled the anticipation before school started each fall when her mother would sort out all the hand-me-downs. Speaking as the fourth daughter, Brenda said, "We all loved getting to wear our older sisters' clothes."[29]

Reading scriptures around the table each morning remains a vivid and pleasant memory for Brenda. She also recalls the thrill she felt when her mother brought Marjorie, the last daughter, home from the hospital. She was, however, rather disappointed when, six and one-half years later, little Russell ruined the perfect string of nine girls in succession. Since then, of course, she has become, along with the other Nelson sisters, a member of the Russell Jr. fan club.[30]

Richard L. Miles, who served in the Germany Hamburg Mission, eventually came courting. Soon thereafter, on December 16, 1975, Dick and Brenda were married in the Salt Lake Temple. They are proud of their progeny: Courtney, Melinda, Tyler Richard, Bryson Nelson, and Rachel. Dick is a real estate developer and Church leader.[31]

SYLVIA

About three months after Russell and Dantzel had left Minnesota for Salt Lake City, their fifth daughter arrived, on June 6, 1955. They named her Sylvia, a name they had loved for years.

Russell recalls, "She came in a hurry. I remember bringing Dantzel to the hospital around seven in the morning. Knowing that there would be a few preliminaries at which I would not be particularly needed, I told her that I would go over to my office, make rounds briefly, and then return to be at her side. When I returned, Dantzel was in labor, and I just barely made it in time to sustain her during Sylvia's arrival."[32]

Very early in her development, Sylvia demonstrated an adventuresome spirit. Russell recalled, "When Sylvia was only two and a half, she wandered away from home to follow her sisters to the Douglas School. She ended up in the arms of a police officer, who sang her to sleep and then brought her safely home, but not until he had her picture taken for the newspaper."[33]

Sylvia has also been known for her courage. Facing a number of health challenges and painful medical procedures, she has always risen above the darkened clouds to bask in the light. Like her sisters, Sylvia is a gifted singer, and she plays the piano, violin, and guitar.[34]

Sylvia's memories of home include Sunday morning scrimmages between the girls as they would contend for slips, curlers, and panty hose. Sometimes the scrimmages would expand to include the complaint, "She's dating my boyfriend!" According to Sylvia, "We were typical teenage girls."[35]

Sylvia has always been a selfless person, and Dantzel knew she could count on her help around the house to lighten a mother's load. These qualities were soon recognized by young David R. Webster, who swept Sylvia off her feet and married her in the Salt Lake Temple on March 15, 1977. The sealing was performed by his former mission president, Elder William Grant Bangerter, who had presided over David's pioneering missionary efforts in Portugal. David and Sylvia are the proud parents of David Reed Jr., Rosalie Brynn, Daniel Jonathan, Sarah Jane, Jacob Russell, Samuel Nelson, and Adam Michael. Dave is a hotelier, has been a bishop, and is a member of a stake presidency.[36]

EMILY

Because Emily's arrival on January 15, 1958, was a full month later than anticipated, she weighed in at ten pounds five ounces. Later that year, Emily developed severe convulsions and became rigid. Dr. Paul Rasmussen diagnosed spinal meningitis as she lay in a coma for several days. Russell tearfully recalled, "How we prayed for her. Finally, we supplicated the Lord in prayer, telling Him that we were so grateful to Him for sending that little spirit to us. We thanked Him most sincerely, and I said, weeping, that if He needed her now more than I needed her, I, as her father, was prepared to release her to Him for His care."[37]

Unaware that Emily would not be called to her heavenly home until thirty-seven years later, Russell wrote of her infant illness, "I suppose it will never be required of me to undergo a test such as Abraham had with Isaac, but this came about as close as I may expect to come. Literally I had come to the point where I sensed that the Lord was asking me if I would be able to yield to His desire in calling her home." Continuing, he said, "Shortly after we united in prayer and let the Lord know that we were willing to release her, she began to improve. Her fever broke and she convalesced. The miracle of her recovery is one for which we shall always be grateful."[38]

A few years later, Emily was out in the yard one day with her father when they heard the familiar chimes of the ice cream wagon approaching. When innocent Emily asked her daddy for a dollar to buy some ice cream, he rather heartlessly responded, "Why don't you earn your money like everyone else?" Tears welled up in little Emily's eyes as she replied, "But Daddy, I don't like to work!"[39]

Notwithstanding her initial reluctance to earn bread by the sweat of her brow, many years later Emily wanted to participate in the Brigham Young University study abroad program in Vienna. To raise necessary funds, she worked as a waitress in a restaurant and got another job at a clothing store.

Always a sweet and gentle daughter, Emily had an inherent

desire to do what is right. Russell reminisced about the time he had been offered a position as professor of surgery in Chicago, which would have meant a move from Salt Lake City. "I called our family council together," he said. "The older girls were understandably reluctant to move and expressed themselves honestly. When it came Emily's turn for expression, she shed a few tears and said, 'If you want to go, Daddy, I'll go with you.' Then I wept when I realized what she was willing to do for me."[40]

Emily excelled academically, and she was an excellent musician, dancer, and seamstress. In 1978, she sang and danced in *A Christmas Carol*, produced by Promised Valley Playhouse in Salt Lake City.[41]

In May 1980 Emily married Bradley E. Wittwer in the Salt Lake Temple. He had served as a missionary in Italy. They were blessed with William Marion, Wendy, Nelson Bradley, Preston Haycock, and their "miracle baby," Jordan White, who was born perfectly normal, notwithstanding that his mother had to undergo chemotherapy during her pregnancy. Following Emily's death on January 29, 1995, the Nelson sisters offered help in Brad's home, and they supported his later efforts to find a new mother for his five children. Their combined prayers were answered when in February 1998 Brad married Julie Veranth.[42] Their daughter, Kennedy, and son, Joshua Russell, are regarded as Nelson grandchildren.

LAURIE

Shortly after Laurie's birth on April 27, 1959, she was whisked away by the nurses to be cleansed and clothed, later to be returned to her proud parents. Russell was seated at Dantzel's bedside while the nurses down the hall at LDS Hospital were engaged in post-delivery activities. Suddenly, Dantzel exclaimed, "I hear our baby crying."[43]

Russell was astonished at her comment, replying, "You've got to be kidding; you've never seen our baby yet." But Dantzel persisted, "That's our baby. I know her voice."[44]

As a scientific skeptic, Russell left the room and sauntered down
the hospital hallway until he saw a long cart that conveyed all the
babies to their respective mothers. Russell recalled, "There was only
one baby crying, and all the babies looked alike to me, so I looked at
the identification tag on each of those babies and found that the one
crying was labeled 'Baby Girl Nelson, Room 571.' This certainly was
an inspiration to me, for Dantzel knew the voice of her child even
though she had never heard it before. It reminded me of the Savior's
statement that His sheep know His voice" (John 10:4).[45]

Laurie, like her mother, has been sensitive to the voice of the
Lord in always striving to do what is right. As with her older sisters,
she developed a great love of music and dance, and she excelled aca-
demically. She also developed acting skills, starring in East High
School's production of *Bye Bye Birdie* and playing the part of
Scrooge's fiancée in the Promised Valley Playhouse production of *A
Christmas Carol.*[46]

Two days after Christmas 1979, Laurie married Richard Moyle
Marsh in the Salt Lake Temple. They have been blessed with six children: Richard Moyle Jr., Douglas Nelson, Kristina Dantzel, Allison,
Stephanie, and Madison Emily, who was born exactly six months
after the passing of her Aunt Emily. Rick Marsh, who served as a
missionary in Ecuador, is a lawyer and a devoted Church leader.

Laurie recalls a family automobile trip to Flagstaff, Arizona,
when they were caught in a snowstorm so severe they could not even
see the road. To their good fortune, they were able to follow the car
ahead of them. Ever the teacher, Elder Nelson said, "Now Laurie, as
long as you follow the light, you'll never get lost." Unfortunately, it
soon became apparent that the person in the car ahead of them was
lost. At this juncture, Professor Nelson slightly revised his previous
counsel: "Be sure you follow the *right* light," he said, "and *then* you'll
never be lost."[47]

Laurie and Rick were living in Virginia when Russell was called
to the Twelve. "It didn't surprise me at all," she said. As Elder Nelson
became actively involved in expanding the Church in Eastern

Europe, he would often stay with Laurie and Rick whenever he had meetings with Eastern European government officials in Washington, D.C. Laurie appreciated the letters she received from her father each week without fail. After her father's apostolic calling, she observed, "As he stayed in our home in Virginia, he smiled more, perhaps because he wasn't facing life-and-death decisions each day. He was more relaxed and at peace."[48]

ROSALIE

Rosalie, born February 7, 1962, holds the distinction of being the longest baby of the entire Nelson clan at 23½ inches upon arrival. She has always stood tall among her peers, though she is now the shortest of the Nelson children. She has excelled in music, dance, and love for other people, especially younger children. In December 1973, several of the Nelson children participated in the Yale Second Ward's production of *The Sound of Music*. Rosalie stole the show as she played the part of Gretl, the baby of the von Trapp family. Years later the ward sponsored another production, Thornton Wilder's *Our Town*. Russell and Dantzel played the roles of Dr. and Mrs. Gibb, while Rosalie played the part of their daughter, Rebecca. She was not only a singer and a dancer but also a choreographer. Her parents recall a garbage can that went missing for several weeks as Rosalie choreographed a garbage can dance routine performed by the East High School dance company.[49]

Because Rosalie was the eighth child, her father affectionately nicknamed her *Ocho,* Spanish for eight. She claims to have inherited the best of all worlds, being near the end of the line in a large family in which there was perhaps more relaxed time as the older children began to leave the nest. With ten children in the family, the Nelsons did not go to restaurants often, so it was a treat when she would meet her dad at the cafeteria of the LDS Hospital, where they would enjoy dining together.

While serving as the general president of the Sunday School,

Russell took Rosalie with him to a Church meeting in Las Vegas and called upon her to speak. Russell reminisced, "Rosalie cheerfully responded with a moving message, based on scripture, that was outstanding. Everyone there was impressed and astounded that such a pretty young lady could be so capable."[50]

While attending Brigham Young University, Rosalie and Michael Ringwood started seeing more and more of each other, and friendship turned to love. They were married in the Jordan River Temple just after Christmas in 1982. They have since welcomed five children into their family circle: Tally Spencer, Melissa, Jeffrey Michael, Kimberly, and Spencer Nelson. Michael, who served a mission in Korea, is a business executive and a former bishop.

MARJORIE

A few hours after Marjorie's arrival on October 5, 1965, Russell was driving home from the hospital when he saw Marsha and Wendy walking home from school. "When I told them the news, their shouts for joy were loud and spontaneous as they confessed that they had harbored great fear that their select society of sisters might be spoiled by the addition of a baby boy," he said.[51]

Striving to provide special recognition for their ninth daughter, the parents decided to name their new infant Marjorie, in honor of Russell's eldest sister and Dantzel's eldest sister, who both bore the same name.[52]

Marjorie's birth was heralded by the local newspaper with the banner headline: "Another Girl; That Makes 9." Featuring a photo of the entire family, the article described the Nelson home as "a girls' dormitory. . . . And the arrival of Marjorie, the ninth daughter, two and a half weeks ago, only intensified the situation. But nobody could be happier."[53] When Marjorie was three, all nine daughters and their parents were again in the news. In anticipation of Father's Day in June 1969, a reporter interviewed the Nelson children for an article titled "Dad Is an Extra-Special Person." The collective summary assessment of their dad was, "He takes time to do things with us . . . he has a good sense of humor . . . he's so nice and kind . . . he's lots of fun to be with . . . he really understands . . . he listens." The interviewer concluded, "And what finer compliments could any father receive!"[54]

Marjorie was always a tenderhearted and sensitive young child. One evening, Russell came home from work to find Dantzel weary from the day's activities, so he offered to help get the children ready for bed. He also had had a rather demanding day, so, hearkening back to his days in the military, he began to give orders: "Take your clothes off and hang them up. Brush your teeth. Put on your pajamas. Say your prayers"—all befitting the demeanor of a drill sergeant.

Marjorie interrupted her father's commands by asking, "Daddy, do you own me?" Her wistful eyes and poignant question caused Russell to realize that he was exercising unrighteous dominion rather than following the Savior's example of leading with love. This penitent father gained an important insight: "We don't own our children; we have them for a short season. As parents, we have the privilege to love them, to lead them, and then to let them go."[55] Marjorie recently remarked, "My parents are pretty much perfect role models in my life. Most importantly, I never doubted that I was loved."[56]

Russell was always conscientious in setting aside time from his busy schedule to celebrate the birthdays of each of his children, but Marjorie's eighth birthday was an exception. President Nelson had been so busily engaged in the annual Sunday School conference that he was unable to spend time with Marjorie during the day. However, she joined her parents that evening for a Sunday School leadership meeting in the Tabernacle. After the meeting, President Harold B. Lee graciously greeted the birthday girl with a hug, a kiss, and a dollar. Her birthday turned out to be the most memorable of her life—kissed by a prophet of God.[57]

Marjorie grew in wisdom and stature, and three weeks before her twenty-first birthday she married Bradley R. Helsten in the Salt Lake

Temple. Their union has been blessed with three children: Jeffrey Marion, Andrew Bradley, and Jane Ann. Brad, who served a mission in Italy, is a lawyer. He has served as an elders quorum president and high councilor.[58]

Unlike her older sisters, with their penchant for maintaining an exclusive sorority, Marjorie was always open to welcoming a baby brother into the fold. But where was he?

CHAPTER 7

IT'S A BOY—FINALLY!

ONE AUTUMN EVENING IN 1957, Dantzel awakened Russell with a special announcement. "During the night, I had a remarkable vision," she said. "It was more than just a dream. I saw a little baby boy. He was a very special, handsome child. He had a round face and lots of hair; he looked just like you! I had a wonderful visit with him."[1]

Russell did not pay undue attention to Dantzel's announcement, even though she was expecting their sixth child. However, intermittently throughout the following years she would indicate that she had received yet another visit from this same little boy. Russell said that her comments eventually became a regular part of their lives, with Dantzel frequently commenting, "I saw him again. He's such a sweet and special young boy."[2]

Subsequent to that first visionary visit, the Nelsons made four more trips to the hospital to bring home Emily, Laurie, Rosalie, and Marjorie as welcome additions to the family. But even with nine beautiful daughters, Dantzel, endowed with unshakeable faith, had the firm conviction that their family was not yet complete. So, notwithstanding the fact that she was nearly forty-six, she selflessly embarked on her tenth pregnancy.[3] Five years and four months after the birth of their "last" child, Marjorie, Russell was awakened by a distinct impression confirming that this time Dantzel would bear a

81

son, the one who had been appearing to her over the years. Russell also felt the strong impression that his name should be Russell Marion Nelson Jr.[4]

Because of Dantzel's age and the fact that she had not been in the best of health, obstetricians were concerned about the prospects of a normal delivery. As her labor was augmented by uterine stimulants, her blood pressure began to soar to dangerous heights. Russell summoned the obstetrician and informed him that Dantzel's life was in danger. Within the hour, on March 21, 1972, she underwent a cesarean section in order to give birth to a twelve-pound baby boy! It was little wonder the delivery had been so challenging.[5]

Russell recalled, "After she awakened, the nurses brought the baby to her side, and as she looked at that fat little round face and the abundance of dark hair, tears welled up in her eyes, and she exclaimed, 'He's the one! He's the one I've seen and known for all of these years!'"[6]

When Russell Jr. was six, his father called upon him one evening to offer the family prayer. At the time, Emily had been in Europe for five months on a Brigham Young University Semester Abroad Program. Russell Sr. had corresponded with her but had not spoken with her by phone. As young Russell prayed, he supplicated the Lord to prompt Emily to telephone the family. At the conclusion of the prayer, Russell and Dantzel peered at each other over their bi-focals and benevolently smiled at the childlike faith of their son. Within two hours, Emily called the family from London. Her parents asked if anything was wrong, to which she replied, "No, I just had a sudden urge to give you a phone call." The next morning, the parents greeted young Russell with the news that his sister had, indeed, called after he had gone to bed. He simply said, "Of course. I knew she would. I prayed for it last night."[7]

Young Russell's faith continued to increase, and as he approached age nineteen he accepted a prophet's call to serve in the vanguard of pioneering missionaries called to labor in Russia. While on his mission, he mastered the very difficult Russian language, and

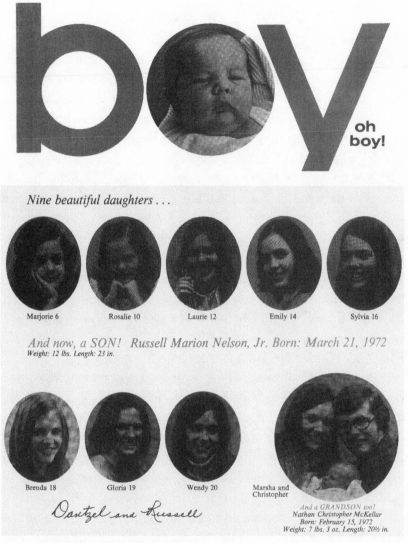

The birth announcement of Russell M. Nelson Jr.

upon his release he served as an interpreter for his father in Russia and later in meetings with Russian dignitaries visiting Salt Lake City, including former premier Mikhail Gorbachev and Ambassador Yuri Dubinin.[8]

As Russell Jr. was contemplating his future career path, his father did not attempt to steer his only son toward a medical career. Rather, he counseled him, "I don't think the Lord cares what you do for a living as long as you serve others well."

Two years after returning home from his mission, Russell Jr. married Britney Timms in the Salt Lake Temple. They are now the parents of Olivia, Nicholas Russell, and Gavin Derek. Russell earned a master's degree in international management at the Thunderbird International School of Business in Arizona. He serves in the Church as a Sunday School teacher.[9]

After his father's calling to the Twelve, Russell Jr. said, "The full impact of the apostolic calling did not hit me at first because my dad had always sat on the stand in Church. The biggest change in my life was that after his calling to the Twelve, the fishing stopped but skiing together on Mondays increased, as did water skiing in the summer."[10] After Elder Nelson returned from an extended ecclesiastical assignment in Europe, it was not unheard of for him to take his only son out of school for half a day so the two of them could become reacquainted on the slopes of Brighton or Alta, east of Salt Lake City.[11] Elder Nelson has long concurred with the counsel of President Harold B. Lee: "The most important of the Lord's work you will ever do will be within the walls of your own homes"[12]—or on the ski slopes with your children and grandchildren.

Despite the nearly twenty-four-year age spread between the Nelson family's oldest child and youngest child, their respective descriptions of their parents' child-rearing practices are almost identical. Marsha said of her parents, "They always put more trust in us than we deserved. They taught us the principles, but then we had to make the decisions. They were always generous in their praise, and we couldn't let them down."[13] Reared in the same home a quarter of a century later, Russell Jr. said, "We've been blessed to have such a wonderful mother who never raised her voice. With our parents, we never wanted to disappoint them or betray their trust."[14]

CHAPTER 8

LIVING AFTER THE MANNER OF HAPPINESS

WILLIAM WORDSWORTH OBSERVED, "The Child is the father of the Man," implying that a mature individual is largely the product of his childhood.[1] In Russell's case, only part of the child "fathered" the man. In the spirit of Paul's admonition to "prove all things [and] hold fast [to] that which is good" (1 Thessalonians 5:21), Russell retained from his parental household the love of music in the home and of family vacations together and a custom of kindness, always speaking respectfully to other family members. But the home of Russell's parents had some spiritual shortcomings, from which he and Dantzel tried to profit. They conscientiously assured that family home evening, family prayer, scripture study, and service in the kingdom were fostered in their own home. They taught their children that all family members are "happiest while serving."[2]

Family traditions are important ingredients in the Nelson extended family of ten children, their spouses, fifty-four grandchildren, and eight great-grandchildren. Once several wholesome traditions become established, their convergence constitutes an abundant life, characterized as living "after the manner of happiness" (2 Nephi 5:27).

MOTHER'S DAY

Mother's Day always seemed to be a wonderful and sacred day to Russell. He rejoiced in the privilege of honoring his own dear mother and of remembering his sisters and Dantzel's sisters, usually with a card or a greeting on the phone, expressing admiration for their sacred role as mothers. Russell also gave flowers to his young daughters with a note that indicated he honored them as prospective mothers.[3] Some of the sons-in-law have perpetuated this tradition with their own daughters.[4]

Russell knows why the Lord blessed him with nine beautiful daughters: "It is because they had such a saintly mother to teach them." He testifies that "God needs good mothers on this earth, and the best way to make good mothers is to send worthy daughters to a good mother to help them appreciate their own worth."[5]

CHRISTMAS

Although busily engaged in his medical practice, Dr. Nelson generally took a few days off prior to Christmas to be available to the children, helping them shop, attending their Christmas programs at school, and assisting them in the delivery of gifts. He said, "I was always amazed to see how much our children were able to do at the last minute with little or no concern for the fact that it was the last minute!"[6]

Christmas Eve was always a time of joyful anticipation as the family lit a fire in the fireplace, read the Christmas story either from Helaman in the Book of Mormon or from Luke and Matthew in the Bible, and focused attention on the meaning of the birth of the Savior of the world. Christmas Eve usually included a visit to the neighbors, caroling from one home to another, and delivering goodies Dantzel and the girls had prepared.[7]

On Christmas morning, Dantzel and Russell were generally awakened by the caroling of their children surrounding their bed. Then came unbridled excitement as the family proceeded to the living room, where a glowing Christmas tree partially sheltered all the presents. The gifts would be passed out by one family member, an assignment that was rotated each year. The recipient and the giver greeted each other with a kiss and a heartfelt expression of thanks.[8]

As the children began to marry and have children of their own, Dantzel would prepare special dinners during the Christmas season and invite two families at a time. Now the children host progressive dinners in clusters for those who live in Bountiful, Murray, Old Mill, or the east bench of Salt Lake City, inviting Russell and Dantzel to each of them.[9]

On Christmas Day 1996, Russell wrote in his personal record, "We spent the morning alone for the first time in forty-nine years. We made up for it in the evening, though, when all of our locally available children and grandchildren joined us for a gift exchange and a wonderful, spiritual time together. How we love them all."[10]

ANNIVERSARIES

Wedding anniversaries have always been special occasions for Dantzel and Russell. While still a practicing surgeon, he made no appointments for operations or office visits on August 31. On that day, he made only the necessary visits to patients in the hospital and then spent the rest of the day with his sweetheart doing whatever she wanted to do. One of the blessings of returning to Salt Lake City in 1955 was being able to celebrate each wedding anniversary in the temple, where Russell and Dantzel renewed and reviewed the covenants they made with each other and with their Heavenly Father. Presents exchanged on anniversaries have always been modest because, said Russell, "We feel that, to a certain extent, every day ought to be a wedding anniversary."[11]

EASTER

When the children were young, Easter traditions included an early morning hunt for eggs, jelly beans, and candy hidden in certain rooms of the house. Then the children methodically counted their prizes and made adjustments for any major discrepancies in order to be fair to the younger children. Although the tradition of hunting for eggs was started by the parents, the subsequent custom of the children sharing their bounty equitably was begun by the older children.[12]

The daughters often received new dresses made by Dantzel, who sometimes sewed late at night to complete each girl's dress on time. When the Nelsons went together to church services on Easter, Russell realized how fortunate he was to have such a talented and devoted wife and such choice, beautiful daughters.[13] His gratitude increased with the arrival of a son and, eventually, the arrival of his grand-children and great-grandchildren.

"SCRAPBOOKING"

It is safe to assume that most English speakers know what a scrapbook is; it is less certain to assume a universal understanding of the verb "scrapbooking." This particular noun-cum-verb refers to the monthly meeting of the Nelson daughters and their mother at one of their homes to work on their respective scrapbooks, bringing them up to date with recent photos and letters from missionaries and others far from home.[14]

The genuine love the Nelson children have for each other is reflected by the fact that on July 15, 1999, seven of the nine married daughters and their families stayed overnight at the Midway home to enjoy the final opportunity to be with their sister Rosalie and her family before their return to Australia for Mike's employment.[15] The Nelsons anticipate the prophetic promise that "the same sociality which exists among us here will exist among us [in heaven], only it will be coupled with eternal glory" (D&C 130:2). The Nelsons have already experienced a sampling of heaven here on earth.

THANKSGIVING

Celebrating Thanksgiving is another favorite family tradition, with as many as six dozen family members present for turkey and all the trimmings, including almonds planted by Dantzel in the mashed potatoes. The person finding an almond is destined for good luck throughout the coming year. As part of the after-dinner program, Dantzel may distribute a sheet of paper to each individual with the heading "This year, I am thankful for . . ." The remainder of the page is blank so that the older family members can provide a thoughtful written response while the younger children respond by drawing a picture. The papers are then collected and read aloud, and everyone tries to guess the author, which, in most cases is not difficult.[16]

MEMORIAL DAY

On Memorial Day, the Nelson family would visit Dantzel's parents and the White extended family at the family home in Perry, near Brigham City. After Dantzel's parents passed away, that tradition was perpetuated by Dantzel's brother, Clark, and his wife, Grace, who continued to invite his parents' increasing posterity to Perry on Memorial Day. After paying their respects to the deceased members of the family at the cemetery, they would all meet at the White farm to have lunch and then a program, games, and a family meeting.[17] Now the group has grown so large that they generally meet at the park in Perry.[18]

Russell cherishes the memory of riding one of the farm horses with each of his young children as they came along. He would nuzzle his nose in their hair and wrap his arms around them. Russell recalled, "I am sure each of the children thought I was hanging on to give them security while they were riding the horse, but to me, I was clinging to a precious moment that I had alone with each loved one as that turn came. On each occasion I offered a prayer of gratitude to my Father in Heaven for the great privilege of being a father to this one, for he knew each to be such a special spirit."[19]

SKIING

For many years, Monday afternoons in the winter have been reserved for skiing, which Dr. Nelson previously shared with some of his medical colleagues, including Dr. Howard C. Sharp and Dr. L. Stephen Richards Jr. In more recent years, Elders Hans B. Ringger, John E. Fowler, and W. Craig Zwick have been occasional skiing companions, along with Russell's children and grandchildren. Of course, he cannot make it every Monday because of travel obligations, but he still tries to reserve that time for the regeneration that comes from smelling the pines and enjoying the solitude of a quiet snowfall on steep mountain slopes where stillness and silence seem so serene.[20] Russell has never taken for granted the blessing of living close enough to the ski slopes that he can work a good forenoon and be on the lift at 1 P.M., ski until 4:30 P.M., and then return home to enjoy dinner with the family.[21]

DADDY-DAUGHTER DATES

Daddy-daughter dates sponsored by the Primary were always a special privilege for Russell. Few fathers have gone on more such dates than he, and none have enjoyed them more than he did. "I looked forward to those occasions much more than the girls ever dreamed," he said, "for I was very proud to be with each one of them."[22] Going with his daughters and daughter-in-law to buy birthday dresses is another annual tradition that he and they continue to cherish.[23] While shopping with his daughters, Elder Nelson possesses the patience of Job, the wisdom of Solomon, and the generosity of Joseph of Egypt.

MEETING AT THE BARBERSHOP

Wayne Pope, Elder Nelson's barber for more than forty years, observed that as Russell Jr. reached boyhood, he would meet his father at the barbershop at regular intervals. As this practice became a firmly entrenched tradition, young Russell, as a teenager, had no

The Nelson family in 1982. Left to right, seated on the floor: Brenda, Gloria, Sylvia; seated in chairs: Emily, Dantzel, Russell Sr., Marsha; standing: Wendy, Laurie, Marjorie, Russell Jr., and Rosalie.

inclination toward growing long hair because he always knew he had an appointment in the near future with his dad and the barber for their regular haircuts. This tradition expanded to the point that a visit to the barbershop once included a great-grandson, two grandsons, a son, and Elder Nelson, getting their hair cut in succession by the same barber on the same day.[24]

SCRIPTURE STUDY

In the Nelson home, scripture reading became a great way to start the day, usually at 6:30 A.M. (followed by family prayer at 6:45 A.M.), at meal times, and at 10 P.M. As the children married, a monthly extended family scripture-study program was instigated while the grandchildren were small. As each nuclear family became larger, however, it was deemed wise for the grandchildren to study the gospel in their own homes with their own parents.[25]

FAMILY HOME EVENING

Family home evening has always been a delightful experience for Russell and Dantzel, and notwithstanding wiggles and giggles from a gaggle of girls, the children enjoyed them as well. In the Nelson home, family home evening always involved a brief lesson and planning their weekly schedule. Activities, such as swimming, were scheduled for another night of the week. In addition to the weekly home evening, Russell maintained a tradition of reading nightly to the younger ones and helping the older ones with their studies so that he was current on their schoolwork while nurturing a cozy relationship.

GATHERING IN MIDWAY

On September 12, 1973, Dantzel and Russell were in the throes of last-minute preparations before leaving for some international surgical meetings in Germany and Spain when Russell received an unexpected phone call from Elder Ezra Taft Benson. Elder Benson said, "We have some family property in Midway, near Heber City, which we don't need anymore. I think this would be a good thing for you and your family. Would you like to see it?"[26]

The Nelsons had become well acquainted with Elder and Sister Benson in 1952 when Elder Benson was called to serve as President Eisenhower's secretary of agriculture. Russell and Danztel were living in Washington, D.C., at the time, and Russell was serving in the bishopric. In March 1953, when Russell was released from the bishopric, Elder Benson was one of the sacrament meeting speakers. After the meeting, he gave Russell a special priesthood blessing.[27]

Elder Benson later visited the Bonneville Stake conference in February 1971 while Russell was still serving as stake president. Two years later, the Saints in Washington, D.C., invited the Bensons and the Nelsons to return to Washington to participate in a special program commemorating the thirtieth anniversary of the Washington Ward chapel. As general president of the Sunday School, Russell had also had contact with Elder Benson on several occasions, so he was familiar with Russell, Dantzel, and their children. Therefore, when Elder Benson suggested that the Nelsons purchase the four-acre piece of property in Midway, the offer was not made by a complete stranger. Somewhat surprised by the proposal, Russell explained to Elder Benson that they were getting ready to leave for Europe in the morning.[28]

Undaunted, Elder Benson replied, "Well then, would you like to see the property right now—today?"

Notwithstanding the inconvenient timing, Russell and Dantzel interrupted their packing and drove to Midway with Elder Benson, who graciously introduced the Nelsons to the little community of Midway and then suggested a fair market price for the property in question. Russell and Dantzel looked at each other, envisaged the future potential of a getaway haven for their family, and shook hands with Elder Benson, confirming their agreement to the purchase.[29]

After the contract was signed, Elder Benson said, "Now don't build a house too close to the road. I would recommend that you build it two hundred feet back from the frontage so you'll have a little more privacy." The Nelsons consulted with Elder Benson on architectural drawings for a four-bedroom house and an outside deck, and he pronounced them to be good. Recently Elder Nelson said, "What he foresaw as something good for our family has come to pass. As time goes on, our gratitude for this property increases, as does our thankfulness for the Bensons. Were it not for them, we would not have our lovely family haven and retreat there."[30]

When the Nelson clan gathers at the Midway home for a little rest and relaxation, the numbers may swell to as many as seventy-two people sleeping over at one time. The four bedrooms are filled to capacity, as is the deck. In the summer, the children love to sleep outdoors. To teach young Russell and all of his cousins the rewards of honest toil, Elder Nelson planted a vegetable garden, complete with several rows of corn, potatoes, carrots, peas, and beets, which he loves. In late summer and fall, the family reaped the fruits of the law of the harvest.[31]

Sharing time at the Midway home has remained a treasured family tradition. Elder Nelson insists that he is not proficient at summer sports, but during the lazy days of summer he can be seen playing golf, bicycling, swimming, fishing, hiking, or pitching horseshoes, always in the company of children and grandchildren.[32] Though this Apostle and father never took up archery, the psalmist described him well: "Lo, children are an heritage of the Lord. . . . Happy is the man that hath his quiver full of them" (Psalm 127:3, 5).

BAPTISMS FOR THE DEAD

Occasionally, the Nelson grandchildren twelve and older will convene at the Salt Lake Temple early in the morning to perform vicarious baptisms for their deceased ancestors. After these sessions, the fathers go to work, the children go to school, and the mothers return home with joy-filled hearts. In recent years, it has been customary for the extended family to spend several days together on a family vacation. It was the children, not the parents or grandparents, who suggested that the first day of vacation be spent at the temple performing baptisms for the dead. The family recently performed more than five hundred baptisms in one day for Russell and Dantzel's deceased ancestors.[33]

REVIEW OF GENERAL CONFERENCE

As the grandchildren have matured, it has become a welcome custom to meet Saturday evening following the general priesthood session of general conference to review the teachings of the day. While Elder Nelson, Russell Jr., the sons-in-law, and grandsons of Aaronic Priesthood age convene in the Conference Center or their local stake center, Dantzel and her daughters join forces in preparing food for the men upon their return. Over soup and homemade doughnuts, the men recount the principles taught in the priesthood meeting, and then each family member recounts an insight or two gained from the preceding sessions of conference.[34]

BALL GAMES

Whenever there is a little space in Elder Nelson's busy schedule, he enjoys taking family members to basketball or football games. In his typically meticulous fashion, Elder Nelson records in his personal record the exact score and perhaps a highlight of the games he attends. On occasion, he and Dantzel will meet at one of the homes of their children to join the family in cheering on the Utah Jazz during a televised game—the only time he watches TV for recreation.

FOURTH OF JULY

When five or six dozen members of the Nelson extended family convene at the family home in Midway on the Fourth of July, they are able to celebrate on their own without help from the community. They have the Nelson family Olympic games, stage their own parade, go boating and water skiing at Deer Creek Reservoir, play tennis, croquet, pitch horseshoes, hold relay races, and conclude with fireworks after sundown. As usual, Dantzel and her daughters take care of the planning, preparation, and prizes.[35]

VACATIONS

The Family: A Proclamation to the World declares, "Successful marriages and families are established and maintained on principles of faith, prayer, repentance, forgiveness, respect, love, compassion, work, and wholesome recreational activities."[36]

The Nelsons have tried to follow that pattern through the years. Vacations together have always been an important ingredient in the Nelson family. The children cheerfully recall riding in the car, listening to their mother read *Winnie the Pooh* while their dad drove. The children found their mother's reading, punctuated by hysterical laughter, to be much more entertaining than the content of the book itself. Dantzel became so tickled that tears trickled down her cheeks as she read. She believes that the *Winnie the Pooh* books were actually written for adults rather than children.[37]

In his own parental home, Russell and his siblings were not carefully taught to observe the sanctity of the Sabbath day. When Dantzel and Russell had children of their own, however, Russell meticulously taught them to show love for the Lord through observance of the Sabbath, and he reminded the general membership of the Church of the Lord's command to "hallow my Sabbaths; and they shall be a sign between me and you, that ye may know that I am the Lord your God"[38] (Ezekiel 20:20).

As a young man, Russell initially questioned the importance of what was taught in Sunday School class because no examinations were ever given. So, as a father, he occasionally "tested" his children to see if they had "caught" what he had taught. On one family vacation, they camped out and went fishing. Actually, the girls fished while their father surgically baited their hooks with worms and then removed the fish from their hooks. Family plans included going to church Sunday morning. To see how well his daughters understood the importance of keeping the Sabbath holy, Russell proposed that they go fishing for a few hours before church services began. He was pleased when Wendy responded in righteous indignation, "Daddy, how could you ask a blessing on fish you had caught on Sunday? And how could you possibly eat them?"[39] The student got an A.

One particularly memorable vacation involved a rafting trip down the Colorado River through the Grand Canyon. Russell recounted in general conference, "As we started our journey, we had no idea how dangerous this trip could be. The first day was beautiful. But on the second day, when we approached Horn Creek Rapids and saw that precipitous drop ahead, I was terrified. Floating on a rubber raft, our precious family was about to plunge over a waterfall! Instinctively I put one arm around my wife and the other around our youngest daughter. To protect them, I tried to hold them close to me. But as we reached the precipice, the bended raft became a giant sling and shot me into the air. I landed into the roiling rapids of the river. I had a hard time coming up. Each time I tried to find air, I hit the underside of the raft. My family couldn't see me, but I could hear them shouting, 'Daddy? Where's Daddy?'

"I finally found the side of the raft and rose to the surface. The family pulled my nearly drowned body out of the water. We were thankful to be safely reunited."

Turning this near tragedy into a profound teaching moment, Elder Nelson said, "I nearly lost my life learning a lesson that I now give to you. As we go through life, even through very rough waters, a father's instinctive impulse to cling tightly to his wife or to his children may not be the best way to accomplish his objective. Instead, if he will lovingly cling to the Savior and the iron rod of the gospel, his family will want to cling to him and to the Savior."[40]

As the older children began to leave the nest, they and their young families began having vacations of their own. On a few special occasions, however, Dantzel and Russell have bravely organized and sponsored vacations for the entire extended family.

Russell and Dantzel had a long-standing goal of visiting the Holy Land with their entire family so they could walk together where Jesus walked. In October 1980, they went to Israel with four of their married daughters and their respective husbands, and in May 1983 they returned to Israel with four more married daughters and sons-in-law, along with their youngest daughter, Marjorie, and Russell Jr.[41]

Seven summers later, as the extended family matured, they traveled in a caravan of cars over the Alpine Loop in American Fork Canyon to spend a wonderful week together at activities in Aspen Grove, the Brigham Young University Alumni Camp in Provo Canyon. Russell recalled with great satisfaction that week together with thirty-eight grandchildren: "Days were warm, nights were cool, and the companionship was great."[42]

The first week in August 1995, the Nelsons celebrated their fiftieth wedding anniversary a couple of weeks early by touring Alaska on a cruise ship with their children and their respective spouses. At the end of the cruise, family relationships had been solidified and each member returned home with memories to last a lifetime.[43]

In June 2000, fifty-six members of the extended Nelson clan traveled by air to Los Angeles, sailed to Catalina Island and Ensenada, Mexico, and then returned to Los Angeles to make Disneyland their final stop.[44]

Trips with the Children

Some of the Nelson family traditions became coupled with Russell's continuing education, sparked by his insatiable desire to learn. Because he was generally out of town 25–30 percent of the year attending medical meetings to advance his pursuit of knowledge, Dr. Nelson usually took with him one or more family members on each trip. This kept him from getting lonesome for his loved ones, gave him a chance to listen to their problems and hopes, and provided him and family members with an opportunity to talk to each other and share ideas and experiences. The selection of which child got to go on which trip was not based on rotation but rather on which child most needed a trip with daddy.[45]

Russell recalled boarding a plane with one of his daughters when he noticed that Elder Mark E. Petersen of the Quorum of the Twelve Apostles was on the same flight. Russell explained to Elder Petersen that his daughter was accompanying him to a professional meeting, adding apologetically that taking her along might be a bit extravagant. Elder Petersen responded, "Extravagant? No, Brother Nelson, it's a wise investment."[46]

Elder and Sister Nelson can recall very few moments when one of the Nelson children gave them cause for concern. Of course, Russell does not credit this great blessing entirely to the occasional trips he took with his children. He contends that the greatest share of credit goes to their mother and to their efforts to rear their children in the knowledge of the Lord and His doctrines.

"Nonetheless, the privilege of having one or more of the family with me on my trips has been the spoonful of sugar that's helped the medicine go down," he said. The "medicine" was his relentless pursuit of excellence through continuing medical education that took him away from his family and loved ones but allowed him to improve the quality of his work.[47]

THE NELSON NEWS

A Church assignment to Italy in 1985 brought Elder and Sister Nelson together with members and missionaries in Milan, Turin, Rome, Naples, Bari, and Siracusa. Near the conclusion of this assignment, Elder Nelson was interviewed on Sicilian television in Siracusa. One of the first statements made by the interviewer was, "I understand that you are not only a renowned surgeon and an Apostle but the owner of a newspaper."

Elder Nelson responded quizzically, "Newspaper?"

"Yes, *The Nelson News*," the reporter responded.

Elder Nelson could hardly believe that word about the family's little monthly newsletter had reached far-off Sicily. He assured the interviewer that he was definitely not in the newspaper business and that *The Nelson News* had a very limited circulation.

The interviewer then asked, "Being the first Apostle in Siracusa in about two thousand years, what is your message?"

Elder Nelson responded in fluent Italian, "Il messagio piu importante che potrei dare e quello di obbedire ai comandamenti di Dio!" (The most important message I could give is to keep the commandments of God!) The interviewer, and many people watching the program no doubt, was astonished to hear a response in Italian.[48]

The monthly edition of *The Nelson News* has become a traditional way of communicating with the entire family, and it is especially appreciated by those living far from home. The *News* is a forum for expressions of love, exhortations, and needed reminders. Each of the Nelson children's families contribute to the *News,* with the editorship rotating throughout the clan. A recent edition consisted of forty-five copies of forty pages each.[49]

In the September 1993 issue, Elder Nelson shared with extended family members the feelings he had while attending a recent testimony meeting with the other members of the Quorum of the Twelve: "To be taught by the Twelve is one thing, but to feel the inspiration that comes to each as he stands to speak is another. The world can never know, nor can we explain, but the faithful Saints will perceive the mutual love and the divine direction that we feel."

As a father, father-in-law, and grandfather, he then closed with this gentle exhortation: "In a way, I understand that each member of the family is subject to extra scrutiny because of the position to which I have been called. I, too, am to live out the final scenes of my life in full public view. Together we sustain each other with fidelity, love, and gratitude to the Lord for all the blessings that we have received. May we never take any of them for granted, or be timid about expressing our reliance on the Lord, from whom all blessings flow. And when difficult days that lie ahead come upon us, we need all the more to be resolute and unwavering in our faith. We are to be the examples. We no longer can afford the luxury of anonymity in going along with the crowd in ordinary behavior. If we are to be lifeguards, we can't resemble all the other swimmers on the beach. As the world is awash in spiritual drift and apathy, Mother and I pray for each of you to be steadfast and strong—well anchored to the everlasting gospel and to the teachings of prophets and Apostles, past and present."[50]

For Elder and Sister Nelson, with more than four dozen grandchildren, it is, of course, challenging to spend a lot of one-on-one time with each grandchild. *The Nelson News,* however, provides a wonderful forum for commendation and praise for the accomplishments of the grandchildren. The baptism and confirmation of each grandchild receives a prominent mention in the *News,* as does participation in a school play, piano recital, and sports event; the earning of the Eagle Scout rank, the Aaronic Priesthood Duty to God

Award, and the Young Women Personal Progress Recognition; as well as mission calls, engagements and marriages, impending birth announcements, and the proclamation of the arrival of another precious child.

In September 1997, Elder Nelson included the following counsel to his children: "Each of you—so distinct and different—supports Daddy by your devoted discipleship. His task is to be worthy of you and never to bring embarrassment to any of you. Thank you for being such a wonderful part of our family team. We love you and express our everlasting appreciation and affection for every member of the family.

"With those blessings, we have an imperative duty that we owe to all the rising generation. There are many yet among us who are 'only kept from the truth because they know not where to find it' (D&C 123:12). We and our posterity are to 'wear out our lives in bringing to light all the hidden things of darkness, wherein we know them; and they are truly manifest from heaven' (D&C 123:13). Our grandchildren are magnificent and trustworthy, for which we are deeply grateful!"[51]

CHAPTER 9

BECOMING A PHYSICIAN

THE DISRUPTIONS OF WORLD WAR II resulted in many shortages, including a shortage of housing. So when Russell and Dantzel married in August 1945, they were fortunate to find a small apartment near the University of Utah.[1]

A wise sage once observed that the honeymoon ends the first time the bride burns the toast. One Sunday, Dantzel put a roast in the oven before she and Russell left for Sunday School. When they returned home from the chapel, half a block away, they found smoke pouring out of their apartment and discovered that the roast had become a burnt offering, filling the apartment with smoke and covering the walls and their possessions with a greasy film. Cleaning the apartment consumed the better part of a week.

That well-done dinner was one of the few roast beef dinners prepared in that apartment. The Nelson budget was so tight that whenever an invitation came from either of their sets of parents for Sunday dinner, Russell and Dantzel eagerly accepted. Their parents knew of the couple's plight and would occasionally give them sacks of groceries, which they gladly received.[2]

After Dantzel graduated from college, she received a teaching contract at Hawthorne Elementary School at 700 East and 1700 South. She was a good teacher and enjoyed her experience at the school, located conveniently near Salt Lake County General

*Russell upon graduating
from the University of
Utah with a bachelor's
degree, June 1945.*

Hospital, on 2100 South and State Street.[3] Russell spent his final
two years of medical school at the hospital.

Finances eventually became so straitened that Dantzel took a
second job, working evenings as a clerk in a music store downtown.
Once, when there was too much month at the end of their money,
they found themselves in the hole by about forty-three dollars. On
this occasion, Russell picked up Dantzel after school and took her
to LDS Hospital, where they each sold a pint of blood for twenty-
five dollars. This gave them enough cash to retire their bills. As the
needle was withdrawn from Dantzel's arm, she said to Russell,
"Don't forget to pay tithing on my blood money!"[4]

Russell will never forget the reaction of Dantzel's mother when
she discovered that he was having Dantzel work two jobs and bleeding her in between. It has been said that behind every successful man
is a surprised mother-in-law. Russell confessed, "I got the general
feeling that she didn't think that Dantzel had married much of a

husband. We laugh about it now, but at that time it was no laughing matter."[5]

By August 1947, when he graduated from medical school at age twenty-two, Russell likely had elevated himself in the eyes of his in-laws. He had completed his four-year course of medical school in just three years by going to school year-round, summers included. He graduated number one in his class and was inducted into the honorary scholastic societies of Alpha Omega Alpha and Sigma Xi. As a graduation present, Russell's parents gave him and Dantzel a check for a thousand dollars, which they sorely needed as Russell embarked on the next phase of his medical career.[6]

LIFE IN MINNESOTA

Following Russell's graduation from medical school, he and Dantzel stuffed all the belongings they could into a two-door, blue Chevrolet that his parents had purchased for them. In September 1947, they drove to Minneapolis, Minnesota, where Russell was to begin an internship at the University of Minnesota Hospitals. His mentor was the internationally renowned surgeon Dr. Owen H. Wangensteen, whom many regarded as one of the outstanding surgical teachers of modern times.[7] Dr. Wangensteen was known for fostering a creative research climate and for supporting his protégés' research initiatives.

Dantzel and Russell arrived in Minneapolis in a rainstorm, knowing absolutely no one in that large city. Finding housing was difficult, so they were fortunate to locate a little apartment in a four-plex that housed three other physicians. They all soon became close friends.[8]

Dantzel remained the breadwinner by finding a teaching job in a school located in the south end of the city near the airport. Her income was around $135 a month; to that, Russell contributed fifteen dollars a month, his pay as an intern at the University of Minnesota Hospitals.[9] One evening, Dantzel asked Russell if he was paying tithing on his monthly wage. He recalled, "Frankly, I had regarded that as just a token payment designed to keep my teeth clean, hair cut, and shoes polished. But when she confronted me with that question, I realized that she was right and I was wrong, and so our tithing was increased to include a tenth of that $15 every month. I have been a full tithe payer ever since, but I often wonder what might have happened if she had not exerted her sweet influence at that moment."[10]

Few members of the Church lived in the Twin Cities at that time, but a great feeling of closeness existed among the small community of Saints. Dr. Frank M. Whiting was asked to direct Thornton Wilder's *Our Town* as a building fund-raising activity. Dantzel and Russell were cast as Dr. and Mrs. Gibb, roles that they would reprise later for the Yale Second Ward. They had a great time preparing for the play, which branch members received enthusiastically. The activity was considered a success because the more than one hundred people who attended donated enough money for the branch president to begin a building program for a new chapel in Minneapolis.[11]

Russell was soon called to be the Sunday School superintendent for the Minneapolis branch. He was pleased when the branch president approved his request to call Brother Keith M. Engar as his first assistant superintendent.[12] Keith later distinguished himself as a professor of speech and theater at the University of Utah. He and his wife, Amy, became, and remained, dear friends of the Nelsons through the years.

At the conclusion of his internship year, Russell successfully competed for advanced surgical training as a resident at the University of Minnesota Hospitals. In order to augment his routine surgical training, he pursued studies leading to a Ph.D. degree, with a major in surgery and a minor in physiology, which would enable him to engage in research under Dr. Maurice Visscher, a demanding and critical, but highly acclaimed, scientist.[13]

The requirements for a Ph.D. degree included passing an examination in a foreign language. Inasmuch as Russell had studied

French for only three years in junior high and high school, he employed as his French tutor an elderly professor who had retired from the faculty at the University of Minnesota. This private tutoring prepared him to pass the French examination[14] and would later prove to be a blessing to French-speaking Saints in Europe and Africa.

Two of Russell and Dantzel's good neighbors were Dr. Don Davis and his wife, Netta, both of whom were devout Catholics. Netta, a petite, attractive brunette in her late twenties, was chronically ill, having suffered from rheumatic heart disease, which had destroyed her mitral valve. The Nelsons and their neighbors watched helplessly as Netta went from petite to emaciated. They literally observed her life slowly slipping away from one day to the next. Eventually, death mercifully released her from her discomfort and breathlessness.

Russell had come to Minnesota with the thought of becoming a general surgeon, but watching Netta Davis die at such a young age generated some inner stirrings to repair human hearts. At the time, such a thought was beyond the realm of practicality because cardiac surgery faced a big impediment. While the heart was temporarily out of commission and undergoing necessary surgical repair, blood somehow had to be circulated and continuously oxygenated.[15]

Russell's interests in research were enhanced when he learned that Dr. Clarence Dennis had received what then seemed to be an enormous grant of $25,000 a year for five years to develop an artificial heart-lung machine. Russell made arrangements through Dr. Wangensteen and Dr. Dennis to begin work in Dr. Dennis's lab in 1948. Being young, Russell recalled, "I didn't realize that the task which lay before us was 'impossible,' and so I started out with the very naive assumption that it wouldn't be very hard to build a heart-lung machine."[16]

Dr. Nelson, Dr. Clarence Dennis, Dr. Karl E. Karlson, Dr. W. Phil Eder, Dr. Frank Eddy, and others labored to make every piece of the heart-lung machine themselves, a project that proved to be very challenging! "We had glass-blowing equipment, a lathe, a drill press, and a machine shop," Russell said. "Every part for the machine was built by one of us." The doctors not only had to learn *what* they needed but also had to learn how to *make* what they needed.[17]

There were chemical challenges as well as mechanical challenges. For instance, it took them many months to work out the optimal chemical titration that would prevent blood from coagulating while it passed through the heart-lung machine and then allow it to coagulate normally again when the experimental animal's heart was beating on its own again.[18]

One by one, these persistent physicians gradually solved many of their problems until they were able, for brief periods of time, to sustain a dog on their heart-lung machine, which would temporarily take over the function of the natural heart and lungs. All the animals later succumbed, however, to a mysterious ailment that the doctors did not understand.[19]

At this point, Dr. Dennis had to travel abroad, and he left Russell in charge of the lab during his absence. When he returned, Dr. Nelson had solved the mystery of why the animals had not survived. They had died from the poisonous effects of bacterial toxins in the blood. Russell had designed experiments which proved that bacterial toxins were not being fully eliminated from the heart-lung machine with the cleaning process then being employed. Once the cleaning process was improved sufficiently to eliminate this problem, the experimental animals began to survive with regularity. Russell based his doctoral dissertation on this research, and three years later he received his Ph.D. degree.[20]

About this time, Russell's parents arrived in Minneapolis for a visit. This was their first trip to see Russell and Dantzel after they had been away for so long, and, of course, they anticipated with considerable expectation the accomplishments of their doctor son. Russell was excited about what his research team had accomplished, and so he invited his father to come to the research laboratory on the fourth floor of Millard Hall. They then went out under the eaves of this musty old building and found a dog that researchers called Una. Russell brought the dog in and fed, watered, and petted it, proudly showing it off to his dad. He then explained, "This is the first dog in medical history ever to survive for thirty minutes with the blood circulation being maintained entirely by an artificial heart-lung machine!"[21]

As he excitedly and enthusiastically shared his accomplishments, his father turned his back toward Russell, shedding a few tears. Russell had not expected his father to be so emotionally moved, great as the achievement was in his own mind. Then, as his father spoke, Russell realized that his tears were not tears of joy at all. "Your mother and I have sacrificed and worked all these years to have a doctor son of whom we could be proud," he said. "Now we find that you're just a dog doctor."[22]

Years later, they shared a good laugh about this incident, but little did his father realize then what a significant, historic achievement Una's survival was. Nor did he realize what ultimate meaning it would have in changing the face of medical and surgical practice in the future.[23]

When the survival of Una was reported to the American College of Surgeons at its Clinical Congress, October 16–23, 1949, in Chicago, it was acclaimed to be a highly significant event. As the Minneapolis surgical investigators were getting more and more confident in their ability to do their work experimentally, they approached the time when they were sufficiently prepared to move the work from the laboratory to the hospital.[24] They faced an interesting obstacle, however, in applying their skills to humans in a hospital operating room.

Elder Nelson recalled, "The heart-lung machine we had built had become so large that there was no way we could get it out of the laboratory. Just like a model ship built in a bottle, there was no way that it could be moved; so we had to start over on a much smaller, compact model which could be used for human surgery in hospitals."[25]

Dr. Richard L. Varco, professor of surgery at the University of Minnesota, told his colleagues of a lady he had operated on who had a hole in her heart. With the limited surgical techniques then available to him, he was unable to repair her heart. So he closed the incision, hoping one day to be able to empty her heart of blood long enough to surgically repair the hole and thus prolong her life.[26]

In March 1951, the first open-heart operation on a human being sustained by an artificial heart-lung machine was performed on this patient in Minneapolis by Dr. Varco and Dr. Dennis. The heart-lung machine performed successfully, but the patient failed to survive because what was thought to be a simple hole in her heart turned out to be a complicated congenital abnormality, and the surgical repair of this complex defect was imperfect. Nonetheless, details of this pioneering operation were presented at the American Surgical Association in Washington, D.C., in April 1951. Dr. Nelson recalled with enthusiasm, "It marked an important transition in surgical history between gaining access to the open, beating heart and knowing what to do once that access had been achieved. A new world of surgical repair of the heart had been made possible."[27]

In the space of four years, researchers had come a long way. When Russell began medical school, he had been taught that the beating heart must never be touched lest it stop. Yet he was constantly encouraged by a passage in the Doctrine and Covenants that states, "Unto every kingdom is given a law; and unto every law there are certain bounds also and conditions" (D&C 88:38). He also knew that the Lord had said there is no blessing given except by obedience to the law upon which that blessing is predicated (D&C 130:20–21). Therefore, he knew that even the blessing of the heartbeat was predicated upon law. The job of researchers was to harness the power contained in the understanding of those laws.[28]

In the midst of the euphoria created by a successful heart-lung machine, Dr. Nelson's surgical training and exciting research work were interrupted by the Korean War, for which doctors were desperately needed. The Surgeon General's Office in Washington, D.C., aware of Dr. Nelson's research and clinical training with Dr. Wangensteen, thought this young surgeon could make a special contribution while fulfilling his obligation for military duty by coming to Washington, D.C.[29] He was selected to form a surgical research unit at the Walter Reed Army Medical Center and to coordinate research activities in military and civilian institutions under army contracts.

Russell and Dantzel had just recently moved into a new home in Minneapolis, so the prospect of military duty was an unwelcome disruption to their family life and to Russell's peaceful pursuit of surgical training. Nevertheless, their eyes turned toward Washington, D.C., as they contemplated their new opportunity for service.[30]

CHAPTER 10

LIFE IN THE ARMY

INASMUCH AS DANTZEL WAS NEARLY ready to deliver their second child, Russell preceded her to Washington, D.C., to find an apartment for their little family. On April 5, 1951, just a few days after Dantzel and Marsha's arrival by plane, Dantzel gave birth to Wendy at the Walter Reed Army Medical Center.[1]

The Nelsons were alone in Washington with no friends. Just a few days after Wendy's birth, the army changed its plans for Russell, now a first lieutenant, and issued orders for his immediate transfer to active duty in Korea. The war was raging at the time, and Lieutenant Nelson's commanding officers felt an urgent need for him to go to Korea to conduct research regarding the causes of death among the wounded at the battlefront. Russell had anticipated a Washington assignment, and he would never have brought Dantzel to the nation's capital had he known he was going to leave her alone with their two small children. Russell recalled, "Prayerfully we supplicated the Lord that we might be able to be faithful to our obligations in the military while still being faithful to our family responsibilities."[2]

At the eleventh hour before Russell's projected departure for Korea, President Harry S Truman suddenly fired General Douglas MacArthur as the commander in chief of military operations in the Far East. Because General MacArthur's office had made the arrangements for Lieutenant Nelson to work in Korea, his travel

Capt. Russell M. Nelson while serving at the Walter Reed
Army Medical Center in Washington, D.C., in early 1953.

orders were canceled. Those orders were later reissued, setting his
departure for June 1951. The change allowed Russell time to make
arrangements for Dantzel, Marsha, and Wendy to travel to Utah
and stay with her parents. Their prayers had been answered.[3]

Russell became a member of a four-man surgical team that lived
together for the entire summer of 1951. They flew from Travis Air
Force Base in California to Honolulu and then to Wake Island,
where they saw remnants of the war fought there six years previously
with Japan. Wake Island was nothing more than a coral reef with an
airport and a few Quonset huts. From there they flew to Tokyo for
their briefings.

During their first night in Tokyo, a small earthquake struck the city. Russell was sleeping in the top bunk of a double bunk bed when the quake hit. The first thing he knew, he was on the floor, the chandeliers were swinging, and the dressers had toppled over. In a bit of an understatement, Russell recalled, "That was a disquieting feeling. The tremors lasted very briefly, and then all was back to normal again."[4]

During a military flight from Tokyo to Taegu, Korea, Russell was surprised to be handed a rifle. When he asked why, the officer replied, "All lieutenants get rifles. Captains and above get pistols." Lieutenant Nelson told the officer that he had never used a rifle before and did not have any idea how to fire one.

"Carry it anyway," the officer brusquely responded.[5]

Russell obeyed, taking the rifle wherever he went. "I remember one day while walking through the streets on the outskirts of a Korean village with my rifle in hand when I was fired upon by some guerillas still hiding in the hills roundabout," he said. "I had no way of defending myself because I didn't know from where the shots were coming and I didn't know how to fire the rifle I had. I sensed that my rifle was more of a hazard to me than a protection."[6]

With his colleagues, Dr. Fiorindo A. Simeone, Major Curtis P. Artz, and Capt. George Schreiner, Lieutenant Nelson visited every mobile army surgical hospital (M.A.S.H.) in Korea, several battalion aid stations, and the battle line where artillery units were firing at the enemy. Reflecting upon the tenuous and unpredictable nature of life on earth, he said, "Just a few days earlier I had enjoyed the peace and comfort of a family reunion in our backyard in Salt Lake City, and now here I was in the midst of a war, being fired upon and caring for the wounded."[7]

"There are no atheists in foxholes," goes the saying. Lieutenant Nelson learned the truth of that statement one night when the mobile army surgical hospital unit he was working in was subjected to an air raid. He and Dr. Simeone ended up sharing a foxhole for much of the night. Russell recalled, "Dr. Simeone, a devout Catholic, and I, a devout Latter-day Saint, prayed unitedly in our foxhole that our mission might be a successful one and that our lives might be preserved."[8]

In addition to visiting Korea, Lieutenant Nelson's medical team also visited and worked in American military hospitals in Japan. They spent considerable time in the Osaka General Hospital, where they examined several patients who had been maimed by frostbite the preceding winter. Lieutenant Nelson reported that "measurements made on these soldiers who had been subjected to frostbite indicated that the blood flow to their extremities was reduced by cigarettes even if the smoke was inhaled secondhand. If a man smoking a cigarette entered the room, measurable differences in the blood flow to the digits could be detected. I think this is the first time I really began to document the harmful effects of cigarette smoking on the circulation. Prior to this, the harmful effects of cigarettes on the lungs seemed to be general knowledge, but it was just about at this time that the effects of cigarette smoking on the circulatory system began to be evident."[9]

As they concluded their work in Korea and Japan, the four-man medical team returned to Tokyo to report that "many of the major blood vessel injuries could be helped by the vascular surgical techniques that our team introduced, that the care of patients subjected to burns could be improved by what they called 'open treatment' rather than massive dressings, and that kidney shutdown or renal insufficiency could be aided by the establishment of an artificial kidney team in Korea." They called for "better hydration of the soldiers during the hot summer months, when already dehydrated men were subjected to bleeding, blood transfusions, and further dehydration."[10]

Lieutenant Nelson was rather disappointed that he did not get to know the Korean people as well as he would have liked, but his work was confined almost entirely to the American and Allied medical forces and to the wounded.[11] He lost fifteen pounds during his "hot and uncomfortable, dusty and demanding" stay, and he returned weighing only 160 pounds. Nevertheless, he said, "It was a fabulous experience."

Russell recalls meeting a special wounded soldier in one M.A.S.H. As his team was visiting that facility, one of the doctors, knowing Lieutenant Nelson was a Latter-day Saint, asked him if he would like to meet a seventeen-year-old boy from Idaho who was a priest in the Church. The doctor thought the young patient would derive some comfort from meeting a fellow Latter-day Saint. On the way to the patient's tent, the doctor told Russell that this young man had received a gunshot wound that had severed his spinal cord, making him a permanent paraplegic.[12]

As he approached the soldier's bedside, Lieutenant Nelson wondered what he could say that would possibly be of comfort to this young man. After they were introduced, the perceptive young man could tell that Dr. Nelson was genuinely compassionate and concerned for his welfare. This fine young priest uttered words that Russell would never forget: "Don't worry about me, Brother Nelson, for I know why I was sent to the earth—to gain experiences and work out my salvation. I work out my salvation with my mind and not with my legs. I'll be all right!" Russell humbly recorded, "The faith of that young man has motivated me ever since. He accepted the fact that he would never walk again as a challenge which would fortify his faith even further."[13]

After a long, hot summer in Japan and Korea, Russell returned to Salt Lake City to find all well with Dantzel, Marsha, and Wendy, and with his and Dantzel's extended families. After a brief reunion, the Nelsons returned to their apartment in Hyattsville, Maryland, outside Washington, D.C., and about a twenty-minute drive from the Walter Reed Army Medical Center, where Dr. Nelson worked.[14]

SHARING THE GOSPEL

At age nineteen, when Russell might otherwise have been able to serve a mission, the nation was at war. He was in medical school, so there was no official mission for him. However, he has had some interesting missionary opportunities throughout his life. In 1951, during the Korean War, Russell worked closely with Jane S. Poole, a nurse at the Walter Reed Army Medical Center in Washington, D.C. She had closely observed Dr. Nelson's behavior, certain aspects of which differed from that of other surgeons. One day, she asked Dr. Nelson what the Mormons believe, giving him an opportunity to share the gospel.[15]

"She was like a sponge craving water," Russell recalled. "She wanted to know more and more, so I gradually introduced more of the doctrine and concepts of the Church and suggested reading materials for her. It wasn't long before she had converted herself and I had the privilege of baptizing her." Jane was a divorced mother with a young son, George, who later served a mission in Australia. Jane has remained true and faithful, periodically writing the Nelsons thank-you notes during the succeeding fifty years.[16]

Russell also became well acquainted with two professional colleagues at the Walter Reed Army Medical Center, Dr. Derwin Ashcraft and his wife, Beverly. One day, they asked Dr. Nelson about his religious beliefs, so he gave them a preliminary overview and loaned them his copy of the Book of Mormon. About a week later, they returned the book to him, saying, "Thanks a lot."

Rather assertively, Russell asked, "What do you mean, 'Thanks a lot'? That is a totally inappropriate response for one who has read this book. You didn't read the book. Please take it back and read it; and then when you have read it, please return it to me."

Somewhat red-faced and embarrassed by this challenge and confrontation, the Ashcrafts retrieved the book, acknowledging that they had only thumbed through the pages. Three weeks later, they returned with tears in their eyes and said, "We have read the book. We know it is true. We want to learn more." Dr. Nelson said, "Now I know you've read the book."

In due course, Dr. Nelson baptized the grateful couple. Not long thereafter, Dr. Ashcraft passed away and Russell lost contact with

Sister Ashcraft. Twenty-six years later, in 1977, Beverly came up to Brother Nelson after he had addressed a Sunday School leadership meeting in Weston, Massachusetts, and asked, "Russell, do you remember me?"

He looked at her radiant countenance and replied, "Yes, Beverly, I do. Tell me what has happened to you in all these years."

She had married a wonderful man named Harold L. Zitting, and they had had several children. He had become a bishop, and they were happily and busily engaged in the work of the Lord. She assured Russell of her gratitude for his sharing the gospel with her so many years before.[17]

Elder Nelson's deep and abiding love for the Book of Mormon and his belief in its converting power have been reflected in his instruction to full-time missionaries. Just as he chastised the Ashcrafts for their casual approach to the book he had loaned them, on more than one occasion he has gently chided missionaries for treating the Book of Mormon as if it were a mere pamphlet instead of being the sacred record it is. He has instructed them that they are not merely trying to see how many books they can distribute; rather, they are trying to share their testimony and offer a personal invitation to each person with whom they place a Book of Mormon.

Although Russell held a relatively lower military rank as a first lieutenant, his assignment as a physician at the Walter Reed Army Medical Center required him to supervise the surgical work of older men of higher rank. One of these men was Maj. Gen. Wallace Graham, personal physician to President Harry S Truman. Dr. Graham was pursuing residency training in surgery at the medical center in addition to performing duties at the White House. Lieutenant Nelson also worked closely with several young and capable men who would later become teachers and leaders in the medical profession.[18]

During his two years in Washington, D.C., Lieutenant Nelson had a variety of responsibilities. These included caring for patients at the Walter Reed Army Medical Center, directing his own surgical research program, and setting up a laboratory that procured the first flame photometer for determining sodium and potassium levels in the blood. He was also part of a collaborative research effort with civilian medical institutions, which brought him in contact with several medical schools and research centers throughout the country.[19]

The research Dr. Nelson had conducted on bacterial toxinemia in shock patients impressed Dr. Edward D. Churchill, professor of surgery at Harvard Medical School and chief of surgical services at Massachusetts General Hospital in Boston. Dr. Churchill offered him a position with his group at Massachusetts General Hospital upon completion of his tour of military duty, but Dr. Nelson explained his intentions to return to the University of Minnesota. Dr. Churchill persisted, suggesting that if Russell were to come to Boston and spend a year adding to "the educational ferment in our institution," he would be properly cared for.

"I'll never forget the kindness and the encouragement extended to me by Dr. Edward D. Churchill," Russell said. "He was truly one of the great giants in American surgical history."[20] Russell gratefully accepted Dr. Churchill's offer upon completion of his military obligation.

Not long after Russell returned from Korea, he was called as second counselor to Bishop L. Blaine Liljenquist of the Washington Ward. The first counselor was Brother George H. Bailey Sr. For nearly two years, Brother Nelson labored with these brethren in a relationship he will always treasure. The call to serve was extended to him by the stake president, J. Willard Marriott, for whom Russell had great admiration and affection. On December 27, 1951, Elder George Q. Morris, Assistant to the Council of the Twelve, ordained Russell a high priest and set him apart as a member of the bishopric.[21]

Little more than two months later, Russell and Dantzel received their patriarchal blessings from the stake patriarch, Brother Joseph Stimpson, "a dear and gentle soul who magnified his calling as a patriarch." Russell and Dantzel have always cherished the promises in their patriarchal blessings.[22]

Elder Ezra Taft Benson was on leave from his Church calling while serving as secretary of agriculture in the cabinet of President Dwight D. Eisenhower, so the Benson family frequently attended the Washington Ward. This was the beginning of a warm relationship the Nelsons enjoyed with the Bensons.[23] It was also while living in Washington, D.C., that Russell and Dantzel became better acquainted with another young couple from Salt Lake City, Neal A. and Colleen Maxwell.

Three months before he finished his military obligation, Russell was promoted to captain. With a humble disclaimer, he observed, "That promotion came not from any merit or commendable performance but simply because I had lived long enough to fulfill the requirement of twenty-one months in service as a first lieutenant, whereupon an automatic promotion was to follow."[24]

The Nelsons had made many friends in the medical profession and in the Church. Those friendships have endured throughout the years, enriching their lives. The Sunday night before their departure for Boston in March 1953, Russell was released from the bishopric. He and Dantzel were honored at sacrament meeting, during which Elder Benson and Bishop Liljenquist offered kind remarks. After the meeting, Elder Benson asked Russell if he would accept an assignment to watch out for a young man in Boston from a fine LDS family in whom he was interested. "I accepted that assignment as I would any assignment given me by my leaders in the Church," Russell said. "With that challenge and blessing from an Apostle, we looked forward to the next chapter in our lives, in Boston, Massachusetts."[25]

CHAPTER 11

CONTINUING THE
QUEST FOR KNOWLEDGE

HAVING FULFILLED HIS MILITARY obligation, Russell joined the staff at Massachusetts General Hospital and Harvard Medical School. This was a privilege he had never imagined would come to him. Once again, Dantzel, who was becoming accustomed to a nomadic lifestyle, embarked with Russell into the unknown. As had been the case elsewhere, they arrived in Boston "not knowing a single soul." They were fortunate to find housing in Belmont, on the lower floor of an unfurnished duplex conveniently located near bus lines Russell could use to travel to work, allowing Dantzel to use the car.[1]

Unfortunately, their arrival in Boston preceded the moving van by nearly a week. But shortly after their arrival, two "ministering angels," John N. and Elizabeth S. Hinckley, appeared at their door. These solicitous Saints provided the Nelson family with sleeping bags and bedrolls, pillows, food, and other needed items until their material goods arrived. To this day, Dantzel and Russell regard the couple's timely appearance as a miracle because the Hinckleys were complete strangers. John served as the local district president in the Church, and the Nelsons and Hinckleys enjoyed pleasant times together during the Nelsons' year in Boston.[2]

Russell's work schedule was demanding, as he was on call at the hospital every other night and every other weekend. He would kiss

Dantzel and the three children goodbye at 6 A.M. one day and greet them again late the evening of the following day. He usually spent only about seven of each forty-eight hours at home, during which time the children were asleep. Almost single-handedly during that year Russell spent at Massachusetts General Hospital, Dantzel cared for their little trio.[3]

Usually, Russell was able to make a trade with his Jewish or Seventh-day Adventist colleagues at the hospital. He would work for them a couple of hours on Saturday, and they would work for him a couple of hours on Sunday. That enabled him at least to attend Sunday School or sacrament meeting and to see his little loved ones, albeit briefly. When he had a free weekend, the family enjoyed seeing the beautiful sights of historic New England.[4]

The Saints met in a house across the street from the Longfellow House on Brattle Street. They labored together to keep the house looking nice, and they produced plays and held banquets and other fund-raising activities so that one day they might have a chapel. Dantzel served in the branch Relief Society presidency while Russell served as secretary of the adult Aaronic Priesthood.[5]

The demands of the hospital made Russell's Church calling quite challenging. He was required to make numerous visits over long distances during his few free evenings, but with careful scheduling, he successfully made those visits.[6] The spiritual welfare of a number of good men became his concern. One of these men was Wilbur W. Cox, whose wife, Nora, served as branch Relief Society president. Evenings in the Cox home were rewarding, and getting to know this good man and his gracious wife was an enriching experience for the Nelsons. It did not take long for Russell to detect the wonderful spirit in Wilbur, whom he learned to love.

In later years, Brother Cox was called to serve as the first president of the Boston Stake.[7] Elder Henry B. Eyring recalled the sage advice he received from President Cox as a young student attending Harvard: "Always treat people as if they're in trouble, and you'll be right most of the time!"[8] Brother Cox subsequently served as a mission president and as president of the Manti Utah Temple. As one of the Twelve in 1985, Elder Nelson ordained Brother Cox to the office of patriarch.[9]

Another friendship started at Church one day when Dantzel and Russell were attracted to a young, hungry-looking couple they saw in Sunday School. They said to each other, "Wouldn't it be nice to invite them to our home for Sunday dinner?" Their invitation was quickly accepted. That was their first encounter with Truman G. and Ann Nicholls Madsen, marking the start of a lifelong friendship with this couple, who, in subsequent years, returned to the area to preside over the New England Mission. They enjoyed many Sundays together, including singing quartet music for various Church meetings.[10]

Russell's year at Massachusetts General Hospital was difficult for Dantzel but rewarding and challenging for young Dr. Nelson. He made many lifelong friends at the hospital and became acquainted with several distinguished surgeons who were also attracted to this great center of learning. Russell was strongly impressed that at Massachusetts General, the patient always came first.[11]

With the arrival of their fourth child, Brenda, Russell and Dantzel felt the pinch of poverty even further. But Russell recalls no murmurings from his wife, even though he felt that she and the children were being imposed upon. Russell recalled, "The children seemed to think it was normal to sleep in sleeping bags on army cots, and they just accepted that as a routine way of life."[12] The family's one luxury was an upright piano, which they bought in Minneapolis for a hundred dollars and transported to Washington and back to Boston. They bought the piano so that their children could have music in the home and become accustomed to its good influence.[13]

After the year in Boston seemed to fly by, Dr. Nelson was eager to return to Minneapolis to complete the work he had begun so many years before. Just two days before Brenda arrived on February 3, 1954, Russell was able to afford a new Ford station wagon. He and Dantzel timed their move so they could drive all the way to Salt Lake

City for family reunions and then backtrack their way to Minneapolis. With all the comfort and convenience of a station wagon, Russell said, "I marveled at the Mormon pioneers making that trek with their children under the circumstances associated with their travel. We developed an even greater feeling of empathy and love for those pioneers as we made that transcontinental trek ourselves" with four little ones under the age of six.[14]

MINNEAPOLIS

The Nelsons returned to their previous home in Minneapolis in April 1954. They had purchased it for $8,800 on a GI Loan that required no down payment. They had one child when they left that home three years previously; they had four little girls when they returned. With only two tiny bedrooms, the home was inadequate. Ever resourceful, Dantzel and Russell, with the help of their friend Bill Groesbeck, converted the attic into a large multipurpose room with knotty pine paneling. Their arms grew sore from pounding nails, but their work yielded a study, recreation room, sewing room, and another bedroom.[15]

It was in the study that Russell spent countless hours pecking away at the typewriter, writing his Ph.D. dissertation on bacterial toxinemia.[16] He successfully defended his dissertation, completed his senior residency with esteemed professors Dr. Owen H. Wangensteen and Dr. Clarence Dennis, and was awarded the Ph.D. degree from the University of Minnesota in June 1954. With a major in surgery and a minor in physiology, Russell said, "I don't think I ever worked so long and so hard for one piece of paper as I did for that one."[17]

Russell was senior resident in Minneapolis on Dr. Wangensteen's staff when a junior resident was assigned to work with him. This young man, Dr. Conrad B. Jenson, had graduated from the University of Utah. "I immediately became impressed with his devotion, his faith, his perseverance, and his exceptional skill," Dr. Nelson recalled. "He was so dependable; whenever an assignment was given to him, the assignment was done and a report given."[18]

The Minnesota research team members were pleased to learn of the first successful open-heart operation with a heart-lung machine, performed in 1953 by Dr. John H. Gibbon Jr. in Philadelphia.[19] As a result, Dr. Nelson's research work in the field of open-heart surgery continued with enthusiasm. The chief problem researchers faced in relation to the heart-lung machine was oxygenating the blood artificially. The pumping seemed to be handled adequately, but the process of oxygenation, or aeration, seemed to damage the blood.

The Minnesota surgical residents who were engaged in this research were meeting one evening with their wives, one of whom, Mrs. Morley Cohen, was pregnant at the time. She listened to the residents talk about problems of children with congenital heart defects that might be repaired surgically. Then, without lifting her eyes from her knitting needles, she asked a simple yet provocative question: "Why don't you do just as I'm doing now? Let the mother breathe for the baby."[20]

Everyone was stunned by her question, and their animated conversation suddenly stopped. They realized that she had made a profound statement that would alter the direction of future research and subsequent practice. That same year in Minneapolis, Dr. C. Walton Lillehei performed open-heart surgery by placing a child with a congenital heart defect on one operating room table and the mother on an adjoining table to facilitate cross-circulation between parent and child. The procedure provided ideal circulatory and respiratory support while the patient's heart was repaired.[21]

This method placed the parent as well as the child at risk during the operation, so not long afterward, the lungs of primates were used to oxygenate blood during operations. Eventually, Dr. Richard DeWall developed the first bubble oxygenator for this purpose.[22]

With Russell's Ph.D. degree in hand and his residency commitments fulfilled, he and Dantzel decided they would head westward, leaving behind tempting offers to stay in Minneapolis or return to Boston. Dr. Nelson felt that his skills, training, and talents were needed in Utah, so with four children and a fifth one on the way, they returned to Salt Lake City to launch the next phase of his medical career.[23]

CHAPTER 12

APPLYING THE HEALER'S ART

After living in Minneapolis, Washington, D.C., and Boston for nearly eight years, Russell and Dantzel packed up their belongings in March 1955 and returned to Salt Lake City. "Previous moves had been to an unknown destination and a known professional opportunity," Russell said. "This time we were moving to a known destination, with friends and family there to greet us, but to an entirely unknown professional opportunity. We had no job, no arrangements made for hospital privileges, and no office location."[1]

Russell's parents moved out of the family home at 974 South 1300 East, and Russell's family moved in. "For us it was a Cinderella transformation. Suddenly to have adequate housing with five bedrooms and three bathrooms made us feel as though we were royalty," Russell recalled.[2]

Upon learning that Dr. Nelson had returned to Salt Lake City, Dr. Philip B. Price, professor of surgery at the University of Utah College of Medicine, extended an offer to his former student to become a full-time member of the faculty as an assistant professor of surgery. Dr. Nelson cheerfully accepted the offer. He could see that this would allow him an opportunity to pursue his research interests and teaching, which he loved, and to enjoy some modest surgical privileges. His office was located on the second floor of the

Salt Lake County General Hospital on the corner of 2100 South and State Street.[3]

Although Dr. Nelson's research and advanced training had pointed him in the direction of thoracic surgery, eventually to include open-heart surgery, he was known as a general surgeon rather than as a heart surgeon when he returned to Salt Lake City. Surgeons fresh out of training do not inherit waiting rooms packed with handpicked patients. Consequently, those who were initially referred to him presented a wide variety of challenges. Dr. Nelson's first year at the university brought patients suffering from uterine cancer who required hysterectomies, patients needing hernia repairs, and patients requiring gallbladder, pancreatic, thyroid, and gastrointestinal procedures.[4]

Dr. Nelson's quest to pursue surgical access to the heart remained unquenchable. Dr. Price kindly provided space for his research in a laboratory in temporary army barracks adjoining the University of Utah Medical School. There, Dr. Nelson continued his unrelenting research into the development of a pump-oxygenator by which open-heart surgery might be performed.[5]

Inasmuch as Dantzel graciously invited Russell to collaborate in the rearing of their children, Russell reciprocated by inviting Dantzel to become a collaborating investigator in his research. One evening, they had a serious discussion about how tiny air bubbles could be introduced into a column of blood gently enough to oxygenate it without destroying its formed elements. Together they reasoned that "the foamed blood could be defoamed and collected in a settling chamber where it could be pumped back to the arterial system of the patient."[6]

Russell described in detail the fruits of their collaboration: "She and I snipped off the closed-end of a rubber nursing nipple that we had used to feed our babies. To that opening we tied an oxygen line. To the larger open end of the nursing nipple we glued a rubber diaphragm, which Dantzel had perforated about a hundred times with tiny pricks of her sewing machine needle. Then we screwed this

This twin-pump heart-lung machine developed by Dr. Nelson was used in 1955 for the first open-heart surgery performed in Utah (photo courtesy of the Salt Lake Tribune, April 7, 1956).

modified nipple onto a glass column into which the venous blood flowed. By turning the oxygen gas on, tiny bubbles were created which ascended along with the blood up this oxygenating column. Then as this column of foamy blood erupted over the top of the oxygenating column, we provided a zone of contact so that that blood would pass over some copper 'Chore-girls,' which were originally made to scrub pots and pans. The 'Chore-girls' were daubed with a compound known as a silicone antifoam which changed the surface tension of the bubbles so that they burst, allowing the gas to escape into the atmosphere. The liquid blood surrounding the bubbles cascaded down the walls of the outer receiving chamber and settled without bubbles, awaiting passage through a pump back to the heart."[7]

The oxygenator performed well when Dr. Nelson tested it on animals. He was now ready to try it on a human patient. Dr. Hans H. Hecht, professor of medicine and one of Dr. Nelson's teachers in medical school, had watched his work with animals with great interest. In November 1955, he referred a patient to Dr. Nelson, knowing that this would be Dr. Nelson's first human open-heart surgery using an oxygenator of his own design. Russell felt the weight of this responsibility heavily, and he consulted his professor of surgery, Dr. Philip B. Price. Dr. Nelson explained that he was ready, but he wanted to counsel with his chief with respect to the ethics involved. Russell asked, "Would it be wise to accept this patient for the operation, or should the patient be sent to Minnesota for the team of my former colleagues there to do the operation?" Dr. Price's encouragement was clear and unmistakable: "By all means, if you feel that you can do it, you should do it, and you will have my sustaining support."[8]

The first patient to undergo such open-heart surgery in Utah was Mrs. Vernell Worthen, thirty-nine, from Price, Utah. She did not appear to be anxious or frightened, and she showed great confidence in her young surgeon. On November 9, 1955, Dr. Nelson operated on her to close an atrial septal defect. All went well. She recovered without complication, and the *Deseret News* featured her in an article twenty-five years later titled, "Utahn's Life Gets Bonus from Heart Surgery: 25 Extra Years to Love, Learn, Live."[9]

This operation put Utah on the map as only the third state in the nation, behind Pennsylvania and Minnesota, where successful open-heart surgery had been performed. The success of this historic event was shared by Dantzel and by Dr. Nelson's medical colleagues, including Richard W. Hardy, who was a medical student with Dr. Nelson at the time and who ran the heart-lung machine during the operation.[10]

After performing successful cardiac operations on a series of patients with the new pump-oxygenator, Dr. Nelson presented a paper on his work at the annual meeting of the American Association for Thoracic Surgery at the Fontainebleau Hotel in Miami Beach, Florida, in 1956. Wanting Dantzel to share in this important experience, he persuaded her to join him on that trip to Florida. The paper was well received, and while in Florida, Dr. Nelson passed the examination of the American Board of Thoracic Surgery.[11]

Together, Russell and Dantzel had worked for his M.D. and

Ph.D. degrees. His certification by the American Board of Surgery in 1954 and his certification by the American Board of Thoracic Surgery in 1956 were the culmination of Russell's medical education and the last of many hurdles he and Dantzel had overcome. Euphoric over the realization of their accomplishments, they decided to travel to Nassau in the Bahamas for a vacation. They rented a car, toured the island, and thoroughly enjoyed themselves, notwithstanding getting badly sunburned on Paradise Beach. They were grateful for their blessings and prayerfully and joyfully celebrated the achievement of the "final" milestone.[12]

In the spring of 1956, the media reported that "Salt Lake City is now one of the few medical centers in the world in which direct-vision open-heart surgery is being performed with the aid of a heart-lung machine." The news article, featuring a photo of young Dr. Nelson with his newly developed heart-lung machine, compared the advantages of using the heart-lung machine in open-heart surgery with the alternative method of inducing hypothermia in patients by packing their bodies in ice to reduce their body temperature and thus lower their demand for oxygen.[13]

In recognition of Russell's development of the heart-lung machine and his pioneering contributions to open-heart surgery, in January 1957 the Salt Lake Junior Chamber of Commerce named the thirty-two-year-old doctor "Outstanding Young Man of the Year" for 1956. Utah's governor, George D. Clyde, presented Dr. Nelson that same year with the Utah Distinguished Service Award, for the young physician truly had put the state on the medical map.[14]

The early days of open-heart surgery were an uncharted frontier. As a result, tragedies occurred, one of which Russell will never forget. A couple who had already lost one child to congenital heart disease before the advent of cardiac surgery lost a second child following Dr. Nelson's unsuccessful ministrations. Then, in 1957, filled with hope and trusting in Dr. Nelson's skills, they brought him their third child who had been born with a malformed heart. Despite his best efforts, the child died following the operation. Sadly, Russell recalled, "In my grief I felt totally inconsolable."[15]

When he arrived home, he told the story to Dantzel, tearfully exclaiming, "I'm through. I'll never do another heart operation as long as I live!" He wept most of the night, which he spent kneeling beside a chair in the living room. All he could think of was the faces of the parents, now childless because his hard-earned skills were seemingly inadequate to do what needed to be done.

"Words cannot describe my feelings of pain, despair, grief, tragedy—these characterizations only scratch the surface of the torment raging in my soul, which caused me to determine that my failures and inadequacies would never be inflicted on another human family," he said.[16]

Dantzel had also spent a sleepless night, and at the break of dawn she told Russell, "If you quit now, someone else will have to learn all over again what you know. Isn't it better to keep trying than to quit now and require others to go through the same grief of learning what you already know?"[17]

Russell recognized that "her compassionate wisdom was not only for me but also for those whom I might serve if I could just work a little harder, learn a little more, and strive further for the perfection that was demanded for consistent success. I listened to her counsel, and I returned to the laboratory and worked even harder to chart the uncharted sea."[18]

In recognition of Dr. Nelson's demonstrated competence and promise as a medical researcher, the John and Mary R. Markle Foundation in March 1957 awarded him a prestigious research grant of $6,000 annually for five years to support his continued cardiovascular research.[19]

Not long afterward, the dean of the University of Utah College of Medicine resigned, and Russell's dear friend and mentor, Dr. Price, became the new dean. Dr. Nelson realized that Dr. Price's replacement as professor of surgery could have a significant impact on the development of his career. The man chosen to be the new professor and head of the department of surgery had long-range plans that did not include Russell's remaining in the department. Thus, after four rewarding years as a full-time member of the faculty at the University of Utah College of Medicine, Russell left his position on the faculty and released the Markle award after having held it for only two years.[20]

Anticipating the foregoing changes, Russell had applied for staff privileges at LDS Hospital. The administrator, Clarence Wonnacott, and Russell's good friend, Dr. Homer R. Warner, welcomed him with open arms and provided laboratory facilities in which his research work could continue. He also received an offer, extended by Dr. Ernest L. Wilkinson, to affiliate with the staff at the Salt Lake Clinic.[21]

In March 1959, Dr. Nelson moved his office to the Salt Lake Clinic, and his research laboratory was moved from the temporary barracks at the University of Utah to the seventh floor of the west wing of LDS Hospital. James W. Henry, his laboratory associate and technician, joined him in the move.[22]

Shortly after shifting his research facilities, Russell received a research grant from the Utah Heart Association to assist in the development of a suction apparatus to help surgeons better see what they are doing during an operation.[23] In 1961, Dr. Nelson received another research grant "to study alterations in cardiac output and blood flow to the major organs of the body during the state of shock caused when the body is weakened by loss of blood."[24] At the end of that same year, he received yet another research grant to study possible beneficial effects of a chemical to correct certain systemic abnormalities in persons undergoing open-heart surgery.[25] Dr. Nelson was clearly a young man in a hurry to discover the laws of successful surgery.

Russell enjoyed his years at the Salt Lake Clinic and was delighted to associate with such well-trained, skilled physicians. He had been there about two years when he received a phone call on June 20, 1961, from his former surgical colleague and fellow resident in

Minneapolis, Dr. Conrad B. Jenson. Inasmuch as Conrad was completing his residency, he wondered if it would be possible for him to become Dr. Nelson's associate. Conrad's father was a prominent physician in Ogden, and Russell had always assumed that Conrad would return to Ogden.

"We spent eight hours on the Fourth of July analyzing the pros and cons of our possible future association," Russell said. "Neither the Salt Lake Clinic nor I could offer him much in the way of specific encouragement, for my work had not been built up to the point where I needed help; yet I realized that he was a special individual who would come along only once in a lifetime. So I determined that I would take him as my associate and persuaded the Salt Lake Clinic to feel the same way."[26]

In a moment of soliloquy, Russell said: "It is interesting in retrospect to look back on important decisions that shape the future of a man's life and see how relatively effortless those decisions seemed to be at the time. The decision to marry Dantzel, the decision to have Conrad as an associate—both seemed to be so easy. Now, with the hindsight of many years, it is apparent that I could not have been more blessed than I have been with such companions with whom I might share this life at home and at work."[27]

After spending four years at the Salt Lake Clinic, Russell realized that his goals would best be served if his practice were independent rather than clinic-oriented. He was interested in research and in teaching, as well as in service in the Church. These interests would require that he spend considerable time away from practicing medicine at the clinic, while his colleagues at the clinic pursued their medical work full time.

"Even though I was able to hold my own with them by producing a fair share of the income and extracting a fair share of the returns," Russell said, "I could see that inevitably there would be those who might resent the time I wanted to spend doing other things in life."[28]

By mutual agreement, Russell left the clinic in April 1963 and

was joined by Conrad a few months later as they initiated a partnership that lasted more than twenty-seven years. Never during that
time did an unkind word pass between them. "It was a genuine
pleasure to work with such a choice soul, a noble Saint, and a fan-
tastic surgeon," Russell said of Conrad.[29]

Dr. Jenson reciprocates Russell's admiration of his skills as a surgeon, rejoining that "Russell has great vision and organizational
skills. One of his great qualities is his ability to anticipate and prepare for the future. He has excellent judgment, and he is very organized and a doer, not just a thinker. He successfully transmitted to
the hospital administrators and his fellow physicians his vision for
developing programs of excellence which would establish the LDS
Hospital as an outstanding center of medical care."[30]

Early in Russell's medical career, he realized that there were distinguished Latter-day Saint physicians, such as Dr. Homer R.
Warner, at the top of his field who were willing to come to the Salt
Lake Valley in order to rear their families in a supportive, moral
environment. "I could see that the LDS Hospital had the great
potential to become a tertiary medical care center of significance,"
he said. "The University of Utah College of Medicine wanted excellence, as did we at LDS Hospital. We could either compete with
each other or unite and combine our strengths."[31]

David B. Wirthlin, an administrator at LDS Hospital, described
the process: "Dr. Nelson was considered to be one of the premier
heart surgeons in the entire country. He received patients from all
over the world, and with his vision and leadership, he made the LDS
Hospital a world-renowned heart center. He knew that the best centers in the world needed the finest doctors who would be involved in
teaching and research; a hospital that provided the latest in design
and equipment in surgical facilities, intensive care units, and hospital
beds; nurses and support staff who were specially trained in the care
of open-heart patients; and a unified staff of surgeons, cardiologists,
internists, and administrators who were all united in providing a

heart center that offered the best care anywhere in the country to every patient."

He continued: "Elder Nelson was the great 'unifier' in this Herculean effort. He was always the oil on troubled waters, and he was able to sooth hurt egos and resolve disagreements with the medical staff, many of whom were known for their impatience and independence. He knew that without a team effort, the ultimate goals could not be accomplished. He was able to articulate to the administration the vision of achieving the best care and the importance of budgeting for the needs in the immediate future and for the long term. I doubt that the accomplishments which were achieved in making the LDS Hospital the finest in heart care could have been achieved without Elder Nelson's constant support and leadership to achieve the very best. He was a natural leader because he demonstrated a level of excellence as a surgeon that demanded respect and admiration. He did not have to seek these responses; they came spontaneously to him."[32]

Dr. Nelson was invited to become the chairman of the combined thoracic surgical residency program with the resources of LDS Hospital, the University of Utah Medical Center, Primary Children's Hospital, and the Veterans Administration Medical Center. This combination of medical facilities provided the necessary volume and variety of patients and the clinical resources necessary to compare favorably with other residency programs in the country. But it was no small feat to bring together the administrators and surgical staffs of each respective organization. Myriad questions were raised about which organization would cover which costs and who would assume responsibility for meeting which challenges. But in the end, after several candid discussions, Dr. J D Mortensen said, "Russ was the catalyst for the development of the combined LDS Hospital-University of Utah thoracic surgical residency, a program he directed for seventeen years. Among his biggest contributions to medicine was his skill as a teacher and administrator."[33]

Dr. Nelson's credibility as an honest broker and negotiator was

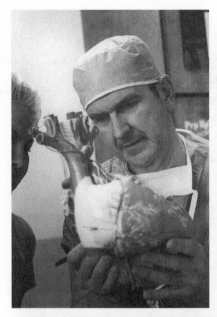

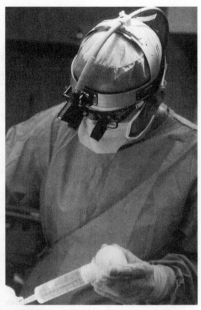

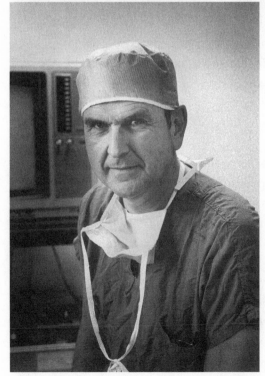

Top left: Using a model of the human heart, Dr. Nelson explains a surgical procedure to a nurse.

Top right: Dr. Nelson performs surgery in 1982.

Left: Following an operation of several hours, Dr. Nelson reflects his weary satisfaction with a successful surgical procedure (photos courtesy of the Church Visual Resource Library).

evidenced by the fact that the agreement among the respective surgical staffs and administrators of four different hospitals was entirely verbal, sealed with handshakes rather than written contracts.

Dr. Nelson long contended that "the duty of a doctor, primarily, is to teach. In Latin, the word *docere* means 'teacher.' A doctor is really functioning at his highest level when he is teaching his patient what is wrong and what can be done about it. Some things can be treated medically or surgically and some things can't. The doctor's duty is to discern and to teach."[34] Dr. Nelson also contended that the physician "does not own his patient." Thus, patients must be given their choice in the course of treatment.[35]

"Another part of a doctor's career is to serve, and to serve when the patient needs it, not according to the doctor's own time preferences. Medicine is a discipline that teaches you to serve selflessly and without regard to your own comfort, whether you're tired, hungry or whatever. You have to subvert your own personal appetites."[36]

Although they considered other surgeons as possible associates over the years, Drs. Nelson and Jenson invited Dr. Kent W. Jones to join their practice in 1977. Dr. Jones had worked with the two surgeons when he was a medical student, and they had observed his work for a decade. They agreed that he was such an outstanding individual that they would like to have him as their professional associate.[37]

Dr. Jones was delighted with the invitation, acknowledging Russell's leadership in helping to make Salt Lake City one of the pioneering centers in coronary artery bypass surgery, the implantation of pacemakers, and the surgical repair of heart valves. In addition to admiring Russell's surgical skills, Dr. Jones also admired the fact that no matter "what setting he is in or what group he is with, he is always himself."[38]

Dr. Jones also has great admiration for Russell's attention to detail and for his vision of the big picture. "He must have had a list of hundreds of people that he sent birthday cards to each year," Dr. Jones said. "He'd sit down every morning and send them out. He never let

Russell M. Nelson in 1961 while serving as second counselor in the bishopric of the Garden Park Ward.

the 'small things of life' fall through the cracks because of what we may think are the 'bigger things in life.'"[39]

As Dr. Nelson's practice grew, Dantzel and Russell were busily engaged in the Garden Park Ward. Hoyt W. Brewster, Russell's former priests quorum adviser, was now his bishop. He called Brother Nelson to be the adviser of the priests quorum, which included more than fifty young men. This was a marvelous assignment that Brother Nelson greatly enjoyed. He was later called to be first assistant to John Matheson in the superintendency of the Bonneville Stake YMMIA. Later, when professor Melvin A. Cook was released from the bishopric of the Garden Park Ward in 1958, Bishop

Brewster called Brother Nelson to serve as his second counselor, with Paul W. Cox as first counselor.

Because Bishop Brewster was the son-in-law of President Joseph Fielding Smith, he felt comfortable in bringing Russell to President Smith's apartment to have this venerable Apostle set apart Brother Nelson as the second counselor in the bishopric.[40] Bishop Brewster, Brother Cox, and Brother Nelson enjoyed serving together for about five and a half years in a ward with more than a thousand members.

In 1955, not long after returning to Salt Lake City, Russell was honored when Elder Richard L. Evans called him to serve as a missionary on Temple Square. He served each Thursday from 4–5 P.M., guiding tourists through the grounds and explaining to them some of the basic principles and doctrines of the Church. He served in this assignment for ten years until he was released in 1965 after being called as a stake president.

Of his Temple Square calling, Russell modestly surmised, "I really don't know how much good I may have done through those efforts on Temple Square, but introducing the gospel to between twenty-four and fifty people a week, fifty-two weeks a year, for ten years meant that thousands could have been introduced to the message of the Restoration."[41]

CHAPTER 13

CALLED TO BE A
STAKE PRESIDENT

Although Russell had had some contact with Elder Spencer W. Kimball in prior years, their first meeting of real substance came when Elder Kimball and Elder LeGrand Richards were assigned to the Salt Lake Bonneville Stake conference in December 1964 to reorganize the stake presidency.

Brother Nelson said, "Frankly, I didn't give the matter a lot of thought other than to lament the end of a very pleasant relationship, having been recently called to serve on the high council with President Frank B. Bowers, President Ira B. Sharp, and President Ferdinand E. Peterson."[1]

On the Wednesday evening prior to stake conference, Russell was shocked by a statement made by his fellow high councilor Joseph G. Jeppson, who said, "It has been revealed to me that you will be our new stake president." This upset Russell tremendously because he had great admiration for Brother Jeppson and was surprised at this impropriety on his part. The next night, however, Russell had a similar impression—not clearly that he would be the stake president, but that he would somehow be involved in the reorganization.[2]

"I remember how poorly I did in my interview with Elder Kimball," Russell said. "He showed me a figure and asked if that represented all the tithing that I had paid in the preceding year. I said I didn't know anything about that particular figure, but I knew I was a full tithe payer."

Elder Kimball said, "Well, I thought you were a little more prosperous than this figure might indicate."

Brother Nelson replied, "I don't know how much money I paid in tithing last year. All I know is that I am a full tithe payer."

When Russell went home and consulted his records, he found that Elder Kimball had tithing records for only the month that the Nelsons had resided in the Yale Second Ward during the preceding year. Elder Kimball's record did not include the tithing the Nelsons had paid the previous months of the year while residing in the Garden Park Ward. Russell thought, "Well, how stupid can I be not to have any idea as to how much tithing I had paid."[3]

The Friday evening before stake conference, the Nelson family sang for the annual stake leadership party. Dantzel accompanied her eight daughters, who gave an impressive performance.[4] The following Saturday afternoon, as the priesthood leaders attended stake conference meetings, Brother Nelson was called out of a meeting to meet with Elder Kimball and Elder Richards.

"We feel that the Lord wants you to preside over this stake," Elder Kimball told Brother Nelson. "During our many interviews, whenever your name has come up the response has been rather routine: 'Oh, he wouldn't be very good,' or 'He does not have time,' or both. Nonetheless, we feel that the Lord wants you. Now if you feel that you are too busy and should not accept the call, then that is your privilege. But we have to remain true to the inspiration given to us to extend you the call to be the president of the Bonneville Stake."[5]

Russell told the Brethren that when he and Dantzel were married in the temple on August 31, 1945, they had made a commitment to "seek . . . first the kingdom of God, and his righteousness," feeling confident that everything else would be added unto them, as the Lord had promised (Matthew 6:33). Brother Nelson added, "The Lord has been so good to us, and there is nothing we desire more than to serve where He wants us to serve, in whatever capacity we are called to serve."

The Brethren asked, "Do you want to call Sister Nelson and get her permission?"

"I would like to call her," Russell said, "but not to get permission, for I know the answer she will give. I have just given it to you, but I think that she would appreciate such a call as a courtesy."

When Russell phoned Dantzel, she said what he thought she would say. "This call to serve upset her plans, however," Russell recalled, "because she had just accepted a personal request from Brother Richard P. Condie to become a member of the Tabernacle Choir. Elder Kimball and Elder Richards counseled her to postpone that assignment, at least for the present, and to lend her support to her husband in this new calling instead."

The Brethren then said, "Let us know whom you would like to call for your counselors."

"May I pray about it?" Brother Nelson asked.

"Yes," they said. "We'll be back in twenty minutes."

Russell said, "I consulted with the Lord about it in prayer and had a clear vision as to who should be called." The day before, when the Brethren asked Brother Nelson whom he would recommend as the new stake president, unequivocally he had said, "Joseph B. Wirthlin." Russell felt that Brother Wirthlin would be a strong leader in the stake, so he called him as a counselor. "It was also clear to me that Albert R. Bowen should be the other counselor," Russell recalled. Because he was older, Albert became the first counselor. That marked the beginning of nearly seven gratifying years the men served together in the presidency of the Bonneville Stake.[6]

Before being set apart, Brother Nelson indicated to Elder Kimball and Elder Richards that one of the most serious problems confronting him as a cardiac surgeon was the surgical procedure of aortic valve replacement on people who would otherwise soon die. Russell discussed the risks, explaining that his colleagues had worked on the procedure for two years and that the mortality rate of patients

President of the Salt Lake Bonneville Stake, 1964.

was about 20 percent. Such high-risk operations usually required an entire night of follow-up care by Dr. Nelson.[7]

"In setting me apart," he recalled, "Elder Kimball blessed me that the quality of my professional work would be increased so that I would have time to perform my duties as stake president without jeopardizing the care that was required by my seriously ill patients; moreover, that my ability to perform cardiac operations would increase, and that the mortality rates would decrease to a more acceptable range."[8]

Dantzel and Russell vividly remembered this blessing during subsequent years as Dr. Nelson's surgical mortality rate fell to less than 5 percent. The blessing Elder Kimball gave him in 1964 redounded to Elder Kimball himself eight years later when Dr. Nelson performed an aortic valve replacement on him during open-heart surgery.[9]

On January 13, 1965, at a special meeting of the stake presidents in the Salt Lake Valley, Elder Kimball warmly embraced Russell and said, "Brother Nelson, are you still the president of the Bonneville Stake?"

"Oh, yes," President Nelson responded

Elder Kimball laughed and said, "After you were called to be stake president, I had all sorts of people tell me they thought you wouldn't last more than two weeks. It delights me to see that you are still serving."

Russell recalled, "That was rather typical of Elder Kimball's marvelous sense of humor."[10]

Notwithstanding Elder Kimball's good-natured teasing of President Nelson, his comments about his being too busy to serve were rather stereotypical of all physicians throughout the Church. President Faust recalled, "Back when I was growing up, many doctors were too busy for Church callings. They were good men, but we assumed they were too busy to serve. Russell Nelson changed all of that in his service as a stake president and as general president of the Sunday School. He has blessed the entire Church, and we now have many fine doctors serving in the kingdom. I give Russell M. Nelson the credit for changing the stereotype that doctors are too busy to serve in the Church."[11]

As if to confirm President Faust's observations, the *Deseret News* published an article about Russell's call as stake president titled "'Make Time' for Church, Doctor Says." The article quoted Dr. Nelson as saying, "You never find time to do anything. One can always make time to do things he feels are important."[12] Several years later, a *Church News* editorial asked the question: "How can a man serve his church in many responsible capacities and still do justice to the work he does in his profession and for his community?" The editorial then answered, "Just ask Dr. Russell M. Nelson . . . one of America's busiest and most respected heart surgeons."[13]

Elder Cecil O. Samuelson Jr. of the Seventy acknowledged that Dr. Nelson's example of serving in the Church had made it much easier for him years later to serve as a stake president and then as a regional representative while working as dean of the College of Medicine at the University of Utah.[14]

About a year after Russell became president of the Bonneville Stake, he received a prestigious offer to become professor of surgery and chairman of the Division of Cardiovascular and Thoracic Surgery at the University of Chicago. He and Dantzel were attracted to this offer and even picked out a home in one of the suburbs of Chicago where they might rear their family. They still remember with fondness the hospitality of a young professor of law at the University of Chicago, Dallin H. Oaks, who, with his wife, June, invited the Nelsons to their home in November 1965 for Sunday dinner. Professor Oaks served as a member of the stake presidency in Chicago.

Brother Oaks had served on a few university committees together with the dean of the University of Chicago Medical School, who knew he was a Latter-day Saint. Thus, when the medical school faculty attempted to recruit Dr. Nelson, the dean mentioned to Brother Oaks that Dr. Nelson might have some serious concerns about moving a large family to Chicago. He asked Professor Oaks if he could invite Dr. and Mrs. Nelson to dinner and speak to them, as fellow Latter-day Saints, about the rewards of living in Chicago.

Elder Oaks recalled, "June and I had never met the Nelsons previously, but our time together in Chicago was delightful."[15] Russell reciprocated similar feelings: "To meet the Oaks family was one of the highlights of that trip to Chicago; it was a memorable experience to be with this talented and faithful family of such great ability."[16] Little did these brethren know that eighteen years and four months later they would both be called to serve as Apostles of the Lord.

Brother Joseph Anderson served as a member of the high coun-
cil of the Bonneville Stake and as the secretary to the First
Presidency, so when Russell returned to Salt Lake City, he informed
Brother Anderson of his offer from the University of Chicago.
Brother Anderson advised President Nelson to counsel with the
Lord's prophet about this important decision, and he arranged for
Dantzel and Russell to meet with President David O. McKay.[17]

When they met in President McKay's Hotel Utah apartment on
December 14, 1965, the prophet was ninety-two years old. As he
greeted them at the front door, he relied on an aluminum walker to
steady his gait. Smiling, he said, "You'll have to pardon my use of
this walker. Sometimes my legs are a bit disobedient!"

He invited Russell and Dantzel into his study, and there they
reviewed the nature of the offer extended by the University of
Chicago. After hearing their story, he closed his eyes, leaned his head
back, and pondered the matter for a while. Then he asked, "And
what would you want to do this for? To get fame? You are already
famous; I know who you are!" He laughed as he said this and then
continued. "How many children do you have?"

"Nine daughters," the Nelsons replied.

"Where is it you live in Salt Lake?" President McKay then asked.

Russell told him they lived on Normandie Circle, where they
had moved in the fall of 1963. Their home was just opposite the
canyon where President McKay's son Llewelyn lived.

"Then," Russell recalled, "he laid his head back on his chair,
closed his eyes, and communed with the Lord in supplicating an
answer that would be a guide for us. Actually, he was nonresponsive
to us for such a long time that I began to wonder if he was still alive.
But then, with that keen, sharp intellect and piercing eye, he looked
at me directly and said, 'Brother Nelson, if I were you I wouldn't be
in a hurry to change neighborhoods. It doesn't feel good to me. No,
Brother Nelson, your place is here in Salt Lake City. People will
come from all over the world to you because you are here. I don't
think you should go to Chicago.'"[18]

Russell recalled, "That was it. In a meeting lasting seventy-five minutes with President David O. McKay, the decision had been made." He called the officials in Chicago and informed them that he was declining their offer and remaining in Salt Lake City. Many of Russell's friends in academic surgery thought he had made a serious mistake, but his faith was secure. He and Dantzel had been privileged to receive a prophet's counsel, and they were going to abide by it.[19] After their experiences in Minnesota, Washington, D.C., and Boston, they finally felt settled in Salt Lake City, experiencing the poetic prediction of T. S. Eliot:

> *We shall not cease from exploration*
> *And the end of all our exploring*
> *Will be to arrive where we started*
> *And know the place for the first time.*[20]

En route to a medical meeting, Russell called Dantzel on January 18, 1970, to let her know he had arrived at Stapleton Airport in Denver, Colorado. She broke the news that President McKay had died. "How we loved this magnificent man—a chosen prophet of God," Russell said.[21]

President Nelson served as stake president from 1964 to 1971. During his presidency, the Bonneville Stake had about six thousand members. The stake presidency during this period remained intact, and President Nelson was grateful for the devotion and loyalty of his faithful counselors.[22]

In summarizing his tenure as stake president, President Nelson said, "Most of all, there was a feeling of faith, unity, and love—love for one another, love for the leadership in the Church, and love for the Lord. That same love was shared by me for the wonderful Saints whom I was privileged to serve."[23]

After post-surgical mortality rates began to decline significantly, Dr. Nelson gratefully confessed the Lord's "hand in all things" (D&C 59:21). With childlike faith, he acknowledged, "Faith is power. Priesthood power is real." With almost boyish wonder, he observed, "When President Kimball—then Elder Spencer W. Kimball of the Quorum of the Twelve Apostles—and Elder LeGrand Richards laid their hands upon my head and blessed me that I could do the work of a stake president and also have time for my medical work, they gave me power to do and to understand and to see what I hadn't before. My capacity increased.

"I was sailing on seas that were largely uncharted, so I had to work, I had to learn. I had to go into the lab and learn what some of the laws were. But even beyond that, there were elements of inspiration and revelation that were very helpful."[24]

To illustrate the process of revelation, he said, "I remember one man I operated on, a stake patriarch from southern Utah. I had previously turned him down for surgery because I knew I didn't know how to repair his defective tricuspid valve. He was a man of great faith, and time and time again, he returned with a plea for surgical help, saying, 'I'm going to die if you don't help me.'

"I allowed myself to be persuaded, not knowing exactly the technique required. The operation had not been done before. I operated upon him, and, in the middle of the operation, I had the most wonderful vision of what should be done—dotted lines as to where the stitches should be laid. I opened his heart up and placed the stitches right where I saw them in that diagram that flashed before my mind, and the operation worked beautifully.

"That serves to illustrate there is this element of faith and this element of power. When you have people praying for you and you're praying yourself, coupled with the power of fasting, which makes you more humble and more teachable, you can learn things, even if it is given you by revelation."[25]

CHAPTER 14

A Prophet's Surgeon

WHILE PARTICIPATING IN AN area conference in Manchester, England, in 1971, President Spencer W. Kimball, who was then acting president of the Quorum of the Twelve, confided in Dr. Nelson that he was having anginal pains. When they returned to Salt Lake City, Dr. Nelson referred President Kimball to Dr. Ernest L. Wilkinson, who could give him the continuing medical care that is best given by a medical cardiologist. Working together, the two physicians tried to determine the nature of his heart problem. On October 9, 1971, Dr. Nelson performed a selective coronary arteriogram and found that President Kimball's heart was being overworked because of severe aortic valve disease. The overworked heart was being undersupplied with blood because of an obstruction in the main arterial supply line to the cardiac muscle.[1]

"Five months later, the hour of decision approached," Russell solemnly recalled. "Neither Dr. Wilkinson nor I recommended a surgical approach because of the complex nature of the heart operation that would be needed and because of President Kimball's being in congestive heart failure at seventy-seven years of age. So President Kimball called a special meeting with the First Presidency. Invited to the meeting in addition to the First Presidency and Sister Kimball were Dr. Ernest L. Wilkinson and myself. President Kimball began the meeting by saying, 'I am a dying man. I can feel my life slipping.

At the present rate of deterioration, it is my belief that I can live only about two more months. Now I'd like my medical cardiologist, Dr. Ernest L. Wilkinson, to present his views about my health.'"

Dr. Wilkinson reaffirmed President Kimball's statement, explaining that "because of congestive failure, occasioned by the extra workload on the heart, strained with an incompetent aortic valve and a high-grade obstruction in the most important artery in the heart, spontaneous recovery would be unlikely and death would ensue in the not-too-distant future."

Then President Kimball called on Dr. Nelson to speak, asking, "What can cardiac surgery offer?"

Dr. Nelson said, "I indicated that the operation, if it were to be done, would be a compound surgical procedure consisting of two components. First, the defective aortic valve would require removal and replacement with a prosthetic aortic valve. Second, the left anterior descending coronary artery would have to be revascularized with a bypass graft."

President Lee asked, "What would the risks be with such procedures?"

Dr. Nelson replied, "We have no experience doing both operations on patients in this age group. Therefore, I cannot give you any risk data based on experience. All I can say is, it would entail extremely high risk."

Then a weary President Kimball said, "I'm an old man and ready to die. It is well for a younger man to come to the Quorum and do the work I can no longer do."

Elder Nelson described the dramatic reaction of President Lee: "At that point President Harold B. Lee, speaking for the First Presidency, rose to his feet, pounded his fist to the desk, and said, 'Spencer, you have been called! You are not to die! You are to do everything that you need to do in order to care for yourself and continue to live.'"

President Kimball responded, "Then I will have the operation performed."

"Sister Kimball wept," Dr. Nelson remembered. "When he spoke those words, my heart sank, for the weight of this decision seemed suddenly to pass to me. But this was a remarkable event. This momentous decision, which shaped the history of the Church, was not based on medical recommendation. It was based strictly on the desire of President Kimball, as an Apostle of the Lord, to be obedient to the inspired direction of the First Presidency of the Church."

After this momentous decision had been made, a brief discussion followed regarding the timing of the operation. It was March 1972, and Dr. Nelson recommended postponing the operation until after general conference. The decision was made to perform the operation on April 12.

"President Kimball attended only one of the seven sessions of general conference in April 1972," Russell recalled. "His breathlessness and inability to exert himself because of his congestive heart failure forced him to listen to the other sessions from his bed."

Russell received a blessing from the First Presidency on the eve of the operation, under the hands of President Harold B. Lee and President N. Eldon Tanner. "They blessed me that the operation would be performed without error, that all would go well, and that I need not fear for my own inadequacies, for I had been raised up by the Lord to perform this operation."

The operation began the next morning, and as the first incision was made, the resident physician exclaimed, "He doesn't bleed!"

Dr. Nelson observed, "From that very first maneuver until the last one, everything went as planned. There was not one broken stitch, not one instrument had fallen from the table, not one technical flaw had occurred in a series of thousands of intricate manipulations. I suppose my feelings at that time may have been like those of a concert pianist rendering a concerto without ever hitting a wrong note, or a baseball player who had pitched a perfect game—

no hits, no runs, no errors, and no walks. For a long and difficult operation had been performed exactly in accordance with the blessing invoked by the power of the priesthood."[2]

President Monson recalled that eventful day. He was seated in the temple with President Lee and the other Brethren. They had been fasting, and their hearts were filled with hopeful anxiety. When the phone rang, President Lee left the room to take the call. President Monson noted, "President Lee was a master at masking his feelings, and he walked back into the room as somber as he could be. He said, 'That was Brother Nelson. Spencer is off the pump!' We all smiled and said a prayer of thanksgiving."[3]

Russell recounted, "Even more overpowering than the feeling that came as we shocked President Kimball's heart and it resumed its beating immediately with vigor, was the manifestation of the Spirit which told me that I had just operated upon the man who would become president of the Church!

"I knew that President Kimball was a prophet. I knew that he was an Apostle, but now it was revealed to me that he would preside over the Church! This feeling was so strong that I could hardly contain myself as we performed the routine maneuvers to conclude the operation. Later on in the week as he convalesced, I shared these impressions with him and he and I wept." Russell added, "I know that he did not take this feeling as seriously as I did because he knew that President Harold B. Lee, who stood before him in the Quorum, was younger and more healthy than he."

Both physician and patient became close during President Kimball's convalescence, which went smoothly. That is not to minimize the burden of pain and anxiety that he experienced. Frequently, Dr. Nelson would visit President Kimball's home and find that he was discouraged, as are most convalescing patients.

"The thing that President Kimball feared most was disability," Russell said. "He did not fear death, but he did not want to be a drain on the Brethren, the Church, or his beloved Camilla. He was

President Spencer W. Kimball and his wife, Camilla, at a party hosted by the general presidency of the Sunday School in honor of President Kimball's eightieth birthday, March 28, 1975.

concerned that although his life might have been prolonged, he might not be able to return to full service in the Church."

In the midst of this postoperative recovery came the death of President Joseph Fielding Smith, in July 1972. Dr. Nelson went immediately to the Kimball home upon learning of the death of President Smith. He and Sister Kimball helped President Kimball get dressed so he could attend the meeting of the Quorum of the Twelve wherein the presidency of the Church would be reorganized. Russell said, "I even sat down at President Kimball's typewriter and wrote a medical report on President Kimball that I hoped would be of some value to President Harold B. Lee as he, the new president of the Church, considered the reorganization."

From that time forward, President Kimball began to gain power and strength. As more was asked of him in the Church, and as more was expected from him, his ability to perform increased remarkably.

The evening after Christmas 1973, Brother Nelson heard the fateful news on television that President Lee had just died and that President Romney and President Kimball were at the hospital, where he had passed away. Dr. Nelson immediately left home, sensing that his place was beside President Kimball. He went into the board of directors' room at LDS Hospital and there found President Kimball and President Romney. Brother Nelson and President Kimball embraced each other and wept. Russell said, "I thought maybe you needed me." President Kimball replied, "I surely do. Thanks for coming."

Russell recalled, "Over the next day or two I began to sense a mood of anxiety, not only among President Kimball and the other Brethren, but in the whole community, for three presidents of the Church had been buried in the three-year period from 1970 to 1973. Now the mantle was to fall upon President Spencer W. Kimball, a man known to have cancer controlled with surgery and radiation, heart disease mended with open-heart surgery, and another illness for which he had just been hospitalized in the preceding month."

Russell added, "As I sensed these anxieties, I was impressed to write a letter to President Kimball on the Sunday he was ordained president of the Church. President Kimball read excerpts from my letter to the Brethren in the temple and again at his first press conference. It gave him a great deal of fortification, particularly with the press as they questioned him pointedly, for he was then able to refer to the letter." The letter read in part, "Your surgeon wants you to know that your body is strong, your heart is better than it has been for years, and that by all of our finite ability to predict, you may consider this new assignment without undue anxiety about your health."[4]

President Kimball became the president of the Church on December 30, 1973, at age seventy-eight. Filled with renewed enthusiasm and the Spirit of the Lord, he encouraged the Saints to "lengthen your stride" and "quicken your pace." It would be a dozen years before he passed away at the age of ninety.

CHAPTER 15

GENERAL PRESIDENT OF
THE SUNDAY SCHOOL

L IKE MANY OTHER DAYS FOR Dr. Nelson, June 4, 1971, began in the hospital. Following a lengthy, difficult open-heart operation, Russell arrived at his office late in the afternoon. When the phone rang, Mrs. Helen Kemp, the receptionist, informed Dr. Nelson that President N. Eldon Tanner was calling. President Tanner got right to the point: "Do you think you could meet with us next Monday around three in the afternoon?"

Russell replied that his schedule required him to be in Hawaii on Monday for a medical meeting, but he told President Tanner that he would change his plans if the Brethren wanted him to. President Tanner asked: "Do you think you could come right now?"

After entering President Tanner's office a short while later, Russell said, "I found that President [Harold B.] Lee was also there. (President Joseph Fielding Smith, president of the Church, was not well that day and was therefore absent.) After they exchanged greetings, President Lee and President Tanner indicated that Brother David Lawrence McKay, who had served more than five years as general superintendent of the Sunday School, was being released to become a mission president. They extended a call to me to serve in this calling, provided that it would not take me away from my medical work, which they did not want to disturb."[1]

Russell was shocked. "I had no idea they were considering such

159

Russell at the time of his call to be the general president of the Sunday School (photo courtesy of the Church Visual Resource Library).

a thing," he said. "Not only that, I had not even realized that Brother McKay was to be released. But without hesitation I replied that my work didn't matter, that if it were necessary for me to sell furniture or take up some other occupation in order to be obedient to the call they were impressed to give, that I would do."[2]

They reiterated their concern that he accept the call only if he could continue in his profession. Russell assured them that if he "would depend upon the Lord, this new challenge could be met."[3]

Following this brief visit in the office of the First Presidency, Russell's life changed considerably. "President Tanner was kind enough to say that he was only sorry that this call would mean the termination of my service as his own stake president," Russell said.[4]

President Monson recalled that, at President Lee's request, "I went to see Russell M. Nelson at home to get his suggestions for counselors in the General Sunday School Superintendency. As I entered the living room I was struck by the sight of boy girl, boy girl, boy girl on every couch." Russell suggested that, for a little privacy,

President Harold B. Lee (left) and President N. Eldon Tanner (right) of the First Presidency with the members of the new general presidency of the Sunday School—Joseph B. Wirthlin, Russell M. Nelson, and Richard L. Warner—and their families.

The newly called presidency of the Sunday School: Joseph B. Wirthlin, Russell M. Nelson, and Richard L. Warner.

*Dr. Nelson greets President and
Sister Harold B. Lee at a Utah
State Medical Association
reception.*

they walk a short distance to the cabin that was built in their back-
yard. There, he indicated that he would be pleased to serve with
Joseph B. Wirthlin and Richard L. Warner.[5] President Nelson and
his counselors were sustained during the closing session of MIA June
Conference on Sunday, June 27, and were set apart by the First
Presidency on July 2, 1971.[6]

The First Presidency invited all the members of the Nelson,
Wirthlin, and Warner extended families to attend the setting apart
of the new Sunday School leaders. This was a large group because
all three men had several children. At the selected hour, all were in
attendance except Russell. As the Brethren were about to proceed,
the phone rang. President Harold B. Lee then explained that Dr.
Nelson "has his finger in someone's heart and can't leave just yet."
Russell's sister Enid recounted that President Lee, showing no impatience, took time to deliver an inspiring impromptu speech. She
recalled that he said, "Many people have asked us: Why would we
choose someone like Dr. Nelson when he is so busy saving lives and
already doing a very important work? We also asked ourselves that
question."[7]

Russell and Dantzel at a Utah State Medical Association dinner, November 1978.

Then, in his deep mellifluous voice of certitude, he said, "I assure you this was not our decision but the Lord's. We asked for guidance and we prayed and talked it over, and this was always the predominant name that came to us. We wanted to make sure the Lord's will was made known. The Lord calls whom He wants. This is not our decision." About half an hour later, Brother Nelson humbly appeared and was set apart for his new calling.[8]

Enid was particularly touched by the propitious nature of President Lee's comments. It just so happened that she had been discussing the fifth article of faith with her Primary class: "We believe that a man must be called of God, by prophecy, and by the laying on of hands by those who are in authority, to preach the Gospel and administer in the ordinances thereof." After hearing President Lee's remarks regarding her brother's call, she was able to testify to her class that she knew "the Lord is in charge."[9]

On that occasion, President Harold B. Lee asked Dantzel how she would cope with raising a large family while her husband served as general superintendent of the Sunday School and worked as a busy heart surgeon. Dantzel replied simply, "When he's home, he's home." President Lee repeated that comment throughout the length and breadth of the Church when encouraging busy priesthood leaders to focus more upon their families in giving them their undivided attention.[10]

Not long after his new call, Brother Nelson received a letter from the First Presidency inviting Sister Nelson and him to attend the first area conference of the Church to be held in Manchester, England, in August 1971. They accepted the invitation but then realized that the date conflicted with Russell's previous commitment to present a scientific paper in Moscow, Russia. Consequently, he sought the counsel of President Tanner regarding how to resolve the conflict. President Tanner said, "You will be able to do both. Don't worry; it will work out."[11]

Russell noted, "That was an interesting challenge because the Manchester meetings were right in the middle of the meetings of the International Surgical Society and the International Cardiovascular Society to be held in Russia. So it would mean commuting from Moscow to Manchester and then back to Moscow in order to be faithful to all concerned."[12]

The Nelsons had been to Russia before and knew that the Russians provided visas with two parts: one part is torn out upon entering the country and the other part is surrendered upon leaving the country, thus making it impossible to enter the country again without another visa. Russell tried to negotiate in Russian, French, and English, and in every way possible to persuade Russian officials to let Dantzel and him leave Russia for Manchester and then reenter Russia to meet his obligations there. Finally, a government official said the only way this kind of an exception could be granted would be for him to appeal to the office of the foreign minister, Andrei Gromyko.[13]

Russell said, "With the aid of the United States embassy, Gromyko's office was contacted and I made my plea. Four hours prior to our flight to England [from Moscow], Gromyko's office delivered an unusual visa for the two of us which permitted us to go to Manchester, participate in that great area conference there, and then return to Russia for the conclusion of our meetings! It was truly an inspiring and faith-promoting experience for us to see the fulfillment of President Tanner's prophetic utterance: 'Don't worry; it will work out.'"[14]

The month previous to the Manchester area conference, President Joseph Fielding Smith's beloved wife, Jessie Evans Smith, passed away. Elder Nelson recalled, "We all felt so compassionate and sympathetic toward President Smith because 'Aunt Jessie' had brought so much youthful vigor and joy into his life." President Smith's bereavement was a cause of great concern inasmuch as his next major assignment as president of the Church was to preside over the Manchester area conference.[15]

Shortly after the Nelsons' arrival in Manchester on August 26, 1971, they were invited to join President Smith and other General Authorities at a special meeting in a hotel room. Brother Nelson learned some powerful lessons in leadership taught indirectly by President Smith as he asked for the reports of each of the leaders in the room. When it was his turn to speak, President Smith stood in presidential dignity and, with the experience of his ninety-four years, said, "Brethren, I want you to know of my great love for you! All my life I've tried to prepare to be able to be of assistance to you in your great ministry. So, if I can be of help to you in any way in the great responsibilities that you carry, that is what I want to do." The thought struck Russell that he really was in the presence of a prophet and a great leader. Rather than giving them dictatorial direction, he expressed his love and sincere desire to help them.[16]

President Smith delivered a profound address at the Manchester area conference. That evening, as the Nelsons spent an intimate moment with him at the hotel, they congratulated him on his talk, telling him how much they enjoyed it and calling it "a masterpiece." President Smith replied, "I didn't come here to fail."[17]

Russell and Dantzel returned to Russia, where Russell presented a paper on aortic valve replacement in patients older than sixty. They then traveled to Leningrad. As they returned to the Hotel Leningrad one evening, Russell received a telephone call from his brother-in-law, Bob Rohlfing, who had gotten through on a poor transoceanic connection. All Russell could hear of the conversation was, "Your mother . . . serious stroke . . . not expected to live . . . come home." Russell said, "Dantzel and I were shocked and saddened by this news and of course had to abandon our plans for remaining longer in Russia."[18]

Once they arrived in New York, they phoned home and found out that Russell's mother was still living. On arriving home, they learned that Joseph B. Wirthlin had asked President N. Eldon Tanner to join him in giving Russell's mother a blessing. She had been in a coma for several days but remained stable until Russell and Dantzel reached her bedside. "When I came into her room, she manifested an awareness of who I was, which was the first glimmer of hope that she might continue to live," Russell said. As her recovery continued, Russell expressed his gratitude to the Lord.[19] She lived nearly twelve additional years.

Shortly after Brother Nelson was called as general superintendent of the Sunday School, a newspaper story mentioned his calling as "head" of the "Deseret Sunday School Union," the official name of the Sunday School organization since its inception on November 11, 1867.[20] The first Sunday School in the Salt Lake Valley was held December 9, 1849, under the direction of Brother Richard Ballantyne. During the following nearly eighteen years, several other Sunday Schools sprang up throughout the valley.

In 1867, the disparate schools were placed under general Church direction and given the name Deseret Sunday School Union to signify that they were united into one union with a uniform curriculum.[21] Over the years, the connotation of "union" generally became associated with labor unions, so President Lee agreed with Brother

Nelson that the time had come to refer to this particular Church auxiliary simply as Sunday School.[22]

The following year, Brother Nelson discussed with President Lee the fact that the presiding authorities in priesthood quorums, the Relief Society, the Primary, and the Young Women's Mutual Improvement Association were called "presidents" and "counselors." In the Sunday School and the Young Men's Mutual Improvement Association, however, the leaders were called superintendents and assistant superintendents. Shortly thereafter, the Church decided that the leaders of all Church auxiliaries should uniformly be called presidents and counselors.[23]

Other more substantive innovations introduced during Brother Nelson's tenure as general president included the formulation of a mission statement that would guide the form and content of the Sunday School curriculum throughout subsequent years. The stated mission of the Sunday School was to teach the gospel of Jesus Christ, to build faith, and to strengthen the family.[24] An outgrowth of that mission was the development of an eight-year cycle of study with the scriptures as the main curriculum. In addition, the weekly hymn practice in Sunday School was changed to the more meaningful "Worship through Music."[25]

In anticipation of the Church's burgeoning growth throughout the earth, the Sunday School's approach to training underwent a dramatic shift. Board members, rather than traveling extensively to offer in-service training visits on specific subjects, began developing permanent resource materials such as *Teaching: No Greater Call*. A natural extension of this process was a uniform program to train new Sunday School leaders and teachers, a prototype of the current teacher-development program.[26] During all of the substantial changes that occurred, Brother Nelson and his counselors engendered among the Sunday School board members great loyalty and mutual love.[27]

CHAPTER 16

WITH PRESIDENT KIMBALL
IN THE PACIFIC ISLES

O NE OF THE HIGHLIGHTS OF Brother Nelson's service as general
president of the Sunday School occurred when he and Sister
Nelson accompanied President Kimball and other Brethren and
their wives to nine area conferences held in the South Pacific from
February to March 1976. Brother Nelson said, "It gave us the
opportunity of being immediately beside the prophet day and night
for a period of three weeks."[1]

They first traveled to Apia, Western Samoa, and as their airplane
touched down, they could see a throng of people, complete with a
brass band, gathered to greet President Kimball. "Governmental
hosts were in attendance, and the streets were lined with waving
crowds, signs, and flowers all the way from the airport to downtown
Apia," Brother Nelson recalled. "A national holiday had been
declared for the visit of the prophet."

As part of the welcoming ceremony, hosted by government and
Church leaders, the Samoan Saints sang a song in their native
tongue about their need for a temple in the Samoan Islands. Brother
Nelson recalled: "Very thoughtfully, they had prepared a translation
of the song and presented it to President Kimball so that he might
follow along and know the substance of their message. When it
came time for his reply, his sense of humor shone forth as he said,
'Now, if I understand your Samoan well, I get the impression that

you are interested in having a temple here.' This brought waves of laughter from the assembled Saints. Then he said, 'I'll have more to say about that at our area conference tomorrow.' The next day he said, 'Before you shall have a temple here, you need to convert your genealogical information from memorized recollections to a written form that can be used in a temple. You also need to get more convert baptisms, for it takes a lot of people to run a temple. So, in essence, when you have done your part, the Lord will do his part and you shall have a temple here.'" The very next year the Saints were delighted with the announcement that a temple was to be built in Samoa.

While President Kimball was in Samoa, several people sought special blessings from him, "including the mission president, President Luapo Iuli Peters, who became quite ill with a high fever on the final day of the area conference. President Kimball selflessly exposed himself to all manner of sickness in order to respond to such requests. Then, while flying from Apia back to Pago Pago, he himself was stricken with a similar febrile illness that came with great suddenness," Brother Nelson recalled.

When they arrived at the hotel, President Kimball had a temperature of 104 degrees Fahrenheit, and both he and Sister Kimball were coughing and feeling miserable. Brother Nelson and D. Arthur Haycock, President Kimball's secretary, responded to President and Sister Kimball's request for blessings, but before doing so, Brother Haycock reminded President Kimball that he and President Tanner were to appear on Samoan television that evening. President Kimball replied, "Have President Nelson take my place." With that pronouncement, Brother Nelson appeared on television for thirty minutes that evening with President Tanner. He later reported that President Tanner's part was brilliant.

The next day the entourage had a 5 A.M. departure from Pago Pago, which meant they had to leave the hotel at about 3:30 A.M. It was merciless to do so because President and Sister Kimball were so ill. When the Brethren got President and Sister Kimball on the airplane and settled with blankets, their fevers raged between 102 and 104 degrees.

"As the long hours of that flight from Pago Pago to Auckland, New Zealand, elapsed, President and Sister Kimball slumbered and later awakened as instructions were given to prepare for the descent," Brother Nelson recalled. "President Kimball had perspired a great deal, which indicated to me that his temperature had fallen; and indeed it had, for it was now 98.9 degrees. He began to button his shirt and cinch his tie, and he asked Sister Kimball to comb his hair. She jokingly responded, 'Which hair do you want me to comb, Spencer?' So their preparations continued for the commitments that awaited him."

President and Sister Kimball were the first ones through the door once the plane landed. "Together they marched like generals inspecting the troops, shaking hands with the people who were lined up to greet them."

Shortly after arriving, President Kimball was scheduled for a television interview. Brother Haycock and Brother Nelson sat in the rear of the room filled with great anxiety for this man whom they had assisted onto the airplane just a few hours earlier and who was now standing before television cameras. President Kimball proceeded to give a marvelous twenty-five minute dissertation on the Church, its history, its mission, and its programs. Brother Nelson said, "It was the finest presentation I have ever heard—thoroughly organized, comprehensive, and humbly and powerfully delivered. Brother Haycock and I looked at each other in utter amazement; we could hardly believe what we were seeing and hearing."

President Kimball then went to a luncheon meeting with Prime Minister Robert Muldoon. "This seemed to be an enjoyable affair for both of them as each gained quick admiration and affection for the other," Brother Nelson said. "We found Prime Minister Muldoon to be a man of great character and courage. When dessert was being served, President Kimball motioned to me and said, 'Brother Nelson, I think I'd better join Sister Kimball in the room.'

So we excused ourselves from Prime Minister Muldoon's company and went to Sister Kimball's room, where she had been since their arrival. President Kimball's illness again became evident, so I took his temperature and found it to be 102 degrees. I couldn't believe the miracle I had just seen. A man so ill had received the blessing of a two-hour remission, which allowed him to perform his duties faithfully and well, as though his spirit had the power to drive the illness, at least temporarily, from his body."

The party later drove from Auckland to Temple View, near Hamilton, where President Kimball was scheduled to meet the Maori queen. President and Sister Kimball were taken to their rooms in the home of the temple president, and they immediately went to bed. President Kimball asked President Tanner to attend the reception with the Maori queen Saturday afternoon since he was ill.

"Sister Kimball and I will also not make it to the cultural activities planned for this evening because of our illness," President Kimball said. "Therefore, will you please excuse us and begin the meeting on time. Express our regrets to the congregation. We will try to conserve our strength in order to make it to the general sessions of the area conference on Sunday morning."

Dantzel went to the stadium to attend the cultural activities at the Church College of New Zealand with President and Sister Tanner and the other Brethren and their wives. Brother Haycock and Brother Nelson remained behind with President and Sister Kimball at the temple president's home. Brother Nelson was reading in President Kimball's room when President Kimball awakened with a start.

"Brother Nelson, what time was that program to begin this evening?" President Kimball asked.

"At seven o'clock, President Kimball."

"What time is it now?"

"It's almost seven."

Noting that President Kimball was soaked in perspiration,

Brother Nelson thought his fever might have broken. Indeed, his temperature was down to 98.6 degrees.

"Tell Sister Kimball we're going," President Kimball said.

Brother Nelson ruminated, "Several thoughts flashed through my mind in that instant, culminating in a decision that it would be unwise for me to say anything about it being medically inadvisable for him to go. So I quickly went in and said to Sister Kimball, 'We're going.' They each hurriedly got dressed and went to the car that had been made available to them."

The Kimball, Haycock, and Nelson entourage drove the short distance to the Church College stadium. Brother Nelson said, "As the car entered the stadium, there was a very loud shout that erupted spontaneously. It was so sudden and so deafening that I wondered if it might have been a clap of thunder. The car was driven around the track to the place where President and Sister Kimball could be ushered to their seats, and Brother Haycock and I took our seats beside our respective companions as well."

Brother Nelson asked Dantzel what caused the enormous shout. She said that when President Tanner began the meeting at 7 P.M., he had excused President and Sister Kimball because of illness. The meeting was to proceed without them so that their strength could be preserved in order for them to join the Saints the following day. One of the young New Zealanders was then called upon to offer the invocation.

"With a faith typical of the Saints in the islands, this young New Zealander gave what Dantzel described as a rather lengthy prayer," Brother Nelson said. During the course of his prayer, he supplicated the Lord thusly: "We are three thousand New Zealand youth. We are assembled here, having prepared for six months to sing and to dance for thy prophet. Wilt thou heal him and deliver him here." Just as the "amen" was pronounced, the car carrying President and Sister Kimball entered the stadium. "They were immediately identified by the assembled throng of thousands, who all spontaneously issued that shout for joy on having their prayers answered so directly!"

Brother Nelson said, "This ability of President Kimball to receive and respond to revelation is one that I've observed on many occasions. I suppose he would regard this as rather an incidental revelation, but to me it was very meaningful because I was there, and I saw it happen."

Continuing his account, he said, "The area conference was to be held outdoors, for there was not an auditorium in New Zealand large enough for the crowd. About fifteen thousand were expected. This was the rainy season in New Zealand, and it had rained every day for at least two weeks. In fact, there was so much concern about the weather that a national day of fasting and prayer had been declared by the government officials the Sunday before the visit of the prophet, to ask for good weather during the conference session the following week. Not only Latter-day Saints but also the entire nation was united in fasting and prayer that this might happen."

On the Sunday morning of the conference, the weather was perfect. "We were blessed with a great outpouring of the Spirit in the sermons that were delivered. Only after the meetings were over did the moisture return," Brother Nelson said.

Following the conference in New Zealand, the group then traveled to Fiji for an area conference in Suva. At the end of the meeting, Brother Haycock and Brother Nelson approached President Kimball with the intention of ushering him immediately to the car that was waiting outside to transport him and Sister Kimball to the hotel. "But with the power of Samson," Brother Nelson said, "President Kimball pushed Brother Haycock and me aside and broke into the crowd of a thousand people who were there and proceeded to shake hands with every one of them."

The next conference was in Tonga, where Brother Nelson witnessed another moving experience. President Kimball prophesied that Tonga would be one of the first nations to send out more missionaries than would be required domestically. "At the conclusion of the meeting, there was not a dry eye," Brother Nelson recalled. "No one moved. The Tongans sang song after song as their means of expressing gratitude to God and to his prophet for the spiritual experience they had enjoyed. In my remarks I indicated that the singing of the Tongan Saints, which I was privileged to observe in a regional meeting assignment three years previously, had led to a change in the format of the Sunday School program for the whole world. The general presidency of the Sunday School was inspired to change the 'Hymn Practice' to 'Worship through Music' because of what I'd seen in Tonga. The power of the Tongan Saints' supplication in musical prayer had set an example that I hoped would be caught by the whole world."

From Tonga, the Brethren and their wives returned to Auckland and then traveled to Australia for regional meetings in Sydney, Melbourne, and Brisbane. Brother Nelson's heart was full of compassion for President and Sister Kimball, who were still struggling with their feverish illness.

The final segment of their trip took them to Tahiti for the ninth and final area conference. Brother Nelson accompanied President Kimball as he received a rather cool reception from the governor of Tahiti, who spoke in French and, through interpreters, asked why they had come. Brother Nelson reported with a smile that "President Kimball won him over in a very short time and invited the governor to come to the area conference, which he did. Elder Bruce R. McConkie gave a talk at that meeting which visibly moved the governor."

Upon reaching home, President and Sister Kimball had chest X-rays which revealed that they both had pneumonia, though Sister Kimball's lungs were clearing. Both Dr. Ernest L. Wilkinson and Dr. Nelson tried to talk President Kimball into going to the hospital, but he pleaded with them not to force him to go. "You brethren just do not understand the urgency that I perceive about the work I must do," President Kimball said. "You must not hospitalize me and slow the work down." They acceded to the words of a prophet and continued to care for him as an outpatient.

Dantzel and Russell still regard the privilege of this three-week association with the Brethren as one of the greatest experiences of their lives. Reflecting on his experiences with President Kimball, Brother Nelson said: "From time to time, I hear people speculate on the question, 'When does the prophet speak as a prophet, and when does he speak otherwise?' This query seems curious to me, as if one were presumptuous enough to sit in judgment on a prophet. In my close associations with President Kimball, spanning two decades and the spectrum from suffering to sublimity, I have never asked that question. The only question I have asked has been, 'How can I be more like him?'"

Continuing, Brother Nelson said: "His saintly life has truly been an inspiration to me, for I have watched him carefully in virtually all circumstances to which one may be subjected. Nothing could bless me and my family more than for us to strive toward the degree of perfection and self-mastery he has achieved. I know that this man, like his predecessors, has been prepared, blessed, inspired, and preserved to preside over the Church as a living prophet. I know that he is directed by the Lord. I have seen it, and I have felt it. I know that Spencer W. Kimball taught and testified as a prophet, that he suffered as have other prophets, that he served as a prophet. He received and responded to revelation as a prophet. He had the courage of a prophet, the kindness and concern of a prophet. He was blessed as a prophet, and he blessed others as a prophet."

CHAPTER 17

CALLED TO BE A
REGIONAL REPRESENTATIVE

A FTER MORE THAN EIGHT YEARS of service as general president of the Sunday School, President Nelson, along with counselors William D. Oswald and J. Hugh Baird, were released during October 1979 general conference. They were succeeded by three General Authorities: Elder Hugh W. Pinnock as president and Elders Ronald E. Poelman and Jack H Goaslind Jr. as counselors.[1]

A few days before general conference, President N. Eldon Tanner called and set apart Brother Nelson as a regional representative. Elder Nelson's new assignment would involve the supervision of fourteen stakes at Brigham Young University. Thus, he began a new chapter of service.[2]

That same year, Dr. Nelson's professional influence continued to expand far beyond the Intermountain West. He accepted invitations to serve as a visiting professor of surgery at the National Institute of Cardiology in Mexico City. He accepted another invitation to serve as the visiting professor of surgery at the Catholic University in Santiago, Chile.[3]

Notwithstanding ever increasing opportunities within his professional career, combined with the time demands of his calling as a regional representative, Elder Nelson always made time for his family. March 21, 1980, was Russell Jr.'s eighth birthday. For his son's birthday, Elder Nelson presented him with a new dirt bike and took

Russell and Dantzel with three of their children and six of their grandchildren in 1982.

him and grandson Nathan McKellar, who had turned eight the previous month, to *This Is the Place* monument to teach them about the privileges and responsibilities associated with baptism. The following week, Elder Nelson baptized Russell Jr.[4]

In June 1980, Elder Nelson gave the devotional address at Brigham Young University, speaking on "What's in a Name?" He challenged the youth to make a name for themselves, to take upon themselves the name of the Lord, to honor the names of their fellow men, to honor the names of Deity, and to prepare themselves for the day when they would be given a new name. Elder Nelson has long maintained that when God's children gain an appreciation of who they really are, they can acquire a vision of their destiny and direction in life.[5] This was but the beginning of what would become Elder Nelson's sustained influence upon the youth of the Church. He was also invited in 1981 and 1985 to speak to the students participating in the University of Utah institute program.[6]

As a regional representative, Elder Nelson exerted a steady, positive influence on stakes at Brigham Young University. From his experience as a father of a large family, he could immediately connect with the youth of university age. For example, on one occasion he was speaking about the Abrahamic covenant, including Abraham's posterity. He recounted Isaac's desire to find a wife for his son, Jacob. To the delight of everyone in attendance, Elder Nelson said, "Well, happily as men are wont to do, Jacob fell in love. In an act I would not recommend today, Jacob kissed Rachel on their first date. But on that occasion Jacob also kissed her father. I wouldn't recommend that either."[7]

In mid-October 1980, Dantzel, Russell, and his sister Enid went on a Mediterranean cruise to the Holy Land, sponsored by Brigham Young University under the direction of Daniel H. Ludlow and David B. Galbraith. This was but one of several trips the Nelsons would take to the Holy Land, and each time, as they walked where Jesus walked, their testimonies of the Savior's divine mission and their appreciation for the Atonement increased. Each visit to the Holy Land animated the scriptures for Elder Nelson. As he read the New Testament, he could envisage the Savior calling His disciples as they cast their nets into the Sea of Galilee, and he could visualize the Savior walking the road to Bethany to visit his friends Martha, Mary, and Lazarus.

Russell reflected upon 1981 as a productive year professionally. He had performed 285 open-heart operations with only five deaths—an operative mortality of 1.7 percent. He consecutively performed the last 95 operations without a fatality. His reputation as a cardiac surgeon transcended the boundaries of the United States, and invitations increased for him to teach surgeons in other countries.[8] During May 1982, Dr. Nelson served as visiting professor of surgery in Montevideo, Uruguay, at the Hospital de Clinicas and associated hospitals.[9]

In 1982, Lane Johnson, assistant editor of the *Ensign* magazine, wrote an interesting and inspiring biographical tribute to Elder Nelson titled "Russell M. Nelson: A Study in Obedience." To gain some background into the professional life of a cardiac surgeon, Lane received permission from Dr. Nelson to observe an open-heart operation. His eloquently graphic description of Dr. Nelson's professional service as a surgeon follows:

> On the operating table under a bright light and surrounded by a jungle of glittering equipment is a sixty-year-old man being covered with special green drapes that leave a long, rectangular opening squarely over the middle of his chest and another opening over his left leg.
>
> Dr. Russell M. Nelson joins seven other members of the surgical team in the room: the senior resident in surgery; a surgical nurse; an anesthesiologist; a heart-lung machine specialist; a computer specialist; and two other nurses, one of whom is in charge of the operating room. I stand slightly apart from them, an observer, scrubbed and wearing sanitized clothing.
>
> Having taken their positions, they begin their work with an alacrity that is somewhat chilling to a newcomer. The senior resident, in one deft stroke, makes a foot-long incision the length of the sternum, following quickly with a cauterizing tool that seals off the numerous small vessels that have begun to bleed into the wound.
>
> Meanwhile, Dr. Nelson is making an incision in the left leg to locate a vein that will be removed. This is to be a quadruple coronary arterial bypass operation—in other words, surgery to bypass obstructions in four arteries that feed the patient's heart muscle. The vein being taken from the thigh will be used for the bypass grafts. There is a snipping of scissors and more cauterizing. I make an unscheduled exit to the hallway for a breath of fresh air and a reassessment of my determination to continue with this assignment.
>
> Then comes the whirring sound of an electric saw. Reentering the room, I am stationed at the head of the operating table, where in full view before me I see that the patient's sternum has been sawed through longitudinally and an ingenious retractor has been placed in the cleft. Several cranks on a short lever spread the

retractor apart—and *there,* between the patient's spread ribs, is his beating heart.

Soft music is playing quietly over the intercom. The surgeons' eyes reveal no amazement, no sense of drama—only deliberate concentration. My weak-in-the-knees feeling soon leaves, and the procedure takes on a magnetic fascination.

An incision is carefully made into the aorta and another into one of the chambers of the heart, which continues to beat. Long sutures are prepared. Tubes coming from the heart-lung machine— the "pump"—are inserted into the incisions, and at a given signal the heart-lung machine whirrs into action. Now the dark venous blood entering the heart is intercepted and routed through the heart-lung machine, which oxygenates it and returns it—now a brighter red—to the arterial system leading to the patient's body. At length the heartbeat slows to a stop and the intricate repairs begin.

The surgeons now wear glasses with powerful magnifiers built into the lenses. Using a very small scalpel, they begin to carefully probe the layer of fat around the heart to locate the arteries in question, which are scarcely distinguishable from the surrounding fatty tissue. They find one, and after a glance at an X-ray displayed on the wall, the surgeon makes a small slit. Then a small catheter is inserted into the slit and pushed carefully up the artery until it suddenly comes to a stop against an obstruction. After a light tap on the catheter, which I can almost feel in my own fingertips, the surgeon says, "That's it. There's just a very narrow opening for blood to pass through."

A section of the pencil-size vein that will serve as the graft is carefully measured and trimmed to the correct length. Then, with the utmost care and an amazing display of teamwork, the two surgeons begin to sew the graft onto the slit in the artery. The tiny, curved needle passes from hand to hand; the hairlike thread is drawn snug; the knots are tied.

After more than an hour of painstaking labor, four grafts have been connected to coronary arteries and to the aorta.

There are smiling eyes all around. He [Dr. Nelson] is clearly the one in control of this operation. He keeps the atmosphere light enough so that all the team members remain relaxed. But there is also an unspoken demand for constant concentration.

Four hours have now elapsed, and things are just about wrapped up. The heart-lung machine has been disengaged and the heart gently shocked into activity with electrodes; the grafts, now fairly bulging with a new blood supply for the heart muscle, have been checked for leaks. The heart is doing well on its own, and the patient is stable. Thoughts now turn to the patient's worried family, and one of the nurses reaches for a telephone: "We're off the pump, we've done four grafts, and Dr. Nelson will be down in about 45 minutes."[10]

One patient recounted how kind and considerate Dr. Nelson was after his operation in assuaging anxieties and giving clear instructions regarding the postoperative regimen for recovery. To assure his patient that the prognosis looked bright, Dr. Nelson drew "a beautiful diagram" of the heart and then sketched in detail the bypasses that had been grafted into the heart. His bedside manner engendered the confidence of his patient.[11]

Elder Nelson is adroit at illustrating gospel principles using medical metaphors, such as when he is teaching priesthood leaders the principles underlying disciplinary councils. "When one inadvertently gets a splinter in one's finger, the splinter will evoke an abscess unless it is removed, but you don't have to cut off the whole finger to make it better," he has taught. "We need to make an adequate excision, but we do not need to take more radical measures than are necessary for proper healing."[12]

Continuing the analogy between medical treatment and spiritual medicine, Elder Nelson said, "Sometimes when the body is ill, all that is needed for a full recovery is a little bed rest for a few days. In some instances, the body will heal much more quickly if the patient takes a pharmaceutical remedy in the form of antibiotics or other medication. In more severe cases, the only way the body will ever be able to heal properly is for a physician to perform invasive

surgery to remove the diseased tissue. So it is with Church disciplinary councils. Sometimes a brief period of probation will be adequate to bring about needed repentance. On other occasions, it may
be necessary to disfellowship members in transgression in order to
restore their spiritual health. Still other members may need to be
excommunicated in order to enable them to experience a cleansing
only made possible through the refreshing waters of rebaptism."[13]

When asked how he remains so unflappable under stress, Russell
recalled the time, as a surgical intern, when he was assisting the chief
surgeon in the amputation of a patient's leg infested with gangrene.
In the heat of the battle, the surgeon lost his composure and jabbed
a knife "loaded with deadly organisms" into Russell's arm.

"I didn't like that too well," Elder Nelson wryly remarked, and
he resolved then and there that "I would discipline my body always
to be subject to domination by my spirit."[14]

Elder Nelson completed his assignment as regional representative to the BYU First Region and was given a new assignment to
supervise the Kearns Utah and Kearns Utah Central Regions.[15] His
love for the youth of the Church was evidenced by his assertive personal involvement in encouraging bishops throughout the regions
to assure that every young high school student had an opportunity
to be enrolled in seminary. His enthusiastic support for the seminary program contributed to a marked increase in seminary enroll-
ment throughout the respective regions.

In mid-July 1983, it became apparent that Russell's ninety-year-
old mother would soon pass away. He wrote in his personal record,
"It is not merciful to subject her to diagnostic testing and a possible
operation. Our prayers must be for her release now." A few days
later, on the evening of July 19, Brother Nelson's mother, Edna A.
Nelson, died in the presence of Russell's father, who had spared
nothing in the way of providing her with compassionate, loving
care. Her funeral four days later was held at the Monument Park
Ward. Speakers included Russell, grandson Thomas R. Rohlfing,

and Wendell J. Ashton, a dear family friend and business associate of Marion Nelson.[16]

Three months later, Dantzel and Russell took their fifth trip to the Holy Land, going for two weeks on a Brigham Young University Mediterranean cruise. During this time, Dr. Nelson conducted a course for Collegium Aesculapium, an organization of Latter-day Saint physicians. He also assisted Elders Mark E. Petersen and Howard W. Hunter in their assignments as instructors to the group. Before this cruise, Elder Petersen had been afflicted with cancer, and it was apparent to all that he was suffering greatly from pain. On the Mount of Beatitudes, Elder Petersen reviewed the Savior's Sermon on the Mount, including the beatitude, "Blessed are they which do hunger and thirst after righteousness." Elder Petersen earnestly surveyed his hillside congregation and said, "None of you know what it really means to hunger and thirst—but I do."

Elder Petersen suffered terribly from both hunger and thirst, and his body was no longer able to metabolize physical nourishment. Yet he forcefully testified of the divinity of Jesus Christ, and his testimony was particularly poignant as he expressed his gratitude for the Savior's suffering in the Garden of Gethsemane and upon the cross on Calvary's hill. This was Elder Petersen's last mission in mortality, and at the end of the trip, he said, "I completed my assignment."[17] A few months later, on January 11, 1984, this revered Apostle of the Lord passed away, creating another vacancy in the Quorum of the Twelve Apostles.

CHAPTER 18

CALLED TO THE
HOLY APOSTLESHIP

D R. NELSON'S MEDICAL CAREER could hardly have been busier or more successful than it was in 1983. That year he had been out of town forty-eight days on various professional engagements, and he had performed 360 operations.[1] The struggling years in medical school at the University of Utah, and his subsequent training in Minneapolis and Boston were bearing fruit. He had sown the seeds of lengthy professional preparation, and now he was reaping the bounteous harvest by blessing people.

When he first entered the research laboratory in 1949, patients with heart disease could rarely be helped with an operation. Now, more than three decades later, the majority of patients with heart disease could be helped through surgery. Dr. Nelson had truly mastered the healer's art, and in the wake of an extremely productive year, he faced 1984 with great professional expectations.

In March, Russell Jr. celebrated his twelfth birthday by skiing with his father at Alta, and his father later had the privilege of ordaining his only son to the office of deacon in the Aaronic Priesthood.[2] On Sunday, April 1, Russell Jr. passed the sacrament for the first time, and he now anticipated attending his first general priesthood meeting with his father the following weekend.[3]

The first week of April was also one of great anticipation for Russell Sr., not only for the forthcoming 154th Annual General

Conference but also because he would have the blessing of participating in a regional representatives' seminar on Friday, April 6. All
the regional representatives from around the world would literally
sit at the feet of the Apostles and be taught the doctrine of the kingdom and instructed in their duties.

While Elder Nelson was seated in the seminar, someone tapped
him on the shoulder and indicated that President Gordon B.
Hinckley, second counselor in the First Presidency, wished to speak
with him. After Elder Nelson entered President Hinckley's office,
President Hinckley asked him if everything in his life was in order.
Elder Nelson was pleased to respond, "Yes." President Hinckley then
stated rather matter of factly, "Good! Tomorrow we will sustain you
as a new member of the Quorum of the Twelve Apostles!"

Elder Nelson was absolutely stunned by this announcement. "In
one short moment," he said, "the focus of the last forty years in
medicine and surgery was changed to devote the rest of my life in
full-time service to my Lord and Savior, Jesus the Christ."[4]

In his heart, *Elder* Nelson wanted to follow the pattern of the
Savior's early Apostles, who, when called, "straightway left their nets
and followed him" (Matthew 4:20). However, *Dr.* Nelson had made
a number of long-term professional commitments. He discussed his
dilemma with President Hinckley, who counseled him to honor his
professional commitments. President Hinckley also suggested that
Elder Nelson excuse himself from the seminar and go home to share
the news with Dantzel and spend time with her.[5]

Bursting with anticipation, Russell returned home only to find
Dantzel was not there. After several anxious minutes, she came into
the house. He quietly suggested that she might want to sit down
because he had some very important information to share. Their conversation involved tearful expressions of mutual love and support.[6]

During the opening session of general conference on Saturday,
April 7, 1984, Russell Jr. and his sister Marjorie were seated in the
Tabernacle when President Hinckley told the Saints, "As you know,
there are two vacancies in the Council of the Twelve Apostles,

*Russell and Dantzel in 1984
when Russell was called to the
Quorum of the Twelve Apostles.*

incident to the passing of Elder LeGrand Richards [January 1983] and Elder Mark E. Petersen [January 1984]. We shall take action to fill these vacancies this morning, and we shall also add to the First Quorum of the Seventy."

The names of the members of the Quorum of the Twelve, including the names of Russell M. Nelson and Dallin H. Oaks, were then presented for the sustaining vote of the Saints. Elder Nelson and Elder Oaks became, respectively, the eighty-fifth Apostle and the eighty-sixth Apostle of this dispensation.[7]

Elder Nelson was no stranger to the members of the Church because he had served as general president of the Sunday School from 1971 to 1979, and Elder Oaks was fondly remembered for his service as president of Brigham Young University from 1971 to 1980. However, their callings to the Quorum of the Twelve surprised many Saints because the previous seven men called to the Twelve had been chosen from the ranks of the General Authorities: Elders Boyd K. Packer, Marvin J. Ashton, Bruce R. McConkie, L. Tom Perry, David B. Haight, James E. Faust, and Neal A. Maxwell. Not since Elder Thomas S. Monson's call in October 1963 had a man been called directly from the general membership as an Apostle.

The sustaining vote of the Saints was enthusiastically in the affirmative for these two great men who would "waste and wear out [their] lives" (D&C 123:13) as special witnesses of the Lord Jesus Christ. In case Elder Nelson had any doubt that he was called of God through revelation, President Spencer W. Kimball, though in frail health, walked over to his chair after the conference session concluded, gave him a hug, and said, "It's right! It's right!"[8]

Because the Brethren are charged not to tell their families of their calls prior to their sustaining, the Nelson children who were not in the Tabernacle learned of their father's call by watching the proceedings on television.[9] When recounting her reactions to her father's call, Wendy said, "He's perfect." Then, choking back the tears, she continued, "If there's anyone who has lived a righteous life, it is he. We had no clue that he would be called because I thought he had several more years of doctoring in store, but he's a perfect example of a disciple of Christ."[10]

The children, of course, reached their parents by telephone as soon as they could to offer their congratulations, love, and support. Their sixth daughter, Emily, who was expecting her second child, experienced such surprise at her father's new calling that she phoned to say the excitement would provoke the onset of labor. Her prediction was self-fulfilling. Little seven-pound Wendy Wittwer arrived the very day her grandfather was sustained as an Apostle.[11]

The next day, during his general conference remarks, Elder Nelson tenderly acknowledged Dantzel as "the fountain from whom flows the nourishing love in our home." He quoted one of the guiding scriptures in his life that fortified him to accept his new calling: "I will go and do the things which the Lord hath commanded, for I know that the Lord giveth no commandments unto the children of men, save he shall prepare a way for them that they may accomplish the thing which he commandeth them" (1 Nephi 3:7).

Elder Nelson also declared, "I have been forged from the stern discipline of law. . . . Desired blessings come only by obedience to divine law, and in no other way. My lifetime thus far has been focused on learning those laws. Only as the laws are known, and then obeyed, can the blessings we desire be earned."[12]

In the concluding session of that historic April conference, Elder James E. Faust began his address in his typically warm way: "I welcome all the new General Authorities. I rejoice in the calls of Elder Oaks and Elder Nelson to the Council of the Twelve Apostles. Brother Nelson has touched my heart deeper than any man. He has held my heart in his hands and has cut into it and sewn in eight bypasses. He and the Lord literally gave me a new heart. And that heart is full of love for him and for Brother Oaks and for all of you."[13]

Earlier, in the fall of 1982, President Faust had taken a stress test and an angiogram. The results indicated some heart vessel blockage. He was told that his problem could be treated either medically or surgically. Because Elder Faust was acquainted with Dr. Nelson, he asked him, "If this were your heart, what would you do?"

Dr. Nelson explored the various medical care options with Elder Faust and then proffered counsel that surgical treatment would most likely give him a better quality of life. Dr. Nelson's personal, professional philosophy is, "Physicians do not own their patients." He is, in his own words, "out of patience with medical doctors who give dictatorial directions." Dr. Nelson has always perceived himself to be a teacher and a servant of his respective patients.

On November 19, 1982, Dr. Nelson performed eight bypasses on Elder Faust, whose strength and vigor were sustained as a result. Thus, Elder Faust's appreciation for Russell M. Nelson is personal and genuinely heartfelt. The operation was the beginning of a warm relationship solidified by their shared apostolic callings.[14]

Sunday evening following the last session of the April 1984 general conference, Elder Nelson requested that all of his available sons-in-law convene at the Nelson home to give him a blessing of comfort. The blessing, he said, "brought a great deal of relief to me."[15] When asked what had precipitated the urgency of a blessing of comfort following his call, Elder Nelson replied, "The gap—the gap between what I was and what I ought to be. The gap seemed to be so very large, and I felt completely inadequate for this holy calling."[16]

On April 12, 1984, Elder Russell Marion Nelson was ordained an Apostle and set apart as a member of the Quorum of the Twelve Apostles. Although President Kimball and President Marion G. Romney were in failing health, they were in attendance, as were all of the Twelve except Elder Marvin J. Ashton, who was en route to an assignment in Australia. President Gordon B. Hinckley served as voice.[17]

A few days later, Elder Nelson conducted his last meeting with stake presidencies of the Kearns Utah Region. "As I said goodbye," he said, "I realized I [wouldn't] have to be released from any more assignments in the Church. What a feeling!"[18]

Elder Nelson also met with Dr. Cecil O. Samuelson Jr., dean of the College of Medicine at the University of Utah, to resign from his faculty position in order to assume his apostolic duties. Dr. Samuelson said, "Early in my own medical training it was unusual for busy physicians to take time to be involved in the community, to take time to serve in the Church, and to take time to be an exemplary family man. Elder Nelson's done all of those. I think if you were to ask him of all the things he feels most strongly about, his family would be at the top of his list."[19]

A day after returning from a stake conference assignment, on April 23, 1984, *Dr.* Nelson performed his last open-heart operation in America.[20] *Elder* Nelson then traveled to Idaho at the end of May to participate in the dedication of the Boise Idaho Temple, where he was invited to speak at two dedicatory sessions. Though he felt that he had spoken a little too long both times, he confided that none of the Brethren had corrected him.[21]

On June 6, the Quorum of the Twelve Apostles met in the Salt

*Elder Nelson meets
President Ronald
Reagan during his visit
to Church headquarters
in September 1984.*

Lake Temple for the first time in more than a year and a half with
no vacant chairs. Elder Nelson said, "It was a thrill to be a part of
that historic occasion."[22]

Notwithstanding his weighty new responsibilities, Elder Nelson
never forgot that he was a father, and throughout the summer following his call, he, Russell Jr., and various grandchildren went fishing several times.[23]

At the beginning of August, the Twelve gathered again in the
temple, and Elder Nelson was asked to provide organ accompani-
ment for the singing of hymns. This he has done ever since at each
of the Twelve's Thursday morning temple meetings.

He reflected upon the time many years before when "I was
impressed to modify my routine by getting up an hour earlier in the
morning to study the scriptures searchingly and dutifully, and also
to teach myself how to play the organ, studying the hymns of Zion
and the masterworks of Bach and others. Jokingly, I told Dantzel
that I was preparing for the next world because heart surgeons
would not be needed then and there. Little did I know that I was
being prepared to serve here and now. Little did I dream that a letter

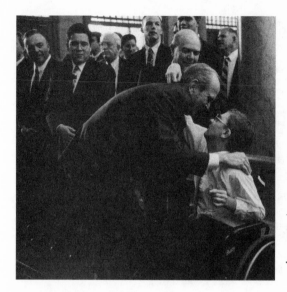

*Elder Nelson embraces
Daniel Bergin of Provo,
Utah, prior to the
priesthood session of
general conference in
October 1996. Daniel's
father, Allen Bergin,
looks on.*

would ever be addressed to me as a member of the Quorum of the Twelve Apostles! In that letter I was asked to be the organist for the Brethren in the Temple."[24]

He continued, "I learned long ago to be obedient to those marvelous, sweet whisperings of the Spirit—those strong promptings to follow counsel. Especially sobering it is to know that, while we may be content with the status quo in life, the Lord would be making something of us beyond our fondest imagination. All he requires of us is to prepare ourselves—to try to iron out our imperfections and to stretch each day to be something more than we otherwise would be."[25]

A scripture that describes Elder Nelson's busy and productive life as a father, surgeon, and Apostle is D&C 72:4: "For he who is faithful and wise in time is accounted worthy to inherit the mansions prepared for him of my Father." Elder Nelson's lengthy preparation as a surgeon, his loving attention to his eternal companion and to his children and grandchildren, and his commitment to building the kingdom all reflect the life of a man who makes every minute count.

In his second general conference address as an Apostle, Elder

Nelson titled his address "Protect the Spiritual Power Line." This sermon endeared him to the membership of the Church for several reasons. First, he demonstrated his humility and humor as he told how he had inadvertently severed the power line of an electric hedge trimmer he was using to manicure bushes and hedges. Second, he showed that he was not above manual labor even though he was a successful surgeon. Third, he confessed his human vulnerability without pomposity or self-righteousness. Fourth, like the Master Teacher, he taught a modern day parable, stating, "Power, if misused, can cut into the very source of that power."[26]

After participating in a multiregional conference for the Saints in Spanish Fork and Payson, Utah, Elder Nelson proceeded to keep his previous commitments by making a presentation in October 1984 on aortic valve replacement to the American College of Surgeons at its annual Clinical Congress in San Francisco.[27]

Upon returning home, he drove to Logan with Russell Jr. to watch the Utah State University football team defeat the University of the Pacific by a score of, according to his personal record, 41–14.[28] Elder Nelson's precise recording of scores of ball games and his meticulous personal record entries of specific travel times and distances between destinations reflects another scripture that epitomizes his life: "Yea, and they did obey and observe to perform every word of command with exactness" (Alma 57:21).

Like Helaman's 2,060 stripling warriors, Elder Nelson has led a life of exactness. His lengthy surgical training required great precision because surgical decisions and procedures are fraught with life-and-death consequences. He has lived his life in the same meticulous way, recognizing that many decisions have life-and-death spiritual consequences.

During the April 1985 general conference, Elder Nelson courageously spoke out against the global epidemic of abortion, testifying, "Life comes from life. It is a gift from our Heavenly Father. It is eternal, as He is eternal. Innocent life is not sent by Him to be destroyed!"[29] Elder Nelson's address immediately followed the magnificent benedictory testimony borne by Elder Bruce R. McConkie just two weeks before he passed away. Elder McConkie declared, "I am one of his witnesses, and in a coming day I shall feel the nail marks in his hands and in his feet and shall wet his feet with my tears. But I shall not know any better then than I know now that he is God's Almighty Son, that he is our Savior and Redeemer, and that salvation comes in and through his atoning blood and in no other way."[30]

Reflecting upon the life of that spiritual giant, who had served for nearly four decades as a General Authority, Elder Nelson said, "Elder Bruce R. McConkie was a great friend. His door was always open to me, and I frequently imposed upon his graciousness, asking him questions that possibly only he could answer." Pondering the fact that Elder McConkie had been diagnosed with terminal cancer more than a year before his death, Elder Nelson said, "I look upon the extra year of life that he was granted as a period for the training of Elder Dallin H. Oaks and me. We are greatly in his debt and miss him very much."[31]

On August 2, 1985, Elder Nelson received an assignment from the First Presidency to serve on the Scriptures Publication Committee, filling the vacancy created by the passing of Elder McConkie. Elder Nelson said, "I feel so humble in receiving such a call, yet thrilled with this new and exciting opportunity for service."[32] Elder Nelson's gospel scholarship perpetuates Elder McConkie's legacy.[33]

At summer's end, Elder Nelson gave an insightful address titled "Truth and More" to the 4,500 faculty and staff convened in the Brigham Young University Marriott Center. In his address, Elder Nelson declared that "truth isn't 'relative.' It is only man's understanding of the truth that is 'relative.'" He cautioned the BYU faculty against using information solely for the purpose of furthering "negative ends." He advocated "a commitment to truth *and more*," including a self-searching sensitivity to our motives for teaching the truth.[34]

During the Saturday afternoon session of general conference on October 5, 1985, Elder Nelson spoke on "Self-Mastery." In his personal record, he made a wry comment afterward: "No rotten eggs thrown, thank goodness!" His counsel, though straightforward, could hardly have offended anyone. Conversely, all were inspired as this Apostle of the Lord, speaking as if he were addressing each of his own children, concluded: "Remember, my dear one, not an age in life passes without temptation, trial, or torment experienced through your physical body. But as you prayerfully develop self-mastery, desires of the flesh may be subdued. And when that has been achieved, you may have the strength to submit to your Heavenly Father, as did Jesus, who said, 'Not my will, but thine, be done'"[35] (Luke 22:42).

In mid-October, Elder Nelson went to Midway to dig a plentiful harvest of beets and carrots from their garden, instructing children and grandchildren that there are "still more in the ground for any who are hungry enough to dig for them." This they did with gusto, and the next day thirteen family members went to the temple for an endowment session together.[36]

The last week of October, Elder and Sister Nelson joined Elder Joseph B. Wirthlin for a mission presidents' seminar in Lisbon, Portugal. Elder and Sister Nelson had some Portuguese language lessons from Brother Lin DePaula of the Church's translation department in anticipation of their trip.[37] Following the seminar, the Nelsons traveled to France, where Elder and Sister Hans B. Ringger joined them for a regional conference in Avignon. There, Elder Nelson was blessed to be able to speak to the Saints in French, though he had not intensively studied the language since 1951, when he passed his Ph.D. language exam at the University of Minnesota.[38]

Piercing a very heavy fog with their prayers, Elder and Sister Nelson caught a flight to Vienna, where they spent the next three days touring the Austria Vienna Mission. After speaking with missionaries earlier in the day, Elder and Sister Nelson agreed to speak at a member-missionary fireside in the evening. Inasmuch as the Vienna stake center has an impressive pipe organ, the stake president, Johann A. Wondra, insisted that Elder Nelson play an organ solo in addition to speaking to the congregation. To the great delight of the Viennese Saints, who know something of good music, Elder Nelson played Bach's *Toccata and Fugue in D*. The Saints were impressed by Elder Nelson's musical skills, but they were even more inspired by his testimony in their native German tongue.[39]

The Nelsons bade *auf Wiedersehen* to Austria and traveled to Madrid to speak to the missionaries in the northern zones of Spain. That evening, Elder Nelson met with priesthood leaders, addressing them in Spanish. As the Lord said, "Every man shall hear the fulness of the gospel in his own tongue, and in his own language, through those who are ordained unto this power" (D&C 90:11).[40]

The first weekend in November, Elder and Sister Nelson were in Lisbon, Portugal, again, where he participated in the reorganization of a stake presidency. Elder Nelson found his tutoring in Portuguese to be helpful during this stake reorganization, which involved numerous interviews and settings apart.[41] Another scriptural injunction that continues to bless Elder Nelson's life and ministry is, "If ye are prepared ye shall not fear" (D&C 38:30). His entire life has been one of preparation "for such a time as this" (Esther 4:14).

When the Nelsons arrived home the evening of November 4, 1985, the security officer who met them at the airport informed them that President Kimball had developed internal bleeding. Elder Nelson immediately went to check on President Kimball's condition while Sister Nelson returned home. The next morning, Elder Nelson returned to President Kimball's Hotel Utah apartment shortly after he had gently passed away at 10:08 A.M. He was present when President Hinckley arrived and called for President Ezra Taft Benson.[42]

Upon President Benson's arrival, President Hinckley, who had served as President Kimball's counselor for four and a half years in the First Presidency, now deferred to President Benson. The First

Russell and Dantzel share a relaxing moment in 1984.

Presidency was now dissolved and Elder Hinckley would do whatever President Benson directed him to do. For the second time in succession, Elder Nelson was present when the mantle of leadership was passed. In 1973, he had been at LDS Hospital when President Harold B. Lee died and President Romney expressed similar deferential sentiments to President Kimball.[43]

The following day, Elder Nelson visited Sister Kimball and learned that he was invited to speak at President Kimball's funeral.[44] The evening before the funeral, Elder Nelson said, "We went to the Utah Symphony concert, which was particularly calming to my troubled spirit, inasmuch as I was anxiously concerned with my assignment to speak that next morning."[45]

Referring to a meeting in the temple on Sunday, November 10, 1985, Elder Nelson said, "There, in one of the sweetest hours of my life, expressions from each of the Apostles supported the immediate reorganization of the First Presidency. President Hunter moved that Ezra Taft Benson be ordained the thirteenth president of the Church.

The motion was seconded by President Hinckley." After expressing his tender feelings on this occasion, President Benson proposed that Elder Gordon B. Hinckley serve as his first counselor and that Elder Thomas S. Monson serve as his second counselor.

"These nominations were enthusiastically sustained," Elder Nelson said. "These three great brethren were then set apart to their respective callings. I could hardly believe that I was there in the circle, participating in the ordaining of the President of The Church of Jesus Christ of Latter-day Saints, and of his counselors. Then, Elder Howard W. Hunter was set apart as President of the Quorum of the Twelve Apostles."[46]

On Thursday, November 14, in a temple meeting with the newly organized First Presidency and the Twelve, Elder Nelson was released from his responsibilities as first contact for the North America Northeast Area. He was then given the "first contact" assignment for Europe and Africa, with special attention to bringing the gospel to the people of Eastern Europe.[47]

Greece was included within his new area of responsibility. So forty-two years after having studied Greek at the University of Utah, Elder Nelson renewed lessons in Greek. Dr. Lica H. Catsakis, a faithful Latter-day Saint dentist in Salt Lake City who helped translate Church materials into Greek, was his tutor. After his first lesson, Elder Nelson humbly remarked, "To say I needed a little brushing up is a mild understatement."[48]

The first day of December, the Nelsons attended the First Presidency's Christmas fireside in the Tabernacle and then capped off the evening with family scripture study at the Nelson home, with Michael Ringwood leading an inspiring discussion on charity, the pure love of Christ.[49]

The following Sunday found Elder Nelson in Frankfurt, Germany, in a special meeting with President Monson, Elders Neal A. Maxwell, Joseph B. Wirthlin, Russell C. Taylor, Hans B. Ringger, and all of the European regional representatives, stake presidents, and mission presidents. During the meeting, President

Monson, who had been first contact for Europe for seventeen years, and Elder Neal A. Maxwell, who followed President Monson, transferred their batons to Elder Nelson, who confessed, "I feel mighty humble in receiving them."[50]

On Sunday, December 15, Elder Nelson participated in a district conference in Athens, Greece, where he concluded his remarks by bearing his testimony in Greek, after working most of the previous night committing each word and phrase to memory.[51] A missionary couple in attendance called the mission president the next morning to report how thrilled the Greek Saints were to hear an Apostle bear testimony in their own language.

The year drew to a close with Elder Nelson speaking at the funeral of his and Dantzel's good friend and voice teacher, Richard P. Condie, former director of the Tabernacle Choir. Russell recounted, "Our courtship was enhanced by our meetings when Dantzel came from Perry for her private vocal lessons with Brother Condie."[52] Elder Nelson had learned the cadence of his calling and "to mourn with those that mourn; yea, and comfort those that stand in need of comfort, and to stand as witnesses of God at all times and in all things, and in all places" (Mosiah 18:9).

CHAPTER 19

BRETHREN IN THE
LORD'S LABOR OF LOVE

THE LORD REVEALED THAT HIS Church should be governed by "three Presiding High Priests," who "form a quorum of the Presidency of the Church," and by "Twelve Apostles, or special witnesses," who "form a quorum, equal in authority and power to the three presidents previously mentioned" (D&C 107:22–24). And notwithstanding differences in backgrounds and personalities, "every decision made by either of these quorums must be by the unanimous voice of the same" (D&C 107:27).

Considering the diverse backgrounds of the members of the Twelve, and also the strength of their personalities, it is a tall order, indeed, to require unanimity in their decisions. The Quorum of the Twelve Apostles, in 2002, included five top-level educational administrators: Elders Boyd K. Packer, Neal A. Maxwell, Dallin H. Oaks (also a jurist), Jeffrey R. Holland, and Henry B. Eyring; five highly regarded business executives: Elders L. Tom Perry, David B. Haight, M. Russell Ballard, Joseph B. Wirthlin, and Robert D. Hales; one nuclear engineer: Elder Richard G. Scott; and one cardiac surgeon: Elder Russell M. Nelson.

Each of these men distinguished himself within his chosen profession prior to his calling as an Apostle, and all of them have had extensive experience serving in Church leadership positions. Prior to their respective calls to the holy Apostleship, five had served as

President Gordon B. Hinckley evokes laughter from members of the Quorum of the Twelve Apostles during his general conference address on October 4, 1997 (photo courtesy of the Ogden Standard Examiner)*.*

mission presidents, six had been regional representatives, seven had served in stake presidencies, and seven had served as a bishop, two of them more than once. These are men of substance, and there is not a shrinking violet within the entire quorum. These impressive spiritual giants were invited to discuss some of the specific contributions Elder Russell M. Nelson makes to the Quorum of the Twelve Apostles.

Elder Boyd K. Packer, acting president of the Quorum of the Twelve, views Elder Nelson as one of the watchmen on the tower for the family.[1] President Packer, also the father of ten children, appreciates the power of good parenting, and he and Elder Nelson both came from homes headed by men who were better fathers than churchmen. In fact, several of the Twelve were reared in homes with a father who did not often accompany his children to church meetings. They would concur that, notwithstanding the blessing and support of all the Church's programs and activities aimed at assisting the family, parents can do a better job than the Church in rearing children.

Elder Maxwell added, "I think of Russell as a father, and patriarch to his clan, but he is not immodest at all in speaking of his own family."[2]

Essential ordinances of the gospel are administered through the Church, Sunday meetings provide essential spiritual nourishment, and branch and ward social activities among a community of Saints generate feelings of warmth and welcome. But the family is the ideal laboratory of love for learning the godly attributes of kindness and compassion, patience and perseverance, faith and forgiveness. These attributes are taught from the pulpit, but they are practiced in the home.

President Packer has said that in the Church's chapels, we organize bishoprics, quorums, and class presidencies, but in the temple we organize families. Family history and the temple are top priorities for Elder Nelson.

After a man is called as a General Authority, one of the Twelve accompanies the newly called, shell-shocked servant of the Lord to his first stake conference assignment. Though Elder Nelson had participated in several stake conferences as a regional representative, Elder L. Tom Perry served as his mentor in his new calling during their assignment to a stake in Toledo, Ohio.

As the two Brethren entered the home of the stake president, one of his daughters was practicing the harp. Elder Perry reported that his junior companion for the weekend aptly observed the young girl's technique in properly plucking the strings. After several minutes, Elder Nelson asked if he could take a turn on the harp. To the amazement of all, he sat down and played "I Am a Child of God"[3] with the alacrity of a veteran harpist.[4] This little incident illustrates an observation of Elder Ballard, who said, "When Russell Nelson sets his mind on something, there is nothing he cannot do."[5]

Elder Haight has been impressed by Elder Nelson's "love for the gospel—you sense it, you feel it, you know how sincere it is." This venerable Apostle, in his mid-nineties, expressed gratitude for Elder Nelson's bright mind and gift of tongues, which enable him to communicate in many different languages.

"We once gave Russell an assignment to visit a given country and immediately he started to get the cards in that particular language out of his briefcase," Elder Haight said. "He is a tremendous addition to the Quorum because of his adaptability and skill. He always does things well."[6]

Just as President Faust has a special relationship with Elder Nelson, who performed life-extending surgery on him, so also does Elder Haight, who holds Elder Nelson in high esteem for being one of the Lord's instruments in saving his life.

Elder Haight recalled, "In January of 1989 I had a rupturing aneurysm of the abdominal aorta, and the list of survivors of such a problem is not very long. When the paramedics brought me to the hospital emergency room, the staff on duty didn't know whom to call, and they could see I was dying and sensed that I wouldn't last long. When they discovered who I was, they called the Church telephone operator, who located Russell Nelson at his home in Midway, and they told him that I was in the hospital.

"The emergency room staff felt I had a bowel obstruction, but Elder Nelson told me later that, as they described the symptoms over the phone, he diagnosed a rupturing aneurysm of the abdominal aorta. Elder Nelson told the emergency room personnel not to cut me open, but to enlist the services of either Dr. Kent Jones or Dr. Donald Doty. He then said, 'I'm on my way.' He drove from Midway as fast as possible.

"It happened that Dr. Jones and Dr. Doty had just completed an operation in the hospital, and they arrived in time to save my life. When I think of Russell M. Nelson, I can piece together some miracles. The emergency staff could have called the wrong specialists.

"I was unconscious for several days. After regaining consciousness, Russell told me later, 'I felt as a fellow member of the Quorum that I had the responsibility on that fateful day to tell your wife, Ruby, that the outlook was bleak and your chance of making it was not good from a medical standpoint. I developed the courage as to how best to say it and motioned for Ruby to come over to a quiet corner of the waiting room to explain it gently.'"[7]

As Elder Nelson began to describe to Ruby the near hopelessness of an eighty-three-year-old man's recovery from a ruptured aneurysm of the aorta, Ruby looked into his eyes and said, "Don't worry about David; he'll be all right." Elder Nelson thought to himself, "Ruby, you're not listening to me." But when he saw her intense look and the positive conviction in her countenance, Russell submissively responded, "I believe so too," and he quietly walked out of the room.[8]

At the following October general conference, Elder Haight related his life-threatening experience and bore a special and profound witness of the events that occurred during his hospital stay. "The terrible pain and commotion of people ceased," he said. "I was now in a calm and peaceful setting; all was serene and quiet. . . . I heard no voices but was conscious of being in a holy presence and atmosphere. During the hours and days that followed, there was impressed again and again upon my mind the eternal mission and exalted position of the Son of Man. . . . I was shown a panoramic view of His earthly ministry. . . . During those days of unconsciousness I was given, by the gift and power of the Holy Ghost, a more perfect knowledge of His mission. . . . My soul was taught over and over again the events of the betrayal, the mock trial, the scourging of the flesh of even one of the Godhead. I witnessed His struggling up the hill in His weakened condition carrying the cross and His being stretched upon it as it lay on the ground, that the crude spikes could be driven with a mallet into His hands and wrists and feet to secure His body as it hung on the cross for public display.

"Crucifixion—the horrible and painful death which He suffered—was chosen from the beginning. By that excruciating death, He descended below all things, as is recorded, that through

His resurrection He would ascend above all things (see D&C 88:6).
. . . I cannot begin to convey to you the deep impact that these
scenes have confirmed upon my soul."⁹ Those who heard Elder
Haight's powerful testimony will never forget the certitude of this
special servant of the Lord.

While Russell and Dantzel were living in Washington, D.C.,
during the Korean War in the early 1950s, they became acquainted
with Neal and Colleen Maxwell. Russell greatly admired young
Neal's energetic administrative acumen as he served in the office of
Senator Wallace F. Bennett, and Neal had reciprocal admiration for
Russell's medical skills. The Maxwells returned to Salt Lake City in
the 1950s, about the same time the Nelsons returned. Russell then
joined the University of Utah medical school faculty while Neal
became one of the university's administrators.¹⁰

Like many of his other colleagues, Elder Maxwell appreciates
Elder Nelson's medical knowledge in assisting the Brethren in making decisions regarding the calling of mission presidents, temple
presidents, and others to serve for extended periods in faraway places
with strange-sounding names. As a couple's medical record is read,
Elder Nelson is often called upon to help the Brethren decide if the
husband or wife might be able to serve in a country where medical
care is not sophisticated. Elder Maxwell hastens to add, "Russell
doesn't go unless invited into that realm."¹¹

Elder Maxwell observed that his "seatmate," Elder Nelson, "is
disciplined and patient in words and editorial changes. He is a
source of refinement. We live in a world of words, and he has several good suggestions and a genuine thoughtfulness about the recipients of the message."

The Quorum of the Twelve spends considerable time in counsel.
Twelve members involved in a given discussion could require an
inordinate amount of time to reach a decision. However, according
to Elder Maxwell, "Russell husbands his commentary and keeps his
counsel reserved and shares it at that point in the discussion when
it is most propitious. I've seen him about to say something, but

then he refrained when he felt the moment had passed. There may have been some missed opportunities when we could have learned more from him. He doesn't feel obliged to comment on everything he observes."[12]

For sixteen years, Elder Nelson served as a member of the Church's Boundary and Leadership Change Committee, which reviews all proposed changes in bishoprics and in stake, ward, and branch boundaries among the more than 26,000 units of the Church. Elder Maxwell observed, "One can become bored and grow detached [in such an assignment], but Russell was always prepared to report on the committee's business in the temple meetings." Whenever any of the Brethren had a question about a given proposal, Elder Maxwell added, "Russell always knew the backup data. He took his assignment very seriously."[13] Elder Hales, who also served on the boundary committee with Elder Nelson, observed, "He immerses himself in the documents and then makes decisions. He measures five times before he cuts once."[14]

Sustained to the holy Apostleship in the same conference as Elder Nelson, Elder Oaks describes his colleague as "a spiritually sensitive man of great faith who does not let his remarkable worldly knowledge deflect him from the impressions of the Spirit or from his insights into the gospel. His spiritual influence is such that everyone becomes more spiritual in his presence. When he comes into the room, you remember who you are. He is a radiant spiritual being."[15]

Elder Oaks called Elder Nelson "the urim and thummim for the Quorum in matters of health. This contribution is also very important to the work." He added, "In the Quorum he is very quiet, and doesn't speak much of the time, in the tradition of President Howard W. Hunter, who spoke little, but his comments were very influential when he did speak. Elder Nelson is less directive than others and less likely to find fault. He doesn't grab a problem or an issue so tightly that he bruises it. He is gentle and wise."[16]

Called to the Twelve eighteen months after Elders Nelson and Oaks, Elder M. Russell Ballard calls Elder Nelson "a Renaissance man. He likes to know about everything, and he looks at something once and he has it forever. He is so disciplined in all ways and emphasizes exactness. There is no greater intellect in the Church." With his typical grin, Elder Ballard continued, "He is a little intimidating because he's so smart, but he is never pompous. His demeanor is a great asset, and his successful medical practice put him in a unique position in dealing with government officials and in building bridges with nations. He has had a tremendous impact in Europe and Asia."

Then, on a personal note, Elder Ballard discussed how moved he was to learn that Elder Nelson had stood by Dr. Donald B. Doty, one of Dr. Nelson's colleagues and close associates, for several hours during an operation in which Elder Ballard had five coronary bypasses. When Elder Ballard asked Elder Nelson why he hovered over him during this critical surgery, Elder Nelson replied simply, "Because you're my brother."

Elder Ballard said, "Sometimes people mistake me for Russell M. Nelson because of our names; however, I consider it a truly great honor to be mistaken for Russell M. Nelson."[17]

A special bond exists between Elder Joseph B. Wirthlin and Elder Nelson. When Russell was called to be the president of the Bonneville Stake in December 1964, he chose Joseph to serve as his second counselor. Then, in June 1971, when Russell was called to serve as the general president of the Sunday School, he chose his trusted friend to be his first counselor. They enjoyed their service together immensely until Elder Wirthlin was called as an Assistant to the Twelve in April 1975.

When invited to discuss Elder Nelson's influence on the Wirthlin family, Elder Wirthlin's countenance brightened. "He saved our precious daughter's life!" he exclaimed.

In May 1973, as Elder and Sister Wirthlin's daughter Ann was giving birth to her third child, her husband, Dr. Kent Farnsworth, became concerned when she began experiencing sharp abdominal pains uncharacteristic of normal labor contractions. The next morning, she delivered a healthy baby girl, but as Ann was wheeled to the recovery room, she felt her life slipping away.

While receiving a priesthood blessing from her father, Ann was blessed that she would live and receive the medical care she urgently needed. A team of surgeons then opened Ann's abdomen and discovered a ruptured liver as a consequence of toxemia of pregnancy. She was suffering from an uncontrollable, profuse loss of blood. Joseph called his good friend, Russell, imploring him to come to the hospital immediately.

When Dr. Nelson arrived, he observed that the attending surgeons had done the best they could with techniques available to them, but he suggested that they apply techniques for stopping hemorrhage that he used during cardiac surgery. As a result, the bleeding was brought under control but not before Ann had received transfusions of more than thirty units of blood. Thirty years later, she is a healthy, happy, vivacious wife and mother. The gratitude that the Wirthlin and the Farnsworth families have for Elder Nelson remains boundless.

In describing Elder Nelson's spiritual gifts and special talents from the perspective of years of serving together, Elder Wirthlin simply replied, "He has them all. Russell is the most Christlike man I have ever known."[18]

The membership of the Quorum of the Twelve is distinguished by at least two pioneers: Russell M. Nelson, in the field of cardiac surgery; and Richard G. Scott, in the field of nuclear engineering. Elder Nelson helped develop the first heart-lung machine, and Elder Scott helped develop the first generation of nuclear submarine engines. Both men have left their nets behind them for the ministry. They view each other, not through the lens of scientific and technological achievements, but through the eternal lens of the gospel.

Elder Scott has been impressed by Elder Nelson's acute awareness of individuals within the Church at large. "His contributions to the Twelve are more in the doctrinal and spiritual area than in terms of organizational concerns," he said. "He continually measures what is

210 FATHER, SURGEON, APOSTLE

being discussed against the doctrine." One of Elder Nelson's significant contributions is "a precision of speech in carefully expressing thoughts in the right words, providing the appropriate tone and balance needed."[19]

Perhaps because for many years Elder Nelson has associated with those of other faiths and with citizens of other countries, "Russell is aware of how the Church appears to those not of our faith, and he is sensitive to the relationships with governments," Elder Scott observed. "Many can teach principles, but to eloquently live them is a great hallmark of this servant of the Lord."[20]

Like Elder Ballard, Elder Robert D. Hales also underwent open-heart bypass surgery. As Elder Hales was recovering, the chief surgeon, Dr. Doty, said, "During the operation, Russell Nelson was literally looking over my shoulder the whole time." Elder Hales concluded, "That's the man!"[21]

Elder David E. Sorensen, executive director of the Temple Department, indicated, "Elder Nelson provides oversight and spiritual guidance to the department, but he emphasizes the doctrine and removes himself from the details."[22] Elder D. Todd Christofferson, executive director of the Family and Church History Department, described Elder Nelson as "a guiding hand who gives counsel and direction by keeping the big picture in mind so we don't get lost in minutiae."[23] However, when one of his Brethren of the Twelve is in a critical, life-and-death situation, Elder Nelson *does* get involved in the details. Elder Hales particularly admired his apostolic colleague's kindness and caring during his various bouts of illness.[24]

Speaking of Elder Nelson's apostolic attributes, Elder Hales said, "There is a purity to his thinking—a grace, really. He has a unique ability as an ambassador in representing the Church with heads of state, and he has a deep sense of commitment to the role of the Twelve in opening the doors of nations." In discussions involving important decisions, "He moderates what is done by referring to principles. That man's a peacemaker who always avoids contention."[25]

In October 1981, Jeffrey R. Holland, then president of Brigham

Young University, had a special university assignment to be in Israel. He decided to take his whole family at personal expense. A Brigham Young University tour group of four hundred Latter-day Saints converged on the Holy Land at the same time, and among this large group were several members of the Russell and Dantzel Nelson family. On October 26, 1981, in the waters of the River Jordan, Jeffrey Holland baptized his son David. Elder Howard W. Hunter then confirmed him a member of the Church, under the gaze of four hundred observers.

Elder Holland recalled: "At that time I knew Russell reasonably well but not intimately. He was so gracious and treated us as family. He was courteous in taking photos and then sent copies to us and to my mother. For years thereafter he remained very solicitous to my mother. I learned at that time that you don't have to be a General Authority (which neither Russell nor I was at the time) to have a great love for your fellow brethren and to enjoy each other as kindred spirits. I think Elder Russell loved me in those days every bit as much as he loves me today."[26]

Elder Holland described Elder Nelson as "a man of integrity who has the attendant courage of one with integrity. When he disagrees on an issue, he finds a way to skillfully, sensitively, and appropriately register a dissenting opinion or point of view. He does not let issues go by if he disagrees, but he is not a 'fusser.' He is very precise and he picks his issues. On many issues on an agenda he doesn't say a word, but he will not let something go past with which he disagrees." Within his council and committee assignments, "he delegates and has great confidence in the people with whom he works."[27]

Continuing, Elder Holland said of his associate, "He works at understanding and pursuing the role of an Apostle as a special witness. He is given to eloquent declaration and admonition, and he is gifted and able in opening the doors to the nations, which he always reminds us can only be done with apostolic keys. He sees a significant portion of his call as apostolic witnessing, meeting governmental officials, and elevating the image of the Church."[28]

When asked to identify one or two spiritual gifts or godly attributes unique to Elder Nelson, Elder Holland said, "He is very, very gentlemanly, courteous and kind—in fact, you could drape the whole Boy Scout Law on Russell."[29]

Jeffrey Holland, himself easily given to humor, appreciates Elder Nelson's "quick wit, a kind of bubble-popping wit." For example, one day when one of the Seventy entered the lunchroom in the Church Administration Building, Elder Nelson politely rose to shake his hand. The Seventy protested, "You only need to stand up for people who are old and gray." With a broad smile, Elder Nelson replied, "You're there!"[30]

As with many of the Brethren, Elder Holland is impressed by Elder Nelson's post-surgical career penchant for precision. "He won't let anything go by if it is untried or untrue." But he makes all corrections and suggestions in a solicitous way. Elder Holland said, "He is not syrupy or mushy, but he is protective of the person making the presentation or reading the document. If he sees something which could be an embarrassment, such as a misspelled word or awkward phraseology, he privately circles the phrase and jots down the question: 'Could this be said better this way?' He then hands the note to the person privately after the meeting, in keeping with the counsel of the scriptures to make corrections privately 'between him or her and thee alone'"[31] (D&C 42:88).

While serving as the president of Ricks College, now Brigham Young University–Idaho, Elder Erying was invited to speak to a group of Saints in Kearns, where Elder Nelson was then serving as a regional representative. Though not an official part of the program, Russell came to the meeting to demonstrate his support. Looking back, Elder Eyring said, "I couldn't believe this busy, distinguished doctor would stay the whole time. Afterward, he acted as if I'd done him a great favor coming down [from Rexburg]."[32]

For several years, Elder Nelson has been a member of the Temple and Family History Executive Council. Elder Eyring has noticed how deeply committed Elder Nelson is to that assignment. Elder

The Quorum of the Twelve Apostles, 1995. Front row: Elder Boyd K. Packer (acting president of the Quorum of the Twelve), Elder L. Tom Perry, Elder David B. Haight, Elder Neal A. Maxwell. Back row: Elder Russell M. Nelson, Elder Dallin H. Oaks, Elder M. Russell Ballard, Elder Joseph B. Wirthlin, Elder Richard G. Scott, Elder Robert D. Hales, Elder Jeffrey R. Holland, and Elder Henry B. Eyring.

Nelson has been engaged in family history for several years and is well acquainted with various computer software products developed to assist individuals and families in their research. Many of his sermons and teachings have concentrated on the blessings of the temple. Elder Eyring has observed that in discussions of challenges facing members of the Church, Elder Nelson often suggests that family history and temple work can become part of the solution.

Agreeing with comments of other Quorum members, Elder Eyring said, "You can always count on Elder Nelson to look at things from the point of view of others, so the message could not be misunderstood."[33]

As commissioner of Church Education, Elder Eyring has a

sensitive eye and ear to good teachers with profound insights. While many of the Apostles extol Elder Nelson's ability to speak Spanish, Portuguese, Mandarin, Russian, German, and French, Elder Eyring has been impressed with his colleague's "spiritual gift of language." In other words, "he uses language to lift us to spiritual heights by saying things in a loftier mode with an inner, spiritual scope. His language shows us the sweep of eternity."[34]

These men who are sustained as prophets, seers, and revelators have come from widely diverse backgrounds and capacities. Notwithstanding their laudable attributes, one of their number wryly remarked that, as they change into their white temple clothing, they are able to see each other's feet of clay. Each in his own way has felt unworthy at the time of his call to the Holy Apostleship. Each is aware that others have talents and strengths that he himself may lack. But each knows that their brotherhood, with its spiritual synergy of combined gifts and talents, when quickened by the spirit, has a potential power that far outweighs individual deficiencies. Thus, they sustain each other with a pure, transcendent love as they literally wear out their lives in the service of their Heavenly Father and His children.

CHAPTER 20

SERVING THE CHINESE

A T A REGIONAL REPRESENTATIVES' seminar Brother Nelson
attended in 1979 in his capacity as general president of the
Sunday School, President Spencer W. Kimball challenged all present
to lengthen their stride in taking the gospel to the entire world.
Among the countries President Kimball specifically mentioned was
China, declaring, "We should be of service to the Chinese. We
should learn their language. We should pray for them and help
them."[1]

Soon thereafter, Russell and Dantzel secured the services of
Mandarin tutors Joe Stringham and Basil Yang, and on Wednesday
evenings they blocked out time to become serious students of
Mandarin. Elder Nelson had determined to be prepared to serve the
Chinese people when the opportunity came.[2]

Not long after he accepted President Kimball's charge to learn
Chinese, Russell attended the annual meetings of the American
Association of Thoracic Surgery. During those meetings, he fortu-
itously sat next to a distinguished Chinese surgeon, Dr. Wu Yingkai.
Dr. Wu, head of the Fu Wai Hospital in Beijing, had worked in the
United States for eight years in the 1930s as a thoracic surgeon.

As Russell took notes on various presentations, he felt strongly
impressed to speak with Dr. Wu, and because he had been studying
Mandarin, he began the conversation in Chinese. This led to a warm

and friendly discussion between the two surgeons. Dr. Nelson extended an invitation to Dr. Wu to visit Salt Lake City and the University of Utah Medical School, which he accepted. "This started the 'Chinese connection,'" Elder Nelson recalled, "and there is no doubt in my mind that the Lord brought Professor Wu and me together."[3] Near the end of 1979, Dr. Wu visited the University of Utah Medical School, delivering a lecture on "Open-Heart Surgery Under Acupuncture."[4]

Upon returning to China after a pleasant experience in Utah, Dr. Wu arranged for a reciprocal invitation to Dr. Nelson to be a visiting professor of surgery at Shandong Medical College in Jinan. As President Kimball's surgeon, Dr. Nelson had frequent contact with him, so he asked President Kimball if he should accept Dr. Wu's invitation. President Kimball enthusiastically responded, "That's what I've been trying to tell you brethren about preparing to be of service to the Chinese."[5]

In mid-September 1980, Russell and Dantzel departed for China.[6] Dr. Zhang Zhenxiang, a kindly Chinese surgeon and a colleague of Dr. Wu, met them upon arrival and served as their interpreter and escort during their stay. As they were driving from the airport to the hotel, Dr. Zhang was pleasantly surprised by Dantzel's lilting pronunciation of *Beijing,* China's capital. "That was the first time I had ever heard a Westerner pronounce Chinese characters so beautifully with the proper musical inflection at the end of a word," he said.[7]

Zhang Zhenxiang was born in China in a small village in the Hebei Province near Tianjin in 1920. At about age five, he was sent to live with his grandfather in Tianjin so he could obtain an education. His uncles assisted his grandfather in teaching him traditional Chinese values of honesty and hard work, and they taught him that his "Heavenly Grandfather was watching all the time." As a young lad, he aspired to become a physician.[8]

Despite disruptions by the Japanese occupation of China in 1937 and the outbreak of World War II in 1941, Zhang graduated with his medical degree in 1946. The Cheeloo Medical College, which would later become the Shandong Medical College, offered him a position on the faculty, which he held at the time he and Dr. Nelson met.[9]

In subsequent years, Russell and Dantzel visited the Shandong Medical College a number of times, and each time, Dr. Zhang invited his medical colleagues from all over the country to attend Dr. Nelson's lectures and operative clinics on cardiovascular surgery. Russell would begin each address in Mandarin and then switch to English, relying on Dr. Zhang to interpret. Dr. Zhang recalled, "Dr. Nelson also taught at the medical school in Qing Dao, a beautiful coastal city in the Shandong Province, and after every lecture he would listen attentively to all the questions raised from the audience and answer every one in detail. He showed great patience, respect, and courtesy for his Chinese colleagues."[10]

Ever the gracious guest, Russell visited the Seniors' (Old People's) University in Jinan and showed great interest in the courses taken by the students, most of them retired people. "He once gave a lecture on the grandeur of nature, teaching of the great Creator, and of prophets and Apostles, and he was welcomed and very much respected wherever he went," Dr. Zhang said. "To the Chinese, he had a Westerner's appearance, but his heart was very close to ours."[11]

Dr. Zhang said, "Dr. Nelson operated in the Shandong Medical Hospital many times, and during each operation he took the position of the first assistant in teaching the surgeons in the hospital how best to perform their operations. Open-heart surgery not only requires knowledgeable, experienced, and skillful surgeons working in close coordination, but also close cooperation between the operating nurse, the anesthesiologist, and the cardiopulmonary perfusionist, who manages the operation of the heart-lung machine."[12]

Open-heart surgery requires sophisticated modern equipment, but in China the operating rooms were not as well equipped as the operating rooms to which Dr. Nelson was accustomed. In addition, the surgeons and nurses had less experience than those with whom Dr. Nelson had worked elsewhere.

"Though it must have been rather challenging for Dr. Nelson, he never complained," Dr. Zhang observed. "He never lost his patience when a surgical nurse misunderstood his request. Dr. Nelson worked very hard and did an excellent job. Everybody was very happy about the result of the operations, and the postoperative course of every patient ran smoothly. The Chinese surgeons and nurses were very pleased because they had learned so much from this caring, patient American surgeon."[13]

At the time of his call to the Twelve in April 1984, Elder Nelson informed President Gordon B. Hinckley that he had made a previous commitment to teach in China. President Hinckley responded: "Honor your commitments; besides, it would be nice to have an ordained Apostle in China."[14] So, with President Hinckley's approval, on April 25, Elder and Sister Nelson departed for China, where Dr. Nelson would serve as visiting professor of surgery at two medical schools—the Shandong Medical College and the Qing Dao School of Medicine. Both schools were located in cities of about a million people.[15]

Their Chinese hosts showed Russell and Dantzel the Great Wall, the Imperial Palace in Beijing, the Yellow River, and the Ling Yen Temple, built in 35 A.D. On May 19, 1984, Dr. Nelson thought he had closed his surgical career in the city of Qing Dao. "It isn't the scenario I would have written, but that is the way it ended—without fanfare and without notice," he said at the time. He and Dantzel left behind many dear friends for whom they would have lasting affection.[16]

In February 1985, ten months after his calling as an Apostle, Elder Nelson received a surprise phone call from China. His good friend Dr. Zhang pleaded for help on behalf of a famous Beijing opera singer. In China, male opera singers must be skilled not only in singing but also in acting and acrobatics. The singer in question had a serious heart condition that prevented him from performing any longer on stage. Because Elder Nelson was no longer practicing surgery, he tried to persuade Dr. Zhang to send the opera singer to Salt Lake City, where some of Dr. Nelson's previous colleagues could perform the needed operation. Dr. Zhang responded that the patient was too ill to make the long journey. And though Zhang is a gentle man, he adamantly insisted that Dr. Nelson *personally* perform the operation in China.[17]

Elder Nelson sought the counsel of President Ezra Taft Benson and President Hinckley. They both agreed that this would be a unique opportunity for Christian service, so they encouraged him to go. Dr. Nelson's former partner, Dr. Conrad B. Jenson, would precede Elder Nelson in making necessary preparations for this important operation.[18]

In a pensive mood prior to his departure for China, Elder Nelson recorded his reflections: "I learned long ago to be obedient to those marvelous sweet whisperings of the Spirit—those strong promptings to follow counsel. Especially sobering it is to know that, while we may be content with the status quo in life, the Lord would be making something of us beyond our fondest imagination. All he requires of us is to prepare ourselves, to try to iron out our imperfections, and to stretch each day to be something more than we otherwise would be.

"On the eve of my third journey to China, this time to help them with an operation on China's most famous opera star, *all* of this has come about because I listened to a prophet's voice. He said that 'We should be of service to the Chinese. We must learn their language. We should pray for them and be ready to help them.' He made this speech at a Regional Representatives' seminar in 1979. I was not a Regional Representative then. I was just an invited guest as president of the Sunday School. But I did *not* hear him say, 'Everyone *except* Brother Nelson should do those things.' So I believed him. I worked, and Dantzel, too, being tutored in Mandarin. Now I don't know what will come of all this, but this much I know: ties between nations will become more secure working side by side in the fields of their need than they will ever be if left only to the political leaders. And the gospel will be preached only among the populous nations of the earth as they learn to trust us and to love us. Then, and only then, will our message of salvation and exaltation have appeal for them."[19]

During the long flight to China, Elder Nelson intensively reviewed his notes on Mandarin so that he would be well prepared to communicate with his Chinese hosts upon his arrival in Beijing. Notwithstanding an early arrival time of 3:10 A.M., Elder Nelson was welcomed by a delegation of Chinese medical professors, including his friends Drs. Zhang, Su, Sung, Li, Yang, Wang, and Yin![20]

The next morning, Elder Nelson met the famous patient, Mr. Fang Rongxiang. After reviewing his case in conference with about fifty other doctors and staff, Elder Nelson explained in detail the procedures that would need to be taken to perform a quadruple coronary artery bypass graft operation. That evening, he and his former partner, Dr. Jenson, rehearsed in detail every step of the procedure they were going to perform. The next morning, they met together in prayer and then entered the operating room fasting. Although Elder Nelson had not performed surgery during the previous eleven months, the operation went flawlessly, much to the delight of his Chinese medical associates.[21]

At that time there was only one cardiopulmonary monitor for postoperative use in the entire hospital, and the Chinese doctors used it sparingly so that "it would last longer." It was their common practice to switch off the monitor as soon as they were sure that a patient's condition was stable. In the United States, on the other hand, the monitor is kept on for at least the first day following an operation. Early in the morning after the operation on Mr. Fang, Elder Nelson went to check on his famous patient. When he saw that the monitor was turned off, he was horrified, fearing the worst. But when he heard Mr. Fang's cheerful greeting from across the room and saw his smiling face as he lay on his bed in a semirecumbent posture, he was greatly relieved. A few months later, Mr. Fang was performing again on the stage![22]

The day after the operation, Dr. Jenson, who had also endeared himself to the Chinese through his careful preparations the preceding week, and Elder Nelson received a surprise visit from a grateful delegation. Mr. Fang's family and friends, the minister of health, the head of the Beijing Opera Company, and various physicians and hospital administrators came laden with gifts of gratitude for their American friends.[23]

After a tearful farewell, Elder Nelson made his way with Dr. Zhang to Beijing, where he would catch his flight home. Unfortunately, all of the nicer hotels were full, so Elder Nelson and Dr. Zhang had to spend the night in a hotel with no heat, no warm water, and no bathing facilities. Dr. Zhang apologized to Elder Nelson for their accommodations, but to prevent any embarrassment, Elder Nelson replied, "I'm not that dirty. I don't need a bath every day."[24]

During one of Dr. Zhang's subsequent visits to Salt Lake City as part of a large delegation of Chinese physicians, he was asked to interpret Elder Nelson's remarks to the group. Everyone was surprised when Elder Nelson began speaking in Mandarin. They were then delighted when Dr. Zhang smilingly interpreted Elder Nelson's address from Chinese to English.[25]

In early May 1986, Elder and Sister Nelson traveled to China with Elder William R. Bradford, president of the Asia Area, and his wife, Mary Ann, and with Brother Ralph and Sister Joan Rodgers, who supervised the Polynesian Cultural Center in Hawaii. On May 7, they went to the Forbidden City in the heart of Beijing, and in the northeast corner of the Imperial Palace grounds, the six Latter-day Saints found a quiet spot in a garden remarkably isolated from the multitudes of people milling about the park. In that tranquil spot, Elder Nelson offered a special apostolic prayer, supplicating the Lord to bless them in their mission to China and to make their ecclesiastical entourage part of the blessings the Lord had in store for the Chinese people.[26]

The delegation was later hosted by Elder Nelson's good friend

Leaders pause during a Brigham Young University Young Ambassadors visit to
China in May 1986. Front row, left to right: William Bradshaw, a Chinese official,
Norma Ashton, Li Peng (China's vice premier), Elder Marvin J. Ashton, Elder
Nelson, an interpreter, and Dantzel Nelson. Middle row: an interpreter, Marjorie
Bradshaw, an interpreter, Mary Ann Bradford, William R. Bradford, Ralph
Rodgers, Joan Rodgers, Virginia Oaks, Harold Oaks, and an interpreter. Back row:
three interpreters and Marta Tullis, LaMond Tullis, and Randy Booth.

Professor Wu Yingkai at the Beijing Heart, Lung and Blood Vessel
Institute, and that afternoon, the brethren met for two hours with
Mr. Ren Wuzhi, director of the Bureau of Religious Affairs of the
State Council for the People's Republic of China. Among other topics, they discussed the desire to organize branches of the Church for
expatriates living in China. In the evening, they and their wives
attended a performance of the BYU Young Ambassadors, who were
accompanied by Elder and Sister Marvin J. Ashton.[27] The Chinese
warmly received the Young Ambassadors, some of whose performances were telecast throughout the nation, reinforcing Brigham
Young University's positive reputation throughout China.

The next day, Elder Nelson met with Dr. Shih Yifan and Dr. Li
Zhenglin, leading physicians at the Peking Union Medical College,
and with Dr. Chen Minzhang, deputy minister of health for the
country. That afternoon, the LDS delegation was joined by Elder

and Sister Marvin J. Ashton and various leaders of Brigham Young University at a special reception given by Mr. Li Peng, China's vice premier.[28]

On May 9, the Nelsons, Bradfords, and Rodgers went to Ba Da Ling to see the Great Wall of China and then traveled to the Ming Tombs. During the day, a special meeting was called for the twenty Latter-day Saints living in Beijing, and during that meeting, the brethren organized the Beijing China Branch of the Church with Brother Forrest M. Anderson as the first branch president.[29] The following day, the brethren met with officials of the Bureau of State Pharmaceutical Administration and with representatives of China Central Television.

On May 13, Elder Nelson gave a lecture at the Shandong Medical College, and in the afternoon he presented a second lecture at the Shandong Seniors' University to more than a thousand retired citizens. He spoke on caring for the elderly in the church and community. To his great surprise, at the conclusion of his address, the university conferred upon him an honorary professorship.[30]

The brethren convened a meeting on May 16 with ten Latter-day Saint expatriates and organized the Xi'an China Branch of the Church with Craig W. Oler as branch president.[31] The next day at the Xi'an Medical College, Dr. Nelson gave a lecture on the history of open-heart surgery, after which the college awarded him an honorary professorship.[32] The Nelsons then bade adieu to the Bradfords and Rodgerses the following day and departed for home.[33]

In early November 1988, Elder Dallin H. Oaks, Brother and Sister Rodgers, and Elder Nelson traveled together to Beijing. On November 7, the brethren held a planning meeting with Beijing branch president Gerrit Gong, who had replaced Forrest Anderson, and others over breakfast at the Great Wall Hotel. Elder Nelson and Elder Oaks had been sent by the First Presidency to meet with Chinese government officials and religious leaders to ascertain whether Chinese members could meet and carry on

Church activities with the approval of the Chinese government, consistent with its laws. They first met with Zhao Puchu, vice chairman of the Chinese People's Political Consultative Conference, who also represented the Buddhist leadership in China. The Imam of the Muslim faith, which has sixteen million adherents in China, and leaders of the Taoist and Catholic religions in China were also present. Their ninety-minute discussion generated amiable feelings.[34]

Still later in the day, the brethren met with the Beijing branch presidency and spoke at a fireside in the branch president's home. Sixty-two people attended, including twenty-five Chinese who were not members of the Church, some of whom had requested baptism.[35]

The next morning, the brethren met with various academic and government officials,[36] and in the afternoon, they met with the deputy director of religious affairs. Elder Nelson recalled, "The Lord blessed us to be able to have a good understanding one with the other, leaving an open door to further communications as needs may arise."[37]

After observing Elder Nelson's actions at close range in various settings with Chinese officials, Elder Dallin Oaks recorded in his personal record: "Russell Nelson is so 'smooth' in his leading role in these meetings. As he spoke with the minister, I had the strong impression that the Lord had raised him up especially for this work, and that his great standing in the Chinese medical community through his personal surgical contributions and his teaching and arranging for Chinese surgeons to study in the United States were heaven-sent opportunities to pave the way for what we are trying to accomplish here. . . . He is a man of great faith and wisdom. The better I know him the better I like him."[38]

The next day, the brethren met in the chambers of Judge Yao Keming of the Beijing People's Higher Court, with whom Elder Oaks, as a former justice of the Utah Supreme Court, had some affinity. Before Elder Oaks returned home to fulfill other assignments, he

Brother Ralph Rodgers and Elder Nelson meet with Mr. Li Xiannian, former president of the People's Republic of China, November 1988.

and Elder Nelson met with and instructed the Beijing branch presidency. Elder Oaks then led the members of the branch in a prayer invoking the Lord's beneficent influence upon the work in China.[39]

Brother and Sister Rodgers and Elder Nelson took a plane from Xi'an to Shanghai on November 11. The following day, Elder Nelson met with Mr. Li Xiannian, former president of the People's Republic of China who then served as one of the nine members on the Politburo. At age eighty, he still presided as the chairman of the State Council. He was widely venerated because of his age and great influence. Although his office was located in Beijing, he was willing to receive Elder Nelson at his winter headquarters in Shanghai.

Mr. Li was familiar with Dr. Nelson's previous visits to China to provide training for several Chinese surgeons, and he recalled having been royally welcomed as a guest of Ralph and Joan Rodgers at the Polynesian Cultural Center in Hawaii. Of Chairman Li, Elder Nelson said, "During the course of our conversation, he assured us that the leaders in China were committed to freedom of religious belief and freedom of their believers to practice the tenets of their individual religious denominations. He assured us of fairness to all religious believers regardless of the number of adherents to their faith, and he indicated that our Church members would be respected and would be protected as would any other believers."[40]

Following this historic meeting, Brother and Sister Rodgers joined Elder Nelson in his hotel room to offer a prayer of thanksgiving for the Lord's influence in arranging for them to be entrusted to represent the Church in China.[41]

A few years later, in early 1990, Elder Nelson received a letter from Dr. Zhang in which he explained that his studies and experiences in China had led him to believe that Elder Nelson's religion was the only one "that made sense." In his letter, Dr. Zhang indicated that his daughter had obtained a job as a pathologist at the University of Toronto. Inasmuch as he was planning to retire soon, and given the tense political situation in China following the Tiananmen Square protest in June 1989, he and his wife contemplated leaving China for Toronto. He asked if Elder Nelson could arrange to have someone teach him the gospel upon his arrival in Canada. Elder Nelson gladly called the mission president, Sidney A. Smith, to arrange for missionaries to visit the Zhang family.

The Zhangs enjoyed their association with the elders and were warmly welcomed by Canadian Church members when they attended meetings.[42] Elder Nelson soon received a phone call from President Smith, who reported that Dr. Zhang and his wife desired baptism. On April 14, Elder Nelson caught a flight to Toronto, where he was met by President Smith, Zhang Zhenxiang and his wife, Zhou Qingguo, their daughter, Yenhui, and her husband, Chiang.[43]

The following day, Easter Sunday, Elder Nelson had the privilege of baptizing Dr. Zhang. After Dr. Zhang's confirmation, Elder Nelson conferred the Aaronic Priesthood upon him and ordained him to the office of priest. Brother Zhang then baptized his wife. That evening, as a benediction to a very moving day, Elder Nelson and Brother Zhang spoke to more than a thousand people at a fire-side at the Etobicoke chapel.[44]

Four months later, in August 1990, Elder Nelson traveled to Toronto to participate in the dedicatory services for the Toronto Ontario Temple. While there, he visited with the Zhangs and shared in the joy of their growing testimonies of the gospel. For Elder Nelson, the highlight of the temple dedication was seeing Dr. Zhang in the temple. "I wept for joy, and so did he," Elder Nelson said.[45]

In the course of interpreting for Dr. Nelson during his travels within China, Dr. Zhang said, "I often wondered: 'How can a man be so friendly, so kind, so loving, so generous, so hard working, so humble, so patient, so considerate and, in one word, so selfless?' After I visited Salt Lake City in 1980 and again in 1985, I gradually began to realize that it was his great faith in God that was motivating him. Faith in God and His gospel has made him completely devoted to spreading the gospel to every corner of the world, for the salvation of the living and the redemption of the dead, and to healing and helping people who are in need."[46]

A year after Brother and Sister Zhang's baptisms, Elder Nelson again traveled to Toronto on assignment at the Toronto Ontario Temple. While there, he escorted Brother and Sister Zhang through a temple session as they received their endowments. Elder Nelson then sealed them as husband and wife for all eternity. "That was an unforgettable experience, coming eleven years after our first meeting in Beijing, China, where our friendship began," Elder Nelson said. "At the request of Dr. Zhang, I also performed the sealing of Dr. Zhang's friend, Daniel Pun, to his wife, and their daughter, Emily, to her parents."[47]

Following area training meetings in Hawaii in November 1994, Elder Nelson and Elder Loren C. Dunn hosted a distinguished group of Chinese government officials at the Polynesian Cultural Center. Among the more than two dozen guests were Li Lanqing, Chinese vice premier; and Li Daoyu, Chinese ambassador to the United States. While there, the vice premier extended an invitation

Elder Neal A. Maxwell and Elder Nelson meet in February 1995 with Vice Premier Li Lanqing and Qi Huaiyuan, president of the Chinese People's Association for Friendship with Foreign Countries.

to Elder and Sister Nelson to visit China. Upon returning home, Elder Nelson contacted Sister Beverly Campbell of the Church's International Affairs Office in Washington, D.C., advising her that he and Elder Neal A. Maxwell might be able to visit China. She discussed the visit with the Chinese ambassador and soon everything was in order for Elders Nelson and Maxwell to be received as Apostles of The Church of Jesus Christ of Latter-day Saints in China.[48]

After a refresher lesson in Mandarin, Elder Nelson and Dantzel and Elder Neal A. Maxwell and his wife, Colleen, departed for the Orient in February 1995.[49] In Hong Kong, the Brethren met with Elders John K. Carmack and John H. Groberg of the Asia Area Presidency to discuss activities and concerns throughout the area. The British had governed Hong Kong ever since they signed a lease with the Chinese government in 1898. At that time, both countries agreed that ninety-nine years later, Hong Kong would revert to Chinese rule. The status of religious organizations within Hong Kong would be uncertain after the official handover in July 1997.

Nevertheless, it was a thrill for the Brethren to see the Hong Kong China Temple under construction.

The following day, the Brethren and their wives, including Elder Carmack, caught a flight to Beijing, where they received a VIP welcome by Su Guang, vice president of the China People's Association for Friendship with Foreign Countries (CPAFFC), and Madame Li Xiaolin, deputy director of the Department of American and Oceanic Affairs within the Chinese People's Association.[50]

Sister Beverly and Brother Pierce Campbell had preceded the Maxwells and Nelsons by a few days in order to prepare for their visit. Sister Campbell described the meeting with the vice premier on the afternoon of February 22, 1995: "The day was balmy, the enormous French doors in the Receiving Hall were opened to the day and the white silk hangings, some twenty feet long, were billowing in the breeze. Indeed, it seemed serene, heavenly, and as though hosts of angels were in attendance. You could feel the Lord's love for His children in China."[51]

During their meeting, Elders Maxwell and Nelson discussed ways in which the Church might help the Chinese people, and they sought the vice premier's counsel regarding initiatives to send educators and doctors to China. These possibilities were also explored with the respective government ministries that supervised such activities.

The vice premier, Mr. Li, listened intently to the three General Authorities and offered a few helpful suggestions regarding ways in which the Church could provide some assistance to China. An outgrowth of this cordial meeting was an appointment the following day with the State Education Commission and its vice director, Zhang Xiaowen, former president of Qing Hua University. In this meeting, the Brethren discussed the possibility of the Church sending retired couples to China to teach English in various institutions throughout the country.[52] This suggestion came to fruition shortly thereafter and has been of great service to the Chinese in recent years.

In the afternoon of February 23, the entourage met at the State

Meeting with Chinese officials in February 1995. Front row, left to right: Liu Yanling (Linda), Colleen H. Maxwell, Elder Neal A. Maxwell, Elder Nelson, Li Lanqing, Qi Huaiyuan, Pierce Campbell, and staff member. Back row: Li Xiaolin, Elder John K. Carmack, Dantzel W. Nelson, Elder Kwok Yuen Tai, Flora Tai, Beverly Campbell, and Wang Jinghua.

Bureau of Religious Affairs, where they were cordially welcomed by Liu Shuxiang, deputy director.[53] Although none of the LDS group was acquainted with these government officials, Mr. Liu was aware of Dr. Nelson's work at the Shandong Medical College and of his life-saving operation on the country's famous opera singer in 1985.

The next day, the Church leaders met with Liu Deyou, vice minister of the Ministry of Culture, and Liu Haiming, assistant director general. This appointment concluded three busy days full of meetings with various governmental dignitaries—meetings that had resulted in the making of new friendships and in the solidifying of old friendships.[54]

On the final evening of their visit, Brother and Sister Campbell arranged a banquet to honor their Chinese hosts, including Dr. Zhang, the Chinese surgeon to whom Dr. Nelson had first taught open-heart surgery. During gracious speeches made by their hosts, Sister Campbell recalled, "We learned that much of what had happened was because Elder Nelson was known to, revered, and valued by the leadership of China because of his service to their people."[55]

In April 1997, Elder and Sister Nelson returned to Hong Kong with President and Sister James E. Faust to participate in a regional conference with Elder John H. Groberg. Nearly 2,800 Chinese Saints attended the April 19–20 conference, and afterward the Brethren visited the beautiful, newly constructed Hong Kong China Temple, which had been dedicated May 26–27, 1996, by President Gordon B. Hinckley and has been a great blessing to the Saints in northeastern Asia.[56]

April 23 was filled with great anticipation as President Faust, Elders Nelson, Groberg, and Kwok Yuen Tai met with Mr. Tung Chee-Hwa, who would soon become chief executive of the Hong Kong Special Administrative Region of the People's Republic of China. This meeting occurred just two months before the British would relinquish control of Hong Kong on June 30, 1997.

In speaking of the importance of the meeting with Mr. Tung, President Faust said, "At that time we didn't know the effect of the handover. The Hong Kong Temple was dedicated a year earlier, and there was a grave concern about the future of the Church there. We were greatly pleased and reassured that religious liberty would continue to be observed and that property rights and our temples and chapels would be respected."[57]

President Faust continued, "We asked Mr. Tung, 'If you were we, what would you do?' and Mr. Tung responded, 'Keep doing what you're doing.'"[58]

Elder Nelson described Mr. Tung as "a very remarkable man, fluent in the English, Mandarin, and Cantonese languages." He gave the Brethren "unequivocal assurance that complete religious freedom would be preserved in Hong Kong. He also shared many other insights into the many challenges that face him. We assured him of our prayers in his behalf and of the loyal support of members of the Church in his courageous efforts to maintain democracy, freedom,

*In April 1997, Elder John H. Groberg, Elder Nelson, President James E. Faust, and
Elder Kwok Yuen Tai meet with Mr. Tung Chee-Hwa (center), who was soon to
become the chief executive of the Hong Kong Special Administrative Region of the
People's Republic of China.*

and private enterprise in this special administrative region of
China."[59]

On February 26, 1999, Elder and Sister Nelson were invited to
a luncheon hosted by the Church in the Ambassador Room of the
Joseph Smith Memorial Building for Chinese ambassador Li
Zhaoxing. He, like many other Chinese officials, had questions
about the Church.

As Joseph Smith was held captive in Liberty Jail in March 1839,
the Lord assured him that the day would come when "the ends of the
earth shall inquire after thy name" (D&C 122:1). Could Joseph have
possibly imagined that one day a high-ranking government official
from far-off China would come to the headquarters of the Church to
learn more of him and to dine in a building memorializing his name?

One reason the Chinese have come to Salt Lake City to learn
more of Joseph Smith is that they, like Dr. Zhang Zhenxiang, know
of the sterling reputation of Dr. Russell M. Nelson, an Apostle of
the Lord Jesus Christ.

CHAPTER 21

THE REFINER'S FIRE

WHEN ELDER NELSON RETURNED to his office on September 17, 1991, following his usual committee meetings at Church headquarters, he received an alarming telephone call from Dantzel. Their fifth daughter, Emily, had just been diagnosed with breast cancer. Concerned, Russell and Dantzel went to see Emily and her husband, Brad. They then drove to Provo to fulfill a commitment to speak to missionaries at the Missionary Training Center. Elder Nelson recalled, "I really didn't feel up to it because of feelings of empathy and concern for our sweet Emily, who bravely received the news of this difficult challenge."[1]

Three days later, a colleague in Dr. Nelson's graduating medical school class, Dr. Joe E. Jack, performed a modified radical mastectomy on this beautiful thirty-three-year-old mother of four. The trauma of the initial diagnosis and subsequent surgery was compounded by the fact that Emily was twenty-one weeks into her fifth pregnancy and was required to undergo chemotherapy following the operation. Family members prayerfully and anxiously awaited chemotherapy's unknown impact upon her developing baby.[2]

When Russell and Dantzel visited the hospital following the operation, they found Emily and Brad in good spirits. They both had claimed the Savior's promise: "I will not leave you comfortless" (John 14:18). A month after the initial diagnosis, on October 17,

Emily underwent her first chemotherapy treatment, which she tolerated well. She was, after all, a spiritually sensitive and resilient young woman.[3]

Less than two months later, on December 6, Emily entered Salt Lake City's Cottonwood Hospital under the care of Dr. Richard Irion, husband of her sister Gloria. Dr. Irion began to induce labor shortly after her arrival, and soon Emily delivered a normal, beautiful, five-pound-seven-ounce baby boy, to be named Jordan White Wittwer. The chemotherapy seemingly had no impact on the baby's perfect little body, and the entire extended family expressed joy and gratitude for the miraculous fulfillment of a priesthood blessing pronounced three months previously.[4]

Three months after giving birth to Jordan, in March 1992, Emily successfully endured her "final" chemotherapy treatment while Russell and Dantzel tended her infant son.[5] Seven months later, Emily's parents and family were delighted to hear the hopeful prognosis she had received from her doctor.[6]

During this same period, Dantzel had felt somewhat weak and lacking in energy. So, a couple of weeks before her sixty-seventh birthday in February 1993, she went to see her physician for a physical checkup. Both her doctor and her husband were relieved to find that Dantzel's heart and arteries were in good condition.[7]

Dantzel's entry in the monthly *Nelson News* at the end of August 1993 had a somewhat foreboding tone: "In this month I have felt less than on top, but I want you all to know how blessed I am to have such a caring and supportive group of cherished loved ones, as you all are. As I have received your calls and visits and caring, each act has lifted me up and made me realize how blessed I am. I see such marvelous things going on in your homes—the love you have for each other—the very special way you are parenting and teaching your beautiful children. . . . Keep up the good work, and keep the spirit of our Heavenly Father in your homes and hearts, always!"[8]

The advent of 1994 was filled with optimism as Emily and Brad left on January 21 for a well-deserved trip to Hawaii.[9] The Hawaiian vacation was propitiously timed, for not long after she returned, Emily began feeling weak again. Toward the end of April, her physician confirmed that she would need more radical treatment for what Elder Nelson called "her unfriendly invader." The evening of April 25, following the monthly family birthday party, Brad and Elder Nelson gave Emily another priesthood blessing of healing and comfort, humbly acknowledging, "Not our will, but Thine be done."[10]

On May 2, a line was inserted into Emily's arm to facilitate intravenous administrations of chemotherapy and to ease the discomfort of multiple samplings of blood for follow-up examinations. The next day, she commenced her treatment with the aid of an intravenous pump.[11]

A month later, on June 1, 1994, Dantzel underwent a surgical biopsy of enlarged lymph nodes on the left side of her neck.[12] Ten days later, the pathologist reported that Dantzel had contracted "large cell lymphoma, non-Hodgkin's type."[13] A biopsy of her pelvic bone marrow revealed tumor cells in that region, causing physicians to classify her illness as Stage IV, the advanced phase of lymphoma. Physicians immediately began an aggressive course of chemotherapy, intermittently administered at monthly intervals for a period of six months.[14]

On Sunday, June 12, family members gathered to fuse their faith as priesthood blessings were administered to both Dantzel and Emily and as their husband and father foresaw that "these ladies will have to endure so much."[15]

With his daughter and his eternal companion both wrestling with life-threatening illnesses, Elder Nelson spent much of July writing a book, *The Gateway We Call Death*, in response to a request to do so by officials at Deseret Book. Working on that book helped him claim the assurances of the precious plan of salvation with its promised blessings of resurrection and reunification with loved ones.

On July 14, Dantzel underwent her second monthly round of chemotherapy. The next day, she and Elder Nelson accompanied Emily, Brad, and their four older children to an orientation at the

*Emily and Dantzel in August 1993, two years after Emily's fateful diagnosis and
seventeen months before she passed away.*

Bone Marrow Transplantation Unit at LDS Hospital to learn more
about Emily's treatment. After the meeting, Elder Nelson observed,
"Those who cared for Emily were so skilled and compassionate, and
we are grateful for their help."[16]

In some people, one of the consequences of chemotherapy and
radiation therapy is the destruction of bone marrow indispensable
for production of blood. Three days after her orientation meeting,
Emily underwent an operation for the extraction of marrow that
would be preserved in case she needed it after her chemotherapy.[17]

On July 28, Emily experienced a hopeful new kind of therapy
in which some of her own blood was removed, spun in a centrifuge
for the harvest of stem cells, and then reinfused into her arm. She
tolerated the procedure well, and the process was repeated until a
sufficient number of cells had been retrieved to provide a healthy
supply of blood.[18] Two weeks later, she completed an intense
ninety-six hours of chemotherapy in which four separate drugs were
pumped into her central circulatory system continuously and

concurrently. Her parents, spouse, and siblings all shared the accolade: "What a courageous young woman!"[19] It seemed to everyone that the life of this beloved mother of five was on the mend, and that her days on earth would be lengthened.

On August 17, Emily received stem cell transplants—six units of her own stem cells that were harvested July 28–30. Fortunately, there were no complications, and hope was renewed with each new round of treatment.[20] On August 22, Russell and Dantzel joined the Wittwers' modified family "home" evening in Emily's hospital room, during which Brad gave special blessings to each of their children. Grandfather Nelson observed this inspirational event from the sideline, commenting afterward, "Father's blessings can be such a comfort and a protection, particularly as children begin a new school year."[21]

The roller-coaster ride from bright hope to dark disappointment continued. The normal count for blood platelets is about 400,000, but by August 23, Emily's count had reached the perilously low level of 4,000. Thanks to all of her siblings, who donated their blood platelets to her, she was rescued from danger.[22] Six days later, after literally being at death's door, Emily called to announce the good news that she was being released from the hospital. Elder Nelson's joy was transparent as he exclaimed, "What a tremendous triumph! It was a victory for Emily, for Brad and their family, for the doctors, nurses, and all who pooled their faith, works, and skill that our sweetheart could receive the chance for a cure that we needed. We were all humbly grateful for her successful completion of that arduous course."[23]

When Dantzel and Russell took Emily to LDS Hospital for an outpatient checkup on September 2, she seemed to be doing well. Not long afterward, while business required Brad to leave town for a few days, Elder and Sister Nelson stayed with Emily to help cook and care for the children.[24] A few days later, when she and her sister Marjorie spontaneously stopped by their parents' home with their respective flocks in tow, Emily seemed to be her old self again.

In mid-September, Dantzel tolerated her fourth chemotherapeutic infusion, and by mid-November, when she completed her sixth treatment, she seemed to be doing well.[25] Russell exclaimed in relief, "That's a real milestone to have the course completed."[26]

On November 22, 1994, three years and two months after Emily was diagnosed with cancer, she, Brad, and Elder Nelson met with Dr. William Reilly, who disclosed the unwelcome news that she needed additional chemotherapy. Emily agreed on the spot to resume treatment. Elder Nelson reflected pensively, "What a great team they were—she was so courageous and Brad was so supportive, and we love them both more than words can express."[27]

Brad's job again called him out of town, so on December 3, Russell and Dantzel went to the Wittwer home to help Emily care for the children. Grandfather Nelson took the three little boys for haircuts and helped with shopping and other errands while Grandmother presided over the kitchen. That evening, Emily joined her parents at a concert of *Viva Voce!*—a choral group in which Emily and her sisters Laurie and Sylvia sang.[28]

Three days after Christmas, Dr. Reilly performed a bone-marrow biopsy on Dantzel to determine the effectiveness of her six-month regimen of chemotherapy. On December 30, the Nelsons received a belated Christmas gift. Dr. Reilly informed Dantzel and Russell that her bone-marrow biopsy was "perfectly normal" and that she was in complete remission.[29]

The good news about Dantzel filled the beginning of 1995 with hope for more miracles. On Sunday, January 8, President Howard W. Hunter dedicated the Bountiful Utah Temple, the forty-seventh functioning temple of the Church. That evening, Elder and Sister Nelson drove with Beverly and Pierce Campbell; Angela McKellar; Marjorie and Brad Helsten; and Emily and Brad Wittwer to Brigham Young University, where Elder Nelson spoke to sixteen thousand youth on "A More Excellent Hope." The program was transmitted by satellite from the Marriott Center to stake centers throughout North America.[30]

The next Sunday was Emily's thirty-seventh birthday, and Russell and Dantzel's thoughts were with their daughter as they participated in a regional conference in Matamoros, Mexico. They conveyed their love and birthday greetings to her by telephone at the conclusion of the day's activities.[31]

Despite the family's hopes and prayers, it became more and more evident that Emily's days in mortality were numbered. On January 27, Elder Nelson recorded in his journal: "While Mother was tending baby Jordan in the adjoining room, Brad and I had an incredible experience with Emily. We were speaking to her about the temple. She had mentioned how grateful she was for her temple endowment and sealing that would perpetuate her family forever. Then she asked the question, 'Do you see Nana and Popsy?'"

Nana and Popsy were family names of endearment for Elder Nelson's deceased parents.

"I replied, 'No, Emily, but I am sure that when the time comes they will be there to greet you and care for you.'

"She mentioned Nana and Popsy again. Then she asked another question: 'Daddy, am I dying now?'

"I said, 'I don't think so sweetheart. You are with Brad and me.'

"She resumed our conversation: 'Now we were speaking about the temple, weren't we?' She threw her arms around my neck, gave me a kiss, and said, 'Daddy, thank-you, thank-you! Thank-you for that great blessing'—referring to the temple."

This was Elder Nelson's last conversation with Emily. He then went into baby Jordan's room, where Dantzel was reading to him. He told her of the sublime experience he and Brad had just had conversing with Emily. Dantzel replied, "I knew you would have a better conversation with Emily if I were in here tending Jordan." Elder Nelson remarked, "That's the kind of a selfless and magnificent person I married."[32]

Emily passed away two days later, on Sunday, January 29, at about 2 A.M. The exact time is uncertain because she literally slept away. As soon as Brad notified the Nelsons, they went to his side. A great outpouring of support followed from all members of the family, including Rosalie, Michael, and their children, who arrived from their home in Texas.[33]

The next evening had been scheduled for the monthly family birthday party but, Elder Nelson observed, "We weren't in much of a festive mood, but we surely were in a cohesive mood. I hope those whose birthdays we commemorated didn't feel too slighted."[34]

On Tuesday, six of the Nelson daughters helped dress Emily in her burial clothes while the other two daughters helped Brad buy new clothing for her little boys so they could look appropriate for the important times ahead. That evening, family and friends called at the mortuary to express heartfelt condolences. The Wittwers and Nelsons were deeply touched and comforted by the great outpouring of love expressed by so many. Among other tributes, Wendy praised Emily in prose that she shared at a family gathering just prior to Emily's funeral:

A Tribute to Our Beautiful Sister
When we look at a yellow rose we see Emily
Beautiful, bright, warm and happy.
Emily delighted in so many small things
Like the beauty of a rose.
We delight in so many beautiful memories of our sweet
    and gentle and sensitive sister.
We love her laugh, we love her beauty, we love her advice,
    we love her willingness to let us all in and be a part of
    her.
We love her husband and his family, we love her children,
    we love her friends and her neighbors.
We love her talents, her perfectionist personality. We love
    the wonderful things she made for us and for our fam-
    ilies. We love the delicious food she made. We love her
    gorgeous clothes. We love her regalness. We love singing
    with her and listening to her beautiful voice. We just

love being with her and doing things with her. We
love the way she looks like our angel mother.
We shall miss her dearly. Our hearts are truly broken. We
know that she was prepared to meet our Savior Jesus
Christ, and we know that His arms were outstretched
to her and she is safe within His arms and is feeling
much better now.
And so, we will always love and cherish our beautiful
Emily. Our prayer is that we can be in tune to know
how to help her and her wonderful family . . . and
that we can prepare ourselves to be with her again
very, very soon.
We love you our sweet sister Emily.[35]

Emily's funeral began at noon on Wednesday, February 1, 1995. Seated on the stand at the Murray South Stake Center were President Gordon B. Hinckley and President Thomas S. Monson, then counselors in the First Presidency. President Hunter was not well, but he extended both written and verbal expressions of love and sympathy. Also on the stand were all of the Twelve Apostles, the seven presidents of the Seventy, most of the locally available members of the Seventy, and the Presiding Bishopric. The Nelsons and Wittwers were deeply moved by the visible expression of support from the Brethren. They were also comforted by the hundreds of cards, letters, and other tangible expressions of support from friends and relatives. Elder Nelson observed, "The goodness of people who wanted to lighten our load and to lift us with their love really did have an encouraging influence."[36]

Marion S. Wittwer, Brad's father, offered the family prayer preceding the funeral, and Elder Joseph B. Wirthlin pronounced the invocation on the service.[37] Emily's close friend Sharon M. Westover then gave a sensitive tribute, recalling the times when tenderhearted Emily would call her to say, "I've been invited to sing in Church."

Then, because Emily found it difficult to sing without crying, she would ask Sharon, "Would you be willing to sing a *solo* with me?"

Elder Nelson paid a tender tribute to his precious daughter, who had fought so valiantly for so long to stay a little longer with those she loved. President Monson and President Hinckley then spoke, extending great sympathy and hope, not only to the Nelson and Wittwer families but also to all in attendance who may have wondered how a loving Father in Heaven could have allowed such a young mother to be plucked from her family at such a seemingly inopportune time. President Monson testified of the Savior's peace, "which passeth all understanding" (Philippians 4:7), and President Hinckley concluded with a powerful testimony of the Resurrection and the promised blessings of the temple. Elder James E. Faust then offered the benediction, imploring the Lord to bless all of Emily's loved ones with His comfort.

The congregation arose, and the organist began to play a reverential recessional. As the pallbearers transported Emily's casket toward the door, Elder Nelson gently scooped up two little motherless boys. Those in attendance thought their hearts would break, but the testimony of the speakers rang true. The Resurrection *is* a reality, and temple ordinances *do* seal families together for eternity. That was the family's assurance as Russell M. Nelson Jr. dedicated his sister's grave.

Brad distinguished himself as he handled the temporary separation from his beloved companion with great dignity, and the Wittwer children—William, Wendy, Nelson, Preston, and Jordan— were eloquent examples of love for their parents, their family, and the Lord. Six-year-old Preston understood quite well the cosmic changes that had occurred. As his Grandfather Nelson was carrying Preston out of the chapel, someone asked how he felt. With unvarnished candor, he replied, "I feel sad, but I understand it's only Mommy's body that has died. Her spirit still lives." He then pointed heavenward and said, "She's with Heavenly Father."

It was extremely difficult for Elder Nelson to lose a devoted daughter in the prime of her life, but it may have been even more difficult for Dantzel. Sensitive to her heartache and pain, Elder Nelson wrote his children, "As the father of the family, I would like to pay special tribute to Mommy. She was a magnificent woman when I married her, but I didn't know how great she was until I saw her handle the vicissitudes of life with such profound faith. She is truly a marvelous mother. I respect her, I honor her, and I love her."[38]

President David O. McKay taught that the most important thing any father can do for his children is to show them he loves their mother. The Nelson children have been taught well.

Shortly after Emily's diagnosis of cancer, and not long before Dantzel's illness was discovered, Elder Nelson was prompted to speak in general conference about "Doors of Death." His words would soon prove to be a source of comfort to his family and a source of reassurance to himself:

"Irrespective of age, we mourn for those loved and lost. Mourning is one of the deepest expressions of pure love. It is a natural response in complete accord with divine commandment: 'Thou shalt live together in love, insomuch that thou shalt weep for the loss of them that die' (D&C 42:45).

"The only way to take sorrow out of death is to take love out of life.

"When our turn comes to pass through the doors of death, we can say as did Paul: 'The time of my departure is at hand. I have fought a good fight, I have finished my course, I have kept the faith' (2 Timothy 4:6–7).

"We need not look upon death as an enemy. With full understanding and preparation, faith supplants fear. Hope displaces despair. The Lord said, 'Fear not even unto death; for in this world your joy is not full, but in me your joy is full' (D&C 101:36). He bestowed this gift: 'Peace I leave with you, my peace I give unto you: not as the world giveth, give I unto you. Let not your heart be troubled, neither let it be afraid' (John 14:27).

"As a special witness of Jesus Christ, I testify that He lives! I also

testify that the veil of death is very
thin. I know by experiences too
sacred to relate that those who
have gone before are not strangers
to leaders of this Church. To us
and to you, our loved ones may be
just as close as the next room—
separated only by the doors of
death.

"With that assurance, brothers
and sisters, love life! Cherish each
moment as a blessing from God
(see Mosiah 2:21). Live it well—
even to your loftiest potential.
Then the anticipation of death
shall not hold you hostage."[39]

After Dantzel underwent chemo-
therapy, her beautiful brunette hair
returned in a cumulous coiffure.

After Dantzel had laid Emily
to rest, she continued her own personal struggle with lymphoma.
Ever since Russell had met her, Dantzel had been a beautiful
brunette, but chemotherapy had robbed her of her raven black hair.
As a result, she wore a wig for many months until her hair grew
back—curly and white.

In May 1995, she went with Russell on an assignment, accompanying President and Sister Monson to a regional conference in
Edmonton, Canada. While they were waiting for their plane, Elder
Nelson excused himself for a few minutes. When he returned to the
boarding area, he walked right past Dantzel without recognizing her.
After fifty years of marriage to a brunette, he had temporarily forgotten that his wife's hair had turned white.[40]

CHAPTER 22

OPENING THE DOORS IN EASTERN EUROPE

FEW TIMES SINCE THE RESTORATION of the Church in 1830 have the doors of so many nations been opened to the preaching of the gospel within such a short period of time as was the case between 1985 and 1991. In the fall of 1978, President Spencer W. Kimball urged every family to pray "that the doors of the nations might be opened to us."[1]

Just as the Lord's Spirit moved upon the ancient Persian kings Cyrus, Darius, and Artaxerxes to allow the captive Israelites to return to Jerusalem to rebuild their temple (Ezra 6:14), so the Lord's Spirit also moved upon various government leaders throughout Eastern Europe. Almost imperceptibly, their hearts were softened toward the Church in preparation for the spreading of the gospel on a grand geographical scale.

In 1985, Elder Nelson was assigned as first contact of the Twelve for Europe and Africa. Elder Hans B. Ringger was simultaneously given the assignment in the Europe Area Presidency to be first contact for the Eastern European countries in which he had previously served for several years as a regional representative. Elders Nelson and Ringger began an important dual ministry—combining their faith, prayers, and service with that of the Saints throughout the world in calling down the powers of heaven to open the nations of Eastern Europe to the preaching of the gospel.

Elder Ringger received university degrees in both engineering and architecture and had been the head of a large architectural firm in Basel, Switzerland, while also serving for many years as a colonel in the Swiss army. As he and Elder Nelson would meet with the officials of various Eastern European communist governments, Elder Nelson, well known as a pioneering American heart surgeon, presented the personable, dignified, diplomatic face of the Church. Meanwhile, Elder Ringger's passport from a neutral country and his incisive, businesslike demeanor served him well as he candidly informed government officials that the Church is not just an American Church but one of worldwide significance, and it would be well for them to sit up and take notice. With their unique backgrounds and personalities, Elders Nelson and Ringger formed a formidable companionship that often disarmed the defenses of government officials.

The work of opening the doors to various nations of the world was a marvelous mosaic of circumstances and individuals whose lives intersected at critical times, often dramatically influencing the course of future events. In 1977, while Brother M. Dale Ensign was serving as the Church's director of public affairs on the East Coast, he invited Sister Beverly Campbell to become his associate. Sister Campbell had her own public relations consulting firm and had established several key contacts within the Washington, D.C., area. She was very skillful at establishing new relationships with members of the international business and political community.[2]

In 1996, Elder Nelson began working closely with Sister Campbell, who had become the director of the Church's newly established International Affairs Office. Sister Campbell recalled: "From the time Elder Nelson received the assignment to open the doors to the Iron Curtain countries, he aggressively pursued every avenue in that regard. He was willing to go anywhere and meet anytime, at any inconvenience or danger to himself. I came to know a man whose judgment was so keen and whose ability to make correct decisions so uncanny, that there was no other explanation than that he had been chosen before the worlds were to be the Lord's servant in these countries for just 'such a time as this'" (Esther 4:14).[3]

President James E. Faust heartily concurred with Sister Campbell's assessment of Elder Nelson's abilities. "Russell M. Nelson has an exceptional intuitive gift for knowing what to do and say with people in different cultures," he said. "He is a natural diplomat."[4]

Before the collapse of communism in Eastern Europe, "Openings and opportunities were mercurial and fleeting," Sister Campbell recalled. "Access to people came to my attention in such unusual ways that I recognized I was seeing the Lord micromanaging His Church on a daily basis. Timing was everything. I observed Elder Nelson's spiritual attributes, and also his surgeon's training in clearly assessing the situation and courageously making cutting decisions, then moving for closure."[5]

In countless instances, Elder Nelson could identify with Nephi of old: "And I was led by the Spirit, *not knowing beforehand the things which I should do*" (1 Nephi 4:6; emphasis added).

CHAPTER 23

EXPANDING THE WORK IN POLAND, CZECHOSLOVAKIA, AND EAST GERMANY

POLAND

OF ALL THE EASTERN EUROPEAN countries that became part of the Soviet Bloc following World War II, Poland was the most successful in maintaining a high degree of public religious worship. The Polish government also often showed a friendly face toward America, and Brother David M. Kennedy, former U.S. secretary of the treasury, was instrumental in cultivating positive relations between the Church and the Polish government.

In the summer of 1977, President Spencer W. Kimball visited Poland, and in the quietude of beautiful Ogrod Saski Park in Warsaw on August 24, he dedicated the land for the preaching of the gospel.[1]

Various missionary couples were subsequently called to serve missions in Poland, but only one couple was allowed in the entire country at a given time. These successive couples courageously cultivated good relationships and won the trust of the government. At the end of May 1986, President Thomas S. Monson, Elder Nelson, and Elder Hans B. Ringger met with various Polish government officials to request permission for additional senior missionary couples to serve in Poland. They also requested permission to acquire property for a chapel. Thanks to the trust generated over the years, both requests were granted.[2]

Three years later, on June 15, 1989, Elder Nelson presided at the groundbreaking service for a new chapel in Warsaw.³ The following year, on July 1, 1990, the Poland Warsaw Mission was established.⁴ One year later, while accompanying the Mormon Tabernacle Choir on its European tour, Elder Nelson dedicated the beautiful, newly constructed chapel in Wola, a district of Warsaw. The chapel, with its gleaming copper roof, is located by a large park with a beautiful tree-lined western border readily visible from a major thoroughfare. With the chapel's completion, it became evident to all that the Church had come to Poland to stay.

CZECHOSLOVAKIA

In January 1986, Elder Nelson expanded his linguistic repertoire when Olga Miller, a resident of Salt Lake City who was born in Czechoslovakia, began tutoring him in the Czech language.⁵ The last weekend of that month, he was able to practice his newly acquired linguistic skills as he and Elder Hans B. Ringger met with a band of thirty Saints in Prague one day and with thirty-five more the following day in Brno. Some of these faithful Czech members had joined the Church before World War II and had remained true to the faith during the Nazi occupation of 1938–45 and the subsequent communist suppression of religious activity following the war.⁶

The person overseeing religious activities within each of the respective Eastern European countries was a communist party official known as the minister of religion. He determined which churches to recognize as legitimate religious organizations, and his approval of religious activities was often arbitrary, having more to do with monitoring religions than with fostering religious worship. Nonetheless, contact with the minister of religion was essential.

Sister Beverly Campbell had developed a relationship with an organization known as the Appeal of Conscience Foundation and with its founder and head, Rabbi Arthur Schneier. When leaders from Eastern European countries were in New York, Rabbi Schneier would invite Sister Campbell to meet with them.[7] In June 1987, he invited her to his study in New York City, where he was hosting Miroslav Houstecky, the Czechoslovak Soviet Socialist Republic's (CSSR) ambassador to Washington, D.C. At the end of the evening, Sister Campbell invited the ambassador to be a guest of the LDS Church in Washington, D.C., where he could meet Elder Nelson and other Church members who were business, civic, and political leaders. Ambassador Houstecky commented on his attraction to "that beautiful building on the D.C. beltway" (the Washington D.C. Temple), and he accepted the invitation.[8]

On the evening of August 4, 1987, Elder and Sister Nelson traveled to Washington, D.C., where they greeted Ambassador Houstecky and his wife, Maria, at the home of Pierce and Beverly Campbell. Following dinner, Elder Nelson and the ambassador retired to the Campbells' library. There, with great clarity and spirit, Elder Nelson presented the Church's desire to openly practice and share its faith in Czechoslovakia. Ambassador Houstecky agreed to lend his best efforts in arranging a future meeting with the Czech minister of religious affairs in Prague.[9]

Five weeks later, Elder Nelson and Elder Ringger traveled to Prague to meet with Vladimir Jankŏ, vice minister and director of the secretariat for church affairs in the CSSR. He was well educated and had a fair command of English. Following their meeting, Elders Nelson and Ringger met with Brother Jiři Šnederfler, the faithful district president who had provided courageous leadership for Church members in the Czechoslovak Soviet Socialist Republic during difficult times.[10]

In December 1987, Elder and Sister Nelson traveled to Washington, D.C., to attend a dinner at the home of Ambassador and Mrs. Houstecky. The Nelsons presented them with an elegant statuette to commemorate their growing friendship.[11] Although it was winter in Washington, one could sense the warming of spring in Czechoslovakia.

Ten months later, Elder Nelson and Elder Ringger traveled to Czechoslovakia to meet again with President Šnederfler and his wife, Olga. After dinner, they planned their strategy for an important meeting scheduled for the next day. Then they offered a special prayer, pleading for the Lord to bless their efforts. The next morning, Elder Nelson, Elder Ringger, and President Šnederfler met with Zdanek Kestl, secretary for religious affairs in the CSSR. The brethren gave him a copy of the Book of Mormon and other supporting materials that had been translated into the Czech language for the review of government officials.[12]

In February 1989, Elder Nelson joined Beverly Campbell at a breakfast in the Czechoslovakian Embassy hosted by Ambassador and Mrs. Houstecky. The spirit of the occasion reflected a growing trust between the ambassador and Elder Nelson and the Church he represented.[13]

Four months later, armed with faith and optimism, Elder Nelson and Elder Ringger again traveled to Czechoslovakia, where, on June 14, they met with the government officials to whom they had previously submitted formal requests for legal recognition of the Church in the CSSR. They were disappointed when the officials informed them that considerable time and study must yet transpire before a definitive response would be made by the government. Nevertheless, it was a productive meeting, and Elder Nelson concluded, "We felt that with the faith and prayers of the members combined with our persistent efforts, our request would ultimately be received in a favorable fashion."[14]

Just two months after the fall of the Berlin Wall and the subsequent shockwave that reverberated throughout the Eastern Bloc countries, Elder Nelson received a telephone call on January 8, 1990, from Ambassador Houstecky. He had been successful in arranging meetings with high-level government officials, and he informed Elder Nelson of another important meeting soon to be held in Prague.[15]

Less than a month later, on February 6, Elder Nelson, Elder

Ringger, and President Šnederfler met with Josef Hromadka, the new deputy prime minister of the Republic of Czechoslovakia. Recalling this significant meeting, Elder Nelson said, "They assured us of freedom of religion and gave us an affirmative response to our pleas for recognition of the Church! They indicated that the formal papers would be signed before the month was over. You can understand how welcome that news was when you remember that we had been going there at least once a year for the last four years only to be politely 'put on hold.'"[16]

Elder Nelson said, "We were so thrilled with this news that we and seven other Czech Saints went to Karlstein to offer an apostolic prayer of gratitude. This is the site where Elder John A. Widstoe dedicated this beautiful country July 24, 1929. For the past forty years the members had not been privileged to worship openly in full dignity, nor had they had the blessings of full-time missionaries, with only limited access to a mission president in Vienna. The termination of these restrictions was a thrill beyond description. For forty years the ancient children of Israel wandered in the wilderness, and the faithful Czech Saints had endured privations of a similar duration."[17]

That evening, Elder Ringger and Elder Nelson took a walk in downtown Prague to Wenceslas Square, where they had walked on many previous occasions. "On every other visit to Prague," Elder Nelson recalled, "there had been practically no one on the streets at night. One's voice would echo across the empty square. But on this evening the place was teeming with people who were laughing and openly conversing one with another. Others were in a more serious frame of mind. Many candles were burning on a growing mountain of wax from the melting of previous candles. Former heroes' pictures were portrayed, wreaths were strategically placed, and flowers were laid in remembrance of the sufferings of the past."[18]

Elder Nelson observed, "The people of Czechoslovakia accomplished a bloodless revolution. Earlier in the day we asked Dr. Hromadka what we, as a Church, could do to be of assistance. His

*Elder Nelson
with Brother Jiří
Šnederfler and Sister
Olga Šnederfler,
faithful pioneers in
Czechoslovakia.*

response was inspiring: 'We don't need material goods or technology; we need a new spirit, we need moral values. We need the Judeo-
Christian ethic back in our curriculum. Please help us to make this
a time of spiritual renewal for our nation!' This, we assured him, we
would strive to do."[19]

On February 22, 1990, Elder Nelson received an early morning
phone call from Elder Ringger announcing that the papers for recognition of the Church in Czechoslovakia had been officially signed
the day before. With unbridled delight, Elder Nelson said,
"Hallelujah! That marked the successful completion of a goal that
we had pursued for several years. What a blessing for that country!
In the temple, the First Presidency and the Twelve were thrilled to
receive that welcome news."[20]

Elder Nelson added: "When that important declaration was
made, I sensed that the real hero in this story was our district president in Czechoslovakia, Jiří Šnederfler, sustained by his dear wife,
Olga. Some two and one-half years earlier, Elder Ringger and I had
learned that recognition could be formally requested only by a
Czechoslovakian member of the Church. So we went to the home of
Brother and Sister Šnederfler. We explained that we had just received

that information from the chairman of the Council of Religious Affairs. Knowing that other Czechoslovakian leaders and thinkers had been imprisoned or put to death for religious or dissident belief, we told Brother Šnederfler that we, as his Church leaders, could not and would not make that request of him. After contemplating only a brief moment, Brother Šnederfler humbly said, 'I will go! I will do it!' As he spoke, his wife, Olga, shed a tear. They embraced and said, 'We will do whatever is needed. This is for the Lord, and His work is more important than our freedom or life.'"[21]

On June 8, 1990, Elder Nelson assisted President Monson in setting apart Richard W. Winder to preside over the Czechoslovakia Prague Mission, beginning July 1.[22] Brother Winder had a great love for the Czech people, having served a mission in Czechoslovakia as a young man from 1948 to 1950, when all missionaries were expelled by the Czech government. Sister Barbara Winder was set apart as his companion, necessitating her release as the general president of the Relief Society.

In conjunction with the Washington, D.C., stake conference commemorating the fiftieth anniversary of its creation, President J. Willard Marriott Jr. hosted a dinner on June 23 for Elder Nelson and several Eastern European ambassadors and other political leaders, including Miloslav Chrobok from Czechoslovakia.[23] The procedure of first becoming acquainted with representatives of Eastern European nations in Washington, D.C., and subsequently meeting their compatriots on the other side of the Atlantic had not only helped build bridges but also established trusting relationships that opened doors to the nations.

EAST GERMANY

Another key nation in initiating the domino decline of communist governments in Eastern Europe was the German Democratic Republic (GDR). During his nearly twenty-year assignment as first contact for Europe, Elder Thomas S. Monson exerted a great apostolic influence upon the Saints and government officials in the GDR. He humbly acknowledges that his ministry in the GDR was built upon the solid foundation of his apostolic predecessors, including Elder Ezra Taft Benson who, following World War II, was assigned by President George Albert Smith to go to Europe to facilitate humanitarian assistance to those needy countries.[24]

Full-time missionaries had been withdrawn from Germany in 1939 before the outbreak of World War II, but at the end of the war a number of local brethren began serving full-time missions within the GDR. However, by 1949, no more full-time missionaries from America were permitted to labor in the GDR, and a decade later, no more locally called missionaries were permitted to proselyte either.[25]

In 1968, Elder Monson made his first visit to the German Democratic Republic. As he met with the Saints in Görlitz, he promised them, "If you will remain true and faithful to the commandments of God, every blessing any member of the Church enjoys in any other country will be yours." In subsequent years a patriarch was called even before the nation's first stakes were organized, in Freiberg in 1982 and in Leipzig in 1984. In June 1985, the Freiberg Germany Temple was dedicated. The only remaining blessing denied the Saints in the GDR was the privilege of sending their youth on missions and receiving missionaries from other countries.[26]

Twenty years after President Monson's first visit to the GDR, he, Elders Nelson and Ringger, stake presidents Frank Appel and Manfred Schütze, and temple president Henry Burkhart met with Erich Honecker, chairman of the State Council of the GDR. On October 28, 1988, the LDS delegation was ushered into a room amidst the glaring lights of television cameras and the flashing cameras of news reporters. At the conclusion of the photo session, the brethren were seated around a large table with representatives of the GDR. Elder Nelson recalled, "They were most cordial to us."[27]

The brethren presented Chairman Honecker with a miniature statue titled "First Steps," depicting a young child walking from her mother to the outstretched arms of her father. After they emphasized the great importance the Church places on the family, Chairman Honecker invited them to make their desires known. President Monson indicated the need for full-time missionaries to be sent to and from the German Democratic Republic. After responding with a thirty-minute description of the progress of the GDR under his administration, Mr. Honecker replied, "President Monson, we know you. We trust you. We have had experience with you. Your request for missionaries is approved." Approval was also given for ten young men to be called from the GDR to serve missions outside their country.[28] Six months later, on March 30, 1989, full-time missionaries from outside Germany entered the GDR for the first time in fifty years.

On November 9, 1989, a Welfare Services Executive Committee meeting at Church headquarters was interrupted with the announcement that the German Democratic Republic had officially opened its borders for residents of the GDR to leave and return from that country without restrictions. The Berlin Wall came down, and Eastern Europe would never be the same again.[29]

Eleven months later, on October 21, 1990, President Monson, Elder Ringger, and Elder Nelson addressed 150 missionaries at the Tiergarten chapel in Berlin. Missionaries who had previously been serving in Berlin were assigned to the Germany Hamburg Mission, presided over by President Robert Peterson. With the unification of East Germany and West Germany, missionaries outside of Berlin were transferred to the newly named Germany Dresden Mission, led by President Wolfgang Paul.

"We could hardly contain our emotions as we recalled that only eighteen months previously, on March 30, 1989, the first group of fourteen missionaries entered the German Democratic Republic with President Paul, and now there are 150 missionaries there with complete freedom to proselyte," Elder Nelson said.[30]

The Brethren then proceeded to the Berlin International Convention Center, which was filled with 2,438 Saints. Elder Ringger represented the General Authorities in realigning stake boundaries, made possible by the crumbling of the Berlin Wall, which had previously circumscribed the entire Berlin Germany Stake.

Following this spiritual regional conference, President Monson, Elder Nelson, and Elder Ringger set apart the new stake presidencies and a newly sustained patriarch. "Then," Elder Nelson recalled, "as a complete surprise, President Monson called me forward to give me a special priesthood blessing in connection with the assignment I had been given to represent the Church in a meeting with the Internal Revenue Service in Washington, D.C., on October 23. We were absolutely astounded that, with all on his mind, he would remember my forthcoming assignment, and that he had been impressed to bestow such a blessing. What a marvelous and inspired leader he is!"[31]

It then came time to bid farewell to Elder and Sister Ringger, who were to return to their home in Switzerland while the Nelsons returned home via Frankfurt and Washington, D.C. "This separation was so tender after our being close partners for five years in my first contact responsibilities for Europe," Elder Nelson said. "Elder Ringger deserves great credit for all that has transpired during our service together."[32]

Elder Nelson had been given a new assignment as first contact of the Twelve to the Pacific Islands, and Elder Dallin H. Oaks would assume first contact responsibilities for Europe. Elder Nelson and Elder Ringger would no longer make weekly phone calls, but they would share sweet memories of intense meetings with government officials and of roller-coaster emotions as they traveled together from country to country. They had missed flight connections, arrived at the wrong hotel, and walked the streets of foreign lands through hail, sleet, and snow. They had been together as Elder Nelson dedicated Hungary, Romania, Bulgaria, and Estonia, and rededicated Russia and Czechoslovakia. They had stood together on many occasions to set apart priesthood leaders to various callings in the kingdom, and they had frequently knelt together, pleading with the Lord for guidance and for the softening of hearts and expressing their gratitude for the opening of doors.

CHAPTER 24

MELTING ICICLES IN
HUNGARY AND YUGOSLAVIA

HUNGARY

IN THE FALL OF 1984, HUNGARIAN National Television sent a film crew to Salt Lake City to spend a month filming a documentary about Latter-day Saints in Utah. Crew members attended sacrament meetings and family home evenings, and they interviewed dozens of individuals from all walks of life and of varying degrees of commitment to the Church. They then returned to Hungary to edit their film and to work on a four-part television miniseries about the Church.[1] The programs were broadcast in November and December 1985.

At the beginning of 1986, the mission home in Vienna, Austria, began receiving dozens of requests for more information about the Church from Hungarians who had seen the TV programs. Inasmuch as no full-time missionaries were then laboring in Hungary, Spencer J. Condie, president of the Austria Vienna Mission, and Brother Karl Trinkl, a native Hungarian living in Vienna, began visiting Hungary to teach the gospel to as many people as possible. Three of the first six Hungarians to join the Church were physicians.

Over the years, the Church had called a few senior missionary couples to establish a presence in Hungary and to visit the few scattered members who had joined the Church in other countries but had then returned to their native homeland. Open proselyting, however, had been out of the question. Baptism was against the law in Hungary, so those who were taught and converted had to obtain visas to visit Vienna, where they were baptized.

On Easter Sunday 1987, Elders Nelson and Hans B. Ringger drove to Budapest with the president of the Austria Vienna Mission. Shortly after arriving, they assembled a small group of Saints on Mount Gellert, a popular picnic spot overlooking the beautiful Danube River. As the descending sun set the clouds ablaze with a glorious amber flame, the picnickers suddenly left, leaving the small group of Latter-day Saints alone.[2] In that beautiful park high on a mountain top, Elder Nelson pronounced an eloquent dedicatory prayer filled with faith and hope for the future of Hungary and its marvelous people and a fervent plea that the Lord would prosper His work in the land.

Two days later, on April 21, Elder Nelson and Elder Ringger met with Dr. Imre Miklos, head of the State Office for Religious Affairs for all of Hungary, and some of his associates. Assisting with interpretation was Miklos Radvanyi, a member of the Church on the staff of the Library of Congress in Washington, D.C.[3] As the meeting drew on, the tension mounted. When it became clear that the cool Hungarian officials saw little utility in meeting with the Church leaders, Elder Nelson felt a sudden spiritual prompting. He looked directly into the eyes of the jaded officials and, with no small risk, quietly stated: "Late Sunday afternoon I went to Mount Gellert, and there I prayed fervently that the Lord's Spirit would be poured out upon this beautiful land, its people, and their leaders, that they would prosper, that families would be happy and strong, and that peace would prevail in this nation. I wanted you to hear of this directly from me rather than indirectly from someone else."

Elder Nelson's remarks touched the officials, who suddenly grew quiet and teary eyed. After a few moments, Dr. Miklos broke the silence, indicating that he and his colleagues would be pleased to cooperate in establishing a Church presence in Hungary.[4] The brethren in the room never doubted the Lord's declaration that His Twelve "shall have power to open the door of my kingdom unto any nation whithersoever ye shall send them" (D&C 112:21; 107:35; 124:128).

Afterward, Dr. Miklos presented Elder Nelson with a book of the beautiful art treasures of Hungary, and Elders Nelson and Ringger were given a tour of the magnificent parliament building, one of the architectural splendors of modern Europe. They then parted company from their Hungarian hosts, anticipating pleasant meetings in the future.

Six months later, on October 12, Elder Nelson hosted a luncheon at the Washington D.C. Temple Visitors' Center in honor of Imre Miklos, his wife, and a delegation of other government officials from Budapest. The setting could not have been better for generating a favorable impression of the Church among all the Hungarian guests.[5] Congressman Tom Lantos of California extended great support in solidifying relationships with Hungary. As a native Hungarian whose wife had joined the Church, Congressman Lantos had a strong desire to see religious freedom extended in Hungary.

In the summer of 1988, Elders Nelson and Ringger returned to Budapest to meet with various government officials. A historic moment arrived at noon on June 24 when Dr. Imre Miklos and other distinguished government officials granted legal recognition to The Church of Jesus Christ of Latter-day Saints in Hungary.[6]

In mid-October 1989, President and Sister Thomas S. Monson and Elder and Sister Nelson attended a seminar for European mission presidents in Budapest, and on October 16, President Monson dedicated the first chapel in Budapest, a large renovated house. Following the dedicatory services, Elder Nelson, joined by a young missionary, Elder Trevor Andreason, granted a television interview. Elder Nelson observed, "The Hungarians were deeply moved when I told them that two and one-half years ago I had offered a prayer of dedication on the country and its people. They immediately

correlated the marvelous changes that had happened in their country with that point in time."[7]

The next day the Hungarian Parliament ratified amendments to
the nation's constitution, making provisions for free elections and
freedom of religious worship, and changing the country's name to
the Republic of Hungary.[8] Elder Nelson recalled the words of the
dedicatory prayer he had offered April 19, 1987: "I invoke an apostolic blessing that this may be the dawning of a new era. . . . May
no unhallowed hand bear sway to hinder the onrolling of Thy work
among Thy people here who hunger and thirst for the truths of the
restored gospel."[9]

The Hungary Budapest Mission was created in June 1990 with
James Wilde as its first president. Today there are more than three
thousand Latter-day Saints and two dozen branches of the Church
in Hungary.[10]

YUGOSLAVIA

In 1969, a tall, lanky Yugoslavian basketball player named
Krešimir Ćosić arrived on the campus of Brigham Young University.
More than three hundred American universities sponsor major bas-
ketball programs, but this young Croatian atheist chose to attend
Brigham Young University. Surrounded by supportive coaches and
athletic department staff, Krešimir warmed to his new environs.
Professors Truman G. and Ann Madsen, professor Hugh Nibley and
his wife, Phyllis, and professor Richard Anderson and his wife,
Carma, took "Kreso" and some of his fellow Yugoslavian students
under their mentoring wings in a manner described by Robert
Browning:

> Were I elect like you,
> I would encircle me with love, and raise
> A rampart of my fellows; it should seem
> Impossible for me to fail, so watched
> By gentle friends who make my cause their own.[11]

Krešimir bedazzled the BYU Cougar fans with his enthusiastic style of basketball, dribbling like a guard, crashing the boards like a power forward, and shooting from anywhere on the court. His coach, the late Stan Watts, said of the Marriott Center, "They say that I built it, Willard Marriott paid for it, and Krešimir Ćosić filled it"—all twenty thousand seats for every game. In 1971, Krešimir was baptized a member of the Church, and in 1973, he declined lucrative offers from the NBA, choosing instead to return to his native Croatia, where he became a player-coach in Zadar and later the coach of the national team. Everyone in the country knew Krešimir Ćosić, and nearly everyone knew he had joined an "American church" while living abroad.

Krešimir was not only a folk hero but also an extremely bold missionary, sharing the gospel with all of his friends. Within a short time, a few enclaves of faithful Saints could be found in various cities. By 1984, there was a small branch in the Serbian capital of Beograd and small branches in Zadar and Zagreb, the capital of Croatia. Senior missionary couples worked in Beograd and Zagreb, but their involvement was primarily confined to shepherding the members.

On October 31, 1985, Elder Thomas S. Monson met with the Yugoslavian Saints, who had been invited from all over the country to a special meeting in a large apartment building in downtown Zagreb that had been renovated into a chapel. That evening, after dedicating the new chapel, Elder Monson asked that the windows be opened as he dedicated the land of Yugoslavia for the preaching of the gospel. Krešimir Ćosić, the district president, served as his interpreter.[12]

Elder Nelson's first apostolic visit to Yugoslavia came in mid-April 1987. In the company of Elder Ringger and the Austria Vienna Mission president, Elder Nelson traveled to Zagreb to meet with Brother Ćosić and Ivan Valek, Zagreb branch president. Brother Ćosić had made arrangements for Elder Nelson to meet with key government officials in both Croatia and Serbia to discuss the possibility of broadening the scope of the Church's activities in Yugoslavia.[13]

The next day, the brethren drove to Beograd, Yugoslavia' s capital, and met with Radovan Samardžić, the nation's minister of religious affairs. Elder Nelson gave him a brief presentation about the Church and its people, including data on the healthy lifestyle of Church members.[14]

Elder Nelson then broached several issues that concerned the Church, including expansion of its missionary force, renewal of visas, purchase of buildings and property (for chapels), and limitations on holding meetings. Minister Samardžić said officials knew something of the Church and of Krešimir's membership in it. He was receptive but insisted that branch meetings be held in buildings with public access rather than in member apartments.[15] At the Church's chapel in Zagreb, government officials would occasionally visit branch meetings. Members, nervous whenever the missionaries referred to "investigators" attending their meetings, assumed that the investigators were government officials.

At the close of their discussion, Elder Nelson presented the minister with a gift, and he reciprocated by giving Elder Nelson a copy of a paperback book he had written. Minister Samardžić then asked Krešimir to autograph a piece of paper that he could take home to his young son, who idolized the athlete.

The mission president had arranged for the Church's local legal counsel, a young woman lawyer, to assist the visiting Church leaders in procuring a suitable building for meetings. When the mission president had called her the previous evening to confirm the appointment with Elders Nelson and Ringger the following day, she sounded somewhat inebriated on the telephone. With unsteady speech, she explained that she had lost two court cases that week and was feeling a little down. "I will meet you tomorrow," she slurred. "Long live Serbia!" When the Brethren met with her the next morning, they noticed that she had obviously applied her makeup with an unsteady hand. Nevertheless, they forged ahead with their search.

The lawyer had, indeed, done her homework, and the Brethren were pleased with some of the alternatives she showed them, especially a substantial three-story house constructed of granite and located in a good neighborhood close to several embassies. Following the search, the mission president apologized profusely to Elder Nelson for having retained a lawyer who was given to drink. Elder Nelson placed his hand on the young mission president's shoulder and said, "Just look at her situation. Here she is, unmarried, living alone, and trying her best to compete in a male-dominated society in a male-dominated profession. The Savior has a soft spot in His heart for young women like her."

During a fireside that evening in Beograd for members and investigators, Elder Nelson again showed compassion when two missionaries struggled unsuccessfully to harmonize while singing a duet.[16] After the elders had sung two verses of the four-verse hymn, Elder Nelson mercifully intervened with a gentle, "Thanks, brethren, I think that will do." All in attendance were grateful to this diplomatic Apostle who saved everyone from embarrassment, including the two elders.

Three years later, Brother and Sister J. Willard Marriott Jr. hosted a dinner in Washington, D.C., for various ambassadors from Eastern Europe, enabling Elder and Sister Nelson to meet Ambassador Dzevad Mujezinovic from Yugoslavia.[17] Shortly after this meeting, Yugoslavia fractured into its component ethnic parts. Fighting between warring ethnic factions during the 1990s halted the Church's budding work. But today, inter-ethnic wounds are beginning to heal, and the Church has resumed its work apace.

CHAPTER 25

THE FORMER SOVIET UNION

FOLLOWING WORLD WAR II, several political leaders and heads of various churches openly condemned communism as an atheistic philosophy that curbed the God-given agency of mankind. Within this context, many individuals living in democratic societies made little distinction between communist leaders and the citizens who were subjected to their repressive rule.

As mentioned previously, during general conference in September 1978, President Spencer W. Kimball proclaimed: "There are many nations where we have not been able to get in, to get visas, or get passports; and it is very important. If we are to fulfill the responsibility given to us by the Lord on the Mount of Olives to go into all the world and preach the gospel to every creature, then we will need to open the doors of these nations.

"I'm hoping that every man and boy listening to me this night will make it a solemn practice in regular life to pray constantly for this great blessing to bless the brethren who are making a special effort to reach the leaders of these nations and to convince them that we have only good for their people. We will make them good citizens, we will make them good souls, and we will make them happy and joyous."[1]

This landmark address required a dramatic change in the thinking of many Latter-day Saints. Into this ecclesiastical cauldron came an Apostle of the Lord who reflected the Lord's counsel to the prophet Samuel of old: "The Lord seeth not as man seeth; for man looketh on the outward appearance, but the Lord looketh on the heart" (1 Samuel 16:7). A man who had looked upon thousands of hearts was called to assist in softening hearts so that the doors of the communist nations, including the Soviet Union, could be opened.

Elder Nelson, through his knowledge of the Russian language, his experiences of sharing his surgical knowledge and skills with Russian physicians, and his love of the Russian people, had become a suitable servant for such a daunting task. Quickened by the Spirit and sustained by the combined prayers of the Saints who followed President Kimball's counsel, he was ably assisted by his faithful associates and a small army of devoted missionaries and inspired mission presidents and their heroic wives. They became instruments in the Lord's hands in softening the hearts of the leaders and in opening the doors of the nations so that empty souls could be filled with the fulness of the gospel.

In early summer 1987, Elder Nelson and Elder Hans B. Ringger traveled to Moscow on a "fact-finding and bridge-building mission."[2] The Brethren had no officially confirmed appointment because their correspondence had gone unanswered, but undaunted they pressed forward with a "brightness of hope" (2 Nephi 32:20). On June 10, as a large communist flag with a hammer and sickle waved briskly over Moscow, Elders Nelson and Ringger sought an audience with the minister of religious affairs.

After waiting much of the day, they were finally given a brief audience with the leaders of the Council of Religious Affairs of the Council of Ministers, including Konstantin Kharchev, chief of the council. Elders Nelson and Ringger asked Mr. Kharchev what the requirements were for a church to gain legal recognition in the Soviet Union. He responded that a minimum of twenty adult Soviet citizens must be willing to sign a document certifying they are members of a given faith. All of these members must live within the same political district, of which there were eleven in Moscow.[3]

The next issue the Brethren raised was the possibility of establishing a small visitors' center or reading room where people could come and read about the Church and learn about the restored gospel. Such an approach had been an effective indirect proselyting method in Warsaw, Poland. Mr. Kharchev curtly responded that no permission would be granted for a reading room until the Church was legally recognized.

Somewhat frustrated, Elder Nelson said, "We have a chicken and egg problem here. You say we can't receive recognition until we have members, but it will be difficult to get any members if we can't have a reading room or visitors' center." Mr. Kharchev responded brusquely, "That is *your* problem. Good day!"[4]

The next day, on a bench outside the Kremlin, Elders Nelson and Ringger prayerfully pondered the challenges that lay before them and explored their available options. Elder Nelson said, somewhat in exasperation, "The bottom line was—we were unable to come up with a plan to meet the requirements for legal recognition."[5]

The Brethren would soon realize, however, the fruition of the Lord's promise that "whithersoever they shall send you, go ye, and I will be with you; and in whatsoever place ye shall proclaim my name an effectual door shall be opened unto you, that they may receive my word" (D&C 112:19). The Brethren had anticipated teaching and baptizing Russians *within* the Soviet Union, but the Lord had alternative plans and His own timetable.

A year later, on July 24, 1988, a Moscow resident named Igor Mikhailusenko was baptized while visiting the United States. A year later, a Russian family from Leningrad—Yuri and Liudmila Terebenin and their teenaged daughter, Anna—were surprised to learn while on vacation in Hungary that some Hungarian friends had recently joined the Church. The Terebenins became interested in the gospel and were subsequently baptized in Budapest on July 1, 1989. Another vacationer from Moscow, Olga Smolianova, was baptized September 23, 1989, while visiting Italy.[6] That same year, Andrei Semionov, from the Russian city of Vyborg near the Finnish

Officials sign a memorandum of agreement related to the construction of a cement plant in Yeravan, Armenia. Seated, left to right: Eduard Asaturovich, Armenian ambassador to the USSR; Hyrair Hovnanian of the Armenian Assembly; Vladimir S. Markariants, prime minister of Armenia; Armand Hammer, Jon M. Huntsman, and Elder Nelson. Standing, left to right: U.S. ambassador Jack Matlock; Liana Dubinin; Levon Sahakian, first deputy prime minister of Armenia; Vasili Kazarian, first secretary of the Armenian Embassy; Yuri Dubinin, Soviet ambassador to the United States; Yuri Christoradnov, chairman of the Council for Religious Affairs; Peter Huntsman, Jennifer Huntsman, and Elder Hans B. Ringger.

border, became acquainted with the Nellie and Aimo Jäkkö family of Finland. Their friendship led to his baptism on February 24, 1990.

These pioneering Russian converts who had been baptized outside of Russia and had then returned home were merely the vanguard of many others yet to come. The Finland Helsinki Mission had sixteen missionaries who had studied Russian at various universities before receiving their mission calls. Mission president Steven R. Mecham received permission from the area presidency to begin having those Russian-speaking missionaries teach the gospel to Russian tourists as they visited Finland.[7]

On August 7, 1989, Elders Nelson and Ringger met at the Heathrow Airport in London, where they were joined by Jon M.

Elder Nelson meeting with Soviet ambassador Yuri Dubinin and his wife, Liana, in December 1989.

Huntsman and his children Peter and Jennifer. All of them were to be guests of Armand Hammer, CEO of Occidental Petroleum, who had invited them to accompany him on his private jet to Russia. The following day, the party met at the office of the Armenian Representation in downtown Moscow. On behalf of the Church, Elder Nelson, Armand Hammer, Jon Huntsman, and the Armenian delegation signed a memorandum of agreement outlining the co-operative construction of a massive building project for homeless victims of the Armenian earthquake on December 7, 1988.[8]

After being with Elder Nelson on this and other occasions, Brother Huntsman observed that he "has a unique gift and talent to put other people at ease." He then added, "I have a great love for him because of his love for other people."[9]

Two months later, while Elder and Sister Nelson were in Washington, D.C., they hosted a luncheon at the Marriott Hotel for Ambassador Dubinin and his wife, Liana.[10] Subsequently, the Church's Washington office of public affairs continued to render yeoman service in arranging frequent contacts between the Brethren and influential government officials from various countries throughout the world.[11]

Dennis B. Neuenschwander, president of the Austria Vienna East Mission, was a former professor of Russian and had worked for many years under the auspices of the Utah Genealogical Society directing the acquisition and filming of genealogical information throughout Europe. He and Brother David Farnsworth, the Church's legal counsel for Europe, were sent to Leningrad in September 1989 to determine how the Church could best meet the needs of an ever-increasing number of Church members who had been baptized abroad and then returned to Russia. During that visit, Brothers Neuenschwander and Farnsworth conferred the Aaronic Priesthood upon Brother Terebenin, who had been baptized in Hungary. Afterward, the three of them visited the Leningrad Council on Religious Affairs, where they were warmly received.[12]

At a seminar for mission presidents held in Budapest, Hungary, in October 1989, Elder Nelson met with President Neuenschwander and with President Steven R. Mecham of the Finland Helsinki Mission. He disclosed that "the First Presidency and Quorum of the Twelve Apostles had decided it was time to take the restored gospel to the peoples of Russia and the Baltic Republics."[13]

A few months later, in April 1990, Elder and Sister Nelson and Elder Ringger traveled to Stockholm, Sweden, where they met President Mecham and his wife, Donna, who were accompanied by Jussi Kemppainen, a Finnish Latter-day Saint. Brother Kemppainen served under President Mecham's direction as president of the Baltic District of the Church, which included Estonia, Latvia, and Lithuania. The five of them took a short flight to Tallinn, Estonia, to participate in a fireside with Saints there.

As they were on their way to the meeting that evening, a television crew stopped them seeking an impromptu interview. It seemed that people living in Eastern Europe were starving for information about religion, which had been denied them for so many years. The recorded interview, later shown on prime-time television, cast the Church in a favorable light.[14] Although only thirty-six Church members lived in Tallinn, about two hundred people attended the fireside, including an interested deputy minister of religion, Ants Liimets.

At 7 A.M. on April 25, 1990, the Church leaders went to a special site known as Laululava. "This is an interesting location, an outdoor amphitheater, where the Estonian people say the soul of their country resides," Elder Nelson said. There, on the brow of a hill overlooking the city of Tallinn, basked in morning sunlight and against the background of the calm, blue Baltic Sea, Elder Nelson dedicated the land of Estonia for the preaching of the gospel. He experienced a feeling of great peace and tranquility as he knelt in prayer and pleaded with the Lord, "Wilt Thou bless the people of this land that as they learn the commandments of God and keep those commandments that they may prosper in the land. . . . May these people become a beacon of faith to this part of the world, that from this point the gospel shall roll forth to the nations to the east, and to the south, and to the neighboring areas beyond."[15] This blessing would prove prophetic in the months ahead.

Later in the morning, the brethren met with Minister Liimets, who was "very cooperative and indicated that he was favorably impressed with the meeting he had attended the night before." The brethren next met with Rein Loik, minister of education, who "was particularly hopeful that we could help them teach about the Lord Jesus Christ in their school curriculum after those doors had been closed for the last half century," Elder Nelson recalled. "We thought how ironic this conversation was in light of the ACLU's objection to prayer at high school commencement exercises in the State of Utah."[16]

Elder Nelson was pleased with the assertive missionary efforts of President Mecham, who had previously asked a taxi driver if he would like to know more about the Church. The driver responded, "No, but my mother would be interested." He was right. The missionaries taught and baptized her, and she was then serving as the branch Relief Society president in Tallin. Her taxi driver son also eventually joined the Church, as did another son and daughter-in-law.[17]

The next morning in Leningrad, the brethren met with Igor M. Vishchepan, representative of the Council for Religious Affairs, and with his associate, Nikolai Kirov. Their discussion about various procedures necessary for the Church to acquire legal recognition required a good deal of time and patience, but the meeting was productive. The brethren warmly parted company and extended an invitation to the officials to attend a fireside that evening. Mr. Kirov indicated that he would attend, which was reassuring because some local Church leaders were anxious about possible police intervention at large public meetings.[18]

In the afternoon, the LDS group retired to the Summer Gardens on the south side of the Neva River just beyond Mars Field in Leningrad. It was here that Elder Francis Marion Lyman had first dedicated the land of Russia on August 6, 1903. The Summer Gardens had been closed for maintenance work, but after prayers and persuasion, the brethren and Sisters Nelson and Mecham successfully prevailed upon the guards at the gate to let them enter for a brief time, giving them the gardens all to themselves. They strolled up to some marble statues, one of which looked like a replica of the sunstones used on the Nauvoo Temple. Directly opposite was a figure titled *Camilla*, the name of President Kimball's wife, and not far away was a statue named *Flora*, the name of President Ezra Taft Benson's wife.[19] At this spot, where *Camilla* and the sunstone converged, Elder Nelson offered a prayer of rededication of the land of Russia for the preaching of the gospel.[20]

A fireside that evening attracted approximately two hundred people, though only fifty-one Church members then lived in Leningrad. The room was filled to capacity, and true to his word, Minister Kirov was there. All in attendance felt the Spirit as Elder Nelson, Elder Ringger, and President Mecham explained the principles of the gospel. At the conclusion of the meeting, ten individuals expressed a desire to be baptized.[21] It was clear that the Lord's

Elder Hans B. Ringger, Sister Dantzel Nelson, Elder Nelson, President Steven R.
Mecham, Sister Donna Mecham, and District President Jussi Kemppainen in the
Summer Gardens in Leningrad.

Spirit was brooding over the Soviet Union and the humble Russian
people.

   While in Leningrad, Elder Nelson learned of Svetlana Artemova,
a young woman in her late twenties who had found the Church in
an unusual way. She had earnestly prayed for the privilege of acquiring a Bible in Russian, but since the communist revolution in 1917,
Bibles had been difficult to obtain. After imploring her husband to
let her go to Finland, Svetlana, her husband, and their young child
traveled to Helsinki in the fall of 1989 in search of a Bible. While
they were taking a walk through a wooded park, she stumbled upon
an object covered by autumn leaves and discovered it to be a dis-
carded Russian Bible. Svetlana was so delighted with her good fortune that she shared news of her find with the first person she saw
in the park. That person happened to be a Finnish member of the
Church, Sister Raija Kemppainen. Sister Kemppainen asked her,

"Would you like to have another book that teaches of the Lord Jesus Christ?" Svetlana was thrilled to receive a copy of the Book of Mormon in Russian, and she was soon baptized in Helsinki.

Svetlana subsequently asked the missionaries to call on a friend in Leningrad. Her friend was not home when the missionaries knocked on her door, but a neighbor opened his door and invited them in. When they announced that they were missionaries from The Church of Jesus Christ of Latter-day Saints, Sasha Teraskin was moved to tears. He had been praying for contact with the Church ever since he had met some Church members in Warsaw, Poland, some time before.

One day, Sasha appeared at a missionary zone conference in Helsinki, requesting baptism. So, following an interview, the missionaries filled a baptismal font with a bucket brigade, quickly transferring water from all available faucets in the chapel into buckets that were then carried to the font. After his baptism and confirmation, he was given the Aaronic Priesthood and ordained a priest. Sasha then baptized his wife, and they returned home to Russia. Not long afterward, he was called to serve as the elders quorum president in Leningrad.

Other responsibilities had later taken Sasha far from Leningrad, but when he learned that Elder Nelson and Elder Ringger would be holding a fireside there on April 26, he and his wife drove eight hundred miles to attend.[22]

The First Presidency and the Quorum of the Twelve Apostles gave approval for the creation of the Finland Helsinki East Mission on May 24, 1990. President Gary L. Browning, a professor of Russian at Brigham Young University, was called to serve as its first president. The new mission initially served people living in Leningrad, Moscow, and Vyborg, Russia; and in Tallinn, Estonia, but it eventually expanded throughout the northern Soviet Union.[23]

In July 1990, new missions were created in Czechoslovakia, Poland, and Hungary. The Finland Helsinki East Mission then provided an umbrella for missionary activities in the USSR. Further south, the Austria Vienna East Mission, under the leadership of President Neuenschwander, directed the work in Yugoslavia, Romania, Bulgaria, and the Ukraine. The Ukraine Kiev Mission was created in February 1992.[24]

After Elder Nelson met with several government representatives from the USSR during their visit to Salt Lake City on June 19, 1990, it became apparent that officials from nearly all of the Eastern European countries felt a need to visit Church headquarters prior to granting legal recognition to the Church in their respective countries.[25] In virtually all cases, after meeting with various Apostles, and often with the First Presidency, and taking a guided tour of Temple Square, they returned home with a favorable impression of the Church.

It has been said that nothing "propinqs" like propinquity,[26] and the frequent diplomatic shuttling from Salt Lake City, Washington, D.C., and Eastern Europe seemed to be bearing fruit. Elder Ringger called Elder Nelson early the morning of September 20, 1990, with the exciting news that governmental recognition of the Church had been officially granted to the branch in Leningrad. Elder Ringger phoned again from Europe a few weeks later to announce that the Church in Vyborg had also been granted official recognition. This recognition was a great tribute to the persistent efforts of mission presidents, missionaries, and Brother David Farnsworth, who had become an expert in drafting documents required for legal recognition in the various countries of Eastern Europe.[27]

On May 10, 1993, Elder and Sister Nelson joined Elder and Sister Ringger in Switzerland for a trip to Minsk, the capital of the newly formed country of Belarus. There they were met by President Howard L. Biddulph of the Ukraine Kiev Mission, his wife, Colleen, and some missionaries. A fireside that evening attracted about five hundred people; at the time, only sixteen members lived in Minsk.[28]

At dawn the next morning, the Latter-day Saint entourage went to Kupala Park, named for the famous Belarus poet Yanka Kupala. As birds overhead beckoned the arrival of a new day, Elder Nelson offered a dedicatory prayer upon the nation of Belarus, which had separated from the Soviet Union on Christmas day 1991. "We rejoice that Thy sons and daughters here who are searching for truth and happiness may now be satisfied and sanctified," he declared. "Let there be a rich harvest of souls who can come unto Thy Son, the Lord Jesus Christ. We dedicate this choice sector of Thy vineyard that it may be a place where missionary work may abound."[29]

From Minsk, the Nelsons traveled to Voronezh, Russia, where they met their son, Elder Russell M. Nelson Jr., and his missionary companion, Elder Dallas Woolf. It had been two years since the Nelsons had seen their son, and, in the unbiased words of proud parents, they found him to be "wise, mature, capable, courteous, wonderful, and a skilled linguist in the Russian language." Continuing, Elder Nelson said, "We had waited more than twenty-one years for the day when we could greet our son at the conclusion of his mission, and it was well worth waiting for!"[30]

Elder Nelson has performed numerous sealings in the temple, but one sealing will long stand out in his memory. In May 1993, while traveling with Russell Jr. at the end of his mission, Elder and Sister Nelson were invited to dinner at the home of Nina and Oleg Barzarsky in the city of Voronezh, where Russell Jr. had labored. Nina had joined the Church, but her husband had resisted accepting the gospel. After dinner, as the Nelsons prepared to say their farewells, Elder Nelson took Oleg by the hand, looked into his eyes and said, "The day will come when you and your dear wife will be sealed in the temple."[31]

Three years later, on May 1, 1996, Nina and Oleg knelt across the altar in one of the sealing rooms of the Salt Lake Temple, where Elder Nelson performed their sealing, with his returned missionary son serving as translator. Oleg reminded Elder Nelson that his prophecy had been fulfilled, and he was pleased to announce that his son was then serving in the Latvia Riga Mission. "It was a great day for Russell Jr. to see the blessing of eternal union come to this family with whom he has worked," Elder Nelson said. [32]

On October 7, 1996, Elder and Sister Nelson attended a reception for Mikhail Gorbachev, former president of the Soviet Union, and his wife, Raisa, who were visiting Salt Lake City. After the formal introductions were concluded, the Nelsons were seated immediately next to the Gorbachevs. During the ensuing conversation, Mr. Gorbachev asked Elder Nelson to explain some of the differences between the LDS Church and the Russian Orthodox Church. This setting provided Elder Nelson an opportunity to extend a formal invitation for Mr. and Mrs. Gorbachev to visit the First Presidency and meet the living prophet of God.[33]

While meeting with the Gorbachevs the next day in the First Presidency's boardroom, President Gordon B. Hinckley told them of the origin of the beautiful Circassian walnut paneling that adorns the room. Mr. Gorbachev was pleased to learn that the wood had come from the region of his birthplace in Russia. Afterward, the Gorbachevs visited Temple Square and the Tabernacle, where they were escorted by a sister missionary from Russia.[34]

In November 1998, Elder Nelson received the assignment to return to Eastern Europe to conduct a series of area priesthood leadership training meetings in the very countries in which he had labored nearly a decade earlier. Between 1985 and 1991, he had made more than thirty trips to Europe to assist in opening the doors of these nations. The Europe East Area of the Church, under the leadership of Elders Charles Didier, F. Enzio Busche, and Wayne M. Hancock, now consisted of approximately fifty countries, thirty-five of which had an organized Church presence. There were now 28,000 members of the Church in Eastern Europe, about half of whom lived in Russia and the Ukraine.[35]

In Prague, Czechoslovakia, about one hundred priesthood leaders met for training,[36] and the next day in Budapest, Hungary, 154 leaders awaited instruction. As his mind raced back to the

On October 8, 1996, Mikhail Gorbachev, former president of the USSR, visited Church headquarters. Left to right: interpreter and assistant to Mr. Gorbachev, Elder Nelson, Raisa Gorbachev, President Gordon B. Hinckley, Mr. Gorbachev, President Thomas S. Monson, President James E. Faust, and Kenneth Knight and Gifford W. Price of the Church's hosting service.

dedication of that country and those early tense negotiations with Hungarian officials in 1987, Elder Nelson said, "I almost wept for joy seeing these priesthood leaders."[37] The next morning, a meeting was held with seventy-five priesthood leaders in Sofia, Bulgaria, five of whom were medical doctors.[38]

Their subsequent stop was Bucharest, Romania, where they met with fifty-four full-time missionaries serving under the leadership of President Robert F. Orton and his wife, Joy.[39] From Bucharest, they took a flight to Kiev, the capital of the Ukraine, where they held an area training meeting with about four hundred brethren.[40] The following day they were in Moscow, where they met with 164 local priesthood leaders.[41]

The trip concluded in St. Petersburg, formerly Leningrad, with training meetings for 223 local priesthood leaders. Elder Nelson ruminated, "Who could have imagined on April 26, 1990, that in less than a decade there would be seven missions in Russia, two more in the Ukraine, and another mission serving the Baltic countries of Estonia, Latvia, and Lithuania? And now there are twelve missions in the former USSR."[42]

On July 13, 2000, Elder Nelson hosted a luncheon at Church headquarters for thirty dignitaries from Russia who were visiting Utah to learn more about the principles of freedom of religion that might be applicable to Russia's fledgling democracy.[43]

CHAPTER 26

WITH THE TABERNACLE
CHOIR IN EUROPE

UNDER THE AUSPICES OF THE First Presidency, the Mormon Tabernacle Choir had planned a historic tour of Eastern Europe for June 1991, but in the fall of 1990, storm clouds were gathering over Europe and the Mediterranean area. A NATO coalition began a massive troop buildup in Saudi Arabia following Iraq's invasion of Kuwait.[1] On Wednesday, January 16, 1991, war erupted in the Persian Gulf as the United States and allied forces attacked strategic targets in Iraq.[2] It seemed that plans for a choir tour might be placed on hold or canceled altogether. Nevertheless, on January 29, Elder Nelson met with Sister Beverly Campbell in Washington, D.C., to plan state dinners to be held in conjunction with the choir's visit to Hungary, Poland, Czechoslovakia, and Russia.[3]

Brother Wendell M. Smoot, president of the choir, began receiving calls from various venues in Europe seeking assurance that the choir tour would not be canceled because of the Persian Gulf War. Concerned for the Church's reputation if bookings for prestigious concert halls were canceled, Brother Smoot sought President Gordon B. Hinckley's counsel on February 1. A couple of days later, President Hinckley assured President Smoot, "The choir will go to Europe this coming summer. The war will be over."[4]

On April 25, 1991, in the aftermath of the war and the uncertainties it had caused,[5] Elder Nelson hosted a breakfast at a hotel in

*Ivan S. Silaev, prime
minister of the Russian
Republic, meets with
Elder Nelson on April
25, 1991.*

Los Angeles for Ivan S. Silaev, prime minister of the Republic of
Russia, and his associates.[6] In that auspicious setting, Elder Nelson
extended an invitation to the prime minister and his colleagues to
attend the Mormon Tabernacle Choir concert and dinner in
Moscow. He then explained the basic tenets of the Church.[7]

The evening of May 22, President Hinckley and Elder Nelson
and their wives met with the members of the Tabernacle Choir in
the fifth floor assembly room of the Salt Lake Temple. The purpose
of the meeting was to prepare the choir members spiritually for their
forthcoming concert tour of Eastern Europe. Both Elder Nelson and
President Hinckley spoke to the choir members, and President
Hinckley pronounced a blessing upon them that their efforts would
be fruitful in softening hearts and opening doors. In that sacred
temple setting, choir members truly sang like angels.[8]

Two days later, Elder Nelson and Elder Dallin H. Oaks were in
Washington, D.C., where they hosted a luncheon honoring Viktor G.
Komplektov, the Soviet Union's new ambassador to the United
States.[9] Elder Nelson said, "We had a marvelous experience dis-
cussing the forthcoming concert tour of the Mormon Tabernacle
Choir, the relief efforts of the Church and the Jon M. Huntsman
family in Armenia, the status of congregations and the work of our

missionaries in the Soviet Union, and the basic beliefs and doctrines of the Church. Initially, the new ambassador was rather reserved and very formal, but two hours later, both he and his counselor, both of whom speak fluent English, were very warm and friendly and supportive of our lofty purposes. The meeting was very successful."[10]

Russell and Dantzel joined 312 members of the Mormon Tabernacle Choir on June 8, 1991, for their historic tour of Europe.[11] The day after its arrival in Frankfurt, Germany, the choir held a late-morning concert on the grounds of the Frankfurt Germany Temple. The commencement of the concert was dampened by rain, but as soon the choir began to sing *Alleluia*, the rain stopped, the clouds parted, and the sun shone directly overhead. Elder Nelson said, "What a magnificent way to encourage the choir in knowing that they were on an errand of the Lord." The next day, the headline over a favorable newspaper article read, "Alleluia Stops the Rain!"[12]

During the concert, Elder Nelson served as host to Friederichsdorf mayor Gerd Schmidt, who expressed disappointment that a meeting with the city council would prevent him from attending the choir concert in Frankfurt that evening. However, after hearing the choir sing on the temple grounds, he rearranged his affairs so he could attend the concert after all.

Choir members then traveled to Strasbourg, France, where they presented a concert at the *Palais d'Congress* before an appreciative audience of about two thousand people on June 11, 1991.[13] The next day, Elder and Sister Nelson and two dozen members of the choir presented a fireside in the Zürich Switzerland Stake Center before about eight hundred members.[14]

The evening of June 13, the choir performed before an audience of 8,400 people in the *Hallenstadion* in Zürich, where professional bicycling races are held. This was the largest audience of the entire tour.[15] The next day, the group departed for Vienna, traveling by bus through the beautiful cities of Innsbruck and Salzburg. On Saturday, June 15, choir members traveled to Hungary to perform in the

Budapest Opera House. The audience's enthusiastic response engendered seven encores.

The choir returned to Vienna the next day for a concert in the famous *Musikverein,* where generations of venerable Viennese composers have had their works performed under the batons of some of Europe's greatest conductors. In a country not easily impressed by foreign choirs and orchestras, the choir received a standing ovation and six encores. Austrian National Television televised the concert and broadcast it later via tape delay to the entire country.[16]

June 18 found the choir in Prague, Czechoslovakia, where it performed in the Smetana Hall before nearly a thousand Czechs. The Nelsons were joined by President Richard W. and Sister Barbara W. Winder of the Czechoslovakia Prague Mission, who were effective bridge builders with the Czech people.[17] The next day, the grand entourage traveled a short distance to Dresden, Germany, where they performed in the *Kulturpalast* for about 2,500 people.

The choir then traveled to Berlin to give both a matinee concert and an evening concert in the *Schauspielhaus.*[18] "During the choir concert, the Parliament of Germany was in session and voted to transfer their future headquarters from Bonn to Berlin," Elder Nelson said. "This decision was announced publicly at the close of the choir concert, which brought an already enthusiastic crowd to the point of ecstatic cheers of celebration!"[19]

On June 22, the choir bade adieu to the bus drivers who had transported them more than 2,700 miles. The group then boarded airplanes bound for Warsaw, Poland, where Elder Nelson dedicated a new chapel in Warsaw and then attended the choir concert at the Wielki Theater that evening.[20]

Two days later, Elders Nelson, Oaks, and Hans B. Ringger were in Armenia, where they were joined by David Farnsworth, David and Jean Horne, Jon M. Huntsman, and Peter and Brynn Huntsman, all of whom ascended a mountain overlooking the city of Yerevan, Armenia. There, on that mountaintop near a large monument representing the mother of Armenia, Elder Nelson and Elder Oaks knelt

together while Elder Oaks pronounced an inspiring prayer of dedication upon the land of Armenia.[21]

Later in the day, a large group of interested people met in
Yerevan for a ribbon-cutting ceremony at a newly constructed precast concrete facility. The plant was designed to produce enough
concrete to fabricate 6,500 apartments per year and provide housing for 25,000 people annually. The project, financed through the
generosity of the Huntsman family, would make a significant contribution to the welfare of half a million people left homeless by the
disastrous earthquake that hit the area in December 1988.
Afterward, in behalf of the Church, Elder Nelson accepted a gift of
land for the construction of a chapel. A brief groundbreaking ceremony followed.[22]

The Latter-day Saint entourage then boarded a plane for
Moscow. Shortly after their arrival, Elders Nelson, Oaks, and
Ringger were interviewed by Soviet National Television. That
evening, the choir performed at the famous Bolshoi Theater before
an audience of about 2,100. At a VIP dinner following the concert,
Alexander Rutskoy, vice president of the Republic of Russia, made
the historic announcement that the Church had been granted full
recognition and registration in the entire Republic of Russia! The
audience cheered the announcement, knowing that the news had
great significance for the future of the Church and the future of this
vast republic, which stretches from Leningrad on the west to
Vladivostok on the east.[23]

Elder Nelson reminisced about the frustrations wrought by the
bureaucratic requirement that twenty Church members live within
every metropolitan district before legal recognition could be granted.
"The mind of man was not able to crack that nut, but the Lord did
it," he said. "If the Lord's servants do the best they can, then the
Lord will open closed doors, but not until they have done all they
can." He likened those early days in the Soviet Union and the Baltic
republics to the time the children of Israel stood on the edge of the
Red Sea, before the Lord parted the sea to enable their escape from

the Egyptians (Exodus 14:15–22). Likewise, under Joshua's leadership, it was not until the priests had actually wet their feet that the Lord stopped the waters of the Jordan River so the people could pass over on dry ground[24] (Joshua 3:15–17).

While in Moscow, the Brethren met with Yuri Christoradnov in the office of the Council of Religious Affairs. "There I was able to transfer the relationship I had established with them to Elder Dallin H. Oaks so that there would be continuity with that office," he said. The three General Authorities and mission president Gary L. Browning then went to the park outside the wall of the Kremlin, where Elder Nelson offered a prayer of gratitude for the remarkable events that had recently transpired in the Soviet Union, the Republic of Russia, and the Republic of Armenia.[25] Elder Nelson is ever mindful that "in nothing doth man offend God, or against none is his wrath kindled, save those who confess not his hand in all things" (D&C 59:21).

The next morning, choir members caught flights to Leningrad, where they were met by guides and tour buses that transported them across the city to the shore of the Baltic Sea. There, a number of choir members decided to go wading, and after a few moments reflection, Elders Nelson and Ringger elected to do the same. Elder Nelson recalled, "As soon as Elder Ringger and I took off our shoes and stockings and rolled our pant legs up to our knees, it seemed like countless choir members gathered, each armed with a camera."[26]

The evening of the following day, in Leningrad's elegant Philharmonic Hall, the choir was greeted with a standing ovation from the 1,200 people in attendance. The concert was inspiring, and there was a spirit about the performance that many teary-eyed Russians had never felt before.[27] The audience remained seated long after the last choir member had exited the stage, basking in the spirit of what they had just experienced. This concert concluded a historic tour that helped bring the Church out of obscurity, softening the hearts and lifting the spirits of thousands.

CHAPTER 27

PIONEERING IN ROMANIA AND BULGARIA

ROMANIA

THE SOCIALIST REPUBLIC OF Romania had one of the most repressive governments among the Eastern European countries, but in March 1987, Elder Nelson expressed a desire to meet with government officials there to open a dialogue on introducing the gospel in Romania.

Elder Nelson joined Elder Hans B. Ringger in Zürich, Switzerland, on Monday, October 19, 1987, and the two of them took a flight to Bucharest, Romania, to test the waters in that country.[1] The next day, they met with the chief of protocol of the State Office of Religious Affairs. Both Elders Nelson and Ringger were able to converse with him in French, but they were told that their official meeting would not be held until Thursday.[2]

While waiting for their appointment, the Brethren toured the Romanian capital, visiting museums and parks and shops, which evidenced a scarcity of consumer goods. They soon had the distinct impression that their appointment had been postponed for two days so that Romanian officials could observe their movements and determine if they were trustworthy. Numerous times, for example, the Brethren were accosted on the streets by individuals trying to exchange currency on the black market.[3]

On Thursday, they finally met with Leon Toader and Dumitru Dan Costea of the State Office of Religious Affairs. The officials informed the Brethren that eighteen million of the country's twenty-three million inhabitants classified themselves as "believers" and that the government legally recognized fourteen different denominations. The Brethren made little tangible progress and were left with the impression that the government was satisfied with the status quo and was not eager to welcome a new religion into the country.[4]

Nearly two years later, President Nicolae Ceaucescu was expelled from office and, following a swift trial, he and his wife, Elena, were summarily executed in Bucharest on Christmas Day, 1989. The resulting political vacuum brought the country to the verge of anarchy.

At the conclusion of a visit to Czechoslovakia, on February 7, 1990, Elder Nelson and Elder Ringger caught a flight to Bucharest, where they were joined by David Farnsworth, the Church's legal counsel for Europe; Peter Berkhahn, the Church's director of temporal affairs; and Brother Nicolai Ciurdea, a Romanian building contractor who had joined the Church in Germany about eight months previously. Elder Nelson said that having Brother Ciurdea with them was providential "because he was able to be our interpreter and also constituted living proof that we have Romanian members of the Church."[5]

During a planning meeting in their hotel room, the brethren could hear the shouting of people parading in the streets below. Street demonstrations were becoming more and more frequent following the fall of the Berlin Wall, and the Romanians were becoming restless in their agitation for democracy and freedom of expression.[6]

The following day, the brethren met with Teofil Pop, minister of justice, who assured the LDS group of freedom of religious activity without discrimination. He asked for assistance, however, in his weighty responsibility to frame new laws and a new constitution in the aftermath of Ceaucescu's execution just six weeks earlier. Brother Farnsworth, who had great expertise and several years experience in this area, was immediately assigned this task, for which Minister Pop was extremely grateful.[7]

The next meeting that same day was with Dr. Sebastian Nicolau, minister of health. The brethren discussed with him how the Church and its members could provide humanitarian relief to the Romanians. After this meeting, the brethren met with Alan Green, U.S. ambassador to Romania, and his assistant, Dennis L. Curry, vice consul. On this same tightly scheduled day, the brethren met with Sorin Botnaru, provincial president of the National Unity Council, and Dan Predescu, a medical doctor serving as mayor of Bucharest. Nearly all governmental officials at the federal and municipal levels had been recently appointed in the aftermath of the collapse of the Ceaucescu regime.[8]

The interpreter for the visiting brethren was Ileana Badescu, who showed them the devastation following the brief, yet bloody, revolution in Bucharest. "Completely destroyed were the museum, the library, and other important buildings surrounding the communist headquarters of Ceaucescu," Elder Nelson said. "These precious buildings were destroyed because the Ceaucescu regime had fortified the museum and library as strongholds in the event of a battle."[9]

Continuing, Elder Nelson recalled, "When Brother Ringger and I had been in Romania in October 1987, we had seen many soldiers working underground, and we were told they were working on a subway. In fact, the underground development was for the security of the Ceaucescu family and close confidantes. Now there were wreaths, flowers, and candles burning in honor of martyrs who were innocently slaughtered in the cause of freedom. It was really sad to watch the mourners, young and old, who had come to Bucharest grieving for their loved ones lost about six weeks previously."[10]

At the meeting with the mayor and the district council, various forms of humanitarian assistance were discussed and religious opportunities within the country were explored. As the day drew to a close, the brethren hosted a dinner for Dr. Elena Voiculescu, a pediatrician; Maria Muga, the Church's legal counsel in Romania; Georg

Radulian, the district leader; Ileana Badescu, the interpreter; and their respective partners. Elder Nelson said, "I was really impressed with the dignity and culture of these wonderful Romanian people. In addition to their native language, all of them understood English and French, and perhaps other languages as well."[11]

Early February 9, 1990, atop a prominent knoll in the snow-covered Cismigiu Gardens, Elder Nelson, joined by Elder Ringger and a few other Latter-day Saints,[12] offered a dedicatory prayer for the country of Romania, calling down the powers of heaven that the gospel might soon be preached to the nation's downtrodden inhabitants. In the local vernacular, *cismigiu* means "one who carries water," an appropriate name for a place where a servant of the Lord pleaded that living water might flow to those with spiritual thirst.

A few hours later, Elders Nelson and Ringger and Brothers Farnsworth and Ciurdea met with Nicolai Stoicescu, who had served as minister of religion for less than three weeks. A member of the Romanian Orthodox Church, he had been a professor of history and had served time in a concentration camp for his religious beliefs. He and two assistants[13] discussed requirements for the Church's recognition as the brethren clarified misconceptions about the Church.[14]

The brethren then visited one of several orphanages in Bucharest. They were ill-prepared for what they saw. "We saw about 150 children between one and three years of age, in pitiful circumstances. In a room about the size of one of our ordinary bathrooms, I counted thirteen children sitting in a circle—all on individual potty chairs. The children were clothed only on the upper half of their bodies. In an adjoining room several children were seated around a table with an attendant dangling a toy in the air. Other toys were on the shelves but the children were not allowed to handle them, nor were the children being taught. It was quite pathetic."[15]

There were thousands of orphans in Bucharest, abandoned on the streets by parents who could not afford to feed or clothe them. The professional caregivers with whom the brethren spoke indicated that caring for orphans was one of the major challenges facing the new government, and they solicited help from the brethren.[16] Upon returning home, Elder Nelson set into motion the calling of humanitarian service missionaries for Romania.

Earlier, as the communist regime was disintegrating in Romania, Elder Nelson had called the Campbell home in Washington, D.C., late one evening to see if Sister Campbell had contacts with the current ambassador. Knowing of the terrible plight in the Romanian orphanages, the Church wished to get medical supplies to the people immediately. When Sister Campbell asked how much time she had, Elder Nelson gently replied, "Noon tomorrow would be best."

The Romanian embassy in Washington, D.C., was surrounded by police because death threats had been made to embassy personnel. With the help of the ambassador's private fax number, an appointment was set, and the ambassador was able to cross police lines so Sister Campbell could convey the Church's interest in finding a safe bank for humanitarian funds and a safe crossing for humanitarian trucks. The ambassador was soon replaced but not before opening avenues for assisting the Romanian people in need.[17]

"To afford relief, members of the Church responded in a most generous and humanitarian manner," Elder Nelson reported. "Particularly do I pay tribute to the Saints in Europe who loaded countless numbers of trucks with needed goods to ease the plight of these unfortunate children."

Several well-trained and professionally prepared Latter-day Saints responded to calls for special service in Bucharest, rendering badly needed voluntary relief. "Certainly their efforts are as historic as those of other pioneers in the annals of Church history,"[18] Elder Nelson declared.

In July 1992, Elder Nelson hosted several distinguished guests from Romania at a luncheon in Salt Lake City. What a dramatic contrast this visit was to the cool reception Elders Nelson and Ringger had received five years previously in Bucharest. Now the Romanians were eager to come to Salt Lake City to meet with Church leaders![19]

Romania was assigned in 1990 to the Austria Vienna East Mission under the direction of President Dennis B. Neuenschwander, and in 1992, humanitarian missionaries served in Romania under the direction of the Hungary Budapest Mission. The Romania Bucharest Mission was created July 1, 1993.[20]

BULGARIA

At the end of October 1988, Elder Nelson and his trusted companion, Elder Ringger, arrived in Sofia, Bulgaria, to begin their first attempts at securing permission to begin the Lord's work in that closed country.

Elder Nelson recalled: "When Elder Ringger and I first arrived in Sofia, Bulgaria, on 30 October 1988, we had been led to believe, through our indirect 'third-party' contact, that we would be met at the airport and that proper appointments had been made. (Incidentally, it had been our experience that most leaders in these totalitarian governments did *not* confirm any arrangements in writing.) So we went to Bulgaria in faith. We arrived late at night. No one was there to greet us. We took a taxi, which delivered us to the wrong hotel. Once we made that discovery, we trudged, luggage in hand, through a snowstorm until we finally found our correct accommodations. Our frustration continued the next day as bilingual telephone operators at the hotel were not able to help us identify either the office or the leaders with whom we needed to meet. We were at a complete dead end. All we could do was to pray for help.[21]

"Our prayers were answered. In a marvelous way, a day later, at 10 A.M., we met with Mr. Tsviatko Tsvetkov, head of the religious affairs department for the country. He had just returned to the city, and his interpreter was available also. Incredible!

"At first, the atmosphere was pretty cold. He didn't know we were coming, and he felt imposed upon. Through his interpreter, he scolded, 'Nelson? Ringger? Mormons? I've never heard of you.'

"I replied, 'That makes us even. We have never heard of you, either. It's time we got acquainted.' Everyone laughed, and we went on to have a great meeting."[22]

They discussed the opportunities that Bulgarian citizens had for religious expression, and Elders Nelson and Ringger acquainted the government officials with the principles and work of the Church. The exchange of information proved rewarding and useful.[23]

As Elder Nelson was preparing for his departure from the airport in Sofia, "The police searched my baggage more thoroughly than I have experienced before. They even looked between the sheets of my pads of paper, looking for anything improper. I guess I shouldn't be surprised. I can imagine how thoroughly a Bulgarian might be searched when he would be leaving one of our airports in the United States. Fortunately, there were no problems and we parted with friendly feelings."[24]

Nearly sixteen months later, Elder Nelson and Elder Ringger returned. On February 13, 1990, they and Brother and Sister Barid King and their two children went to a secluded grove of trees in the *Park Na Svobodata*, which means "Liberty Park." Authorized by the First Presidency and the Twelve Apostles, Elder Nelson offered a dedicatory prayer for the country of Bulgaria. A gentle snowfall added to the sacred serenity of the occasion, as suggested by the words of Orson F. Whitney:[25]

> *Pale through the gloom the newly fallen snow*
> *Wraps in a shroud the silent earth below*
> *As tho 'twere mercy's hand had spread the pall,*
> *A symbol of forgiveness unto all.*[26]

Later that day, the Brethren met with Lubomir Popov, deputy minister of foreign affairs, and his colleagues.[27] Elder Nelson recalled, "Whereas our first meeting in 1988 had been a little tense, this meeting was much more cordial, based on the warmth of the friendship begun at the previous visit."[28]

The next meeting was at the International Foundation, which is responsible for faculty and student educational exchanges. The Brethren discussed a request by foundation officials, Mikhail Tachev and Valentin Mitev, to have LDS English teachers and graduate students come to Bulgaria to teach English.[29] Before the fall of communism, Bulgaria's educational system had strongly emphasized that all students learn Russian. Eventually, however, some leaders in Eastern European countries sensed the important economic and political necessity of building bridges with western Europe and the United States by having students learn English.

During their visit, Elders Nelson and Ringger were interviewed by journalists from Bulgarian radio and a newspaper sponsored by the Agrarian Party. These interviewers seemed sincerely interested in learning more about the Church, and the Brethren hoped that the interviews would result in a wider, positive image of the Church in Bulgaria.[30]

Four months later, on June 23, 1990, Elder and Sister Nelson attended a dinner hosted by Brother J. Willard Marriott Jr. and his wife in Washington, D.C. Among other invited guests was Ambassador Velichko Velichkov from Bulgaria.[31] The Lord has revealed that "the power of my Spirit quickeneth all things" (D&C 33:16)—something that was certainly evident in the Church's developing relations with leaders in Bulgaria.

On June 29, 1990, Todorow Tzakov of Bulgarian TV traveled from Sofia to Salt Lake City to meet with Elder Nelson and to learn more about the Church.[32] A few months later, Mikhail Tachev, head of the International Foundation, paid a courtesy call to Elder Nelson, praising the work of LDS missionary sisters and senior couples who had begun teaching English in Bulgaria.[33] He was grateful to the Church, and it was clear that the icebergs were beginning to melt. Contacts with Bulgarian students studying English provided excellent referrals, and many Bulgarians have since joined the Church. The Bulgaria Sofia Mission was created July 1, 1991.[34]

CHAPTER 28

THE MIDDLE EAST:
TURKEY AND JORDAN

O N JUNE 15, 1988, ELDER Nelson and Elder Carlos E. Asay, Europe Area president, flew to Ankara, Turkey, where they were joined by Brother Blaine C. Tueller, assistant to Brother David M. Kennedy. Brother Kennedy was then serving as an international ambassador for the Church, representing the First Presidency.[1] The next day, the brethren met with O. Nuri Gursoy of the presidency of Turkish religious affairs and head of the Foreign Relations Department.

Reflecting upon that meeting, Elder Nelson recalled, "It's amazing how blessed we are sometimes when circumstances arise without warning. When we were meeting with Mr. Gursoy, his assistant opened a flask of fluid and walked toward me with the open flask. I didn't know what was coming. I didn't know whether we were to have a drink as we do in the islands of the Pacific in a kava ceremony. I felt impressed to hold my hands in the shape of a cup. He then poured the liquid into my hands, and I rubbed my hands together and found it to be an alcoholic-perfumed liquid, similar to aftershave lotion. My actions turned out to be the correct thing to do. Only later was I informed that this is a custom in some Turkish offices as a symbol of peace and goodwill."[2]

Brother Kennedy arrived by air later that afternoon from the United States, after which he and Elder Nelson visited several officials

Elder Nelson and Professor Truman G. Madsen together in Jerusalem in 1988 with special envoy of the First Presidency, Brother David M. Kennedy.

of the Turkish government. One of these was A. Kurtcebe Alptemocin, minister of finance. Elder Nelson said, "This was an interesting meeting because twenty-five years ago Dr. Alptemocin and his wife were students in Düsseldorf, Germany, and they came into contact with the LDS missionaries and had a very favorable experience with them, so our reception was very warm and friendly."[3]

Discussions with Turkish government leaders were cordial, but the vast majority of Turks are adherents of Islam, which is an integral part of Turkish culture. Although the Turkish constitution nominally allows freedom of religion, proselytizing members of other faiths is prohibited. However, individuals who come to Turkey as members of the LDS Church are free to practice their religion within carefully prescribed limits.

On December 7, 1989, Elder Nelson met with Ismet Miroglu, who had come to Salt Lake City from Istanbul. As general director of the Turkish State Archives, he had come to request the help of the Church in microfilming Turkish genealogical records. After the meeting, Elder Nelson said, "That was a marvelous experience in light of the fact that in June 1988, when I met with leaders in Turkey, they were less than enthusiastic about the prospects for our Church's involvement in their country."[4]

In recent years, the Church has had a few senior missionary couples in Turkey to help shepherd the small number of members living there.

JORDAN

After leaving Turkey on June 21, Elder Nelson, accompanied by Elder Asay and Brothers Kennedy and Tueller, traveled to Amman, Jordan. They were met at the airport by Jordanian senator Mohammed Kamal, formerly Jordan's ambassador to the United States. As a member of the Jordanian parliament, he was in charge of foreign affairs, and he provided a gracious reception in behalf of the Hashemite Kingdom of Jordan.[5]

The brethren were granted an audience with Crown Prince Hassan Bin Talal, brother of King Hussein, with whom they visited for nearly an hour. A portion of their discussion was recorded by television cameras and shown across the nation in the evening news telecast. Elder Nelson said of the forty-year-old prince, who had been educated in Great Britain, "He was very cordial to us, offering the support of his office to any efforts we might wish to make in Jordan."[6]

Senator Kamal then accompanied the brethren during a visit to Jordan's prime minister, Zaid Rifai. After the meeting, their hosts arranged to have Elders Nelson and Asay driven to the top of Mount Nebo outside Amman. There they beheld the plains of Moab, the Dead Sea, Jericho, the Jordan River, and the Sea of Galilee—the same vista Moses saw before he "disappeared into a cloud . . . and went to God" (Deuteronomy 34:1–12).[7]

The next day, Elder Nelson and his associates were pleasantly surprised at the news coverage their visit received on television and in the print media. The *Jordan Times* included a photo of Elders Nelson and Asay and Brothers Kennedy and Tueller meeting with the crown prince, and the accompanying story was complimentary. The following day, another article appeared indicating that the prime minister had met with "former United States Treasury secretary David Kennedy and renowned heart surgeon Russell Nelson."[8]

Less than three months after Elder Nelson's visit to Jordan, on September 7, 1988, Brother Kennedy hosted a dinner in Salt Lake City honoring Senator Mohammed Kamal, General Hemidi Al-Fayez, and Elie Atallah, distinguished officials of the Hashemite Kingdom of Jordan. Through the efforts of Senator Kamal and his colleagues, the Church later obtained a lease on a building that formerly housed the Swiss embassy in Amman. This building comprises the Church's physical presence in Jordan and became known as the Brigham Young University Center. The building provides living accommodations for a senior couple serving as representatives of the Church, and it houses a small library of resource materials, meeting rooms for the small branch of the Church in Amman, and rooms for Brigham Young University students visiting Jordan.[9]

CHAPTER 29

ENCOMPASSING THE EARTH

THE FIRST DAY OF JUNE 1992, Elder Neal A. Maxwell and his wife, Colleen, and Elder and Sister Nelson embarked on a historic trip around the world, generally flying westward until they had encompassed the earth, arriving safely home three weeks later.

Their first port of call was Hong Kong, where they met with 120 missionaries during the day and spoke to seven hundred Saints at a fireside that evening.[1] They next took a flight to Kuala Lumpur, Malaysia, where they met with the local leaders, instructed fifty full-time missionaries, and spoke at a fireside with approximately 250 members and investigators, most of whom were of Chinese or Indian descent.[2] The following day, they spoke at a session of district conference attended by 450 Saints.[3]

On June 7, the Maxwell-Nelson entourage arrived in Bangkok, Thailand.[4] Just three weeks before, a civil uprising had left in its wake a number of charred buildings. Palpable tension still filled the air. As the Brethren prepared to participate in the general session of the Bangkok District conference, the mission president, Larry White, humbly expressed his desire that Elder Maxwell pronounce a special blessing upon the troubled land.[5]

Although King Bhumibol Adulyadej still reigned in Thailand, his political influence had greatly eroded in recent years and months. A general climate of political instability existed throughout the

*Elder and Sister Nelson before the
Royal Palace in Bangkok, Thailand,
on June 8, 1992.*

nation, especially following a recent coup by the country's military
leaders. As the district conference drew to a close, Elder Maxwell
pronounced a blessing upon the Thai people and their king that
there would be a "spirit of reconciliation" among the king, the military leaders, and the people. Although the king's role had become
largely titular, because some of the five hundred people attending
the conference were friends of the royal family, President White felt
certain that news of this special blessing would reach the king.[6]

On June 9, the group left Bangkok for New Delhi, India. The
following day, Thailand's king, armed with renewed self-confidence,
invited the general of the military, who had led the coup, to visit
him at the palace. To everyone's surprise, and with the general's support, the king appointed Anand Panyarachun, a former prime minister, to serve as the interim prime minister until general elections
could be held.[7] The political stability that followed has been conducive to the growth of the Church. Latter-day Saint observers in

Thailand could concur with Moroni that "God has not ceased to be a God of miracles"[8] (Mormon 9:15).

On June 11, the Maxwells and Nelsons boarded a bus for the Taj Mahal in the city of Agra. Elder Nelson turned to Dantzel and said, "You had better enjoy this; it might be the last time you see the Taj Mahal." The weather was so blistering hot and oppressive that Dantzel responded, "I certainly hope so!"[9]

During a brief tour of downtown New Delhi, the temperature was 107 degrees. But the Apostles and their wives were undaunted as they held a meeting with twenty-five full-time and district missionaries, and then a fireside with about a hundred members and investigators.[10] The following day, the Brethren and their wives met with forty full-time missionaries in Bangalore and spoke at a fireside to more than 150 members and investigators, including some who had traveled twenty-four hours from Rajahmundry to meet two Apostles of the Lord Jesus Christ.[11]

After these meetings, the Maxwells and Nelsons caught a flight to Bombay, where they were met by Dr. Devendra Saksena, his wife, Hem, and their two sons. Dr. Saksena had been in surgical training with Dr. Nelson and had since become one of India's foremost cardiac surgeons. Their reunion was a pleasant experience.[12]

The group departed from Bombay for Karachi on June 15 and then traveled on to Islamabad, Pakistan. Though Pakistan had a population of about 120 million, only about one hundred members of the Church lived there. Several faithful senior missionary couples were patiently and discretely proselyting among the small number of Christians in this predominantly Muslim country. Thirty-six people, including thirteen native Pakistanis, attended a fireside that evening.[13] The next day, the Brethren and their wives boarded a flight to Karachi, where twenty people attended a meeting that evening with the Brethren.[14]

From Karachi, the four traveled to Abu Dhabi, in the United Arab Emirates, and then caught a connecting flight to Amman, Jordan, where they were welcomed by Saleh Alzu'bi, secretary general

Elder Neal A. Maxwell, Elder Nelson, Sister Nelson, Sister Colleen H. Maxwell,
Elder Spencer J. Condie, and Sister Dorothea S. Condie in the Garden of
Gethsemane in June 1992.

of Jordan's House of Parliament, whose son was attending Brigham
Young University.

Following a meeting with officials at the University of Jordan,
Dr. Ali Kamal took Elders Maxwell and Nelson to the bedside of his
brother, Senator Mohammed Kamal, who was in the King Hussein
Medical Center following a stroke. Senator Kamal had been a great
friend and advocate for the Church in the Hashemite Kingdom of
Jordan, but to the disappointment of his visitors, he was unable to
speak. In a gesture of faith, goodwill, and comfort, Elders Maxwell
and Nelson invited Kamal's loved ones to join hands in a circle
around the senator's bed, and Elder Nelson pronounced a blessing
of peace and comfort upon the senator and his family members.[15]

The group then traveled to Mount Nebo, where the Lord took
Moses unto Himself after the forty-year sojourn in the wilderness.
Elder Nelson read from Deuteronomy 34 of how Moses stood upon
Mouth Nebo and saw the promised land into which the Israelites
would go while he remained behind.[16] The next evening, a fireside

Russell M. Nelson at the organ in the Brigham Young University Jerusalem Center for Near Eastern Studies.

was held in the Amman branch of the Church with twenty-three in attendance, including six Jordanians and five Filipinos.

After partaking of legendary Jordanian hospitality for two days, the Brethren and their wives prepared to cross the Allenby Bridge, which spans the Jordan River separating Jordan and Israel. There they bade adieu to their Jordanian friends and walked into the welcoming arms of Professors Truman G. and Ann Madsen, who for several years had directed the Brigham Young University semester abroad program in Jerusalem.[17]

The Madsens showed their guests several significant biblical sites. Especially poignant was their early morning visit on June 20 to the Garden Tomb on Shabbat, the Jewish Sabbath. The couples spent considerable time in quiet conversation and reverent sharing of testimonies of the reality of the Lord's resurrection. After they returned to the BYU Jerusalem Center, the Brethren addressed a sacrament meeting of about 250 members of a Church Educational System travel group. Deferring to his colleague, senior in years of apostolic service, Elder Nelson spoke briefly so that Elder Maxwell could have adequate time to deliver an inspiring sermon on the Savior's atoning sacrifice. As they listened, the congregation looked upon sacred sites in the distance through large semicircular windows behind the pulpit. Following the meeting, the group traveled a short distance to the Sea of Galilee, where Jesus loved to be.[18]

The next day, the entourage went to Mount Tabor, which many biblical scholars believe to be the Mount of Transfiguration. There, atop that lofty mount, Ann and Truman Madsen and Russell and Dantzel Nelson performed a song from their distant past together in Boston: "The Lord Bless and Keep You." Mount Tabor may or may not be the Mount of Transfiguration, but it certainly was a place of spiritual regeneration that Sunday afternoon.[19]

The following day, the Maxwells and the Nelsons departed for home a bit travel weary but fortified by memories of faithful Saints throughout the world who are striving to keep their sacred covenants, notwithstanding challenging circumstances in which they live.

CHAPTER 30

APOSTLES IN AFRICA

IN AUGUST 1992, ELDER NELSON and Elder Richard G. Scott embarked on a historic trip to Africa, visiting fifteen countries in fifteen days. Their first stop was Nairobi, Kenya. Disregarding any travel weariness after their arrival, the Brethren spoke to the full-time missionaries, held an evening fireside attended by two hundred members, and participated in priesthood leadership and Relief Society training meetings. The Brethren were pleased to find that remarkable progress had been made in the Lord's work since Elder James E. Faust had dedicated Kenya the previous year.[1]

The next day, Elder Nelson and Elder Richard P. Lindsay of the area presidency traveled to Lusaka, the capital of Zambia, where they called on Dr. Boniface M. Kawimbe, the minister of health. When asked how the Church could be of help to his country, he replied, "What we would like to have are ideas and skills so that we can manage our own resources better." Elder Nelson said, "I thought his answer was a marvelous example of the principles of welfare that we teach. It is much better to teach a person how to fish than to give him one."[2]

The next morning, the Brethren, accompanied by a few local members, climbed a grassy knoll on the campus of the University of Zambia near Gama Lake. After several children sang "I Am a Child of God,"[3] Elder Nelson then prayerfully dedicated Zambia, imploring the Lord to "bless this people that they may be receptive to the gospel of Jesus Christ."[4]

Following that sacred event, Elders Nelson and Lindsay met with Roger Chongwe, Zambian minister of legal affairs. Following their cordial meeting, and as the Brethren began to make their way to the door, Minister Chongwe said, "Before you go, I would be grateful if you would lead us in a prayer." In accordance with his desires, they all knelt in a circle, and Elder Nelson offered a prayer invoking the Lord's blessings upon this struggling country and its people. The minister's request reflected the dramatic change in the spirit of the country's new leadership.[5]

Meanwhile, Elder Scott and Elder Earl C. Tingey of the Africa Area Presidency traveled to the beautiful Gaborone Game Preserve, where a band of faithful Saints gathered as Elder Scott dedicated the land of Botswana. Invoking the power of the Holy Apostleship, he prayed, "I humbly dedicate this land to the teaching of the gospel, to the preaching of truth, to the tearing down of barriers of prejudice and misunderstanding, to the unrolling of the priesthood authority that ordinances may be performed for salvation here and for eternity. . . . Bless the mothers and fathers of the families, Father, that they may nurture and strengthen their children to walk in Thy holy paths."[6]

On August 21, Elder Nelson joined Elder J Ballard Washburn of the Africa Area Presidency on a journey to Windhoek, Namibia. True to the name of the city, which means "windy corner" in the Afrikaans language, the Brethren were greeted by warm winds and even warmer members and investigators at an evening fireside.[7] The next day, Elders Nelson and Washburn climbed a hill high above the city, joined by about seventy-five members, including the mission president and his wife. There, overlooking the colorful Kalahari Desert, Elder Nelson offered a dedicatory prayer for the land of Namibia. He besought a blessing that the gospel would flourish in the land, prayed for the safety of the missionaries, and invoked a blessing upon the nation's leadership. He further pleaded, "Wilt

Thou bless the people that they may be receptive to Thy holy mind and will, and come unto Thee, as Thou hast made possible through the ordinance and covenant of baptism. Wilt Thou bless the people that they may be at peace one with another and that they may have adequate for their needs and for their sustenance."[8]

August 23 found Elders Nelson, Scott, and Tingey in Brazzaville, Congo. As they approached the entrance of the airport, they were greeted by beautiful strains of "Come, Come, Ye Saints,"[9] sung in French by about seventy Saints. Most had walked great distances from their homes to see the Brethren, and tears welled up in their eyes as they enthusiastically greeted the three General Authorities with *bienvenue* and *bon soir*.

Because of the great civil unrest in Zaire, now called the Republic of Congo, missionaries there were limited to three senior missionary couples. In mid-afternoon of August 24, Elders Scott and Nelson climbed a hill overlooking the rapids of the Congo River and there knelt together as Elder Scott pronounced a beautiful prayer and blessing of dedication upon the new Republic of Congo.[10] He prayed:

"We, two of Thy servants, . . . dedicate this Republic of Congo to the unrolling of Thy gospel, to the preaching of Thy word, to the testimony of Thy Beloved Son, and to the conversion of those spirits who are willing, now and in the future, to embrace Thy holy word. We rebuke those forces in this land that come from whatever source, tradition, external influence, selfishness, to be hedged up and bound by hearts that are obedient and willing, by righteous prayers and righteous acts of service in Thy Son's behalf."[11]

On August 27, after an arduous and circuitous trip, Elders Nelson, Scott, and Tingey spoke to the missionaries serving in the Ivory Coast. They then met with Dr. Ekre Alaen, the minister of health, and with Madame Amon, the wife of the Nigerian ambassador, who was in Paris. Dr. Alaen, a medical cardiologist, would speak in French to Elder Nelson, who would respond in English. Then,

Elder Richard G. Scott and Elder Nelson greet Fidel Francis Bogler and his family in Abidjan, Ivory Coast, Africa, August 27, 1992.

after a while, they would switch and Elder Nelson would speak in French and Dr. Alaen would respond in English.

In the evening, the Brethren spoke at a fireside to nearly nine hundred people. Afterward, Elders Nelson and Scott shook hands with every person present. Elder Nelson recalled, "When you consider that the Church had been in this country for only five years, that was a remarkable congregation."[12]

The following day, after arriving in Ghana, the Brethren were impressed by the strength of the leaders they met in Accra.[13] On Saturday, August 29, Elders Nelson, Scott, and Tingey held a five-hour meeting with 120 predominantly African missionaries who seemed well versed in the scriptures and highly motivated. In the afternoon, the Brethren held a press conference to answer many sincere queries about the Church.[14]

The next day, Sunday, Elder Scott and Chris Chukwurah, president of the Ghana Accra Mission, traveled to Cape Coast to speak to a gathering of more than 2,400 Saints. Meanwhile, Elders Nelson and Tingey and Elder Emmanuel Kissi, a regional representative, attended a conference of the Accra Ghana Stake held on the University of Ghana campus and attended by about 1,500 members.[15]

Later in the day, Elders Nelson and Scott flew to London, where they parted company—Elder Scott staying in London and Elder Nelson heading for home in time to participate in his extended family August birthday party and to celebrate with Dantzel their forty-seventh wedding anniversary.[16]

Nine years later, Elder and Sister Nelson visited West Africa. On November 16, 2001, after several months of great expectations punctuated by disappointments caused by bureaucratic delays, about 1,300 Saints congregated in Accra to participate in the groundbreaking ceremony for the Accra Ghana Temple. The country's vice president, Alhaji Aliu Mahama, represented the newly elected government.[17]

The day began hot and humid, but as the groundbreaking service commenced, a cloud covered the sun and a gentle breeze began to caress the moistened faces of the congregation. All were able to sit in comfort during the entire ceremony. A beautiful choir sang, after which Elder Nelson spoke briefly and pronounced a dedicatory prayer of gratitude and blessing on that sacred spot. Several Saints then took shovels and turned over soil that would become even more sacred in the coming months.[18]

At the cornerstone laying of the Logan Utah Temple, President George Q. Cannon testified, "Every foundation stone that is laid for a temple, and every temple completed . . . lessens the power of Satan on the earth, and increases the power of God and Godliness, moves the heavens in mighty power in our behalf, invokes and calls down upon us the blessings of eternal Gods and those who reside in their presence."[19] As construction moves forward on Africa's second temple, and with a third temple announced for Nigeria, the future bodes well for the African continent and its humble inhabitants who

Elder Nelson paid a courtesy call on President J. A. Kufuor of Ghana in November 2001.

have waited so long for all the blessings of the restored gospel in their lives.

While in Accra, Elder Nelson, Elder H. Bruce Stucki, area president, Elder Emmanuel O. Opare, Area Authority Seventy, and two stake presidents from Accra visited the presidential palace, where they met the newly elected president of the Republic of Ghana, John A. Kufuor.[20] The room was filled with newspaper reporters and representatives of television and radio media. After a cordial conversation, President Kufuor excused the media and asked Elder Nelson to offer a prayer for him, his associates, and the nation as a whole. Elder Nelson graciously complied, and the brethren concluded their visit with feelings of gratitude for the government's support and cooperation in allowing missionary work and temple construction to go forward. President Kufuor acknowledged, "The Church has come to stay and is part of this nation now."[21]

CHAPTER 31

ACCOMPANYING PRESIDENT HINCKLEY TO CENTRAL AND SOUTH AMERICA

TRAVELING AND ATTENDING MEETINGS with the president of the Church is always a rare privilege and a welcome blessing. In mid-January 1997, Elder and Sister Nelson accompanied President and Sister Hinckley to Central America.[1] Early on January 20, the Hinckleys, the Nelsons, and Elder William R. Bradford and his wife, Mary Ann, met with three thousand Saints packed into the Anayansi Atlapa Convention Center in Panama City. The Brethren encouraged the Panamanian Saints to live up to their covenants and to hold and be worthy of a current temple recommend.[2]

In Costa Rica, the General Authorities went to the presidential palace to meet with José Maria Figueres, president of Costa Rica. President Figueres, a West Point engineering graduate, was gracious to his guests and seemed sensitive to the privilege of hosting the prophet of the Lord.[3]

The Brethren and their wives then spoke to 6,208 members gathered in the National Auditorium. Among other things, the prophet reminded the Saints of the importance of fellowshipping new converts.[4] At the conclusion of President Hinckley's remarks, the Saints stood and, while waving white handkerchiefs, sang "God Be With You Till We Meet Again."[5] The prophet responded in kind, waving his white handkerchief and blowing kisses to them. Everyone knew they were in the presence of a living prophet.[6]

After a brief night's sleep, the entourage embarked for Managua, Nicaragua, at 7 A.M. Upon their arrival, a police escort led them across the city to the Olof Palme Auditorium, where more than two thousand Saints silently and reverently stood to welcome them. President Hinckley edified these Saints, who had been oppressed by civil war and natural disasters, as he said, "How we love you. . . . You have suffered much in years past. I am grateful better days are here. . . . Jesus loved the poor of the earth and He blessed them. We bless you with His divine authority."[7]

Afterward, Elder Nelson recalled, "What was to have been a routine trip to the airport turned into a near tragedy. President and Sister Hinckley and Brother David Sayer of Church Security were being driven in the car in front of us, following the police escort complete with sirens and flashing lights. Suddenly a truck sped into an intersection on our right and put on his brakes to avoid a collision. The truck stopped, but his load of metal channel irons kept coming and hit the right rear of the Hinckleys' car in front of us.

"Those channel irons were twelve to twenty feet long. Like javelins, they struck the rear window, the wing window, and the window of the right rear door, completely shattering all three windows. The rear window of the Hinckley's car was totally gone! President Hinckley foresaw the event and ducked his head forward. Sister Hinckley had done the same. Both escaped without injury. Sister Hinckley had several slivers of glass on her face, but they were easily removed. When we looked at the car, and we saw the dent in the chrome between the windows where the flying metal impacted the car, we realized that the good Lord had protected His prophet and Sister Hinckley in a miraculous way."[8]

The passengers regrouped and resumed their drive to the airport. From Managua, they flew to San Pedro Sula, Honduras, and that evening, under a full moon and cloudless sky, the three General Authorities and their wives spoke to a crowd of 8,100 Saints who waved their handkerchiefs in unison as the prophet entered the San Pedro Sula National Stadium.[9] Reminding the

Saints of the importance of true conversion, he said, "It is important that these [converts] be so well converted that they will never leave the Church."[10]

El Salvador was the next stop, and following President Hinckley's interview by the editor of a major newspaper, an evening meeting was held in the National Auditorium with more than ten thousand members and friends in attendance. President Hinckley told the Saints, "Fathers and mothers, you have nothing more precious than the little children to whom you have given life. Take care of them, teach them, love them, bring them up in the nurture and admonition of the Lord."[11] Following the prophet's address, Elder Nelson concluded, "Many lives had been affected for good, for this and for succeeding generations."[12]

On Saturday, the General Authorities participated in a regional conference for the priesthood leaders of the twelve stakes in Guatemala City, and the following day, two general sessions of the regional conference were held outside at the Pedrera Stadium. Twenty thousand people attended the first session and more than fifteen thousand attended the second session. President Hinckley encouraged the Saints in Guatemala to pay their tithing, assuring them that "the safety of our people lies in living the gospel of Jesus Christ. There is no other way."[13]

During this eight-day Central American journey, President Hinckley delivered nineteen major addresses in seven countries to a total of 87,855 people. In addition, the prophet also held special meetings with the full-time missionaries in each of the countries.

Summarizing President Hinckley's teachings for *The Nelson News,* Elder Nelson wrote: "He taught fundamental doctrines, and gave these people hope, encouragement, and love. He challenged them to keep the commandments and to qualify for all the blessings that the Lord has in store for His faithful children. He closed every talk with an apostolic blessing that evoked tears of joy. He and Sister Hinckley seemed to gain physical vigor day by day, belying the fact that he is 86 and she is also in her eighties. Surely they were and are blessed by the Lord."[14]

In August 1997, Elder and Sister Nelson accompanied President and Sister Hinckley to regional conferences in Montevideo, Uruguay; Asunción, Paraguay; and Quito, Ecuador. Speaking before more than eight thousand Saints in Quito, "President Hinckley began with a word of apology for a hoarse voice, but after expressing words of greeting and appreciation, he gained power and strength to give one of the finest discourses we have ever heard him give," Elder Nelson recalled. "He counseled the people on what to teach their children, basing his text on Isaiah 54:13, 'All thy children shall be taught of the Lord; and great shall be the peace of thy children.' When he finished, there was not a dry eye in the house. The sister who gave the benediction could hardly speak through her tears. President Hinckley was literally lifted and inspired by the Lord."[15]

Nearly two years later, in 1999, the Nelsons participated with President and Sister Hinckley in the largest regional conference ever held in the Church. The conference involved forty-nine stakes in and around Santiago, Chile.

On the Sabbath day, after one of the longest dry spells in Santiago's history and pursuant to persistent prayers for moisture, the rain came in great abundance. Before the general session of the regional conference, the Hinckleys and Nelsons drove through torrential rains to meet with the nearly one thousand missionaries serving in the greater Santiago metropolitan area. Then, with some trepidation, the party proceeded to an open-air soccer stadium for the regional conference.[16]

Elder Nelson recalled, "As soon as we got to this huge stadium the rain stopped. We were cooled by the cloud cover and blessed with the quiet reverence of all those people who jammed the facility. We were told that more than 55,000 were in attendance, and President Hinckley observed that this was the largest assembly of Latter-day Saints in one place in the history of this dispensation. He promised the Saints that 'if you will live the gospel, if you will live in faith, if you will do what you ought to do, not only will you be blessed, but this entire people will be blessed because the God of heaven will smile upon you with love for you and for the land of which you are a part.'"[17]

Elder Nelson said, "Our words of description could never begin to do justice to the marvel of this event. We were all crying because the Spirit was so strong. No one wanted to leave. The Saints all waved white handkerchiefs and the prophet waved to them. Never have we seen such a sight."[18]

As soon as the Church leaders got in the car to be transported to the airport, "the rains resumed and the windshield wipers went back and forth in rhythm with our hearts beating with gratitude for this sublime experience."[19]

The Hinckleys and Nelsons proceeded to Bogotá, Colombia, where they participated in the final four sessions of the dedication of the Bogotá Colombia Temple. Elder Nelson recalled, "In this magnificent temple, we all had the feeling that heavenly beings were with us. It was incredible. The Spirit was so strong! In each session, President Hinckley gave the dedicatory prayer, which is a spiritual and literary masterpiece."[20]

CHAPTER 32

MINISTRY IN LATIN AMERICA

MANY YEARS BEFORE BEING called as an Apostle and receiving his subsequent assignment as first contact of the Twelve for Mexico from 1994 to 1997, Elder Nelson had spent a number of months sharing his medical knowledge and surgical skills with physicians in several different Latin American countries. Throughout the years, Elder Nelson has studied with private tutors who have helped him improve his ability to speak and understand Spanish. This study has paid great dividends, enabling him to communicate with Spanish-speaking Saints in their native tongue. Elder Nelson is especially grateful for the tireless tutoring efforts of S. Shane Littlefield.

HONDURAS

On June 1, 1991, Elders Rex E. Pinegar, Ted E. Brewerton, Gardner H. Russell, Carlos H. Amado, and a company of forty other faithful Saints joined Elder Nelson in ascending the lofty Honduran mountain peak El Picacho. There, overlooking Tegucigalpa, the capital city, Elder Nelson offered a dedicatory prayer for Honduras. Delivering the prayer in Spanish, he prayed to the Lord "that all of the covenants made to Abraham, to Isaac, and to Jacob and their posterity may reach Thy sons and daughters here. . . . Bless Thine elect

*Elder Nelson,
President Gordon B.
Hinckley, and
President Thomas S.
Monson greet
Ambassador Gustavo
Petricioli of Mexico,
June 30, 1992.*

to hear Thy voice and to obey Thy commandments. Bless Thy missionaries to find the humble and the elect who love Thee sincerely."[1]

GUATEMALA

In the autumn of 1991, Elder and Sister Nelson joined Elder Marvin J. and Sister Norma Ashton in Guatemala City, where a small congregation of Saints, on October 18, had assembled on the grounds of the Guatemala City Guatemala Temple. In that sacred setting, Elder Ashton offered a beautiful dedicatory prayer upon the land of Guatemala and its people. Previous dedicatory prayers had been given for all of Latin America, and later for all of Central America, but each individual country had never been specifically dedicated for the preaching of the gospel.[2]

BELIZE

After presiding at a mission presidents' seminar in Flores, Guatemala, Elder Nelson traveled to the Central American country of Belize, formerly known as British Honduras. Accompanied by the area president, Elder Ted E. Brewerton, and his wife, Dorothy, they

In August 1998, Elder Richard J. Maynes and Elder and Sister Nelson inspect the newly dedicated Missionary Training Center in Lima, Peru.

met with missionaries in Belize City. They then drove nineteen miles to the hillside town of Burrell Boom, where, on December 7, 1992, Elder Nelson pronounced a prayer of dedication for the country of Belize. Later, during a meeting in Belize City for members and friends of the Church, Elder Brewerton dedicated the new chapel in which they met.

VENEZUELA, PERU, AND ECUADOR

Following a regional conference in Caracas, Venezuela, in 1997, Elder and Sister Nelson visited Lima, Peru, and Quito, Ecuador. In Ecuador, they took a brief break for sightseeing, including having

Elder Nelson standing amid the Inca ruins of Machu Picchu in the Peruvian Andes, October 1994.

their pictures taken while standing at the equator with one foot in the northern hemisphere and one foot in the southern hemisphere at an altitude of ten thousand feet. They also visited the site where the Guayaquil Ecuador Temple was under construction, concluding their weekend by participating in a regional conference attended by 9,500 faithful Saints.[3] Two years later, in August 1999, Elder Nelson was privileged to participate in the dedicatory services of the Guayaquil Ecuador Temple with President Gordon B. Hinckley, President James E. Faust, and Elders Francisco Viñas and Walter F. González.[4]

BRAZIL

Miraculous growth has occurred in Brazil during the past sixty years since a young Elder James E. Faust served as a missionary there in 1939. At that time, only about two hundred members of the Church lived in the country.[5]

In mid-May 1997, Elder Nelson participated in the reorganization

Dr. Marco Maciel,
vice president of
Brazil, greets Elder
Nelson during a visit
to Brazil in August
2001.

of the stake presidency of the Sorocaba Brazil Barcelona Stake. A few
days later, on May 18, he dedicated—in Portuguese—the newly
constructed Brazilian missionary training center, which can accommodate more than six hundred missionaries.[6] In 1999, Elder Nelson
returned to Brazil, where he presided at four regional conferences
during that year alone.[7]

BOLIVIA

During the weekend of February 14–15, 1998, Elder and Sister
Nelson participated in a regional conference in La Paz, Bolivia, with
7,580 Saints. Also in attendance were two prominent Bolivian government officials.

The general session of another regional conference was held the
following weekend in a large coliseum in Cochabamba. Elder
Nelson reported that torrential rain beat upon the coliseum's metal
roof, creating a deafening noise. "There were 4,358 members in
attendance at the general session, and because of the noise of the
rain, the acoustics were most challenging. The much-needed rain
stopped midway in the meeting and we were able to give our mes-
sages with better understanding than those who had spoken earlier
in the meeting. The Saints had prayed earnestly for rain because the
last good rain they had was in November of 1996 when President

Hinckley came to break ground for the temple. The Saints had been praying that an apostolic visit on this occasion might also be accompanied with rain to bless the lives of the people who depend upon their crops for their sustenance. Their prayers were answered in a most emphatic way!"[8]

Some of the greatest challenges facing the Church in Latin America continue to be rapid growth and retention of members. Economic constraints also present a roadblock to many faithful members. In North America, sacrament meeting attendance is higher than stake conference attendance, and attendance at regional conferences is lower than stake conferences. In Latin America, however, attendance at regional conferences tends to be much higher than sacrament meeting attendance. It seems that many families cannot afford to send all of their members to sacrament meeting each week; however, when an Apostle or a member of the First Presidency presides at a regional conference, families make any sacrifice in order to attend.

Elder Nelson's fervent enthusiasm for family history has spread to many missions, stakes, and districts in Latin America. In those missions where investigators and recently baptized members are introduced to and become involved in family history, retention tends to be much higher than elsewhere. Because families are extremely important to Latin Americans, and because Elder Nelson's family is first and foremost in his own life, there is an immediate bond between Latino members and this disciple of the Lord.

CHAPTER 33

MEETING THE SAINTS
IN THE ISLES OF THE SEA

THE PROPHET ISAIAH UNDERSCORED the Lord's love for those who dwell on the islands of the sea. In prophesying of the gathering of scattered Israel, he declared that "the Lord shall set his hand again the second time to recover . . . his people . . . from the isles of the sea," and "the isles shall wait for his law," "and on mine arm shall they trust."[1]

Members of the Church have long held Polynesians and other island dwellers in high esteem. Many have read the account of young Joseph F. Smith's missionary experiences while serving in the Hawaiian Islands. His love for the humble Hawaiian people engendered affection and admiration among the Saints generally. Elder Matthew Cowley's stories of the faith of the Maoris in New Zealand are legendary. Elder Russell M. Nelson has also observed the faith of the islanders in the South Seas, as demonstrated during his trip with President Kimball in 1976. Thus, when Elder Nelson received the assignment to serve as first contact to the Pacific Area, he was delighted.

In May 1994, Elder Nelson participated in the sesquicentennial celebration of the establishment of the Church in French Polynesia. The festivities began in Papeete's Tipaerui Stadium the day after his arrival. In attendance were the vice president of Tahiti and five of his cabinet ministers and leaders of the Roman Catholic Church and

*Elder and Sister Nelson in
Tahiti in November 1992.*

Evangelical denominations. The throng also included former mission presidents and their companions, several returned missionaries, and more than three thousand Saints, all of whom enjoyed a program of cultural songs and dances. For Elder Nelson, the best part of the program was leisurely shaking hands with hundreds of faithful Tahitian Saints.[2]

Early on a Sunday morning, a small group of Saints met in the western shadows of the Papeete Tahiti Temple. There, on those sacred grounds, Elder Nelson offered a dedicatory prayer for French Polynesia, which had not been previously dedicated as a separate nation. He fervently implored the Lord, "Wilt Thou bless these islands with a rich portion of Thy holy Spirit, that its citizens and their visitors may learn Thy commandments and be obedient to them, that they may prosper in Thy love."[3]

The following morning, nineteen Saints flew to Takaroa, an island in a circular coral reef in which every home has a front-door view of the ocean and a rear-door view of the lagoon. The island has a population of around five hundred residents, three hundred of whom attended commemoration services that day in a beautiful chapel built in 1891. After the services, Elder Nelson joined others in snorkeling along the coral reefs. He recalled seeing a fascinating variety of fish, including four sharks. "But they were not the least bit interested in us,"[4] he said.

On May 10, the LDS leaders took a flight to the island of Raiatea, where they held a commemorative program for the Raromatai Stake. More than eight hundred people attended, including several governmental leaders.[5] The next day in Papeete, Gaston Flosse, president of French Polynesia, participated in commemorating the 150th anniversary of the Church in French Polynesia. At noon, Elders Nelson, Rulon G. Craven, and Jean-Michel Carlson were granted a private audience with President Flosse, his vice president, and all nine cabinet ministers. After fruitful discussions and an exchange of gifts, the Tahitian dignitaries lined up to say goodbye in the customary Tahitian way with a kiss on each cheek. Elder Nelson observed, "The Church has certainly come out of obscurity in French Polynesia."[6]

TONGA

In mid-August 1991, Elder and Sister Nelson arrived in Nuku'alofa, Tonga, where they were met by Elder Douglas J. Martin, a brass band, and many local leaders. En route from the airport to the hotel, the Nelsons observed two dozen archways decorated with green leaves, decorative woven mats, and banners commemorating the centennial celebration of the Church in Tonga. Some archways had a Book of Mormon theme, others depicted President Benson, and still others bore the message "Come Unto Christ," in Tongan.[7]

Elder Martin and Elder John H. Groberg and his wife, Jean, joined the Nelsons for a visit to King Taufa'ahou Tubou IV. The Latter-day Saints presented the king with a letter from the First Presidency confirming a donation of hospital supplies and equipment to the people of Tonga. The gift commemorated one hundred years since the first missionaries to Tonga, Elders Alva J. Butler and Brigham Smoot, had met with King Jiaoji (George) Tubou of Tonga in July 1891. The king gave them permission to teach the gospel

*Queen Halaevalu Mata' aho of Tonga is greeted at Church headquarters by Elder
Nelson, Elder John H. Groberg and his wife, Jean, President Gordon B. Hinckley,
and President Thomas S. Monson.*

throughout the islands. The present monarch graciously accepted
the gift and reminded his guests that he is the great-great-grandson
of the man who authorized the first two elders to teach in Tonga.[8]

On the Sabbath, Elder Nelson offered the dedicatory prayer for
the new the Nuku'alofa Seventh Ward chapel, where the Nelsons
attended sacrament meeting. In the afternoon, Elder Nelson
unveiled and dedicated a historical monument at the Liahona Stake
Center. About seven thousand Saints from seven stakes then
attended an outdoor meeting held on the sports field at the Liahona
High School.[9]

The centennial services were held Monday at the Atele Indoor
Stadium with about two thousand people attending. King Tubou IV
spoke at the meeting, after which the Nelsons had lunch with the
king and queen of Tonga, followed by a program of cultural dances
and songs that proceeded despite torrential rains. Fortunately, the

Russell and Dantzel receive a tapa cloth welcome by Tongan Saints.

guests of honor enjoyed the festivities while seated beneath a protective shelter.[10]

The group then traveled to Vava'u, where the centennial celebration was held August 23 with Church members, political dignitaries, and leaders from other religious denominations. At the luncheon festival that followed, the police magistrate, though not a member of the Church, spoke of his great admiration and respect for the Church. He even testified that Joseph Smith was a prophet of God. At the end of the meeting, Elder Nelson told him he merited baptism in the Church, to which the officer replied, "I am just about ready."[11]

Saturday featured a music marathon. Afterward, Elder Nelson presented medals to the winners and leaders of various brass bands. First prize went to the band from the Wesleyan Church, second prize to the LDS Church brass band, and third prize to the Catholic band. When Elder Nelson complimented the other churches on their participation, they replied, "It's our celebration too." A parade was then held in the capital city of Neiafu, consisting of trucks, tractors, and wagons appropriately decorated with balloons and banners telling the story of one hundred years of Church history in Tonga. A luncheon was then held with entertainment provided by members

*Tofilau Eti Alesana, Samoan
prime minister, and his wife,
Pitolua, meet with President
Thomas S. Monson and Elder
Nelson on October 5, 1990.*

from outlying islands, some of whom had traveled as far as 250
miles.[12]

The festivities on each island were great bridge builders for
members of the Church. The Tongan government even issued two
commemorative postage stamps depicting the temple in Tonga. The
first-day issue of the stamps was August 19, the national holiday
declared for the centennial celebration.[13]

SAMOA/AMERICAN SAMOA

May 1992 found Elder and Sister Nelson and Elder James M.
Paramore and his wife, Helen, in Apia, Samoa. The Samoans were
still recovering from the devastation of hurricane *Val* the previous
December. Russell observed that "the regenerative power of nature is
marvelous, with new vegetation springing back to life so the
Samoans again have enough to eat."[14] The American visitors
observed that there were still many rooftops missing from homes,
churches, and schools.

The Brethren paid a courtesy call on Prime Minister Tofilau Eti
Alesana, presenting him with a check for $25,000, a gift from the
Church to assist in the restoration of schools. When Elder Nelson
invited the prime minister and his wife to attend the forthcoming

*Elder Nelson is warmly
greeted by the Saints in
Western Samoa in March
1987.*

regional conference, he said he would be honored to attend. Two days later, true to his commitment, the prime minister came to the regional conference, attended by nearly twelve thousand Samoans. Elder Nelson invited him to be the first speaker, and he gave "eloquent praise" to Church members and expressed gratitude for the influence of the Church in Samoa.[15]

AUSTRALIA AND NEW ZEALAND

Elder Nelson enjoyed his service in the South Seas and was pleased to travel to Australia and New Zealand on various occasions to participate in priesthood leadership training meetings and regional conferences. One particularly memorable trip "down under" was in 1993 when he and Dantzel traveled to New Zealand.

On November 6, a group of leaders gathered just north of the Hamilton New Zealand Temple, where Elder Nelson offered a dedicatory prayer on the country of New Zealand. Notwithstanding the fact that the Church had long been established in that beautiful country, a careful study of Church records could not confirm that a dedicatory prayer had ever been given. Therefore, the First Presidency and Twelve authorized Elder Nelson to dedicate the land. Invoking the keys of the Holy Apostleship, he prayed, "Wilt Thou bless this land with a rich portion of Thy Spirit, that its citizens and visitors may learn Thy commandments and obey them that they may prosper in Thy sight. . . . We know that this nation is rich with the blood of Israel, our Father. Bless them to find Thee."[16]

A week later, the Nelsons were in Sydney, Australia, where Elder Nelson dedicated the land of Australia for the preaching of the gospel. Because of a heavy rainstorm, wisdom dictated that the prayer be offered inside the Sydney Australia Temple rather than on the grounds near the temple. Elder Nelson prayed, "Let there be a renewal of missionary zeal, that Thine elect may be gathered here prior to the second coming of Thy Son. . . . May they enter the waters of baptism and take His holy name upon them. May they remain faithful and worthy to receive the ordinances and covenants of Thy holy temple."[17]

PHILIPPINES

In January 1996, Elder Nelson embarked alone for the Philippines, where he was welcomed by the area president, Elder Ben B. Banks and his wife, Sue. On January 13, Elders Banks and Nelson spoke to the missionaries of the Philippines Cebu Mission and concluded the day with a four-hour priesthood leadership training meeting with Filipino priesthood leaders.[18] On Monday, following Sunday's regional conference, Elder Nelson attended the Manila Philippines Temple in Quezon City.

After speaking to a hundred temple workers at the Manila Philippines Temple, a similar number of missionaries of the Philippines Bacolod Mission, and more than five hundred priesthood leaders, Elder Nelson concluded his journey with a regional conference in Bacolod, attended by more than three thousand Filipinos.[19] As in many other areas of the developing Church, many Filipino Saints are unable to attend church meetings every Sunday because of transportation costs, so family members often take turns attending on alternate Sundays. But when an Apostle of the Lord comes to town, they invariably make the sacrifice to attend regional conferences in goodly numbers.

Five years later, in mid-January 2001, Elder Nelson presided at a seminar in Manila for mission presidents and their wives serving in thirteen missions and in the missionary training center in the Philippines. On January 19, thousands of demonstrators gathered only a couple of blocks from the hotel where the seminar was held to demand the resignation of President Joseph Estrada. The military, cabinet members, and police joined in demonstrations of "no support," and the streets were crowded with automobiles honking in defiant rhythm. Elder Nelson concluded the day, declaring, "It's all very interesting but not exactly conducive to a good night's sleep. I fervently prayed for peace."[20]

After a fitful and noisy night, the area presidency and Elder Nelson conducted an area training meeting for Church leaders throughout the Philippines. At the close of the day, Elder Nelson invoked an apostolic blessing upon the citizens of the Philippines and upon the nation, pleading that peace would return and that governmental rule would be restored in righteousness. The next day, he spoke at an afternoon devotional service for Saints from four Manila stakes. Then, after a torturous journey through heavy traffic, he spoke to the members of four stakes in Quezon City,[21] where he learned that a peaceful transition of presidential power had occurred.

Elder Nelson concluded his second week in the Philippines at regional conference meetings on Saturday and Sunday in Cebu City. The next morning, he bade adieu to his hosts and caught a flight to Taipei, Taiwan. Because of a delayed arrival, Elder Nelson "ran like a rocket" through the long concourses of the airport to catch his flight to San Francisco. Once on the plane, he was able to stretch out and claim the sleep of a man anxiously engaged in the work of the Lord.

CHAPTER 34

ASSIGNMENTS ON
ANCESTRAL SOIL

WHETHER DISPATCHED IN THE summer to the hot and humid Philippines or in the winter to the frigid Republic of Russia, Elder Nelson accepts every assignment with enthusiasm and anticipation. He looks forward to meeting with Saints, full-time missionaries, investigators, and temple workers. He also enjoys meeting with government officials with whom he can build bridges and cultivate friendships. And he especially enjoys assignments to the lands of his ancestors.

In the summer of 1987, while Elder Nelson was serving as first contact of the Twelve for all of Europe, he and Sister Nelson took Russell Jr. with them to Scandinavia and Great Britain to participate in the sesquicentennial commemoration of the arrival of the first Latter-day Saint missionaries in England and to trace the steps of Nelson family ancestors. It was in July 1837 that Heber C. Kimball and other brethren arrived in Liverpool, England, and began teaching the gospel in the church of Reverend James Fielding in Preston. The reverend's brother, Joseph Fielding, had immigrated to Canada, where he had joined the Church and later answered the call to serve a mission in his native England.[1]

Now, 150 years later, the Saints in England were celebrating the introduction of the restored gospel to this beautiful, sceptered isle.

On the evening of July 24, 1987, the Church sponsored a banquet at the Savoy Hotel in London. Attendees included President Ezra Taft Benson and Sister Benson, President Gordon B. Hinckley and Sister Hinckley, former Prime Minister Edward Heath, and Lord Rhodes Boyson and Lady Boyson. Sir Rhodes had served as minister of education in the British cabinet.[2]

Several other distinguished members of the Church in the international business community were also present.[3] Elder and Sister Nelson were privileged to sit at the head table between the Bensons and the Boysons. Each guest received a Wedgwood plate and a commemorative reproduction of the 1841 edition of the Book of Mormon, similar to the one presented to Queen Victoria by Lorenzo Snow at the behest of Brigham Young. The original of that copy is located in the library at Windsor Castle.[4]

The next day, the Nelsons traveled from London to the Benbow Farm, near the town of Ledbury. It was here that Wilford Woodruff, during his second mission to England, in March 1840, taught the gospel to the United Brethren, an offshoot of the Wesleyan Methodist Church. During his stay in this area of southwestern England, Elder Woodruff baptized six hundred members of the United Brethren in a small pond on the Benbow property.[5] The Church subsequently purchased a narrow tract of land leading to the pond, and on July 25, 1987, Elder Nelson dedicated a permanent plaque located near the pond. The plaque attached to a stand tells of Elder Woodruff's missionary efforts in baptizing all but one of the United Brethren.[6]

The Nelsons then drove southward to Cardiff, Wales, where they met with and presented gifts to various civic leaders. A beautiful Welsh choir sang a song titled "Tydi A Roddaist," which Elder Nelson later retitled "Hosanna" after writing lyrics for it in English.[7] Men of the Mormon Tabernacle Choir sang the song during the priesthood session of general conference the following October:

Hosanna

Through time's immortal endless stay
In love he guides our way.
Beyond the realms of heaven's beam,
Our great God, Elohim.
Hosanna to his holy name—
Our Fathers' God is still the same.
That holy night in Bethlehem
His Son was born among men.
To ransom from a timeless grave,
Each child of God to save.
Hosanna to his holy name—
Our Fathers' God is still the same.
His priesthood power restored to earth
To bless each soul given birth.
Our song of prayer to him we raise,
Proclaiming joy and praise.
Hosanna to his holy name—
Our Father's God is still the same.[8]

On Sunday, July 26, members throughout the entire British Isles participated in the 150th anniversary of the Church in Great Britain. Two members of the First Presidency, four members of the Quorum of the Twelve, and seven members of the First Quorum of the Seventy were allocated among commemorative meetings held in London, Birmingham, Glasgow, Belfast, Dublin, Bristol, and Plymouth.[9]

The next day, Brother V. Ben Bloxham, an expert in Church and family history in Great Britain, assisted the Nelsons in locating the records office in Taunton, Somerset County, where they found the parish register for Ditcheat, where Russell's great-grandmother, Emma Jane Hillard, was christened on April 2, 1826. The Nelsons entered the little village church, which was erected in the twelfth century, and they obtained a copy of the marriage certificate for Emma Jane Hillard and Stephen Williams, who were married in

Bristol on December 26, 1845. Stephen and Emma Jane were among the early British converts to the Church.[10]

The Nelsons proceeded to Hungerford, in Berkshire, where Elder Nelson dedicated another plaque and bench in commemoration of the birthplace of Elder James E. Talmage on September 21, 1862.[11] Later in the week, they drove through the beautiful Cotswolds to Stratford-upon-Avon, where Shakespeare and several of Dantzel's ancestors were born.[12] On July 30, they visited the little village of Loxley, where Sarah Howkins, Dantzel's great-grandmother was born in 1827. The town of Ratley, located nearby, is the birthplace of Sarah's parents, Daniel and Mary Green Howkins.[13]

The search for headstones of deceased ancestors is of little avail in most cemeteries throughout the British Isles and continental Europe because the incumbents of graves are generally exhumed every twenty years or so. Thus, headstones merely indicate the most recent deceased tenant of the burial plot. This long-standing custom prompted Shakespeare to write his own prescient epitaph preceding his death on April 23, 1616. On a memorial stone laid above Shakespeare's remains in the chancel of the Trinity Church in Stratford-upon-Avon are the words:

> *Good friend, for Jesus' sake forbear*
> *To dig the dust enclosed here.*
> *Blest be the man that spares these stones*
> *And curst be he that moves my bones.*[14]

The Nelsons enjoyed visiting family history sites as well as Church history sites, including the city of Preston, where missionaries held their first meetings after arriving in 1837. The Nelsons then went to the River Ribble, where George Watts won the footrace to the river's edge to became the first British convert to be baptized, on July 30, 1837, exactly one hundred fifty years before.[15]

They next strolled to Avenham Park, not far from the river. President Hinckley dedicated a plaque in this park as part of the activities commemorating the emigration of nearly 80,000 Saints from Great Britain to Utah. The Nelsons then proceeded to the house at 15 Wadham Road, which had served as young Elder Hinckley's *digs* during the early days of his mission in England in 1933.[16] They also visited the flat on St. Wilfrid Street, where Heber C. Kimball and his missionary companions had lived.

The following day, they drove through the picturesque villages of Clitheroe, Chatburn, and Downham with their narrow, winding streets and quaint little houses of stone. Elder Heber C. Kimball taught and converted many people in these towns who eventually emigrated to Zion. Of this journey with his parents, Russell Jr. said, "Dad invited me along on this trip so I would see that the Church is more than a chapel on Gilmer Drive in Salt Lake City."[17]

NORWAY

Norway was the home of Russell's great-grandfather Johan Andreas Jensen, a tempestuous sea captain who joined the Church in 1854. Johan's daughter, Russell's Grandmother Nelson, was also born in Norway. Whenever Elder Nelson returns to Norway, he feels a certain kinship with this particular ancestor and with his Norwegian cousins.

In conjunction with an assignment in Europe, Elder and Sister Nelson traveled to Norway in 1997 to assist in bringing the Church out of obscurity in that land. In June, they accepted an invitation to participate in the one-thousandth anniversary of the founding of Trondheim, a city not far from the little village of Daloe, where Elder John A. Widstoe (1872–1952) was born. Accompanied by Elder John E. Fowler of the presidency of the Europe North Area, and his wife, Marie, the Nelsons first landed in Oslo, where they met with forty missionaries. That evening, they attended a banquet arranged by Brother Erland Petersen, a former mission president in Norway and now an official at Brigham Young University. Attendees included Carsten Smith, a Norwegian Supreme Court justice who had recently received an honorary doctorate from Brigham Young University, and his wife, Lucy, president of Oslo University. Members of the Norwegian Parliament and several other dignitaries were also present. Following the banquet, the Nelsons and Fowlers spoke at a fireside attended by nearly a thousand Saints.[18]

On June 10, 1997, the Nelsons, Fowlers, and Norway Oslo Mission president Bernt Lundgren and his wife, Violet, flew to Tromsø, north of the Arctic Circle. There they met with the city's mayor and with the director of Tromsø University. They concluded the day with another fireside.[19]

The next day the retinue flew to Bodø, where Elder Nelson met with missionaries and Church members in this northern outpost of Zion. On June 12, the Nelsons and Fowlers traveled to Trondheim, where they were greeted by leaders from the University of Trondheim. They presented copies of *The Family: A Proclamation to the World* and statuettes of a pioneer handcart family sculptured by Norwegian-born artist Torlief Knaphus to the president of the university and to the mayor's office. When Elder Nelson referred to his Norwegian heritage during a luncheon at the university's medical school, he established an immediate bond of friendship with his hosts. They seemed genuinely pleased to learn that Elder John A. Widstoe, the fifty-fourth Apostle of this dispensation, had lived near Trondheim as a young lad, and that Elder Nelson, the eighty-fifth Apostle of this dispensation, also shared Norwegian ancestry.[20]

The next day, the group caught a flight to the beautiful coastal city of Bergen, where Elders Nelson and Fowler were interviewed by the editor of the newspaper *Bergen Tidende*. He later wrote a complimentary full-page story about Elder Nelson's apostolic visit to Norway. Elder Nelson spoke at a fireside that evening, and on June 14, he and the others flew to Stavanger, where Elders Nelson and Fowler participated in a district conference.[21]

The following March, the Nelsons hosted a dinner in Salt Lake City for Georg Geiber-Mohn, a Norwegian Supreme Court justice.

He was accompanied by his son, Fredrik, and Svein Ludvigsen, a member of Norway's Parliament. Through the gentle influence of Elder Nelson and other Brethren, the persistent efforts of the full-time missionaries, and the faith of the Norwegian members, the Church is, indeed, coming out of obscurity in Norway.

CHAPTER 35

THE FAMILY AND
THE TEMPLE

SAMUEL JOHNSON OBSERVED, "When a man knows he is to be hanged in a fortnight, it concentrates his mind wonderfully."[1] The imminent prospect of death places in bold relief the things that matter most in life. Elder Nelson related just such an experience he had November 12, 1976:

"I was in an airplane going from Salt Lake City to St. George to participate in a function at Dixie College. We were in one of those small commuter airplanes. There were about six passengers in it. The pilot had just announced that we were over the halfway point between Salt Lake City and St. George—we were past the point of no return. I thought, 'Well, that's a weird announcement to make.'

"Shortly after that, the engine on the right wing of the airplane burst open in flames, spewing oil all over the right side of the plane. The propeller became starkly still and the whole engine was on fire. We then went into a dive earthward. I assumed that my life was going to be terminated right then and there.

"The poor lady across the aisle from me was in absolute hysterics. She was right there where the flames were the brightest. But the pilot had turned off the ignition that fed more gas into the fire and had purposely been in a steep dive hoping that the flames might be extinguished, which was what happened. Then, with the power still left in the other propeller—which he then turned on just as we were about ready to have our moment of impact—he was able to glide us, following a highway, until we could make an emergency landing.

"I'm pleased to report that I was really prepared. I knew I was facing death and I was calm. I knew that the most important thing I had ever done was to marry Dantzel White in the temple on August 31—that all of the children that have come into our home were born in the covenant—all faithful; and I was ready to die."[2]

TEMPLES

Elder Nelson has a great love for the temple and boundless gratitude for the eternal covenants made and the ordinances performed therein. For him, there is virtually a seamless transition from families to family history to temple ordinances. And, as evidenced by his reactions to his near-death experience, he anticipates a seamless transition from mortality to the eternal realms beyond.

In addition to their first-contact responsibilities with area presidencies serving in twenty-nine different areas of the world, members of the Quorum of the Twelve Apostles also serve on various executive councils overseeing the building of the kingdom. The Priesthood Executive Council directs the work of the priesthood, the auxiliaries, and the development of Church curriculum. The Missionary Executive Council oversees the proclaiming of the gospel and the development of the supporting materials and services needed in missionary work. The Temple and Family History Executive Council, under the direction of the First Presidency, helps facilitate the construction and operation of temples and the expansion of family history work.

In 1990, Elder Nelson was assigned to the Temple and Family History Executive Council, an assignment he has enjoyed for the past thirteen years. During his first few years on the committee, he worked under the direction of Elder Neal A. Maxwell. Since 1998, Elder Nelson has been the council chairman, ably aided by Elder

Henry B. Eyring. A dozen years ago, activities within the Temple Department, Family History Department, and Church Historical Department were rather predictable. In 1990, for example, only one temple, the Toronto Ontario Temple, was dedicated, bringing the total number of temples in operation throughout the world to forty-four. Over the next five years, three more temples were dedicated. The rate of temple construction, however, accelerated from 1996 to 1999. The Hong Kong China and Mount Timpanogos Utah Temples were dedicated in 1996, the St. Louis Missouri and Vernal Utah Temples were dedicated in 1997, and the Preston England and Monticello Utah Temples were dedicated in 1998.[3]

As President Howard W. Hunter addressed the Saints in his new calling as president of the Church in 1994, he said: "I invite the Latter-day Saints to look to the temple of the Lord as the great symbol of your membership. It is the deepest desire of my heart to have every member of the Church worthy to enter the temple. It would please the Lord if every adult member would be worthy of—and carry—a current temple recommend. . . . Let us be a temple-attending people. Attend the temple as frequently as personal circumstances allow. . . . If proximity to a temple does not allow frequent attendance, gather in the history of your family and prepare the names for the sacred ordinances performed only in the temple."[4]

Although President Hunter's leadership was truncated by death in March 1995, the Saints heard the clarion call. Many of them sought temple recommends, notwithstanding inordinately long distances that might prevent them from actually attending a temple. During general conference in October 1997, President Gordon B. Hinckley informed the Saints that seventeen temples were under construction, noting that "there are many areas that are remote, where the membership is small and not likely to grow very much in the near future." Then, he made a breathtaking announcement: "We will construct small temples in some of these areas, buildings with all of the facilities to administer all of the ordinances."[5]

The trump had sounded, and in 1999, fifteen additional temples were dedicated. During the year 2000, thirty-four more temples were dedicated, including nine temples in Mexico alone. The next year, five temples were dedicated, and in 2002, seven temples were dedicated and two others were rededicated after extensive remodeling (the Freiberg Germany and Monticello Utah Temples).[6]

As the number of temples has increased, so, of course, has the number of temple presidents called each year. Elder Nelson is aware that correct teaching of principles to temple presidents has a spiritual urgency and life-and-death consequences not unlike those he encountered as a cardiovascular-thoracic surgeon. He teaches that the Lord will never withdraw His covenant, so why, he asks, would His children want to withdraw from that covenant?

To help temple presidents and matrons explain the protective importance of the sacred temple garment, Elder Nelson will place an orange in a bowl filled with water, which represents the world. With the peeling intact, the orange continually floats to the top, impervious to its potentially invasive surroundings. But when Elder Nelson removes the protective peeling, the orange immediately sinks to the bottom. A picture is worth a thousand words, and those who see this demonstration always remember it.[7] In a wicked world in which people either sink or swim, God's children constantly need all of the protection available to them.

In addition to the leadership he provides on the Temple and Family History Executive Council, Elder Nelson has written and spoken extensively about the temple. A few excerpts from his teachings follow:

"Each temple is symbolic of our faith in God and an evidence of our faith in life after death. The temple is the object of every activity, every lesson, every progressive step in the Church. All of our efforts in proclaiming the gospel, perfecting the Saints, and redeeming the dead lead to the holy temple. President Hinckley declared that 'these unique and wonderful buildings, and the ordinances administered therein, represent the ultimate in our worship. These ordinances become the most profound expressions of our theology.' Ordinances of the temple are absolutely crucial. We cannot return to God's glory without them. . . .

"In the temple we receive an endowment, which is, literally speaking, a gift. We need to understand the spiritual significance of it and the importance of keeping the sacred covenants and obligations we make in receiving this gift. . . .

"In each temple the sealing authority of the priesthood is exercised. Jesus made reference to that authority when He instructed Peter and other Apostles, 'I will give unto thee the keys of the kingdom of heaven: and whatsoever thou shalt bind on earth shall be bound in heaven: and whatsoever thou shalt loose on earth shall be loosed in heaven' [Matthew 16:19]. . . . Just as priesthood is eternal—without beginning or end—so is the authority of that priesthood. Consequently, the ordinances and covenants of the priesthood also transcend time. . . .

"Because a temple is sacred, the Lord asks that it be protected from desecration. Anyone may enter who is willing to prepare well for that privilege. . . . Judges in Israel who hold keys of priesthood authority and responsibility help us prepare by conducting temple recommend interviews. . . . Succinctly stated, an individual is required to keep the commandments of Him whose house it is. He has set the standards. We enter the temple as His guests. . . .

"The wearing of the temple garment bears great symbolic significance and represents a continuing commitment. Just as the Savior gave us an example of His ability to endure to the end, wearing the garment is one way we demonstrate enduring faith in Him and in His eternal covenants with us. . . .

"Because the ordinances and covenants of the temple are sacred, we are under absolute obligation not to discuss outside the temple that which occurs in the temple. Sacred matters deserve sacred consideration. . . .

"The teachings of the temple are beautifully simple and simply beautiful. They are understood by the humble, yet they can excite the intellect of the brightest minds. . . .

"An eternal perspective helps us maintain complete fidelity to the covenants we make. President Packer emphasized that 'ordinances and covenants become our credentials for admission into [God's] presence. To worthily receive them is the quest of a lifetime; to keep them thereafter is the challenge of mortality.' . . .

"Each temple stands as a symbol of our membership in the Church, as a sign of our faith in life after death, and as a stepping-stone to eternal glory for us and our family. I pray that each member of the Church will prepare for the marvelous blessings of the temple."[8]

FAMILY HISTORY

Between 1993 and 1998, Elder Monte J. Brough, then one of the seven presidents of the Seventy, served as executive director of the Family History Department. He came to the assignment with excellent preparation and expertise, having started his own highly successful computer company prior to his call as a General Authority. He developed a close and compatible working relationship with Elder Nelson in the latter's capacity as a member of the Temple and Family History Executive Council. As the number of temples in operation began to increase exponentially, it became readily apparent that the pace of family history work had to quicken in order to ensure an adequate number of names for all the temples.[9]

In the spring of 1998, Elder Nelson, Elder Brough, and others engaged in family history work met with several business executives of the leading computer and Internet companies in America. During their discussions with these experts in their respective fields, the brethren learned that fully one-fifth of all Internet activity pertained to family history.[10]

The evening following that meeting, Elder Brough lost a night's sleep deliberating on ways the Church could capitalize on Internet technology. He arose the next morning, prompted to sketch out six areas in which the Internet could assist members in pursuing their family history. Elder Brough then met with Elder Nelson to discuss his ideas.[11]

Elder Nelson supported these promptings, but many of the Brethren were concerned about Internet pornography. Some remained unimpressed by demonstrations of Internet technology because of difficulty linking up to a server, and others were simply put off by the technical jargon used in describing the possible use of the Internet for family history research.[12]

President Thomas S. Monson has observed that Elder Nelson "has a curiosity that leads to learning. He is never content but always wants to know more, and he can wrap his mind around the latest technology."[13] Just as he had facilitated understanding among patients, administrators, and staff at various hospitals, Elder Nelson patiently and adroitly put complicated technological terms into a language that all of the Brethren could readily comprehend. In June 1998, the Brethren approved FamiLink, a computer website designed to assist Latter-day Saints and people of other faiths to more efficiently conduct family history research. Under the guidance of Elder Nelson, the website name was later changed to FamilySearch (familysearch.org). President Gordon B. Hinckley announced the launching of the website during a May 1999 press conference.[14] FamilySearch is so popular that it receives nearly fifteen million hits a day!

The extraction and linkage of the Freedman Bank Records was another exciting development. At the conclusion of the Civil War, the United States government organized the Freedman's Bureau (1865–72) to assist four million newly freed slaves to find employment and housing. An adjunct to this bureau was the Freedman Bank, which was organized to protect the savings of freed African-Americans. Unfortunately, fraudulent activities led to the bank's failure. Despite this tragedy, much residual good has come a century

and a half later from the records of 480,000 names maintained by
the bank.[15]

About a dozen years ago, Sister Marie Taylor of the Family and
Church History Department became aware of the existence of
microfilmed records of the Freedman Bank that had been housed in
the National Archives. When she made the Brethren aware of this
valuable resource, they agreed that it would be wise to extract these
records so they could be made available to the descendants of the
original bank patrons.[16] Over the course of the next eleven years,
about five hundred inmates from the Utah State Prison volunteered
to participate in this massive extraction project. At a press conference on February 26, 2001, the Church announced the availability
of the Freedman Bank records on CD.[17]

On April 16, 2001, Elders Nelson, Richard G. Scott, D. Todd
Christofferson, and W. Craig Zwick, along with Brother Bruce L.
Olsen of Church public affairs participated in ceremonies launch-
ing the American Family Immigration History Center on Ellis
Island. The Church had been a partner with the U.S. Department
of Interior, the National Park Service, and the Ellis Island–Statue of
Liberty Foundation in extracting and indexing records of all the
immigrants who passed through Ellis Island.[18]

Noted TV news journalist Tom Brokaw was the master of ceremonies, and speakers included Lee Iacocca, former CEO of Chrysler
Corporation and head of the Ellis Island–Statue of Liberty Foundation; and Gale Norton, secretary of the Department of the
Interior. Elder Nelson represented the Church in announcing the
gift of an automated database consisting of the names of twenty-four
million immigrants who came to America through Ellis Island from
1892 to 1924.

"This magnificent gift represents the work of more than twelve
thousand volunteers who worked for a period of seven years to
transcribe the written information as recorded on microfilm to the
digitized form that could be read by computer," Elder Nelson

Elder Nelson participates in ceremonies launching the American Family Immigration History Center on Ellis Island. Seated to his right is newsman Tom Brokaw, and seated beside him are Gale Norton, secretary of the Department of the Interior; and Lee Iacocca, head of the Ellis Island–Statue of Liberty Foundation.

announced. "This represented a donation of more than 5.6 million hours of tedious labor. These volunteers did all of that transcription work from 3,678 rolls of microfilm, each containing thousands of immigrant entries. If those rolls of film were stacked upon each other, they would be more than three times the height of the Statue of Liberty from the hem of her flowing robe to the tip of her torch."[19]

Elder Nelson's remarks were interrupted by spontaneous applause. Following the program, the Brethren were interviewed by media from all over the world.

As with temple work, Elder Nelson practices the doctrine he teaches with regard to family history research. Excerpts from his teachings, which include words from the prophets, follow:

"Perhaps the greatest example of vicarious work for the dead is the Master Himself. He gave His life as a vicarious atonement, that all who die shall live again and have life everlasting. He did for us what we could not do for ourselves. In a similar way we can perform ordinances for those who did not have the opportunity to do them in their lifetime. . . .

"Ordinances for the dead had to await the Atonement and post-mortal ministry of the Savior. . . .

"'This is the spirit of Elijah, that we redeem our dead, and connect ourselves with our fathers which are in heaven. . . . This is the power of Elijah and the keys of the kingdom of Jehovah.' . . .

"This doctrine and its ordinances are laden with love and are intended to perpetuate the sweetest of all relationships—in families forever."[20]

"Family love is wonderful. . . . Nothing is as predictable as the love of children for their parents or the love of parents for their children.

"Recently I was tenderly hugging one of our . . . granddaughters and said to her, 'I love you, sweetheart.'

"She responded rather blandly: 'I know.'

"I asked, 'How do you know that I love you?'

"'Because! You're my grandfather!'

"That was reason enough for her. Indeed, we do love our grandchildren. We also love our grandparents. I cherish the memories of life with three of my four grandparents. . . .

"Elijah came not only to stimulate research for ancestors. He also enabled families to be eternally linked beyond the bounds of mortality. Indeed, the opportunity for families to be sealed forever is the real reason for our research. . . .

"Our grandparents watch—and wait—for us to identify them, be linked to them, and provide temple ordinances for them."[21]

"'Let us, therefore, as a church and a people . . . offer unto the Lord an offering in righteousness; and let us present in his holy temple . . . a book containing the records of our dead . . . worthy of all acceptation' (D&C 128:24)."[22]

CHAPTER 36

A LIFE OF CITIZENSHIP
AND SERVICE

MANY MEDICAL PRACTITIONERS focus so intently on their personal practice that they have little time or inclination to serve on committees or in leadership positions in medical societies. Many university professors and researchers become so caught up in the pressure to "publish or perish" that they make no time for citizenship within the university or the community. Many Church leaders concentrate their efforts on church and family to the exclusion of any professional or civic involvement. Few individuals have struck a better balance in meeting the demands of profession, citizenship, church, and family than has Russell M. Nelson.

The Lord has said, "I, the Lord, am merciful and gracious unto those who fear me, and delight to honor those who serve me in righteousness and in truth unto the end" (D&C 76:5). Elder Nelson's willingness to sacrifice personal preferences for the good of his family, profession, and the Church have garnered him many honors, including leadership responsibilities. He modestly observed, "The honor of leadership is not as important as the good that one is able to accomplish with that privilege."[1]

In recognition of Dr. Nelson's contributions to the field of cardiovascular surgery, in May 1964, he was elected president of the Utah Heart Association. Far from merely assuming a titular role in this influential organization, he was proactive in advancing knowledge about the prevention and treatment of heart disease. He also actively marshaled resources for continued research in this area.

In 1967, the University of Utah College of Medicine awarded Dr. Nelson fellowship in Medici Publici, an organization that recognizes medical school graduates of the university who have gained prominence through their significant contributions to the field of medicine.[2] That same year, he received a distinguished alumnus award from the University of Utah.[3]

Notwithstanding the demands on his time from teaching, conducting research, performing operations, and serving as a stake president from 1966–72, Russell was chairman of the Division of Thoracic Surgery at LDS Hospital. He was also actively engaged in the American Heart Association and served on its central committee from 1967–69. During this same period, 1967–68, he became president of the Utah Chapter of the American College of Surgeons. In 1969, he became "national secretary of the Society for Vascular Surgery and secretary for the Thoracic Surgery Directors Association for the United States and Canada."[4]

The fall of 1969, Dr. Nelson became president-elect of the Utah State Medical Association, assuming that responsibility for one year in 1970.[5] During this same period, the University of Utah College of Medicine was creating a program in bioengineering to look into the potential of an artificial heart. Dr. Nelson was named as director of medical services in the team to staff the new Artificial Heart Test and Evaluation Facility.[6]

Dr. Nelson's skills as a teacher of surgery were also recognized nationally when he was elected president of the Thoracic Surgery Directors Association in 1971.[7] That same year, he became a member of the Advisory Council of Thoracic Surgeons of the American College of Surgeons, the largest organization of surgeons in the world. Three years later, he was accorded another high honor when he was elected chairman of that organization's advisory council.[8]

For six years, Russell served as one of the directors of the prestigious and highly influential American Board of Thoracic Surgery.

This fifteen-member board examines and certifies specialists in thoracic surgery, applications for which are received from surgeons throughout the world. One of his esteemed colleagues, Dr. Benson B. Roe, recalled the "arduous procedure of constructing, gathering, editing, discussing, and reviewing the questions in which the entire fifteen man board participated." Board directors are nominated by the American Association of Thoracic Surgeons, the Society of Thoracic Surgeons, the American Surgical Association, the American College of Surgeons, and the American Medical Association. Their individual and collective efforts involved "thousands of highly skilled professional man hours, all without remuneration."[9]

In recognition of his countless contributions to the field of medicine, Brigham Young University conferred an honorary Doctor of Science degree on Dr. Nelson in 1970.[10]

In June 1974, Dr. Nelson was elected president of the Society of Vascular Surgery, "so named because when it was formed in 1947, heart surgery had never been accomplished and surgeons worked only on the blood vessels."[11] The first successful open-heart surgery employing extracorporeal circulation was performed in 1953. Two years later, Dr. Nelson performed the first such operation in Utah.

The ever-increasing circle of Russell M. Nelson's professional influence extended to international spheres as the Republic of Argentina expressed its appreciation for Dr. Nelson's "pioneering contributions to the field of heart diseases" and for his unselfish service in teaching his surgical skills to Argentine cardiovascular surgeons by awarding him a Gold Medal of Merit on August 31, 1974.[12]

As an exception to a prophet's being without honor in his own country, the Kiwanis Club of Salt Lake City presented Dr. Nelson with the 1974 Health Service Award that same year.[13]

In the fall of 1975, Dr. Nelson presented a paper on "Ten-Year Follow-up on Patients of Aortic Valve Replacement" to the Societé Internationale de Chirurgie in Edinburgh, Scotland, before more than two thousand researchers.[14] Toward the end of 1976, Dr. Nelson was elected chairman of the American Heart Association's Council on Cardiovascular Surgery. The AHA has fourteen scientific councils and 120,000 members.[15] When this honor was brought to the attention of President Spencer W. Kimball, he wrote Dr. Nelson a complimentary letter expressing his gratitude for Russell's service to him personally and to the Church.

THE CHURCH OF JESUS CHRIST OF LATTER-DAY SAINTS
47 EAST SOUTH TEMPLE STREET
SALT LAKE CITY, UTAH 84111

SPENCER W. KIMBALL, PRESIDENT

November 19, 1976

Dr. Russell M. Nelson
1347 Normandie Circle
Salt Lake City, Utah

Dear Brother Russell:

How pleased we are to learn of the honor that has come to you in your election as chairman of the American Heart Association's Council on Cardiovascular Surgery. We extend our sincere commendation to you.

We are proud of you and of the well deserved recognition you have received in the field of thoracic surgery, not only in the State of Utah and throughout the nation, but internationally as well.

We esteem and commend you also, Brother Russell, for the wonderful influence for good you continue to be as a worthy emissary of the Church and for your effective efforts in your leadership of the Sunday School.

I am, personally, so grateful to you for the special courtesies and services you have extended to me and for our association as we travel together.

May our Heavenly Father's choicest blessings be with you, and with your lovely Dantzel and your family, as you continue to meet the opportunities, challenges and responsibilities which come to you.

Faithfully yours,

President

In recognition of his invaluable teaching of heart surgeons in Mexico, the American Heart Association awarded Dr. Nelson the International Service Citation in March 1979 while he was attending national meetings in Dallas.[16] Three months later, Dr. Nelson received the Golden Plate award from the American Academy of Achievement. During its annual "Salute to Excellence" banquet on June 23, Dr. Nelson was cited as a "pioneer in open-heart surgery, as well as a religious leader, humanitarian and model parent." The award ceremonies were conducted by the actor Ed Asner. Others attending included actress Olivia de Havilland, Dr. Michael E. DeBakey, Dallas Cowboys football coach Tom Landry, actor James Stewart, and Nobel Prize winner Dr. Linus C. Pauling.[17]

On February 1, 1980, Dr. Nelson was named vice chairman of the LDS hospital board of governors.[18] In 1984, just two months after being called to the Quorum of the Twelve Apostles, Elder Nelson received the Gold Heart Award from the Utah Heart Association in recognition of and appreciation for his contributions as a pioneering heart surgeon.

"The new Apostle said Charles A. Lindbergh gets credit for some of the early pioneering efforts in the [field of circulatory support]," the *Church News* reported. "Lindbergh's sister-in-law was dying from mitral stenosis, a heart condition in which a valve cannot open. Lindbergh, who knew something about valves in airplane engines, insisted if an engine valve could be [repaired] so could a heart valve—and contacted a French surgeon [Alexis Carrel]. Unfortunately, said Elder Nelson, she died before her mitral valve could be [corrected]."[19]

Dr. Nelson was cited for his pioneering participation with the team that built the first heart-lung machine at the University of Minnesota while he was a resident there. His subsequent successful construction of a heart-lung machine enabled his first open-heart operation in Utah in 1955.

In late September 1985, Elder Nelson was awarded an honorary professorship from the Shandong Medical College, located in the city of Jinan, Shandong Province, China.[20] Four Chinese physicians from that medical college were working at LDS Hospital when Dr. Li Shouxian represented the president of Shandong Medical College in conferring the award of honorary professor during a luncheon at the University of Utah.[21]

Luncheon host Dr. Cecil O. Samuelson Jr., of the University of Utah College of Medicine, said, "Dr. Nelson is a distinguished Utah medical alumnus. His accomplishments in science and medicine, as well as his contributions as an LDS Church leader, continue to bring great credit to the University of Utah. We are pleased to host this event and be a part of this singular honor for Dr. Nelson."[22]

In January 1985, Elder Nelson honored a commitment he had made two years previously to be the guest speaker at the annual meeting of the Seattle Surgical Society. After presenting the keynote address and then discussing the papers of all the other presenters, he was awarded an honorary membership in the Seattle Surgical Society.[23]

Toward the end of March that same year, East High School of Salt Lake City granted "Distinguished Alumnus" awards to Senator Jake Garn, Mr. Valois Zarr, and Elder Russell M. Nelson. A slide presentation was prepared to highlight the achievements of each of the recipients. Near the conclusion of the program, Marion C. Nelson, Russell's father, who had been a student body president seventy years previously in 1915, was introduced to the audience and received a standing ovation.[24]

In April 1993, Elder Nelson received the Legacy of Life Award from the LDS Hospital-Deseret Foundation's Heart and Lung Institute. Several General Authorities were present at the banquet in which the award was given, including President Gordon B. Hinckley and President Thomas Monson. Elder Nelson's medical colleagues sang his praises as a visionary man and extolled his accomplishments during his forty-year medical career. Robert N. Sears, chairman of the institute's Community Advisory Council, presented the Legacy of Life Award to Elder Nelson, who responded,

Elder Nelson and Elder Neal A. Maxwell meet with President George Bush in September 1991.

"Tonight, recognition has been given to researchers who have brought light and hope where little existed before, as well as to patients whose cries for relief have strongly motivated everyone here. . . . Even more courageous are they who endure risk in reaching for fruits of that research for a better life."[25]

David P. Gardner, a former president of the University of Utah, said, "Russell Nelson is a person I have respected, not for any one of his many accomplishments, but because he is accomplished in so many aspects and conventions of life."[26]

Richard M. Cagen, an administrator at LDS Hospital, described Elder Nelson as one of the "giants who built LDS Hospital's cardio-thoracic surgical program." He underscored Elder Nelson's far-reaching impact as a teacher of other surgeons, concluding, "His influence has never stopped, and we don't think it ever will."[27]

Also attending the banquet were Blair and Lillie Anne Bradshaw. Sister Bradshaw recounted how anxious she felt after her husband's heart surgery at the hand of Dr. Nelson. "Elder Nelson took time to come and write in my journal, draw a picture and explain thoroughly to me what had happened and to set my mind at ease," she said. "We love him."[28]

In accepting the accolades bestowed upon him, Elder Nelson humbly approached the microphone and recited a poem he had written:

> *Our God is my maker;*
> *Parents dear are my guide;*
> *An angel wife my true love;*
> *Children choice are my pride.*
>
> *Our Lord is my light;*
> *His endless truth, my law.*
> *My joy is in service to others;*
> *My message is—my life.* [29]

Nearly two decades after the close of his surgical career, in recognition of his pioneering contributions to open-heart surgery and the development of the heart-lung machine, the American Heart Association presented Elder Nelson with the Heart of Gold Award on April 13, 2002. Following a video presentation highlighting his many medical achievements, Dr. Donald B. Doty, one of Russell's surgical colleagues and former associates, expressed his feelings about Dr. Nelson's transition from surgeon to Apostle: "I think Elder Nelson's contributions in cardiac surgery pale to what he's done since he's been an Apostle. In cardiac surgery we, as surgeons, affect the lives of individuals in a very profound way, but it's always one-on-one. We can only take care of one patient at a time. But when one is in the position of healing lives spiritually, then thousands can be affected at any one time."[30]

Dr. Doty then presented the Heart of Gold award, after which Elder Nelson expressed gratitude to his colleagues in the medical profession, his family, and his "beloved associates in the sacred work to which we have been called."[31] President James E. Faust, who attended the award ceremony, commented several days afterward

Elder Nelson speaks with President Bill Clinton prior to a breakfast meeting in the White House for members of a newly formed Religious Freedom Abroad Advisory Committee, January 6, 1997.

that Elder Nelson's response to the award had brought to mind Psalm 119:46: "I will speak of thy testimonies also before kings, and will not be ashamed."[32]

In addition to his citizenship and service within the medical profession and the community, Elder Nelson accepted an invitation by President William Jefferson Clinton to become a member of the nation's Religious Freedom Abroad Advisory Committee. Elder Nelson's vast experience in Eastern Europe in negotiating the legal recognition of the Church and subsequently acquiring visas for missionaries made him one of the most qualified members of this committee.

On January 6, 1997, President Clinton and Vice President Al Gore and their wives hosted a breakfast for Elder Nelson and about ninety other representatives from various religious denominations. President Clinton asked Elder Nelson to extend his personal regards to President Hinckley, and Vice President and Mrs. Gore acknowledged with fondness the compilation of their family history recently presented to them by Elder Neal A. Maxwell.[33]

On July 1–2, Elder Nelson attended advisory committee meetings at the State Department in Washington, D.C., led by Assistant

Secretary of State John Shattuck. Elder Nelson returned for similar meetings on October 8, 1997.[34]

On January 23, 1998, committee members again met in Washington, D.C., to present a report on their first year's activity and to offer recommendations to Secretary of State Madeleine K. Albright. Elder Nelson once again met with the committee on March 12 to hear testimony from people from the Sudan, Cuba, Egypt, and China. That fall, Elder Nelson attended three more advisory committee meetings.[35]

On May 17, 1999, Elder Nelson attended the advisory committee's final meeting. Congress decided that the task initially given to the committee would be performed by the U.S. Commission on International Religious Freedom as authorized by the Religious Freedom Act, which was unanimously passed by Congress in 1998.[36] The person elected as chairman of the commission was Michael K. Young, dean of the George Washington University Law School and a member of the McLean First Ward in Virginia.[37] Elder Nelson had released Brother Young as president of the New York New York Stake a decade earlier.

As shown by his lifetime of service, Elder Nelson has claimed the Savior's promise to those who continually render unselfish service: "Give, and it shall be given unto you; good measure, pressed down, and shaken together, and running over, shall men give into your bosom. For with the same measure that ye mete withal it shall be measured to you again" (Luke 6:38).

CHAPTER 37

THE ABUNDANT LIFE

THE SAVIOR DECLARED, "I AM come that they might have life, and that they might have it more abundantly" (John 10:10). With boundless joy and rejoicing in their rich posterity, Russell and Dantzel have truly led abundant lives. After many years of scarcity, as measured in time together and worldly wealth, their abundance now includes the riches of eternity. Lehi alerted his son Jacob to the fact that "it *must* needs be, that there is an opposition in *all* things" (2 Nephi 2:11; emphasis added).

And so it is that the abundant life includes much sacrifice that is eventually rewarded with comfort, prolific laughter, and countless tears—the inexplicable joy of birth and the numbing grief of death.

Few individuals have devoted as much time and energy to their chosen profession as Russell M. Nelson did to the emerging field of cardiovascular-thoracic surgery. He is one of the pioneers in developing the heart-lung machine so essential to the performance of open-heart surgery. His quest for surgical perfection became almost an obsession as he continued to enhance and expand his medical education throughout his career. His unrelenting quest was rewarded by ever-decreasing surgical mortality rates and ever-increasing confidence placed in him by his medical colleagues and patients. The year before his calling as an Apostle, he had performed 360 surgical procedures.

When called to serve as an Apostle, Russell, like Peter and Andrew of old, straightway left his nets and followed the Savior's injunction to become a fisher of men (Matthew 4:18–20). As he disengaged from a profession in which he had invested forty intensive years of his life, he came to the Holy Apostleship empty so that he would have room for the fulness that would follow.

AN AMBASSADOR FOR THE LORD

In this dispensation, the Lord has revealed that "the twelve traveling councilors are called to be the Twelve Apostles, or special witnesses of the name of Christ in all the world" (D&C 107:23). Elder Nelson's responsibilities have taken him to 110 nations of the earth, with a typical year involving several stake or regional conferences in England, Brazil, Guatemala, Venezuela, Ecuador, Hong Kong, Taiwan, Uruguay, Paraguay, Utah, Kentucky, Idaho, Florida, California, and Montana, and area training meetings in Africa and Brazil.[1]

One year at Church headquarters, he met with international ambassadors, political leaders, and dignitaries visiting Salt Lake City from Mexico, India, Spain, China, Russia, American Samoa, Western Samoa, Thailand, Jordan, Tonga, Romania, Zambia, the Republic of the Congo, the Ivory Coast, and French Polynesia.[2] On such occasions, Elder Nelson exemplifies well that he "can talk with crowds and keep [his] virtue or walk with kings—nor lose the common touch."[3] Regardless of the size of each guest's country of origin, he treats all with respect and dignity. His infectious smile, warm handshake, and ability to greet many dignitaries in their native tongue immediately put them at ease in his company.

And, of course, when visiting ambassadors learn of the Nelson's ten children and fifty-plus grandchildren, they know they are in the presence of someone who firmly believes that the family is the basic unit of society.

Under the authorization of the First Presidency and the Twelve,

Elder Nelson has been privileged to dedicate the lands of Australia, Belarus, Belize, Bulgaria, El Salvador, Estonia, French Polynesia, Honduras, Hungary, Namibia, New Zealand, Romania, and Zambia. He has also rededicated Russia, which had been dedicated previously by Elder Francis M. Lyman in 1903, and Czechoslovakia, which had been dedicated by Elder John A. Widtsoe in 1929. Elder Nelson was also present when Elder Dallin H. Oaks offered the dedicatory prayer for Armenia, when Elder Marvin J. Ashton dedicated Guatemala, and when Elder Richard G. Scott dedicated Nicaragua and the Democratic Republic of Congo.

Elder Nelson's perfect pitch and musical ear have been a boon to him in learning several foreign languages with varying degrees of fluency. As in the parable of the talents, he has invested considerable time and effort in magnifying his linguistic abilities. The Lord has revealed "that every man shall hear the fulness of the gospel in his own tongue, and in his own language, through those who are ordained unto this power" (D&C 90:11). It is convenient for Church leaders to rely on native interpreters when they travel abroad, but they make a special connection when they can share the gospel in a foreign tongue. Elder Nelson makes that special connection, even if only through a brief testimony, for example, in Greek or Czech.

THE LORD'S PROPERTY

On January 2, 1999, Elder Nelson made the droll comment, "We went skiing for the first time this year," implying a little procrastination on his part. Two days later, he went skiing again with his daughter Gloria and her husband, Rich.[4] Some might think a man in his mid-seventies to be a bit foolhardy to go skiing twice in three days, but Elder Nelson knows better. The Apostle Paul asked the profound question, "What? Know ye not that your body is the temple of the Holy Ghost which is in you, which ye have of God, and ye are not your own? For ye are bought with a price" (1 Corinthians 6:19–20).

As an Apostle of the Lord, Elder Nelson humbly acknowledges that he is the Lord's property, and, as such, he is determined to take excellent care of his body temple. He works hard, he studies hard, and he plays hard. For him, recreation is *re*-creation.

Not infrequently, Elder Nelson will note in his daily record that one day during the summer months he spent four hours mowing the lawn at the family's Midway house. During the winter months, he may record that after a heavy storm, he took "two hours to shovel all the snow out of the driveway this morning." Or, he will mention how rejuvenated he felt after having spent the day in the garden at Midway digging potatoes, beets, carrots, and other vegetables. Just six days before his seventy-fifth birthday, he went to Midway to help young Russell move furniture.[5] Elder Nelson could easily hire others to mow the lawn, shovel the snow, and harvest the vegetables, but then they, not he, would be the beneficiaries of the physical toil that garners stronger, though aching, muscles and a good night's rest.

One of his occasional skiing partners, Elder W. Craig Zwick of the Seventy, recalled the time he and Elder Nelson were ascending a snow-covered mountain on a ski lift with three-person chairs. A third man who joined them seemed to be melancholy and dejected, so Elder Zwick indicated to him that he was in the presence of an Apostle of the Lord. At this point, the emotional dam burst and the young man unloaded his burdens about the causes of his unhappiness. As his sad story drew to a close, Elder Nelson gently admonished the unhappy gentleman to begin reading the Book of Mormon each and every day without fail. He promised the young man that he would find that book to be a great source of comfort and a blessing in his life. Elder Zwick concluded, "Even while skiing, Elder Nelson is always an Apostle of God."[6]

For Elder Nelson, skiing is not just a valuable source of recreation and physical exercise; skiing also provides an opportunity to meditate in the serene surroundings of snow-bedecked pines. High on each mountain top, he revels in the beauties of nature and returns home rejuvenated in mind, body, and spirit.

In the General Authority lunchroom, Elder Nelson generally confines his disciplined palate to a bowl of soup, while many others prefer roast beef, mashed potatoes, and gravy. He never criticizes what others eat, but he is aware of the need to discipline the natural appetites of the body.

Wherever his assignments lead him, he insists on taking a brisk walk, either upon arrival from a long flight, before or after a lengthy meeting, just before retiring after a lengthy day's activities, or first thing in the morning. A couple of years ago, he was staying overnight in the mission home of the Denmark Copenhagen Mission while the mission president and his wife were in Iceland. When he arose at daybreak to take his early-morning constitutional, he found that the streets were laid out in oblique angles in a heavily wooded area. He had difficulty seeing any familiar landmarks or maintaining a sense of direction. As he began to feel that it was time to return to the mission home, he suddenly realized that he was hopelessly lost. Ever resourceful, he called the Church operator in Salt Lake City and asked her to connect him with the home of the president of the Copenhagen Denmark Stake. President Johan Koch got out his map of the city and gave Elder Nelson meticulous directions for returning to the mission home.

On assignments to the South Pacific or the Philippines, Elder Nelson generally follows a daily schedule of meeting for a few hours with a large group of missionaries, then meeting with government officials or members of the press, then holding priesthood leadership training meetings with local leaders, and finally speaking at an evening fireside for members and investigators. It's easy to understand why, after ten days or two weeks of such a schedule, Elder Nelson takes an hour off to go snorkeling around a coral reef.

At the conclusion of the year 2000, Elder Nelson gratefully acknowledged that he was "blessed with another year without illness or injury, still never missing a day of work because of illness since grade school."[7] Elder Nelson not only takes excellent care of his body but also continually stretches his mind. In his daily record, the following entries are typical: "I just completed my fifteenth tutoring session in Portuguese," "Wednesday evening Dantzel and I had another lesson in Mandarin Chinese," and "I took a computer training class in GospeLink at Deseret Book."

He wastes no time watching trivia on television. His daughters have observed that whenever their father would come home in the evening and find the children watching television, he would turn it off. At that point, they all knew it was time to read a book or engage in some more productive activity. At home, at work, or at play, Elder Nelson lives a life that anticipates the Lord's promise: "For he who is faithful and wise in time is accounted worthy to inherit the mansions prepared for him of my Father" (D&C 72:4.)

OPPOSITION IN ALL THINGS

Emily's untimely death and Dantzel's battle with cancer truly constituted a refiner's fire for Elder Nelson. Just because one is called to be an Apostle does not guarantee a charmed life devoid of unrelenting "opposition in *all* things" (2 Nephi 2:11; emphasis added).

It has been said that sacrifice is giving up something good for something better, but "I'll confess to a bit of naiveté," Elder Nelson said. "If we had known that the interval between my getting my doctor's degree and our finally going into practice would be twelve and a half years with six children added, we might not have been so enthusiastic from the beginning."[8] Young Dr. Nelson had to forego many years of income during his lengthy education, and Dantzel had to postpone her dream of owning a house with bona fide furniture. Their little girls also made sacrifices of which they were not really aware, such as sleeping in sleeping bags atop army cots.

Elder Nelson recalled that in those early years of marriage, he and Dantzel didn't know many scriptures, but they consciously adopted the following scripture as a guideline: "Wherefore, seek not the things of this world but seek ye first to build up the kingdom of

God, and to establish his righteousness, and all these things shall be added unto you" (JST, Matthew 6:38).

In the aftermath of their sustained sacrifices came the "something better," when the successful surgeon finally had the means to take his children with him on professional trips, and to take his daughters and their respective husbands on a trip to the Holy Land, gaining a certain closeness with each of them in the process. The brisk headwinds of his early career eventually became friendly tailwinds in his later life.

Elder Nelson's gentle, unflappable spirit in the face of affliction is reflected in his reaction to the demise of an old refrigerator: "Our Midway refrigerator, faithful for twenty-three years, developed a terminal rattle of death; we were advised to replace it. So Mother picked out a new one. We enjoyed installing it later in the afternoon."[9] He has always been a Christian gentleman in dealing with his fellow human beings, but when he describes the old fridge as having been "faithful" and as suffering a "terminal rattle of death," we gain a glimpse into his boundless empathy for the suffering and discomfort of others—even inanimate objects like old refrigerators.

A LIFE OF SERVICE

As a surgeon who identified closely with each patient and compassionately counseled concerned relatives, Russell suffered the agony of occasional unsuccessful operations early in his career. But with Dantzel's continual encouragement, he persisted until the mortality rate of his surgical procedures became among the lowest in the nation.

For Elder Nelson, who spent forty years in the medical profession, service and caregiving have become second nature to him. Thus, whenever the Brethren need extended medical care, it is Elder Nelson who hovers over them and reports on their medical condition. He made frequent hospital visits when President Ezra Taft Benson, Elder Bruce R. McConkie, Elder Marvin J. Ashton, and President

Howard W. Hunter were hospitalized for extended periods of time. Whenever any of his apostolic colleagues have undergone surgery, Elder Nelson has stood by the side of the chief surgeon as a demonstration of confidence, love, and support for both patient and physician.

While monitoring Elder Ashton's chronically ill condition in 1994, Elder Nelson informed the First Presidency that Elder Ashton's passing was near. He recalled at the time, "Elder Ashton was always so willing to teach me and to show me a better way of doing and thinking."[10] This comment typifies Elder Nelson's life and his relationship with other people. He views his brethren in the Church as his teachers in the language of the Spirit. He is always willing to learn from stake presidents, mission presidents, young missionaries, children, and grandchildren. He is both a perpetual teacher and a receptive learner. He is always sowing seeds, and he continues to reap a bounteous harvest "with fruit of life eternal from the seed [he] sowed in tears."[11]

STRIVING FOR PERFECTION

Unlike most physicians, who are notorious for their illegible scrawl, Elder Nelson has beautiful handwriting. "When I operated on someone's heart, it was absolutely critical that they follow my instructions regarding their recovery," he said. "I wanted to make sure they could read and understand those instructions exactly."[12]

Dr. Conrad B. Jenson, Elder Nelson's medical colleague and fellow surgeon for many years, observed that "all surgeons are compulsive."[13] For that, their patients should be grateful. Surgeons, including Elder Nelson, are also perfectionists. But Elder Nelson is not the kind of perfectionist that criticizes or shows impatience toward others. Helen Hillier, who served as his secretary for nearly sixteen years, calls Elder Nelson a "compassionate perfectionist."

"Actually, his perfectionism made my job easier, because I could always count on a good end product," she said. "Though his expectations were always high, he offers correction so gently that one never feels put down." She added, "He is the most disciplined person I've ever known."

Because of Elder Nelson's predictable gentility and unflappable disposition, she said, she never had anxiety about doing something wrong or misunderstanding instructions.

Sister Hillier recalled numerous occasions when Elder Nelson, while on an extended trip, would send dictation tapes to her through an emissary who arrived home a day or two ahead of him. His thoughtfulness allowed her to spread out the workload while he was gone so she was not overburdened when he returned to the office. She was also grateful that once Elder Nelson made his travel plans, often several months in advance, he seldom changed those plans. "He always did things right the first time," she said.[14]

Elder Nelson's current secretary, Bonnie Marchant, has been impressed with his transcendent love for the Lord, the Church, and the First Presidency, of whom he always speaks with great reverence and respect. She has observed how much he loves all the Brethren and cares deeply about them and their families. It is also clear to all, she said, that he "loves, respects, admires, and adores Sister Nelson, and he loves his family dearly."[15]

Both of his secretaries have been impressed with Elder Nelson's perfect organization of his workload. Sister Marchant observed, "He is brilliant and processes information at the speed of light. He likes everything neat and tidy and to have the work done immediately so that everything is done at the end of the day." Notwithstanding Elder Nelson's penchant for perfection, his secretaries concur that he makes gentle corrections without ever making others feel that they are being put down. "He always remembers who he is and acts accordingly," Bonnie said.[16]

Though he sets high standards for himself, his compassion for those who struggle and fall short is a hallmark of his life. After a discussion with some brethren regarding the brusqueness of a certain priesthood leader, Elder Nelson summarized the discussion by saying, "And, of course, we wouldn't want him any other way." In this regard, he shares the charity exhibited by President David O. McKay, who, when told of a fault of a given individual, replied, "Well, a dog has to have a few fleas to know he's a dog."

Elder Nelson is quick to proffer an important word of caution: "An erroneous assumption could be made that if a little of something is good, a lot must be better. Not so! Overdoses of needed medication can be toxic. Boundless mercy could oppose justice. So tolerance, without limit, could lead to spineless permissiveness."[17]

Dr. Jenson, who participated in numerous operations with Dr. Nelson, said of him, "His approach to surgery was always pretty relaxed. He was always in control in difficult circumstances. He was very considerate and polite with a kind demeanor during surgery as in his private life."[18]

The precision Elder Nelson demonstrated in performing surgery has carried over into the way he performs the work of the Lord. This is exemplified by his evaluation of the hymns selected for a particular regional conference several years ago. After reviewing the program in advance, he queried, "Is everyone in Idaho on a diet?" When asked why he posed the question, he responded, "Well, we have an abundance of lettuce in the program. The suggested hymns are 'Now *Let Us* Rejoice,' '*Let Us* Oft Speak Kind Words,' and '*Let Us* All Press On.'" Two of the hymns were changed.

Elder Nelson's expectations have always been high for himself, but he also expects a lot from his associates. Stake presidents and mission presidents who have received a visit from him unanimously concur that his counsel to them has reflected the spirit of the Lord's counsel in D&C 43:8–9: They have been instructed, edified, and taught how to better direct the affairs of the kingdom, they have been sanctified by the Spirit, and they have been invited to make a commitment to improve. While visiting a mission home in South America, Elder Nelson noted a dearth of paintings of the Savior and of pictures of the temples. His observations were gently proffered and the deficiencies were remedied.[19]

Shortly after being called to the Seventy, Elder D. Todd Christofferson accompanied Elder Nelson on a stake conference assignment to Mexico. After the conference, Elder Christofferson said, "Elder Nelson, if at any time I need correction, please feel free to give it to me." Elder Nelson responded, "I will; that's one of the ways we show our love for one another."[20]

The unwritten order of the Church prescribes that the person who presides at a meeting is always the last to speak so that if something previously taught needs to be corrected, the presiding officer can then unobtrusively do so.

On one occasion, Elder Nelson was invited to speak at a funeral. At the conclusion of his remarks, the young bishop who was conducting the services proceeded to give a ten-minute sermon *after* the Apostle had spoken. Following the benediction, in keeping with his calling to regulate the Church and to teach and edify, Elder Nelson took the new bishop aside and gently taught him that after the presiding officer has spoken, the meeting is over. The bishop was sincerely grateful for the instruction and for the gentle manner Elder Nelson gave it.

While he and Sister Nelson were accompanying the Mormon Tabernacle Choir to Europe in June 1991, they agreed to speak to the missionaries of the Switzerland Zürich Mission. This mission has traditionally been one of the most challenging missions in the world, and the mission president, Keith K. Hilbig, now of the Seventy, and his wife, Susan, eagerly awaited to see what this Apostle of the Lord would tell their missionaries after several successive months of few baptisms.

In the dignity of his sacred calling, Elder Nelson approached the pulpit with a warm smile and said, "In behalf of the First Presidency and Quorum of the Twelve, who comprise the Missionary Committee of the Church, I thank you for all you do to build the kingdom." He then gave them helpful instruction and encouragement.

Because of their low productivity, some of the missionaries had anticipated a "Scotch blessing." Instead, they received an apostolic blessing, sincere appreciation, and edifying instruction. That month, the mission had fifteen baptisms, the most of any month that year.

Shortly after his calling to the Twelve, Elder Nelson was invited to speak to the Brethren on "Obedience and Sacrifice Bring Forth the Blessings of Heaven." He began his instruction by examining the Latin roots of *sacrifice.* The first half of the word is derived from *sacer,* meaning "sacred"; the second half comes from *facere,* which means "to do" or "to make." Thus, the word *sacrifice* literally means "to make sacred."[21] In essence, the hollowing brought about by sacrifice prepares us for

Elder and Sister Nelson after fifty-seven years of marriage.

the hallowing—the blessings that follow. Several of his apostolic colleagues have commented that one of Elder Nelson's strengths is his precision of speech. He is seldom, if ever, misunderstood.

In his general conference address in April 1995, he encouraged the Saints to become a peculiar people. In order to understand the true meaning of the Apostle Peter's phrase, Elder Nelson pointed out that the Hebrew word *segullah,* which was translated as "peculiar" in the King James version of the Old Testament, meant "valued property" or "treasure." In the New Testament translation from the Greek, *peripoiesis* had been translated as "peculiar" and in other contexts as "possession," such as, for example, "those selected by God as His own people."[22] Thus, having gained a more precise meaning of the word, the Saints who listened had a greater desire to truly become a peculiar people as mandated in the scriptures.

Two young missionaries recently received some important instruction from Elder Nelson in proper word usage. Their mission president had delegated chauffeuring duties to them to drive Elder and Sister Nelson to their next destination. The elders were seated in the front seat of the car, and the Nelsons were seated in the back seat. As they conversed, the elders continually referred to Elder and Sister Nelson as "you guys." Elder Nelson asked the driver, "Will you please pull the car over to the side of the road?" He then said, "Please turn off the ignition. Now, both of you, please turn around and look at Sister Nelson. Does she look like a guy?"[23]

In a few brief moments, those young elders of Israel had learned an invaluable lesson on respect and on the accurate use of language that would help them become Christian gentlemen and better missionaries.

An Ever-Expanding Circle of Love

The Prophet Joseph Smith taught, "Love is one of the chief characteristics of Deity, and ought to be manifested by those who aspire to be the sons of God. A man filled with the love of God, is not content with blessing his family alone, but ranges through the whole world, anxious to bless the whole human race."[24]

This profound statement describes Elder and Sister Nelson precisely. They not only concentrated their love and best efforts in rearing a wonderful family, but for many years, Dr. Nelson also quite literally ranged throughout sixty-five countries sharing his surgical skills in order to alleviate human suffering. Now he and Dantzel frequently leave their loved ones behind so they can extend their love to those outside their family circle—their brothers and sisters in the gospel living in many other lands throughout the earth.

No one appreciates the Nelsons' inclusive inclinations more than Brad Wittwer and his wife, Julie. After Brad's first wife, Emily (Elder and Sister Nelson's sixth daughter), passed away, he wondered whether former relationships would remain the same within the Nelson family circle. All of Brad's apprehensions were assuaged during the Alaskan cruise the family took several months after Emily's death. Emily's absence was ironic because she had been the moving force behind planning the cruise, which became a time of healing, with plenty of time to talk and meditate.

Russell and Dantzel reassured Brad of their eternal love for him as the husband of their deceased daughter and as the father of their grandchildren, and they supported him in his efforts to find a new mother for his children. In fact, Russell said, "It was more than an expression of support. We told him to get moving!" During the cruise, Brad also spoke privately with each of Emily's sisters. Notwithstanding the green light from all family members, it was not until several months later, after the first anniversary of Emily's death, that Brad finally mustered the courage to begin dating.[25]

He was so busy playing the role of "Mr. Mom" that he relied on the efforts of well-meaning friends to help him find the right person. A work colleague from San Francisco introduced him to Julie Veranth, a beautiful young woman who had never been married but who was adventuresome enough to accept the challenge of inheriting a ready-made family. After dating for seven months, they became engaged, and in February 1998, Elder Nelson sealed Brad and Julie in the Salt Lake Temple. The Nelsons truly view Julie as a ministering angel sent to bless their lives and the lives of others they hold dear.

Julie recalled, "I was completely overwhelmed the first time I attended the monthly Nelson extended family home evening because everyone was so full of love, and they showed sincere and complete acceptance of me."[26] With her marriage to Brad, she now participates in the Nelson sisters' monthly scrapbooking activities and in all other Nelson family events. She was particularly grateful to spend time one-on-one with family members during a family vacation to Mexico and California. When Julie gave birth to

Kennedy Macree Wittwer, Russell and Dantzel proudly claimed her as their fifty-second grandchild, and the even more recent arrival of Joshua Russell in September 2002 as their fifty-fourth.

When the Nelson sisters sing together, they invite Julie to sing with them, even though she feels she does not belong in their league. Their acceptance of her is evidence of the gospel of inclusion and of an ever-expanding circle of love that they learned from their parents.

The eternal love Russell and Dantzel have for each other readily expands to their children, to the spouses of their children, and to their grandchildren and great-grandchildren. It extends to the Brethren, their wives and families, and to all members of the Church. And it radiates to all the inhabitants of the 110 nations they have visited—and beyond.

CHAPTER 38

THE THINGS OF HIS SOUL

IN FULFILLING HIS MAJOR RESPONSIBILITIES as a father, surgeon, and Apostle, Elder Nelson has become a teacher *par excellence.* Whether the venue be the pulpit during general conference, an area priesthood leadership training meeting, a mission tour, a youth fireside, or the 1993 Parliament of the World's Religions in Chicago, Illinois, he inspires as he teaches because his teaching reflects the meticulous preparation of a surgeon who is dealing with matters of life and death. His thoughts are carefully ordered from the beginning of his remarks, when he opens up a topic for examination and then sutures truths together, until he reaches the conclusion of each address.

A central theme of many of Elder Nelson's sermons is eternal identity and the conviction that if God's children know who they really are, they will establish priorities in their lives so that they can reap the gospel's promised blessings—especially within their families and homes.[1] Elder Nelson contends, "When we know who we are and what God expects of us—when His 'law [is] written in [our] hearts'—we are spiritually protected. We become better people."[2]

An apostolic colleague of an earlier era, Elder John A. Widtsoe, taught, "A prophet is a teacher of known truth; a seer is a perceiver of hidden truth, a revelator is a bearer of new truth."[3] A review of the following excerpts from Elder Nelson's teachings reveals that he

Ever the master teacher, Elder Nelson underscores the importance of a principle during general conference in October 1986.

is, indeed, a teacher, a perceiver, and a bearer of truth—in other words, a prophet, seer, and revelator.

THE GREAT PLAN OF HAPPINESS

The Prophet Joseph Smith taught that the atonement of Jesus Christ is the central doctrine of the gospel and that all other teachings are an appendage to it.[4] Elder Nelson has stated, "Before we can comprehend the *Atonement* of Christ, we must first understand the *Fall* of Adam. And before we can comprehend the Fall of Adam, we must first understand the *Creation*. These three pillars of eternity relate to one another."[5]

The Creation

"The Creation culminated with Adam and Eve in the Garden of Eden. They were created in the image of God, with bodies of flesh and bone. Created in the image of God and not yet mortal, they could not grow old and die. 'And they would have had no children' nor experienced the trials of life. (Please forgive me for mentioning children and the trials of life in the same breath.) The creation of Adam and Eve was a *paradisiacal creation,* one that required a significant change before they could fulfill the commandment to have children and thus provide earthly bodies for premortal spirit sons and daughters of God. . . ."[6]

The Fall

"Scripture teaches that 'Adam fell that men might be; and men are, that they might have joy.' The Fall of Adam (and Eve) constituted the *mortal creation* and brought about the required changes in their bodies, including the circulation of blood and other modifications as well. They were now able to have children. . . ."[7]

The Atonement

"Paul said, 'As in Adam all die, even so in Christ shall all be made alive.' The Atonement of Jesus Christ became the *immortal creation*. He volunteered to answer the ends of a law previously transgressed. And by the shedding of His blood, His and our physical bodies could become perfected. They could again function without blood, just as Adam's and Eve's did in their *paradisiacal* form. . . .

"The Creation required the Fall. The Fall required the Atonement. The Atonement enabled the purpose of the Creation to be accomplished. Eternal life, made possible by the Atonement, is the supreme purpose of the Creation."[8]

Premortal Existence

"It is good to consider where we have been [in the premortal existence]. . . . I suspect we were terrified, at first, when told we would forget Father, friends, and facts we formerly knew so well. I can believe we were calmed when informed our Father in Heaven would provide prophets and scriptures to guide us and would provide a means whereby we could communicate with Him through prayer and the spirit of revelation. But still we may have been a bit insecure when we learned that faith—faith to believe the intangible—was the key to success in our journey. Faith was to be the critical component in our safe return to our Father in Heaven. . . .

"Your enemy [on earth] is neither hot sands of the desert, nor smoking guns of foes in pursuit, but heated efforts of the adversary to undermine your marriage and/or the sanctity of your family unit. For the monument of your life to rise from its pedestal of preparation to your appointed site of destiny, you must go where the Lord wants you to go. Wherever it is, go. Go with the same faith that allowed you to leave your heavenly home in the first place."9

Body and Spirit

The crowning event of the earth's creation was the clothing of Heavenly Father's spirit children with a body of flesh and bone. As a surgeon, Elder Nelson has an almost childlike wonder at our Heavenly Father's most complex and wonderful creations—His children.

"We are dual beings. Each soul is comprised of body and spirit, both of which emanate from God. A firm understanding of body and spirit will shape our thoughts and deeds for good.

"The marvel of our physical bodies is often overlooked. . . . Your body, whatever its natural gifts, is a magnificent creation of God. It is a tabernacle of flesh—a temple for your spirit. A study of your body attests to its divine design."10

"Let's mention the magnificence of the eyes with which we see. . . . A self-focusing lens is at the front of each eye. Nerves and muscles synchronize the function of two separate eyes to produce one three-dimensional image. . . .

"As we admire good stereophonic equipment for sensing sound, ponder the magnificence of the human ear. . . . A tiny tympanic membrane serves as the diaphragm. Minute ossicles amplify the signal that is then transmitted along nerve lines to the brain, which registers the results of hearing. . . .

"The human heart has four important valves. . . . They open and close over 100,000 times a day—over 36 million times a year. . . . Each day the heart pumps enough fluid to fill a 2,000-gallon tank. . . .

"I marvel at a computer and admire the work it can do, I respect even more the mind of man that developed the computer. . . .

"Pain itself is part of the body's defense mechanism. . . . The defense of the body also includes chemical antibodies manufactured in response to infections acquired along life's way. . . . Closely related to the concept of self-defense is that of self-repair. . . . The concept of self-renewal is remarkable. . . .

"Another concept that is truly remarkable is that of autoregulation, which controls the temperature of the body and . . . limits the time you can hold your breath. . . .

"Think of the backup provided by a number of organs that are paired, such as the eyes, ears, lungs, adrenal glands, kidneys, and more. . . .

"Protection against germs and injury is provided by the skin. . . .

"The magnificence of man is matchless. Remember, glorious as this physical tabernacle is, the body is designed to support something even *more* glorious—the eternal spirit that dwells in each of our mortal frames."[11]

"Not an age in life passes without temptation, trial, or torment experienced through your physical body. But as you prayerfully develop self-mastery, desires of the flesh may be subdued."[12]

"The great accomplishments of this life are rarely physical. Those attributes by which we shall be judged one day are spiritual."[13]

"Development of the spirit is of eternal consequence. The attributes by which we shall be judged one day are those of the spirit. These include the virtues of integrity, compassion, love, and more. Your spirit, by being housed in your body, is able to develop and express these attributes in ways that are vital to your eternal progression.

"Spirit and body, when joined together, become a living soul of supernal worth. Indeed, we are children of God—physically and spiritually. . . .

"We will regard our body as a temple of our very own. We will not let it be desecrated or defaced in any way. We will control our diet and exercise for physical fitness. . . .

"Who are we? We are children of God. Our potential is unlimited. Our inheritance is sacred. May we always honor that heritage—in every thought and deed."[14]

Moral Agency

"If you truly believe in God and believe you are one of His children preparing to return to Him. . . . And if it truly is your objective, can there be any action appropriate for you to do other than to keep His commandments?

"Agency is a divine gift to you. You are free to choose what you will be and what you will do. And you are not without help. To counsel with your parents is a privilege at any age. Prayer provides communication with your Heavenly Father and invites the promptings of personal revelation. And in certain circumstances, consultation with professional advisers and with your local leaders in the Church may be highly advisable, especially when very difficult decisions must be made. . . .

"As you continue to face many challenging choices in life, remember, there is great protection when you know who you are, why you are here, and where you are going. Let your unique identity shape each decision you make on the path toward your eternal destiny. Accountability for your choices now will bear on all that lies ahead."[15]

Addiction or Freedom

"Agency, or the power to choose, was ours as spirit children of our Creator before the world was (see Alma 13:3; Moses 4:4). It is a gift from God, nearly as precious as life itself. . . .

"We are free to take drugs or not. But once we choose to use a habit-forming drug, we are bound to the consequences of that choice. Addiction surrenders later freedom to choose. Through chemical means, one can literally become disconnected from his or her own will! . . .

"My spiritual prescription includes six choices which I shall list alphabetically, A through F . . . : Choose to Be Alive, Choose to Believe, Choose to Change, Choose to Be Different, Choose to Exercise, and Choose to Be Free."[16]

Perfection Pending

It is not only daunting but also sometimes discouraging to perpetually fall short of achieving goals in life. Elder Nelson has provided some encouraging insight into the continuing quest for perfection:

"'Perfect' in Matthew 5:48 comes from the Greek word *teleios*, meaning 'complete,' and is derived from the Greek word *telos*, which means 'to set out for a definite point or goal.' Thus, this scripture conveys the concept of conclusion of an act. Therefore, *perfect* in this scripture also means 'finished,' 'completed,' 'consummated,' or 'fully developed,' and refers to the reality of the glorious resurrection of our Master.

"Before His crucifixion Jesus so taught, 'Behold, I cast out devils, and I do cures to day and to morrow, and the third day I shall be perfected' (Luke 13:32). . . .

"So the admonition 'to be perfect' should not cause depression among us. To the contrary, it should bring us great joy and jubilation. The Lord knew that the procedure would be long and challenging. . . .

"Those who are really *seeking* to do His will are recipients of His blessings, for He knows the intent of our hearts. . . .

"Be not discouraged when imperfections of yours and of your loved ones seem more than you can bear. And please, 'continue in patience until ye are perfected.'"[17]

PROCLAIMING THE GOSPEL

When Elder Nelson speaks to missionaries in the field or in the Missionary Training Center, he teaches them the doctrines of the Church and shares helpful insights into how to connect with the people they will teach.

"As you invite others to come unto Christ, don't loom so large that you stand in the way. Don't block the view. To put Jesus first, you need to lose yourself. John the Baptist made this statement regarding the Lord: 'He must increase, but I must decrease' (John 3:30). And remember: having character is better than being one.

"As a missionary, you will want to 'open your mouth.' This is crucial! The Lord cannot proclaim His good news of salvation through silent servants.

"Start a conversation with comments that are complimentary. Listen carefully when a name is given. And if you didn't hear it well or didn't understand it, ask again, or have it spelled. No sound is sweeter to an individual than the sound of his or her own name—pronounced correctly. On occasions, I will pursue the name a bit further by asking what it means, or where the name came from. That usually provides a nice bridge to a conversation about the family—children, parents, and one's ancestors.

"The spirit of Elijah is permeating this planet. If I were a missionary today, I would learn which of our Family History Centers is located in my area, and I would become acquainted with the director. I would give to my friends a copy of the pamphlet *Welcome to the Family History Center* and introduce them to the director.

"If there is a new baby in the family, let that be the subject of your connection. Or if there is a marriage or a death in the family, hearts are tender and spirits are especially receptive to the teachings of the Lord.

"In our dispensation, the Lord specified prerequisites to baptism in D&C 20:37. You should underline and internalize that scripture. Its language is not optional; it is imperative. We are to retain each precious convert, with a friend, with a calling, and with continuing nourishment by the good word of God.

"Every missionary yearns for the power to persuade and convince. Nothing you will learn can ever match the power of pure testimony. A testimony is never static. It is either becoming stronger or weaker. It is established by the exercise of faith. It is fortified by work."[18]

Newton's Laws of Motion

"I would like to talk to you about different kinds of laws. These laws were first described about three hundred years ago by Sir Isaac Newton—known as Newton's laws of motion. An understanding of these laws will help you in your missionary work. Let us study the laws, and see how they may be applied to the work you and I have been called to do.

"First, law number one: *A body at rest tends to remain at rest. A body in motion tends to remain in motion.*"

Showing a slide of a sleeping missionary, Elder Nelson then continued:

"This illustrates that a body at rest tends to remain at rest. This sleepy elder has trouble separating himself from his mattress. For him, the hardest part of the day is getting out of bed and on his way. There used to be a saying that I remember so well: 'When you wake up, get up; and when you get up, wake up.' Or to paraphrase a scripture—'with all thy getting, get going.'

"The same principles can apply in missionary work. Whether learning to ride a bicycle, or to ski on water, or to be a missionary, the challenge is to get up and move. But once in motion, momentum is in your favor and you will tend to stay in motion.

"Exercise is good for the heart. We know that during the exercise of walking, or bicycling, the big muscles of the thigh do a third of the work of pumping blood through the circulatory system, leaving only two thirds of the work for the heart. The body at rest requires the entire workload of circulation to be done by this heart.

Elder Nelson conveys a sense of earnestness during his April 1996 general conference talk.

"Mental health is improved by exercise too.

"It is not just coincidence that we use the word exercise when we talk about exercising the priesthood. When we speak of magnifying our calling, that suggests effort and commitment as well. The body in motion tends to remain in motion.

"Returning to the basic laws of motion, it is important to recognize that motion is always affected by friction. Friction causes resistance to motion. You and your companion moving together could be impeded by friction, just as your work will be facilitated by smoothing out those contacts. We talk about having the rough edges polished in the work of the Lord, and that we do by working together. When we have areas of controversy or disagreement, the smoothing influence of conversation will apply oil to the surfaces to reduce the friction. And love is the greatest lubricant of all.

"The Lord wants us to be doers, not just hearers—to be in motion, exercising and growing—all succinctly described by Newton's first law of motion.

"The second law of motion deserves our attention. *When a force is applied to a body in motion, any change is determined by the size of the force, and the mass of the object. The greater the force, the greater the acceleration.* On the other hand, the greater the mass of the object, the smaller will be the acceleration.

"Now, how can we apply this law to missionary work? We can look at this in the two parts of this law. First, we can consider forces that move objects, and then second, we can consider the mass of the objects that are to be moved by those forces. What forces might be harnessed to provide power for our work? First is the force of our thoughts. There is no action that we will ever take that doesn't take root in our mind first as a thought.

"'Let virtue garnish thy thoughts unceasingly; then shall thy confidence wax strong in the presence of God' (D&C 121:45).

"The next force of great power is the force of repentance. If you are carrying the burden of unconfessed sin, discuss it with your priesthood leaders before you depart for your mission. Don't handicap your work by this extra load.

"Another powerful force that will move you is the force of instruction. Seek instruction daily from the various resources available to you—the scriptures, your companion, your mission president, your zone leader.

"'He that refuseth instruction despiseth his own soul; but he that heareth reproof getteth understanding' (Proverbs 15:32).

"Another great force is the power of love. It is the power by which great teachers teach. It is the power by which great leaders lead. It is the power by which great missionaries preach.

"Newton's third law of motion teaches us that *for every action there is an equal and opposite reaction.* So, as missionaries for the Lord, every action you make in righteousness will evoke a reaction from the adversary who is threatened by your very presence. This adversary will be competing for your body and your soul.

"But remember: ' . . . there is nothing that the Lord thy God shall take in his heart to do but what he will do it' (Abraham 3:17). He has restored His church and kingdom in these latter days to fill the earth—to prepare the earth and its people for His second coming."[19]

NOTHING IS IMPOSSIBLE

Elder Nelson is a devout optimist who firmly believes the prophecy that the gospel shall "roll forth unto the ends of the earth, as the stone which is cut out of the mountain without hands shall roll forth, until it has filled the whole earth" (D&C 65:2; Daniel 2:34). He worked against tremendous odds to successfully create a heart-lung machine, but he optimistically persevered and succeeded. On occasion, when Elder Nelson has met with missionaries, especially in parts of the world where baptisms are few and far between, he has imbued them with greater faith by sharing with them his conviction that "with God nothing shall be impossible" (Luke 1:37).

He cites the example of Gideon's troops facing formidable odds against the Midianites. Gideon began with 22,000 men while the menacing Midianites had 137,000 troops (Judges 7:4; 8:10). Notwithstanding these six-to-one odds, the Lord had Gideon eventually reduce his troops to only 300 men, increasing the odds to 457 to one. But Gideon's troops were, nevertheless, victorious (Judges 7–8).

The odds were against Abraham and Sarah ever having children, especially when she was ninety. But the faith of these aged prospective parents was bolstered by the divine decree: "Is any thing too hard for the Lord?" (Genesis 18:14).

Elder Nelson has said: "I admire those who strive to be more worthy by overcoming a personal fault or who work to achieve a difficult goal. . . .

"My heart reaches out to those who feel discouraged by the magnitude of their struggle. . . .

"Suppose for a moment you are a member of a team. The coach beckons you from the bench and says: 'You are to enter this contest. I not only want you to win; you shall win. But the going will be tough. The score at this moment is 1,143,000,000 to six, and you are to play on the team with the six points!

"That large number was the approximate population of the earth in the year 1830 when the restored Church of Jesus Christ was officially organized with six members. . . .

"How is it possible to achieve the 'impossible'? Learn and obey the teachings of God. . . .

"'Dispute not because ye see not, for ye receive no witness until after the trial of your faith' (Ether 12:6). . . .

"'If ye have faith, nothing shall be impossible unto you' (Matthew 17:20).

"Imagine, if you will, a pair of powerful binoculars. . . . Let the scene on the left side of your binoculars represent *your perception* of your task. Let the picture on the right side represent the *Lord's perspective* of your task. Now, connect your system to His. By mental adjustment, fuse your focus. Something wonderful happens. Your vision and His are now the same. You have developed 'an eye single to the glory of God' (D&C 4:5; see also Mormon 8:15). With that perspective, look upward—above and beyond mundane things about you."[20]

BECOMING STANDARD-BEARERS

"I was told a tender account during the holiday season just past. While children reenacted the Christmas story, one child held high a star wrapped in aluminum foil, mounted on a broomstick. Later, someone commended the child for his stamina in holding that star so high for such a long period of time. The child, who had spoken no lines, joyfully replied, 'I had the most important part in the play. I showed people how to find Jesus.'

"As His standard-bearers, we are to help the honest in heart to find Jesus. We don't wave flags. And generally we don't carry stars mounted on broomsticks. Instead, as standard-bearers for Jesus the

Christ, we willingly and gratefully take His sacred name upon us. We enlist in His cause by covenant."[21]

"I testify to you that this work is divine, that this is the Church of Jesus Christ."[22]

HONORING THE PRIESTHOOD

"The Church of Jesus Christ of Latter-day Saints is neither a democracy nor a republic. His is a kingdom—the kingdom of God on earth. His is a hierarchical church, with ultimate authority at the top. The Lord directs His anointed servants. They testify to all the world that God has again spoken. The heavens have been opened. A living linkage has been formed between heaven and earth in our day. . . .

"Often we speak of *keys* of priesthood authority. Fifteen living men—the First Presidency and the Twelve—have been ordained as Apostles and have had *all* keys of priesthood authority conferred upon them. President Gordon B. Hinckley recently explained that 'only the President of the Church has the right to exercise [those keys] in their fulness. He may delegate the exercise of various of them to one or more of his Brethren.' . . .

"Honoring the priesthood also means to honor your personal call to serve. A few do's and don'ts may be helpful:

"**Do** learn to take counsel. Seek direction from file leaders and receive it willingly. **Don't** speak ill of Church leaders. **Don't** covet a calling or position. **Don't** second-guess who should or should not have been called. **Don't** refuse an opportunity to serve. **Don't** resign from a call. **Do** inform leaders of changing circumstances in your life, knowing that leaders will weigh all factors when prayerfully considering the proper timing of your release. . . .

"Now for counsel more specific. **Husbands and fathers:** With your dear partner, shape attitudes at home. Establish a pattern of prayer. . . . Your manners of courtesy at home and of reverence in the chapel will be copied by members of your family. . . .

"Now to **young men** who bear the Aaronic (or preparatory) Priesthood: If you honor it, and prepare for and are worthy of a call to be a missionary, I promise: You will then 'speak in the name of God the Lord' and bring His light to searching souls. To them you will be as a ministering angel, remembered with love forever (see D&C 13). . . .

"To our beloved **presidents and bishops**: When one who presides over you comes into a meeting where you have been presiding, please consult with him immediately for instruction. . . . Be certain to allow adequate time for a message from him. . . . When a presiding General Authority has spoken, no one speaks following him. . . .

"Now for comments about the **stake high council.** It has no president. It has no autonomy and meets . . . only upon call from the stake presidency. Although high councilors may be seated in the order of their call to the council, no one member has seniority over another. . . .

"In contrast, **seniority** is honored among ordained Apostles—even when entering or leaving a room. President Benson related to us this account:

"'Some [years] ago Elder Haight extended a special courtesy to President Romney while they were in the upper room in the temple. President Romney was lingering behind for some reason, and [Elder Haight] did not want to precede him out of the door. When President Romney signaled [for him] to go first, Elder Haight replied, "No, President, you go first."

"'President Romney replied with his humor, "What's the matter, David? Are you afraid I'm going to steal something?"'

"Such deference from a junior to a senior Apostle is recorded in the New Testament. When Simon Peter and John the Beloved ran to investigate the report that the body of their crucified Lord had been taken from the sepulcher, John, being younger and swifter, arrived first, yet he did not enter. He deferred to the senior Apostle, who entered the sepulchre first (see John 20:2–6). Seniority in the apostleship has long been a means by which the Lord selects His presiding High Priest. . . .

"'The Melchizedek Priesthood holds the right of presidency, and has power and authority over all the offices in the church in all ages of the world' (D&C 107:8). This power holds 'the keys of all the spiritual blessings of the church' (D&C 107:18). May we fully honor that priesthood."[23]

"The potential of the priesthood is so vast that our comprehension of it is a challenge. . . .

"They who *receive* ordinations or callings have obligations of obedience, loyalty, and understanding of the power of the priesthood."[24]

HONORING WOMANHOOD

"You young men need to know that you can hardly achieve your highest potential without the influence of good women, particularly your mother and, in a few years, a good wife. Learn now to show respect and gratitude. Remember that your mother is your *mother*. She should not need to issue orders. Her wish, her hope, her hint should provide direction that you would honor. Thank her and express your love for her."[25]

"A worthy woman personifies the truly noble and worthwhile attributes of life. A faithful woman can become a devoted daughter of God—more concerned with being righteous than with being selfish, more anxious to exercise compassion than to exercise dominion, more committed to integrity than to notoriety. And she knows of her own infinite worth. . . .

"Blessings of the priesthood are shared by men and women. All may qualify for baptism and the gift of the Holy Ghost. All may take upon themselves the name of the Lord and partake of the sacrament. All may pray and receive answers to their prayers. Gifts of the Spirit and testimonies of the truth are bestowed regardless of gender. *Men and women receive the highest ordinance in the house of the Lord together and equally, or not at all* (see D&C 131:1–3)."[26]

"From our study of Eve, we may learn five fundamental lessons of everlasting importance regarding the relationship between priesthood and womanhood:

"She labored beside her companion (see Moses 5:1), and she and Adam bore the responsibilities of parenthood (see Moses 5:2).

"Eve and her husband worshipped the Lord in prayer and heeded divine commandments of obedience and sacrifice (Moses 5:5).

"Adam and Eve taught the gospel to their children. . . .

"All the purposes of the world and all that was in the world would be brought to naught without woman—a keystone in the priesthood arch of creation."[27]

"When our tenth child was born, a friend asked me what I would wish for our son. To this question I replied, 'Inasmuch as life's loftiest career is not available to him—that of motherhood—whatever he pursues will be of lesser importance.'

"My inquiring friend may have thought my reply a bit strange, but I was genuinely sincere. Daughters are remarkable in many ways, whether they become mothers in this life or not. Viewed from an eternal perspective, every righteous woman may one day realize this great blessing. For women to be honored by their Creator with that unique potential makes them truly special. Each of our son's nine older sisters might have that glorious possibility of attaining what to me is a most noble destiny—motherhood.

"Sons have their own unique potential destiny. Regardless of career selection, they may bear 'the Holy Priesthood, after the Order of the Son of God' (D&C 107:3). To bear that priesthood worthily in the Lord's behalf becomes the aim of their noblest desire. But the divine design and capacity for motherhood have been entrusted to daughters.

"Napoleon Bonaparte was once asked to describe the greatest need of France. To this question he gave his famous one-word answer: 'Mothers.' Someone else said that God could not be everywhere, so He gave the world mothers.

"As Nancy Hanks Lincoln lay on her deathbed, she said to her nine-year-old son, 'Abe, go out there and amount to something.' Abraham spent the balance of his lifetime trying to fulfill his mother's stated ambition. Some years later he said, 'All that I am or ever hope to be, I owe to my angel mother.'"[28]

EDUCATION FOR ETERNITY

"Because of our sacred regard for each human intellect, we consider the obtaining of an education to be a religious responsibility. Yet opportunities and abilities differ. I believe that in the pursuit of education, individual desire is more influential than institution, and personal faith more forceful than faculty. Our Creator expects His children everywhere to educate themselves. . . .

"Preparation for your career is not too long if you know what you want to do with your life. How old will you be thirteen years from now if you *don't* pursue your education? . . .

"Where is wisdom? It pulses and surges with the Lord's light of truth! With that light He lifts us toward eternal life."[29]

Learning

"May I suggest four steps to facilitate the learning process: The first is to have a great *desire* to know the truth. . . . The second step would be to study with an *inquiring* mind. . . . The third step is to *apply* or practice your learning in your daily lives. . . . The fourth and very important step in the learning process is to *pray* for help. . . .

"Now may I offer important words of warning: Learning, if misused, can destroy your goals. Let us consider some safeguards to protect you from such an undesirable end.

"Your faith must be *nourished*. . . . Enrich that faith additionally with private scriptural study. . . . Nourish the gifts of the Spirit on the same daily basis that you feed your physical body. Choose your *role models* wisely. . . . Remember that the Bible, Book of Mormon, Doctrine and Covenants, and the Pearl of Great Price are the standards by which you should measure all doctrine. Avoid *poisons of faith* such as sin, pornography, or barely abiding the letter of the law instead of embracing the ennobling spirit of the law."[30]

Listening

"The time to listen is when someone needs to be heard. . . .

"Husbands and wives, learn to listen, and listen to learn from one another. . . .

"Members, learn to listen, and listen to learn from Church leaders. . . .

"Above all, God's children should learn to listen, then listen to learn from the Lord."[31]

Studying the Scriptures

"Where do we obtain the guidance we need? We turn to Him who knows us best—our Creator. He allowed us to come to earth with freedom to choose our own course. In His great love, He did not leave us alone. He provided a guide—a spiritual road map—to help us achieve success in our journey. We call that guide the standard works, so named because they—the Holy Bible, the Book of Mormon, the Doctrine and Covenants, and the Pearl of Great Price—constitute the *standard* by which we should live. . . .

"In your journey through life, you meet many obstacles and make some mistakes. Scriptural guidance helps you to recognize error and make the necessary correction. You stop going in the wrong direction. You carefully study the scriptural road map. Then you proceed with repentance and restitution required to get on the 'strait and narrow path which leads to eternal life.'"[32]

"Study of the Book of Mormon is most rewarding when one focuses on its *primary* purpose—to testify of Jesus Christ. . . . *Historical* aspects of the book assume *secondary* significance. . . . The Book of Mormon was written *anciently* for *our day*. . . .

"Each individual who prayerfully studies the Book of Mormon can also receive a testimony of its divinity. In addition, this book can help with personal problems in a very real way. Do you want to get rid of a bad habit? Do you want to improve relationships in your family? Do you want to increase your spiritual capacity? Read the Book of Mormon!"[33]

OBEDIENCE AND THE LAW
OF SEQUENTIAL STRESS

Elder Russell M. Nelson is adept at using medical metaphors to get to the heart of a matter. Following is but one of many insightful, engaging examples:

"The mitral valve is one of four valves within the heart. This delicate and durable structure is situated between the left atrium and the left ventricle. It is a check valve, regulating the flow of freshly oxygenated blood from the lungs into the heart's powerful pump. Your own mitral valve opens and closes about 100,000 times a day—36 million times each year. . . .

"The mitral valve opens widely to let blood enter the pump, and then it snaps securely shut when blood is ejected from the heart. The work of the heart goes on day after day, year after year, with or without your awareness.

"But things can go wrong with the mitral valve. If for any reason the mitral valve doesn't close completely, blood is regurgitated backwards. The high pressure exerted by the heart is then impelled directly back to the lungs. If that were to go on very long, it would result in failure of both the heart and the lungs. Let me describe one condition that can create just such a problem.

"One of the mitral valve's cords may rupture spontaneously. When that occurs, *sequential stress* on the adjoining cords is immediately increased. Then the neighboring cords are much more prone to rupture. And when they break, the entire mitral valve loses it competence, and the patient's life is in serious jeopardy. . . .

"Fishermen also understand the danger of sequential stress as it relates to integrity of their nets. To the untrained, a small tear may seem to be relatively insignificant. But the experienced fishermen knows about sequential stress. A broken strand in his net may allow the loss of a fish or two, but more important, it causes undue strain on adjacent strands. Before long a small hole becomes larger and larger. Eventually the entire net is worthless.

"Applying the metaphor of the mitral valve, let us depict a model of spiritual integrity. Imagine that one of those supporting cords is broken—the cord of honesty, for example. If that cord breaks, the law of sequential stress immediately imposes additional strain on the neighboring cords of chastity, virtue, benevolence, and so on.

"None of us is immune to temptation, and the adversary knows it. Satan would deceive, connive, or contrive any means to deprive us of potential joy and exaltation. He knows that if one little cord of control can be snapped, others are likely to give later under increased strain. . . .

"A surgeon can repair or replace a mitral valve that has lost its integrity. But no surgical procedure can be performed for loss of spiritual integrity of heart. Such breakdown is under individual control.

"The wise fisherman inspects his nets regularly. Should any flaw be detected, he repairs the defect, without delay. . . . So the wise assess personal cords of integrity on a daily basis. You are the one to identify any weakness. You are the one to repair it. . . . That process of repair you know as repentance, and, mercifully, you don't have to begin it alone. Help can be received through counsel with trusted parents and Church leaders. But their aid is more likely to be helpful if you will seek it not merely to satisfy a formality, but with 'real intent' to reform yourself and to come closer to Christ. He is the Ultimate Physician. . . . Repentance may not be easy, but it is worth it. Repentance not only bleaches, it heals!"[34]

CHAPTER 39

A SPECIAL WITNESS OF THE NAME OF CHRIST

MODERN-DAY SCRIPTURE OUTLINES some of the many responsibilities of Apostles. Among their several duties, they are "to
build up the Church, and regulate all the affairs of the same in all
nations" (D&C 107:33). The Twelve also have the authority "to
ordain and set in order all the other officers of the Church" (D&C
107:58), and to open the doors of the nations for "the proclamation
of the gospel" (D&C 107:35). Elder Nelson's participation in such
duties has been discussed heretofore in considerable detail.

One of the most sacred of all apostolic responsibilities is to be
one of the "special witnesses of the name of Christ in all the world"
(D&C 107:23). Elder Nelson has been such a witness, bringing
healing balm to those with broken hearts and contrite spirits as he
testifies that Jesus Christ is "our Master and more."[1]

CREATOR

"Under the direction of the Father, Jesus bore the responsibility
of Creator. . . . The Gospel of John proclaims that Christ is the
Creator of all things: 'All things were made by him; and without him
was not any thing made that was made' (John 1:3; see also D&C
93:21). . . .

JEHOVAH

"Jesus was Jehovah. . . . Jehovah—the great I Am, the God of the Old Testament—clearly identified Himself when he personally appeared in His glory as a resurrected being to the Prophet Joseph Smith and Oliver Cowdery in the Kirtland Temple on 3 April 1836. I quote from their written testimony:

"'We saw the Lord standing upon the breastwork of the pulpit, before us; and under his feet was a paved work of pure gold, in color like amber.

"'His eyes were as a flame of fire; the hair of his head was white like the pure snow; his countenance shone above the brightness of the sun; and his voice was as the sound of the rushing of great waters, even the *voice of Jehovah*, saying:

"'I am the first and the last; I am he who liveth, I am he who was slain' (D&C 110:2–4; emphasis added; see also D&C 76:23)."²

ADVOCATE WITH THE FATHER

"Jesus is our Advocate with the Father (see 1 John 2:1; D&C 29:5; 32:3; 45:3; 110:4). The word *advocate* comes from Latin roots meaning a 'voice for' or 'one who pleads for another.' . . .

"He is also known as the Mediator of the new testament, or new covenant (see Hebrews 9:15; 12:24). Comprehending Him as our Advocate, Intercessor, and Mediator with the Father gives us assurance of His unequaled understanding, justice, and mercy (see Alma 7:12)."³

IMMANUEL

"Jesus was foreordained to be the promised Immanuel. Remember Isaiah's remarkable prophecy: 'The Lord himself shall give you a sign; Behold, a virgin shall conceive, and bear a son, and shall call his name Immanuel' (Isaiah 7:14). . . . The Hebrew name—the title of which Isaiah prophesied, *Immanuel*—literally means 'with us is God'! (Isaiah 7:14, footnote *e*). . . . *Immanuel* could be such only at the will of His Father."[4]

SON OF GOD

"Jesus alone bore His responsibility as the Son of God, the Only Begotten Son of the Father (see John 1:14, 18; 3:16). Jesus was literally 'the Son of the Highest' (Luke 1:32; see also v. 35). . . .

"The unique parentage of Jesus was also announced to Nephi, who was thus instructed by an angel:

"'Behold, the virgin whom thou seest is the mother of the Son of God, after the manner of the flesh. . . .

"' . . . Behold the Lamb of God, yea, even the Son of the Eternal Father!' (1 Nephi 11:18, 21).

"From His Heavenly Father, Jesus inherited His potential for immortality and eternal life. From His mother, Jesus inherited death (see Genesis 3:15; Mark 6:3)."[5]

ANOINTED ONE

"Jesus was the Anointed One. Because of this fact, He was accorded two specific titles. One was *the Messiah*, which in Hebrew means 'the anointed.' The other was *the Christ*, which comes from the Greek word that also means 'the anointed.' Thus, 'Jesus is spoken of as the Christ and the Messiah, which means He is the one anointed of the Father to be His personal representative in all things pertaining to the salvation of mankind' (Bible Dictionary, "Anointed One," 609)."[6]

SAVIOR AND REDEEMER

"Jesus was born to be Savior and Redeemer of all mankind (see Isaiah 49:26; 1 Nephi 10:5). He was the Lamb of God (see 1 Nephi 10:10) who offered Himself without spot or blemish (see 1 Peter 1:19) as a sacrifice for the sins of the world" (see John 1:29). . . .

"Jesus fulfilled His glorious promise made in preearthly councils by atoning for the fall of Adam and Eve unconditionally and for our own sins upon the condition of our repentance. His responsibility as Savior and Redeemer was indelibly intertwined with His responsibility as Creator."[7]

JUDGE

"Closely allied to the Lord's status as Savior and Redeemer is His responsibility as Judge. . . .

"'As I have been lifted up [upon the cross] by men even so should men be lifted up by the Father, to stand before me, to be judged of their works, whether they be good or whether they be evil—

"' . . . Therefore, according to the power of the Father I will draw all men unto me, that they may be judged according to their works' (3 Nephi 27:14–15)."[8]

EXEMPLAR

"Another overarching responsibility of the Lord is that of Exemplar. To people of the Holy Land, He said, 'I have given you an example, that ye should do as I have done to you' (John 13:15; see also 14:6; 1 Peter 2:21). To people of ancient America, He again emphasized His mission as Exemplar: 'I am the light; I have set an example for you' (3 Nephi 18:16; see also 27:27; 2 Nephi 31:9, 16). . . .

"Are you vexed by your own imperfections? For example, have you ever locked your keys inside the car? Or have you ever moved from one room to another, to accomplish a task, only to find you had forgotten what you wanted to do? (Incidentally, troubles of that nature don't disappear as you grow older.) Please do not be discouraged by the Lord's expression of hope for your perfection. You should have faith to know that He would not require development beyond your capacity. Of course you should strive to correct habits or thoughts which are improper. Conquering of weakness brings great joy. You can attain a certain degree of perfection in some things in this life. And you can become perfect in keeping various commandments. But the Lord was not necessarily asking for your errorless and perfect behavior in all things. He was pleading for more than that. His hopes are for your full potential to be realized: to become as He is! . . .

"That precious promise of perfection could not have been possible without the Lord's Atonement and example."[9]

MILLENNIAL MESSIAH

"One of the Lord's ultimate responsibilities lies yet in the future. That will be His masterful status as the Millennial Messiah. When that day comes, the physical face of the earth will have been changed: 'Every valley shall be exalted, and every mountain and hill shall be made low: and the crooked shall be made straight, and the rough places plain' (Isaiah 40:4). . . .

"He will govern from two world capitals, one in old Jerusalem (see Jeremiah 3:17; Zechariah 14:4–7; D&C 45:48–66; 133:19–21) and the other in the New Jerusalem, 'built upon the American Continent' (Articles of Faith 1:10; see also Ether 13:3–10; D&C 84:2–4). From these centers He will direct the affairs of His Church and kingdom. Then He 'shall reign for ever and ever' (Revelation 11:15; see also Exodus 15:18; Psalm 146:10; Mosiah 3:5; D&C 76:108)."[10]

DIVINE ATTRIBUTES

"His mission was the Atonement. That mission was uniquely His. Born of a mortal mother and an immortal Father, He was the only one who could voluntarily lay down His life and take it up again. . . .

"If I were to ask which characteristic of His life you would identify first, I think you might name His attribute of love. That would include His compassion, kindness, charity, devotion, forgiveness, mercy, justice, and more. Jesus loved His Father and loved His mother. He loved His family and the Saints. He loved the sinner, without excusing the sin. And He taught us how we can show our love for Him. He said, 'If ye love me, keep my commandments.' . . .

"Another expression of our Savior's love was His service. . . .

"A second aspect of the Savior's exemplary life was His emphasis upon sacred ordinances. During His mortal ministry He demonstrated the importance of the ordinances of salvation. . . .

"A third aspect of the Lord's exemplary ministry is prayer. . . .

"A fourth aspect of the Lord's example is the use of His divine knowledge. . . .

"A fifth aspect of the Lord's ministry . . . is His commitment to endure to the end. . . .

"These five aspects of His ministry—love (including obedience and service), focus on ordinances, prayer, use of knowledge, and a commitment to endure to the end—can be applied in our own lives. Surely the best evidence of our adoration of Jesus is our emulation of Him. . . . With all my heart I pray that the transforming influence of the Lord may make a profound difference in your lives."[11]

BREAD OF LIFE

"Facing you, I am reminded of military days long ago when our platoon heard shouts from a sergeant: 'Attention!' 'Right face!' 'Left face!' 'About face!' We learned to respond to those orders with instant precision. In retrospect, I don't recall ever having heard his command to 'face upward.' Yet scriptures tell us to 'look to God and live.' . . .

"Sadly, many individuals don't know where to find God, and exclude Him from their lives. When spiritual needs arise, they may look to the left, the right, or round about. But looking to other people on the same level cannot satisfy spiritual shortages. When the immortal spirit is starved, hunger persists for something more filling. Even when material success comes, there is a hollow ache—if living well falls short of living worthily. Inner peace cannot be found in affluence accompanied by spiritual privation.

"Members of The Church of Jesus Christ of Latter-day Saints invite all to come unto Christ and enjoy the spiritual feast that His gospel provides. The Saints savor a sweet spiritual nourishment that sustains them through life. This sustenance comes because they have made covenants to take upon themselves the name of the Lord and strive to obey His precepts. Strength comes in recognizing and in being grateful for the Lord's gifts of immortality and the opportunity for eternal life. . . .

"The Lord said, 'Look unto me in every thought; doubt not, fear not' (D&C 6:36). I have learned that such faith gives emancipating power. Facing God first lets us decide firmly what we shall not do; then we are free to pursue what we ought to do."[12]

THE RESURRECTION AND THE LIFE

"I thank God for His Son, Jesus Christ, for His mission in mortality, and for His ministry as the resurrected Lord. He brought about His own resurrection. Testimonies of thousands, from ancient and modern times, attest to the truth that the resurrected Jesus is the Savior of mankind. He brought about a universal resurrection: 'For as in Adam all die, even so in Christ shall all be made alive' (1 Corinthians 15:22; see also Mosiah 3:16).

"His sacrifice and His glory assure that 'the spirit and the body shall be reunited again in its perfect form; both limb and joint shall be restored to its proper frame, even as we now are at this time' (Alma 11:43).

"Gratefully and positively, I affirm that there is life after life, first in the spirit world and then in the Resurrection, for each and every one of us. I know that God lives and that Jesus the Christ is His Son. He is 'the resurrection, and the life' (John 11:25). He lives. He is my Master. I am His servant. With all my heart, I love Him, and I testify of Him."[13]

EPILOGUE

F OUR DECADES BEFORE THE Savior came to dwell on earth, Alma prophesied, "The Son of God shall come in his glory; and his glory shall be the glory of the Only Begotten of the Father, full of grace, equity, and truth, full of patience, mercy, and long-suffering, quick to hear the cries of his people and to answer their prayers" (Alma 9:26). After the Savior had atoned for our sins and had overcome the bands of death through the Resurrection, He appeared to the ancient Nephites and urged them to "be perfect even as I, or your Father who is in heaven is perfect" (2 Nephi 12:48). Becoming perfect involves acquiring the attributes cited by Alma, including patience and mercy.

It has been nearly two decades since Dr. Russell M. Nelson set aside his scalpel, sternal saw, and sutures. Nevertheless, physicians throughout the country continue to inquire about his health and well-being. They still admire his pioneering contributions to the field of cardiovascular and thoracic surgery, and his extraordinary surgical skills have left an indelible impression upon the medical profession. But even more important than his skills and accomplishments are the pleasant memories his colleagues have of his countless acts of kindness toward them and their families.[1] Past patients, medical interns and residents, nurses, and administrators all refer to his boundless patience and thoughtful, compassionate deeds.

King Benjamin taught his people that one hallmark of having received a remission of sins is to "have no more disposition to do evil, but to do good continually" (Mosiah 5:2). This scripture aptly describes Elder Nelson, who has disciplined himself to the point that impatience, anger, and contention are completely foreign to him. By contrast, the godly attributes of patience, compassion, and kindness are more than second nature to him. He has nurtured these attributes to the point that they epitomize him.

Elder Nelson's penchant for hard work and efficient use of time has redounded as a blessing upon the Saints. The Prophet Joseph Smith taught, "Happiness is the object and design of our existence; and will be the end thereof, if we pursue the path that leads to it; and this path is virtue, uprightness, faithfulness, holiness, and keeping all the commandments of God."[2] Russell and Dantzel Nelson have pursued the path of which the Prophet speaks and have reaped the reward of living "after the manner of happiness" (2 Nephi 5:27).

The Declaration of Independence sought to assure the "unalienable rights" of "Life, Liberty and the pursuit of Happiness." But it did not *guarantee* happiness, and sometimes we must be content with the happiness of pursuit. When Russell M. Nelson began his lengthy medical studies and subsequent career, he did not directly pursue happiness; rather, he sought increased knowledge and a concomitant ability to alleviate suffering. When he and Dantzel married, they did not directly set upon a course of having as many children as possible; rather, they tried to listen to the promptings of the Spirit. Elder Nelson did not aspire to the Holy Apostleship, but, as President Monson said of him, "He'll happily go anywhere he's sent and leave a trail of happiness behind."[3] Elder Nelson and Sister Nelson have simply lost their lives in the service of others, and in the process they have reaped the reward of happiness.

Only our Father in Heaven knows what the future holds for this exemplary couple. They are no strangers to heartaches and tears, but they readily resonate to the sound of hearty laughter and expressions of affection from those they hold dear. Regardless of whether their remaining years on earth are brief or lengthy, they will leave behind a legacy of love that will persist in perpetuity among all those who have observed firsthand their pattern of happiness. May their lives become a pattern for each of us.

May this book provide an incentive for each of us to emulate the lives of Elder and Sister Nelson by living the gospel with exactness, tempered with patience and compassion, wisely using our time on earth to serve the Lord and His children, including our own families.

APPENDIX

Dr. Russell M. Nelson had been serving as director of the Cardiovascular-Thoracic Surgical Residency at the University of Utah Affiliated Hospitals since 1967 when he was called to the Quorum of the Twelve Apostles in 1984. During that seventeen-year period, fifty-seven surgeons received their specialty training in the surgical residency program.

SURGEONS TRAINED BY DR. RUSSELL M. NELSON AND HIS MEDICAL COLLEAGUES

Resident	Period of Training
Becker, Albert A.	November 1974–June 1975
Berk, Arnold D.	July 1969–June 1971
Berry, Charles	July 1982–June 1984
Brezing, Richard	July 1981–June 1983
Burdette, Fred	July 1975–June 1977
Bustos, Manuel	July 1968–June 1971
Butler, Charles F.	July 1977–June 1979
Cabi, Ahmet Turgut	July 1964–June 1966
Collins, Michael P.	July 1978–June 1980
Depp, David A.	July 1972–June 1973; July 1975–June 1976
Esmaili, Saeed	July 1976–June 1978
Ferrero, Alessandro	July 1976–June 1978
Gonzales, Alejandro G.	July 1959–June 1961
Gresen, Arthur A.	July 1972–June 1974
Guibone, Roy A.	July 1966–June 1968
Horton, Vern H.	October 1971–September 1973
Jaeger, Vincent J.	July 1978–June 1980
Joyce, Lyle D.	July 1980–June 1982
Judson, John P.	July 1977–June 1979

Katz, Saul	July 1974–June 1976
Kim, Chang Suh (Charles)	July 1974–June 1975
Kolff, Jack	January 1974–February 1974
Kotselas, Evangelos	July 1962–June 1963
Kwan-Gett, Clifford S.	July 1970–June 1971;
	July 1972–June 1973
McGough, Edwin C.	July 1970–June 1972
Miller, Hyman	July 1975–June 1977
Morales, Rodolfo A.	July 1973–June 1975
Nellis, Noel	July 1968–June 1970
Pearce, Maunsel B.	July 1968–June 1969;
	July 1971–June 1972
Peterson, Charles A.	July 1962–June 1964
Place, Robert	July 1979–June 1981
Planz, Edward	July 1980–June 1982
Pliam, Michael	January 1975–December 1976
Po, Vicente	July 1961–June 1963
Prian, Gregory W.	July 1977–June 1979
Propp, John	July 1982–June 1984
Quinton, Ronald R.	July 1981–June 1983
Randono, John	July 1981–June 1983
Ranganath, Halemane S.	July 1973–June 1975
Robinson, George C. (Terry)	July 1978–June 1980
Roohanipur, Manoochehr	July 1972–June 1974
Saksena, Devendra	July 1968–June 1970
Salaymeh, Muhammed T.	July 1965–June 1967
Santos, Arthur	July 1983–June 1985
Schorlemmer, Gilbert	July 1983–June 1985
Sethi, Gulshan K.	July 1970–June 1972
Shore, Richard T.	July 1969–June 1971
Smith, Glade R.	July 1982–June 1984
Smith, Mont	July 1979–June 1981
Stanton, Michael	July 1979–June 1981
Stark, Roger	July 1980–June 1982
Thorne, J. Kent	July 1983–June 1985
Torres, José	July 1963–June 1965
Vana, Milton	July 1975–June 1977
Vaughn, Cecil C.	July 1967–June 1969
Wertheimer, Mark	July 1972–June 1974
Zwart, Hans	July 1970–December 1970;
	July 1971–June 1973

NOTES

NOTES TO PREFACE

1. John L. Hart, "Elder Nelson, Pioneer Heart Surgeon, Honored," *Church News,* 20 April 2002, 4.
2. Gordon B. Hinckley, remarks at the Heart of Gold award ceremony, 13 April 2002; "Elder Russell M. Nelson Is Given American Heart Association Award," *Ensign,* July 2002, 76.
3. Russell M. Nelson, "The Creation," *Ensign,* May 2000, 85.
4. James E. Faust, interview by author, 17 January 2002.

NOTE TO ACKNOWLEDGMENTS

1. Jeffrey D. Keith, "Feeling the Atonement," *Brigham Young University 2001–2002 Speeches,* (Provo, Utah: University Publications, 2002), 113–20.

NOTES TO CHAPTER 1

1. Ford Stevenson, "Church Marks 150 Years in Scandinavia," *Church News,* 15 July 2002, 8–10.
2. Ibid. The sculptor was Dennis Smith. The unveiling of a second statue, *Kristina,* occurred at the Copenhagen Harbor on July 6. Brother Smith sculpted this statue in honor of his own great-grandmother, who emigrated at age sixteen.
3. Ibid.
4. Russell M. Nelson, *From Heart to Heart* (Salt Lake City: Russell M. Nelson, 1979), 7.
5. Thomas Gray, "Elegy Written in a Country Church Yard," in *The Poem: An Anthology,* ed. Stanley B. Greenfield and A. Kingsley Weatherhead (New York: Appleton-Crofts, 1968), 143–47.
6. Andrew Jenson, *History of the Scandinavian Mission* (New York: Arno Press, 1979), 3–43.
7. Joseph Smith, *History of the Church of Jesus Christ of Latter-day Saints,* ed. B. H. Roberts, 2d ed. rev., 7 vols. (Salt Lake City: The Church of Jesus Christ of Latter-day Saints, 1932–51), 5:423.
8. The Journal History of the Church of Jesus Christ of Latter-day Saints, Church History Library, 13 October 1852, 2.
9. *Our Yesterdays: A History of Ephraim, Utah 1854–1979,* ed.

and pub. the Centennial Book Committee (Ephraim, Utah: 1979), 8–10.

10. Ibid., 118.

11. Ibid., 12.

12. Warren Metcalf, "A Precarious Balance: The Northern Utes and the Black Hawk War," *Utah Historical Quarterly* 57 (1989): 25; Deloy J. Spencer, "The Utah Black Hawk War, 1865–1871," master's thesis, Utah State University, 1969, 54–55.

13. Ibid., 34.

14. Josiah F. Gibbs, "Black Hawk's Last Raid—1866," *Utah Historical Quarterly* 4 (1931): 108.

15. *Mormon Immigration Index Family History Resource File* (Salt Lake City: The Church of Jesus Christ of Latter-day Saints, CD-Rom Library, 2000).

16. Ibid.

17. Nelson, *From Heart to Heart*, 7.

18. *Mormon Immigration Index.*

19. The daughter of Christen Hansen and Kristine Nielsen, she was known in America as Margrethe or Margrete (Grethe) Christena Hansen. She is listed in the Danish IGI under both Hansen and Christensen. In the *Mormon Immigration Index*, she is listed as Grethe Christensen.

20. Nelson, *From Heart to Heart*, 15.

21. Keith A. Hunsaker, "The Life and Educational Contributions of Superintendent A. C. Nelson," master's thesis, University of Utah, 1941, 9.

22. Ibid., 5–6.

23. Nelson, *From Heart to Heart*, 15.

24. Parley P. Pratt, *Key to the Science of Theology* (Salt Lake City: Deseret Book, 1978), 72.

25. Nelson, *From Heart to Heart*, 16–18.

26. Hunsaker, "The Life and Educational Contributions," 16.

27. Nelson, *From Heart to Heart*, 18.

28. Ibid.

29. Jenson, *History of the Scandinavian Mission*, 65.

30. Gerald Haslam, "The Norwegian Experience with Mormonism, 1842–1920," doctoral dissertation, Brigham Young University, 1981, 67.

31. Ibid., 67.

32. Jenson, *History of the Scandinavian Mission*, 65–66.

33. *Mormon Immigration Index.*

34. Nelson, *From Heart to Heart*, 7, 15.

35. Ibid., 8.

36. *Mormon Immigration Index.*

37. Nelson, *From Heart to Heart*, 8.

38. Anna S. D. Johnson, "The Seventh Handcart Company," *The Relief Society Magazine*, volume 35 (1948): 449–51, 501.

39. *Our Yesterdays*, 81.

40. Inger Höglund and Caj-Aage Johansson, *Stegitro: Jesu Kristi Kyrka av Sista Dagars Heliga i Sverige 1850–2000* (Stockholm, Sweden: Informationstjästen, 2000), 242.

41. Nelson, *From Heart to Heart*, 8.

42. *Mormon Immigration Index.*

43. Ibid.

44. Ibid.

45. Nelson, *From Heart to Heart*, 8.

46. Ibid., 8–9.

47. Ibid., 10; the Swedish name of Andersson was eventually changed to Anderson.

48. Ibid., 12.

49. Ibid., 12, 15. On November 5, 1999, Elder Nelson was invited to be the guest speaker at the Snow College Founder's Day celebration in Ephraim. While there, he offered the dedicatory prayer for

the newly remodeled Noyes Administration Building. During that visit, he saw a historic document containing the names of his grandparents Andrew C. Anderson and Sarah E. Anderson on the list of citizens of Ephraim who signed a petition on October 17, 1897, granting land for the construction of the Sanpete Academy, which later became Snow College (Russell M. Nelson, personal record, 5 November 1999).

50. Ibid., 9.

NOTES TO CHAPTER 2

1. Russell M. Nelson, *From Heart to Heart* (Salt Lake City: Russell M. Nelson, 1979), 23.
2. Ibid.
3. Ibid.
4. Ibid.
5. Ibid.
6. Ibid.
7. Ibid.
8. Ibid., 24.
9. Marjory Nelson Rohlfing, interview by author, 30 May 2002; *Through Our Eyes: 150 Years of History as Seen through the Eyes of the Writers and Editors of the Deseret News*, ed. Don C. Woodward (Salt Lake City: Deseret News, 1999), 89.
10. Nelson, *From Heart to Heart*, 24.
11. *Through Our Eyes,* 98.
12. Nelson, *From Heart to Heart*, 25.
13. Ibid., 26.
14. Ibid., 27.
15. Ibid., 39–40.
16. Russell M. Nelson, interview by author.
17. Thomas S. Monson, interview by author, 8 June 2002.
18. Nelson, *From Heart to Heart*, 41.
19. Ibid., 208.
20. Monson, interview.

NOTES TO CHAPTER 3

1. Russell M. Nelson, *From Heart To Heart* (Salt Lake City: Russell M. Nelson, 1979), 40.
2. *Through Our Eyes: 150 Years of History as Seen through the Eyes of the Writers and Editors of the Deseret News*, ed. Don C. Woodward (Salt Lake City: Deseret News, 1999), 103.
3. Nelson, *From Heart To Heart*, 29.
4. Russell M. Nelson, interview by author; Thomas S. Monson, interview by author, 8 June 2002.
5. Nelson, *From Heart to Heart*, 29.
6. Ibid., 29.
7. Ibid., 29–30.
8. Ibid., 30.
9. Ibid.
10. Ibid.
11. Ibid., 30, 32.
12. Ibid., 32.
13. Nelson, interview, 9 February 2003.
14. Ibid., 151.
15. Ibid., 32.
16. Ibid.
17. Ibid.
18. Ibid., 32–33.
19. Ibid., 33.
20. Ibid.
21. Ibid.
22. Russell M. Nelson, personal record, 31 May 1994.
23. Nelson, *From Heart to Heart*, 33.
24. Ibid.
25. Enid Nelson DeBirk, interview by author, 3 June 2002.
26. Ibid.
27. Ibid.
28. Nelson, *From Heart to Heart*, 34.
29. Ibid.
30. Ibid., 36.

31. Ibid., 34.
32. Ibid., 34, 36.
33. Ibid.
34. Marjory Nelson Rohlfing, interview by author, 30 May 2002.
35. Nelson, *From Heart to Heart*, 36.
36. Ibid., 37.
37. Ibid.
38. Ibid.
39. Ibid.
40. Gerry Avant, "Elder Nelson: Husband, Father Are Highest Titles," *Church News*, 16 February 1986, 4–5.
41. Nelson, *From Heart to Heart*, 38.
42. Ibid.
43. Ibid.
44. Ibid.
45. Ibid., 39.
46. Ibid.
47. DeBirk, interview.
48. Ibid.
49. Ibid.

NOTES TO CHAPTER 4

1. Russell M. Nelson, *From Heart to Heart* (Salt Lake City: Russell M. Nelson, 1979), 42.
2. Ibid., 42, 44.
3. Ibid.
4. Ibid., 44.
5. Ibid.
6. Ibid., 44–45.
7. Ibid., 45.
8. Ibid., 48.
9. Ibid.
10. Ibid., 46.
11. Ibid., 51.
12. Ibid., 48.
13. Ibid.
14. Ibid., 51.
15. Ibid.
16. Ibid.
17. Ibid., 51, 55.
18. Ibid., 55.
19. Ibid.

NOTES TO CHAPTER 5

1. Russell M. Nelson, "Nauvoo: Place of Revelation, Gathering, and Faith," address at Nauvoo Illinois Temple dedication, session 3, 28 June 2002.
2. Dantzel W. Nelson, interview by author, 7 January 2002.
3. Russell M. Nelson, *From Heart to Heart* (Salt Lake City: Russell M. Nelson, 1979), 58; Boyd K. Packer, interview by author, 16 January 2002.
4. Nelson, interview.
5. Ibid.
6. Ibid.
7. Ibid.
8. Ibid.
9. Ibid.
10. Ibid.
11. Ibid.
12. Nelson, *From Heart to Heart*, 57.
13. Ibid.
14. Ibid.
15. Ibid., 58.
16. Ibid.
17. Ibid.
18. Ibid., 59.
19. Ibid.
20. Ibid.
21. Nelson, interview.
22. Ibid.
23. Enid Nelson DeBirk, interview by author, 3 June 2002.
24. Russell M. Nelson, personal record, 6–21 June 1982.
25. Nelson, *From Heart to Heart*, 59–60.
26. Ibid., 60.
27. Ibid.
28. Ibid., 89.
29. Ibid., 60.
30. Ibid.
31. Russell M. Nelson, "Identity, Priority, and Blessings," *Ensign*, August 2001, 9.

32. Sylvia N. Webster, interview by author, 2002.
33. Nelson daughters, interview by author, 2002.
34. Brenda N. Miles, interview by author, 10 January 2002.
35. Rosalie N. Ringwood, interview by author, 4 January 2002.
36. Nelson, interview.
37. Ibid.
38. Gloria N. Irion, interview by author, 10 December 2001; Miles, interview.
39. Irion, interview.
40. Wendy N. Maxfield, interview by author, 3 January 2002.
41. Russell M. Nelson, interview by author, 23 May 2002.
42. Marsha N. McKellar, interview by author, 5 January 2002.
43. Nelson, *From Heart to Heart*, 60–61.
44. Conrad B. Jenson, interview by author, 21 May 2002.
45. Robert D. Hales, interview by author, 29 May 2002.
46. Thomas S. Monson, interview by author, 8 June 2002.
47. Nelson, *From Heart to Heart*, 61–62.

Notes to Chapter 6

1. Russell M. Nelson, *From Heart to Heart* (Salt Lake City: Russell M. Nelson, 1979), 68.
2. Ibid.
3. Ibid., 68, 70, 213.
4. Ibid., 213.
5. Russell M. Nelson, "Endure and Be Lifted Up," *Ensign*, May 1997, 70–73.
6. Marsha N. McKellar, interview by author, 5 January 2002.
7. Nelson, *From Heart to Heart*, 213, 215, 217.
8. Ibid., 220.
9. Ibid.
10. Wendy N. Maxfield, interview by author, 3 January 2002.
11. Dantzel W. Nelson, interview by author, 7 January 2002.
12. Nelson, *From Heart to Heart*, 220.
13. Nelson, interview.
14. Nelson, *From Heart to Heart*, 220.
15. Maxfield, interview.
16. Nelson, *From Heart to Heart*, 81.
17. Ibid.
18. Ibid., 225.
19. Gloria N. Irion, interview by author, 10 December 2001.
20. Nelson, *From Heart to Heart*, 225.
21. Ibid.
22. Ibid.; Irion, interview; Jeffrey R. Holland, interview by author, 23 January 2002.
23. Nelson, *From Heart to Heart*, 227.
24. Ibid., 88.
25. Ibid.
26. Ibid., 232.
27. Ibid.
28. Ibid.
29. Brenda N. Miles, interview, 10 January 2002.
30. Ibid.
31. Ibid.
32. Nelson, *From Heart to Heart*, 95, 97.
33. Ibid., 109.
34. Sylvia N. Webster, interview by author, 2002.
35. Nelson, *From Heart to Heart*, 239–40.
36. Ibid., 240.
37. Ibid., 243.
38. Ibid., 243, 245.
39. Russell M. Nelson, "Woman—of Infinite Worth," *Ensign*, November 1989, 21; Russell M. Nelson, interview by author.
40. Nelson, *From Heart to Heart*, 245.
41. Ibid.
42. Bradley E. Wittwer and Julie V.

Wittwer, interview by author, 14 January 2002.

43. Nelson, *From Heart to Heart*, 246.
44. Ibid.
45. Ibid.
46. Ibid., 246, 248.
47. Ibid.
48. Ibid.
49. Ibid., 250, 252, 253.
50. Ibid., 253.
51. Ibid., 254.
52. Ibid., 257.
53. "Another Girl; That Makes 9," *Deseret News,* 26 October 1965, B1.
54. Rose Mary Pedersen, "Dad Is an Extra-Special Person," *Deseret News,* 14 June 1969, B16.
55. Russell M. Nelson, "Listen to Learn," *Ensign,* May 1991, 22.
56. Marjorie N. Helsten, interview by author, 11 January 2001.
57. Nelson, *From Heart to Heart,* 259–60.
58. Ibid.

NOTES TO CHAPTER 7

1. Russell M. Nelson, *From Heart to Heart* (Salt Lake City: Russell M. Nelson, 1979), 261.
2. Ibid.
3. Ibid.
4. Ibid.
5. Ibid., 263.
6. Ibid., 265.
7. Ibid., 268, 271.
8. Russell M. Nelson, personal record, 7–8 October 1996.
9. Russell M. Nelson Jr., interview by author, 2 January 2002.
10. Ibid.
11. Nelson, personal record.
12. Harold B. Lee, *The Teachings of Harold B. Lee,* ed. Clyde J. Williams (Salt Lake City: Bookcraft, 1996), 280.

13. Marsha N. McKellar, interview by author, 5 January 2002.
14. Nelson Jr., interview.

NOTES TO CHAPTER 8

1. "My Heart Leaps Up," in *William Wordsworth: Selected Poems* (New York: Random House, 1993), 164.
2. Rosalie N. Ringwood, interview by author, 4 January 2002.
3. Russell M. Nelson, *From Heart to Heart* (Salt Lake City: Russell M. Nelson, 1979), 207.
4. Ibid.
5. Ibid., 207–8.
6. Nelson daughters, interview by author, 2002.
7. Russell M. Nelson, personal record, 25 December 1996.
8. Nelson, *From Heart to Heart,* 208.
9. Ibid., 208–9.
10. Ibid., 209.
11. Brenda N. Miles, interview by author, 10 January 2002.
12. Nelson, personal record, 15 July 1999.
13. Nelson daughters, interview.
14. Nelson, *From Heart to Heart,* 209.
15. Russell M. Nelson Jr., interview by author, 2 January 2002.
16. Nelson, *From Heart to Heart,* 209.
17. Ibid.
18. Nelson daughters, interview.
19. Nelson, *From Heart to Heart,* 209–10.
20. Russell M. Nelson, interview by author.
21. Nelson, *From Heart to Heart,* 210.
22. Ibid.
23. Nelson, personal record, several entries.
24. Ibid., 14 December 2001.
25. Nelson, interview.
26. Nelson, *From Heart to Heart,* 193–94; Nelson, interview.

27. Ibid., 81, 84.
28. Nelson, interview.
29. Ibid.
30. Ibid.
31. Nelson family members, interview by author, 2002.
32. Nelson, personal record, several entries; Nelson, interview.
33. Nelson, interview.
34. Ibid.
35. Nelson children, interview by author, 2002.
36. "The Family: A Proclamation to the World," *Ensign,* November 1995, 102.
37. Dantzel W. Nelson and Gloria N. Irion, interview by author, 7 January 2002.
38. Russell M. Nelson, "Reflection and Resolution," *Brigham Young University 1989–90 Devotional and Fireside Speeches* (Provo, Utah: University Publications, 1990), 59–67.
39. Nelson, interview.
40. Russell M. Nelson, "Set in Order Thy House," *Ensign*, November 2001, 69.
41. Nelson, personal record, 8–19 May 1983; 17 October–2 November 1980.
42. Ibid., 7–13 July 1990.
43. Nelson daughters and Brad Wittwer, interview by author, 2002.
44. Nelson, personal record, 12–18 June 2000.
45. Nelson, *From Heart to Heart,* 211.
46. Ibid.
47. Ibid.
48. Nelson, personal record, 27 February 1985.
49. Nelson Jr., interview.
50. Nelson, personal record, 26 September 1993.
51. Ibid., 27 September 1997.

NOTES TO CHAPTER 9

1. Russell M. Nelson, *From Heart to Heart* (Salt Lake City: Russell M. Nelson, 1979), 63.
2. Ibid.
3. Ibid.
4. Ibid., 63, 66.
5. Ibid., 66.
6. Ibid.
7. Ibid., 67.
8. Ibid., 67–68.
9. Ibid., 68.
10. Ibid.
11. Ibid., 70.
12. Ibid.
13. Ibid., 70–71.
14. Ibid., 71.
15. Russell M. Nelson, interview by author.
16. Nelson, *From Heart to Heart*, 71.
17. Ibid.
18. Ibid.
19. Ibid.
20. Ibid., 72.
21. Ibid.
22. Ibid.
23. Ibid., 73.
24. Ibid., 72–73.
25. Ibid., 73.
26. Ibid.
27. Ibid.
28. Ibid.
29. Ibid., 74.
30. Ibid.

NOTES TO CHAPTER 10

1. Russell M. Nelson, *From Heart to Heart* (Salt Lake City: Russell M. Nelson, 1979), 75.
2. Ibid.
3. Ibid., 75–76.
4. Ibid., 76.
5. Ibid.
6. Ibid., 77.
7. Ibid.
8. Ibid.

9. Ibid., 77–78.
10. Ibid., 78.
11. Ibid.
12. Ibid.
13. Ibid., 79.
14. Ibid.
15. Ibid., 123.
16. Ibid.; Russell M. Nelson, interview by author.
17. Ibid., 123–24.
18. Ibid., 79.
19. Ibid.
20. Ibid., 79–80.
21. Ibid., 80.
22. Ibid., 81.
23. Ibid.
24. Ibid., 83–84. Dantzel and Russell had come to love Washington, D.C., and had enjoyed nearby museums and historical sites. One day in January 1952, Russell started watching the televised proceedings of the inaugural ceremonies for President Dwight D. Eisenhower while Dantzel was caring for their little ones. It suddenly occurred to him that he was in Washington, D.C., just a few miles away from where the inauguration was taking place. He left the apartment, drove downtown as far as he could, parked the car, and then walked the rest of the way to the White House. He watched the remaining inaugural festivities on Pennsylvania Avenue in front of the White House, recalling, "I was thoroughly inspired by the entire proceedings."
25. Ibid., 84.

NOTES TO CHAPTER 11

1. Russell M. Nelson, *From Heart to Heart* (Salt Lake City: Russell M. Nelson, 1979), 85.

2. Ibid.
3. Ibid.
4. Ibid., 86.
5. Ibid.
6. Ibid., 89.
7. Ibid., 86.
8. Henry B. Eyring, interview by author, 14 March 2002.
9. Nelson, *From Heart to Heart,* 86; Russell M. Nelson, interview by author.
10. Ibid.
11. Ibid., 87.
12. Ibid., 89.
13. Ibid.
14. Ibid., 89–90.
15. Ibid., 91.
16. Ibid.
17. Ibid.; "Russell M. Nelson Awarded Ph.D. in Surgery at Minnesota," *Church News,* 29 January 1955, 13.
18. Nelson, *From Heart to Heart,* 91.
19. Mark M. Ravitch, *A Century of Surgery: The History of the American Surgical Association,* 2 vols. (Philadelphia: J. B. Lippincott, 1981), 2:970.
20. Nelson, *From Heart to Heart,* 92.
21. Ibid.
22. Ibid., 93.
23. Ibid.

NOTES TO CHAPTER 12

1. Russell M. Nelson, *From Heart to Heart* (Salt Lake City: Russell M. Nelson, 1979), 95.
2. Ibid.
3. Ibid. Russell became a full-time member of the faculty surgical staff along with Dr. Price, Dr. William H. Moretz, and Dr. Ralph C. Richards, general surgeons; and Dr. Petter A. Lindstrom, neurosurgeon.

4. Russell M. Nelson, interview by author, 23 May 2002.
5. Nelson, *From Heart to Heart*, 97.
6. Ibid.
7. Ibid., 97–98.
8. Ibid., 98.
9. Twila Van Leer and Arva M. Smith, "Utahn's Life Gets Bonus from Heart Surgery: 25 Extra Years to Love, Learn, Live," *Deseret News*, 15 December 1980, B8.
10. Nelson, *From Heart to Heart*, 98.
11. Ibid., 99.
12. Ibid.
13. William C. Patrick, "Complex Machine Adds New S. L. Medical Stride," *Salt Lake Tribune*, 7 April 1956, 19–20.
14. "U. Medic Named 'Man of Year' by S. L. Jaycees," *Deseret News*, 25 January 1957, B2.
15. Nelson, *From Heart to Heart*, 99.
16. Ibid.
17. Ibid., 99–100.
18. Ibid., 100.
19. "Professor at University Wins Top Medical Scholarship," *Salt Lake Tribune*, 8 March 1957, C15.
20. Nelson, *From Heart to Heart*, 100.
21. Ibid.
22. Ibid.
23. "Research Grants Awarded 3 Doctors in Utah," *Deseret News*, 25 May 1959, A12.
24. "Heart Grants Awarded," *Deseret News*, 18 January 1961, C6.
25. Nelson, interview.
26. Nelson, *From Heart to Heart*, 100; Conrad B. Jenson, interview by author, 23 May 2002.
27. Nelson, *From Heart to Heart*, 103.
28. Ibid.
29. Ibid.
30. Jenson, interview.
31. Nelson, interview.
32. David B. Wirthlin, interview by author, 28 May 2002.
33. "Award Honors Elder Nelson for Contributions in Medicine," *Church News*, 24 April 1993, 7.
34. Gerry Avant, "Elder Nelson: Husband, Father Are Highest Titles," *Church News*, 16 February 1986, 4–5.
35. Nelson, interview.
36. Avant, "Elder Nelson," 4–5.
37. Nelson, *From Heart to Heart*, 103.
38. Kent W. Jones, in "Heart of Gold: Russell M. Nelson," produced by Bonneville International Corporation, KSL, and Freebairn Entertainment, 2002, video-cassette.
39. Jones, interview.
40. Nelson, interview.
41. Nelson, *From Heart to Heart*, 124.

NOTES TO CHAPTER 13

1. Russell M. Nelson, *From Heart to Heart* (Salt Lake City: Russell M. Nelson, 1979), 113.
2. Ibid.
3. Ibid.
4. As observed by the author.
5. Nelson, *From Heart to Heart*, 114.
6. Ibid., 114–15; "Bonneville Stake Sustains New Leaders at Conference," *Church News*, 12 December 1964, 4.
7. Nelson, *From Heart to Heart*, 115.
8. Ibid., 116.
9. Ibid.
10. Ibid.
11. James E. Faust, interview by author, 17 January 2002.
12. Maurice A. Jones, "'Make Time' for Church, Doctor Says," *Deseret News*, 12 December 1964, 16.
13. "The Fruits of Faith," *Deseret News*, 28 June 1971, A12.

14. Cecil O. Samuelson Jr., interview by author, 23 April 2002.
15. Dallin H. Oaks, interview by author, 1 February 2002.
16. Nelson, *From Heart to Heart*, 149.
17. Ibid., 149–50.
18. Ibid., 150.
19. Ibid., 150–51.
20. T. S. Eliot, "Little Gidding," in *T. S. Eliot: Collected Poems 1909–1962* (London: Faber and Faber, 1963), 222.
21. Nelson, *From Heart to Heart*, 151.
22. Ibid., 119.
23. Ibid., 122.
24. Gerry Avant, "Elder Nelson: Husband, Father Are Highest Titles," *Church News*, 16 February 1986, 4–5.
25. Ibid.

NOTES TO CHAPTER 14

1. Russell M. Nelson, *From Heart to Heart* (Salt Lake City: Russell M. Nelson, 1979), 162.
2. Ibid., 163–65.
3. Thomas S. Monson, interview by author, 8 June 2002.
4. Nelson, *From Heart to Heart*, 165, 166, 168.

NOTES TO CHAPTER 15

1. Russell M. Nelson, *From Heart to Heart* (Salt Lake City: Russell M. Nelson, 1979), 125.
2. Ibid.
3. Ibid.; "The Fruits of Faith," *Deseret News*, 28 June 1971, A12.
4. Nelson, *From Heart to Heart*, 125, 127.
5. Thomas S. Monson, interview by author, 8 June 2002.
6. Nelson, *From Heart to Heart*, 127; "Sunday School Superintendency Is Reorganized," *Church News*, 3 July 1971, 3–4.
7. Enid Nelson DeBirk, interview by author, 3 June 2002.
8. Ibid.
9. Ibid.
10. Nelson, *From Heart to Heart*, 155.
11. Ibid., 127, 129.
12. Ibid., 129.
13. Ibid.
14. Ibid.
15. Ibid., 152.
16. Ibid., 153.
17. Ibid.
18. Ibid., 131.
19. Ibid.
20. Ibid.
21. *Deseret News 2001–2002 Church Almanac* (Salt Lake City: Deseret News, 2000), 99.
22. Nelson, *From Heart to Heart*, 158.
23. Ibid.
24. Ibid., 137.
25. Ibid., 138.
26. Ibid., 137–38.
27. At general conference in April 1975, Russell's counselor Joseph B. Wirthlin was the last man to be called as an Assistant to the Twelve. Russell's other counselor, Richard L. Warner, was called as a regional representative. Russell said, "Just a week prior to that, we had mused in reflection on the choice nature of our callings and service together in the Church. This taught me again to savor service and servants as they now are, for change will come and the moments we cherish will soon become memories." B. Lloyd Poelman and Joe J. Christensen were called to be President Nelson's new counselors in the Sunday School general presidency, each bringing unique talents to their assignments. Three years later, Brother Poelman was released to serve as a mission

president. Brother Christensen became first counselor and William D. Oswald became second counselor. On May 7, 1979, Brother Christensen was called to preside over the Missionary Training Center in Provo. On August 14 of that same year, President Marion G. Romney set apart Brother Oswald as first counselor and Brother J. Hugh Baird as second counselor in the Sunday School general presidency (Nelson, personal record, 7 May 1979; 14 August 1979).

NOTE TO CHAPTER 16

1. All information in this chapter comes from Russell M. Nelson, *From Heart to Heart* (Salt Lake City: Russell M. Nelson, 1979), 175, 176, 177, 178, 179–80, 181, 182, 183–85, 186.

NOTES TO CHAPTER 17

1. Russell M. Nelson, personal record, 6 October 1979.
2. Ibid., 1 October 1979.
3. Ibid., 3–11 March 1979; 24 August–1 September, 1979.
4. Ibid., 21, 29 March 1980.
5. Russell M. Nelson, "What's in a Name?" BYU devotional, 24 June 1980; manuscript in possession of the author.
6. Russell M. Nelson, "Invisible Cables," 6 February 1981; "A Call to Serve," 31 March 1985; manuscripts in possession of the author.
7. Russell M. Nelson, "Thanks for the Covenant," *Brigham Young University 1988–89 Devotional and Fireside Speeches* (Provo, Utah: University Publications, 1989), 55.

8. Nelson, personal record, 30 December 1981.
9. Ibid., 10–26 May 1982.
10. Lane Johnson, "Russell M. Nelson: A Study in Obedience," *Ensign*, August 1982, 18–24.
11. James E. Faust, interview by author, 7 January 2002.
12. Russell M. Nelson, interview by author.
13. Ibid.
14. Johnson, "Russell M. Nelson," 20.
15. Nelson, personal record, 31 December 1982.
16. Ibid., 16–19 July 1983.
17. Ibid., 14–29 October 1983.

NOTES TO CHAPTER 18

1. Russell M. Nelson, personal record, December 1983.
2. Ibid., 21, 25 March 1984.
3. Ibid., 1 April 1984.
4. Ibid., 6 April 1984.
5. Russell M. Nelson, interview by author.
6. Ibid.
7. Gordon B. Hinckley, "The Sustaining of Church Officers," *Ensign*, May 1984, 4–5.
8. Neal A. Maxwell, interview by author, 1 March 2002.
9. Nelson, personal record, 7 April 1984.
10. Wendy N. Maxfield, interview by author, 10 December 2001.
11. Nelson, personal record, 7 April 1984.
12. Russell M. Nelson, "Call to the Holy Apostleship," *Ensign*, May 1984, 52–53.
13. James E. Faust, "The Magnificent Vision Near Palmyra," *Ensign*, May 1984, 67.
14. James E. Faust, interview by author, 17 January 2002.

15. Nelson, personal record, 8 April 1984.
16. Nelson, interview.
17. Nelson, personal record, 12 April 1984.
18. Ibid., 15 April 1984.
19. Cecil O. Samuelson Jr., interview by author, 23 April 2002.
20. Nelson, personal record, 21–23 April 1984.
21. Ibid., 28 May 1984.
22. Ibid., 6 June 1984.
23. Ibid., 15, 30, June 1984; 27 August 1984.
24. Nelson, interview.
25. Ibid.
26. Russell M. Nelson, "Protect the Spiritual Power Line," *Ensign,* November 1984, 30–32.
27. Nelson, personal record, 25 October 1984.
28. Ibid., 27 October 1984.
29. Russell M. Nelson, "Reverence for Life," *Ensign*, May 1985, 11–14.
30. Bruce R. McConkie, "The Purifying Power of Gethsemane," *Ensign*, May 1985, 11.
31. Nelson, interview.
32. Ibid., 2 August 1985.
33. Elder Nelson's previous general conference address contained six scriptural references within the text and forty-five additional scriptural references interspersed among the thirteen footnotes (Nelson, "Reverence for Life").
34. Russell M. Nelson, "Truth and More," *Ensign,* January 1986, 69–73.
35. Russell M. Nelson, "Self-Mastery," *Ensign,* November 1985, 30–32. During the same general conference, Elder M. Russell Ballard was sustained as an Apostle on October 10. The First Presidency and the Twelve later ordained him to the office of Apostle and set him apart as a member of the Quorum of the Twelve Apostles (Nelson, personal record, 10 October 1985).
36. Nelson, personal record, 14–15 October 1985.
37. Ibid., 22, 25 October 1985; subsequent Portuguese lessons in 1997–98 were tutored by Lyle Black.
38. Nelson, personal record, 27 October 1985.
39. Elder Nelson's German tutor was Rick Sutherland.
40. Nelson, personal record, 31 October 1985.
41. Ibid., 2–3 November 1985.
42. Ibid., 4–5 November 1985.
43. Ibid., 5 November 1985.
44. Ibid., 6 November 1985.
45. Ibid., 8 November 1985.
46. Ibid., 10 November 1985.
47. Ibid., 14 November 1985.
48. Ibid., 26 November 1985. During his years as a General Authority, Elder Nelson has also received valuable language instruction from William D. Cocorinis, a friend and professor of Greek at the University of Utah.
49. Ibid., 1 December 1985.
50. Ibid., 8 December 1985.
51. Ibid., 15 December 1985.
52. Ibid., 27 December 1985.

NOTES TO CHAPTER 19

1. Boyd K. Packer, interview by author, 17 February 2002.
2. Neal A. Maxwell, interview by author, 1 March 2002.
3. *Hymns,* 301.
4. L. Tom Perry, interview by author, 19 February 2002.
5. M. Russell Ballard, interview by author, 27 February 2002.

6. David B. Haight, interview by author, 1 March 2002.
7. Ibid.
8. Russell M. Nelson, interview by author.
9. David B. Haight, "The Sacrament—and the Sacrifice," *Ensign*, November 1989, 59–61.
10. Maxwell, interview.
11. Ibid.
12. Ibid.
13. Ibid.
14. Robert D. Hales, interview by author, 29 May 2002.
15. Dallin H. Oaks, interview by author, 1 February 2002.
16. Ibid.
17. Ballard, interview.
18. Joseph B. Wirthlin, interview by author, 4 April 2002.
19. Richard G. Scott, interview by author, 12 February 2002.
20. Ibid.
21. Hales, interview.
22. David E. Sorensen, interview by author, 29 May 2002.
23. D. Todd Christofferson, interview by author, 30 May 2002.
24. Hales, interview.
25. Ibid.
26. Jeffrey R. Holland, interview by author, 23 January 2002.
27. Ibid.
28. Ibid.
29. Ibid.
30. Ibid.
31. Ibid.
32. Henry B. Eyring, interview by author, 14 March 2002.
33. Ibid.
34. Ibid.

NOTES TO CHAPTER 20

1. Russell M. Nelson, personal record, 19 February 1985.
2. Russell M. Nelson, interview by author.
3. Ibid.
4. Nelson, personal record, 11–12 December 1979. This was the annual Philip B. Price lecture. Dr. Price had been the head of the Department of Surgery and the dean of the Cheeloo Medical College before World War II. After the war, he became the first professor and chairman of the Department of Surgery at the University of Utah.
5. Ibid., 2, 9 May 1980; Nelson, interview.
6. They were accompanied by Dr. Price, then eighty-five years old, and by Dr. and Mrs. Randy Shields.
7. Zhang Zhenxiang, interview by author, Toronto, Ontario, Canada, 7 May 2001.
8. Ibid.
9. Ibid.
10. Ibid.
11. Ibid.
12. Ibid.
13. Ibid.
14. Nelson, interview.
15. Dr. Nelson's surgical nurse, Jan Curtis, accompanied them (Nelson, personal record, 25 April–22 May 1984). This trip to China was a follow-up to his earlier visit in 1980 when he instructed Chinese physicians and demonstrated for them the surgical procedures that address congenital and acquired cardiac problems. Some of these Chinese medical school professors had visited Salt Lake City in 1981 for further instruction and observation of Dr. Nelson's surgical techniques.
16. Ibid.

17. Nelson, personal record, 11 February 1985; Zhang, interview.
18. Nelson, personal record, 11 February 1985.
19. Ibid., 19 February 1985.
20. Ibid., 2 March 1985.
21. Ibid., 4 March 1985.
22. Zhang, interview.
23. Nelson, personal record, 5 March 1985.
24. Zhang, interview.
25. Ibid.; Nelson, interview.
26. Nelson, personal record, 7 May 1986.
27. Ibid.
28. Ibid., 8 May 1986.
29. Ibid., 9 May 1986.
30. Ibid., 13 May 1986. The Nelsons, Bradfords, and Rodgerses traveled the next day by air to Xi'an, where they were met at the airport by government officials and medical leaders. The following day the group visited the Museum of Qin Pottery Figures, which features hundreds of life-size terra-cotta figures made more than two thousand years ago, yet only discovered in the last quarter century. This exhibit is touted as the eighth wonder of the world. In the evening, the entourage was greeted at an official reception by the governor of Shaanxi Province, Li Qingwei (Nelson, personal record, 15 May 1986).
31. Ibid., 16 May 1986.
32. Ibid., 17 May 1986.
33. Ibid., 18 May 1986. On October 7, 1988, President Gordon B. Hinckley and Elder Nelson met in Salt Lake City with several visitors from the People's Republic of China, including representatives from the Agricultural Bank of China and steel executives who came to visit the Geneva Steel

Plant in Orem, Utah (Nelson, personal record, 7 October 1988).
34. Gerrit W. Gong, personal journal, 7 November 1988.
35. Nelson, personal record, 7 November 1988.
36. Ibid., 8 November 1988.
37. Ibid.
38. Dallin H. Oaks, personal journal, 5–8 November 1988.
39. Gong, personal journal, 9 November 1988. The next day Elder Nelson met with several physicians on the faculty of Shandong Medical College, many of whom had been in the Nelson home in Salt Lake City. He was honored at a dinner sponsored by Sun Daren, the vice governor of Shaanxi Province. Later, he visited the apartment of John and Rachel Nutter, who taught English at the Shaanxi Teachers University (Nelson, personal record, 10 November 1988).
40. Nelson, personal record, 12 November 1988.
41. Ibid.
42. Zhang, interview.
43. Nelson, personal record, 14 April 1990.
44. Ibid., 15 April 1990.
45. Ibid., 25 August 1990.
46. Zhang, interview.
47. Nelson, personal record, 12 April 1991.
48. Beverly Campbell, interview by author, 7 August 2001.
49. Nelson, personal record, 10 February 1995.
50. Ibid., 21 February 1995. Also in the welcoming groups were Elder and Sister Kwok Yuen Tai of the Asia Area Presidency and Beverly and Pierce Campbell from Washington, D.C., who had come

to China in advance in order to prepare for this apostolic visit.

51. Campbell, interview.

52. Nelson, personal record, 23 February 1995. Zhang Xiaowen was accompanied by Wang Zhongda, deputy director, and Chen Yue, deputy chief.

53. His assistants, Xue Hui, section chief; Guo Wei, director of the Department No. 2; and Lu Jinguang, of the Bureau of Religious Affairs, were also present.

54. Nelson, personal record, 24–26 February 1995. Elder and Sister Maxwell and Elder Carmack then parted ways to travel to Singapore, Elder and Sister Tai went to Shanghai, the Campbells departed for Washington, D.C., and the Nelsons caught a flight to Korea, where Elder Nelson presided at the Kwang Ju/Chung Cheong regional conference over the weekend.

55. Campbell, interview.

56. Nelson, personal record, 20 April 1997.

57. James E. Faust, interview by author, 17 January 2002.

58. Ibid.; "Church Leaders Meet with Hong Kong Official," *Ensign,* July 1997, 78.

59. Nelson, personal record, 23 April 1997.

NOTES TO CHAPTER 21

1. Russell M. Nelson, personal record, 17 September 1991.

2. Ibid., 20 September 1991.

3. Ibid., 17 October 1991.

4. Ibid., 6 December 1991.

5. Ibid., 6 March 1992.

6. Ibid., 22 October 1992.

7. Ibid., 4 February 1993.

8. Ibid., 26 August 1993.

9. Ibid., 21 January 1994.

10. Ibid., 25 April 1994.

11. Ibid., 2–3 May 1994.

12. Ibid., 1 June 1994.

13. Ibid., 10 June 1994.

14. Russell M. Nelson, interview by author.

15. Nelson, personal record, 12 June 1994.

16. Ibid., 14–15 July 1994.

17. Ibid., 18 July 1994.

18. Ibid., 28 July 1994.

19. Ibid., 15 August 1994.

20. Ibid., 17 August 1994.

21. Ibid., 22 August 1994.

22. Ibid., 23 August 1994.

23. Ibid., 29 August 1994.

24. Ibid., 2 September 1994.

25. Ibid., 14 September 1994; 12 October 1994; 14 November 1994.

26. Ibid., 14 November 1994.

27. Ibid., 22 November 1994.

28. Ibid., 3 December 1994.

29. Ibid., 28, 30 December 1994.

30. Ibid., 8 January 1995.

31. Ibid., 15 January 1995.

32. Ibid., 27 January 1995.

33. Ibid., 29 January 1995.

34. Ibid., 30 January 1995.

35. Ibid., 31 January–1 February 1995.

36. Ibid., 1 February 1995.

37. Ibid.

38. Ibid.

39. Russell M. Nelson, "Doors of Death," *Ensign,* May 1992, 72–74.

40. Nelson, interview.

NOTES TO CHAPTER 22

1. Spencer W. Kimball, "Fundamental Principles to Ponder and Live," *Ensign,* November 1978, 45–46.

2. M. Dale Ensign, interview by author, 8 August 2001.
3. Beverly Campbell, interview by author, 7 August 2001.
4. James E. Faust, interview by author, 17 January 2002.
5. Campbell, interview.

NOTES TO CHAPTER 23

1. Martin Berkeley Hickman, *David Matthew Kennedy: Banker, Statesman, Churchman* (Salt Lake City: Deseret Book, 1987), 354.
2. Russell M. Nelson, personal record, 1 June 1986; Russell M. Nelson, "Drama on the European Stage," *Ensign*, December 1991, 9.
3. Nelson, personal record, 15 June 1989.
4. Nelson, "Drama," 9. Walter Whipple was the first president of the mission.
5. Nelson, personal record, 14 January 1986.
6. Ibid., 25–26 January 1986.
7. Beverly Campbell, interview by author, 7 August 2001.
8. Ibid.
9. Nelson, personal record, 4 August 1987.
10. Ibid., 10 September 1987.
11. Ibid., 11 December 1987.
12. Ibid., 20 October 1988.
13. Ibid., 21 February 1989.
14. Ibid., 14 June 1989.
15. Ibid., 8 January 1990.
16. Ibid., 6 February 1990.
17. Ibid.
18. Ibid.
19. Ibid.
20. Ibid., 22 February 1990.
21. Nelson, "Drama," 10–11.
22. Nelson, personal record, 8 June 1990.
23. Ibid., 23 June 1990.
24. Thomas S. Monson, "Thanks Be to God," *Ensign*, May 1989, 50–53; Ezra Taft Benson, *A Labor of Love: The 1946 European Mission of Ezra Taft Benson* (Salt Lake City: Deseret Book, 1989).
25. Dorothea S. Condie (former resident of the GDR), interview by author.
26. Thomas S. Monson, *Faith Rewarded: A Personal Account of Prophetic Promises to the East German Saints* (Salt Lake City: Deseret Book, 1996), 5–7, 35–38, 66–67, 88–106, 121–37.
27. Nelson, personal record, 28 October 1988; "LDS Leaders Meet with E. Germans," *Salt Lake Tribune*, 29 October 1988, A1.
28. Monson, "Thanks Be to God," 50–53; Nelson, "Drama," 10.
29. Nelson, personal record, 9 November 1989.
30. Ibid., 21 October 1990.
31. Ibid.
32. Ibid.

NOTES TO CHAPTER 24

1. Dorothy Stowe, "Film Makers Satisfy Europe's Curiosity," *Church News*, 11 November 1984, 10.
2. Others attending the dedication were Elder Wayne and Sister Linea Johnson, Elder Jean Marc Frey, Elder Zolton Nagy-Kovac, Dr. Peter Varga, and Spencer J. Condie, president of the Austria Vienna Mission.
3. Russell M. Nelson, personal record, 21 April 1987. Imre Miklos was joined by Laszlo Pozsonyi. In the afternoon, the brethren also met the vice premier, Jozsef Marjai.
4. Russell M. Nelson, interview by author.

5. Nelson, personal record, 12 October 1987.
6. Ibid., 24 June 1988; "Hungary Recognizes Mormon Church," *Salt Lake Tribune*, 6 July 1988, A14. Other officials included Ferenc Banadics, Sarkadi Nagy, and Ferenc Nagy.
7. Ibid., 16 October 1989; "Meetinghouse Dedicated in Hungary," *Church News*, 11 November 1989, 3–4.
8. Russell M. Nelson, "Drama on the European Stage," *Ensign*, December 1991, 12.
9. Nelson, personal record, 17 October 1989.
10. Nelson, "Drama," 12.
11. "Paracelsus," in *The Poetical Works of Robert Browning*, 2 vols. (London: Smith, Elder & Co., 1902), 1:25.
12. Nelson, "Drama," 12.
13. Nelson, personal record, 15 April 1987.
14. Ibid., 16 April 1987.
15. Ibid.
16. Ibid., 18 April 1987.
17. Ibid., 23 June 1990.

NOTES TO CHAPTER 25

1. Spencer W. Kimball, "Fundamental Principles to Ponder and Live," *Ensign*, November 1978, 43–44.
2. Gary L. Browning, *Russia and the Restored Gospel* (Salt Lake City: Deseret Book, 1997), 18; Russell M. Nelson, personal record, 9–12 June 1987.
3. Nelson, personal record, 10 June 1987; Russell M. Nelson, interview by author.
4. Nelson, interview.
5. Ibid.
6. Browning, *Russia*, 20.

7. Ibid., 20–21.
8. "Church Will Help Armenian Homeless," *Church News*, 19 August 1989, 3–4. The brethren were pleased that Soviet ambassador Yuri Dubinin and Jack Matlock, U.S. ambassador to the Soviet Union, had accepted invitations to attend this meeting (Nelson, personal record, 8 August 1989).
9. Jon M. Huntsman, in "Heart of Gold: Russell M. Nelson," produced by Bonneville International Corporation, KSL, and Freebairn Entertainment, 2002, videocassette.
10. Also attending were Valery Sorokin, Ralph and Carole Hardy, and Beverly Campbell.
11. Nelson, personal record, 13 October 1989.
12. Browning, *Russia*, 23–24.
13. Ibid., 24.
14. Nelson, personal record, 24 April 1990.
15. Ibid., 25 April 1990; "Dedicatory Prayer for Estonia," 25 April 1990.
16. Nelson, personal record, 25 April 1990.
17. Ibid.
18. Ibid., 26 April 1990.
19. Ibid.
20. Ibid.
21. Ibid.
22. Ibid.
23. Ibid., 24 May 1990.
24. Dennis B. Neuenschwander, interview by author, 22 May 2002; *Deseret News 1999–2000 Church Almanac* (Salt Lake City: Deseret News, 1998), 398.
25. Nelson, personal record, 19 June 1990.
26. Attributed to former U.N. secretary general Carlos Romulo.

27. Nelson, personal record, 2 November 1990. When they visited President Ezra Taft Benson at his home on November 16, Elder Faust and Elder Nelson were delighted to see how much his health and strength had improved. In the afternoon, Elder Nelson met with Rashid Kaplanov, a distinguished scientist from Moscow who spoke thirty languages fluently and desired to learn more about the Church. He already had a copy of the Book of Mormon in English, but he desired a copy in Turkish, so Elder Nelson presented him with a copy of *Selections from the Book of Mormon* in Turkish. For the initial phase of introducing the gospel to certain countries where few Latter-day Saints live, the Book of Mormon is only partially translated in order to hasten the process of getting at least some of the book into the hands of the members (Nelson, personal record, 16 November 1990).

28. Ibid., 10 May 1993.

29. "Dedicatory Prayer for Belarus," 11 May 1993; "Four European Lands Dedicated: Apostles 'Turn Keys, Unlock Doors' for Gospel in Nations of Latvia, Lithuania, Belarus, and Albania," *Church News*, 12 June 1993, 3, 6.

30. Nelson, personal record, 11 May 1993.

31. Ibid., 1 May 1993.

32. Ibid., 1 May 1996.

33. Ibid., 7 October 1996.

34. Ibid., 8 October 1996; Nelson, interview. After the departure of the Gorbachevs, Elder Nelson attended a luncheon at the Lion House for participants at a Religious Freedom Conference, sponsored by Brigham Young University. Guests included several governmental leaders in charge of religious affairs from Russia, Ukraine, Slovakia, Mexico, and other countries. Elder Nelson was pleased to greet each of them in their respective languages, and they were all interested in learning more about the Church after having attended general conference two days earlier. On Tuesday, December 9, 1997, Elder Nelson hosted a luncheon for Vasiliy Alexandrovich Starodubtsev, governor of the Tula Oblast, a province in western of Russia. He was accompanied by Anatoliy Sergevich Kopylov, vice governor of the Tula Oblast. Elder Nelson wished that his son could have been present to help interpret for his Russian guests (Ibid., 9 December 1997).

35. Ibid., 13 November 1998.

36. Ibid., 14 November 1998.

37. Ibid., 15 November 1998.

38. Ibid., 16 November 1998.

39. Ibid., 17 November 1998.

40. Ibid., 18 November 1998.

41. Ibid., 19 November 1998.

42. Nelson, interview.

43. Nelson, personal record, 13 July 2000. Elder Bruce Porter of the Seventy, himself an expert in Russian politics, also attended, as did Russell Jr. Elder Nelson recalled, "Our visitors were really impressed that one of the Twelve Apostles had a son who had served as a missionary in Russia and who had maintained his fluency in the Russian language seven years after his release."

NOTES TO CHAPTER 26

1. Tom Morganthau et al., "Bracing for War," *Newsweek*, 21 January 1991, 16–19; Russell Watson et al., "The Edge of the Abyss," *Newsweek*, 21 January 1991, 20–22, 24.

2. "Special Issue: America at War," *Newsweek*, 28 January 1991.

3. Russell M. Nelson, personal record, 29 January 1991. A special meeting was held with the First Presidency on March 6, 1991, during which they discussed an invitation from Jon Huntsman for Church representation at the June dedication of his precast concrete plant in Yerevan, Armenia. The First Presidency designated Elder Dallin H. Oaks and Elder Nelson to represent the Church on that occasion (Nelson, personal record, 6 March 1991). The next day, Russell M. Nelson Jr. received his mission call to serve in the Finland Helsinki East Mission—Russian speaking (Nelson, personal record, 7 March 1991).

4. Jay M. Todd, "An Encore of the Spirit," *Ensign*, October 1991, 42–43.

5. Thomas Matthews, "The Secret History of the War," *Newsweek*, 18 March 1991, 28–32, 36–39.

6. Mr. Silaev was accompanied by Vladimir Volodin, Mikhail Kouristchev, Dimitry Zubov, Alexei Tsaregorodsev, Valeriy V. Rishin, and Alla Zakharova.

7. Nelson, personal record, 25 April 1991.

8. Ibid., 22 May 1991.

9. He was accompanied by his counselor for cultural affairs, Alexander P. Potemkin. Also present were several faithful, distinguished Latter-day Saints: Brother and Sister Ralph Hardy; Beverly and Pierce Campbell; Nolan D. Archibald, CEO and president of Black and Decker; Layne W. Cannon, vice president of WordPerfect Corporation; Sterling Colton, senior vice president and general counsel for the Marriott Corporation; attorney Marcus G. Faust; Clayton Foulger and Sidney Foulger, vice president and chairman, respectively, of Foulger-Pratt Construction.

10. Nelson, personal record, 24 May 1991.

11. Ibid., 9 June 1991.

12. Ibid., 10 June 1991; Todd, "An Encore," 44.

13. Ibid., 11 June 1991; Ibid., 38.

14. Ibid., 12 June 1991; Ibid., 46.

15. Ibid., 13 June 1991; Ibid., 43–44.

16. Todd, "An Encore," 44.

17. Ibid., 38–40, 46; Nelson, personal record, 18 June 1991.

18. The afternoon concert was primarily for Latter-day Saints; the evening program was for the general public. It was a joyful privilege for Elder and Sister Nelson to host Kurt Löffler and Günter Behncke, who, as officials of the East German government, had hosted President Thomas S. Monson and the Nelsons at a concert in that same hall in October 1988.

19. Nelson, personal record, 20 June 1991; Todd, "An Encore," 46. The choir rested on Friday, June 21, so the Nelsons enjoyed a walk around East Berlin with Elder Albert Choules of the area presidency and his wife, Marilyn. That evening, Elder Nelson spoke to the theme "Be Not Weary in Well-Doing" at a fireside attended by

about eight hundred members gathered at the Berlin Germany Stake Center (Nelson, personal record, 21 June 1991).

20. Nelson, personal record, 22 June 1991; Todd, "An Encore," 45–47. As guests of Karen and Jon M. Huntsman on June 23, the Nelsons boarded the Huntsman Gulfstream jet bound for Yerevan, Armenia. There they were greeted by a host of dignitaries and television cameras. They then went to the Republican Children's Hospital to unveil plaques and tour the facilities. Also present were Senator Jake Garn, Congressman Wayne Owens, Utah governor Norman Bangerter, Elder Dallin H. Oaks, Elder Hans B. Ringger, BYU president Rex Lee, and Geneva Steel president Joe Cannon, and their respective spouses.

21. Ibid., 24 June 1991. Brother David Horne was a faithful Church service supervisor of the Yerevan concrete plant. Not long after this visit, he was tragically burned in a gas explosion in his apartment. Brother Jon Huntsman rushed back to Armenia to bring him to Salt Lake City in his private plane so he could receive expert medical care. Unfortunately, Brother Horne's injuries were so severe that within a short time he passed away, claiming the Lord's promise and blessing that "every one that hath forsaken houses, or brethren, or sisters, or father, or mother, or wife, or children, or lands, for my name's sake, shall receive an hundredfold, and shall inherit everlasting life" (Matthew 19:29).

22. Ibid.

23. Ibid.; Todd, "An Encore," 41–42, 48; Gerry Avant, "Russia Recognizes LDS Church," *Deseret News*, 25 June 1991, A1; Paul Rolby, "Russia Recognizes LDS Faith," *Salt Lake Tribune*, 25 June 1991, A1; Gerry Avant and Matthew Brown, "Church Is Recognized by Russian Republic," *Church News*, 29 June 1991, 11–12.

24. Russell M. Nelson, interview by author.

25. Nelson, personal record, 25 June 1991.

26. Ibid., 26 June 1991.

27. Ibid., 27 June 1991; Todd, "An Encore," 35.

NOTES TO CHAPTER 27

1. Russell M. Nelson, personal record, 19 October 1987.

2. Ibid., 20 October 1987.

3. Ibid., 21 October 1987; Russell M. Nelson, interview by author.

4. Nelson, personal record, 22 October 1987.

5. Ibid., 7 February 1990.

6. Ibid.

7. Ibid., 8 February 1990; Minister Pop was accompanied by his office manager, Nicolae Zaharra.

8. Ibid.

9. Ibid.

10. Ibid.

11. Ibid.

12. Ibid.

13. Ibid., 9 February 1990. Others attending were David Farnsworth, Brother Nicolai Ciurdea, and Maria Muga, the Church's Romanian legal counsel, and her driver.

14. Mr. Constantinescu and Mr. Carstoiu.

15. Nelson, personal record, 9 February 1990.
16. Ibid.
17. Ibid.
18. Campbell, interview.
19. Russell M. Nelson, "Drama on the European Stage," *Ensign*, December 1991, 13.
20. Nelson, personal record, 17 July 1992.
21. *Deseret News 1999–2000 Church Almanac* (Salt Lake City: Deseret News, 1998), 380; Nelson, "Drama," 13.
22. Nelson, "Drama," 13.
23. Ibid.
24. Nelson, personal record, 1 November 1988.
25. Ibid., 13 February 1990.
26. Orson F. Whitney, "The Wintry Day, Descending to Its Close," *Hymns*, 37.
27. Minister Popov was also chairman of the Committee on the Matters of the Bulgarian Orthodox Church and the Religious Cults. He was assisted by Tsviatko Tsvetkov, with whom the Brethren had met during a previous visit, and by legal counsel Oleg Penkov and Antonia Terzieva, interpreter for the Ministry of Foreign Affairs.
28. Nelson, personal record, 13 February 1990.
29. Ibid.
30. Ibid.
31. Ibid., 23 June 1990.
32. Ibid., 29 June 1990.
33. Ibid., 26 October 1990.
34. *Church Almanac*, 286.

NOTES TO CHAPTER 28

1. Russell M. Nelson, personal record, 15 June 1988; Martin Berkeley Hickman, *David Matthew Kennedy: Banker, Statesman, Churchman* (Salt Lake City: Deseret Book, 1987), 334–65.
2. Nelson, personal record, 16 June 1990.
3. Ibid., 17 June 1990.
4. Ibid., 7 December 1989.
5. Ibid., 21 June 1988.
6. Ibid. The LDS entourage was hosted at a luncheon in the home of Mr. and Mrs. Fuad T. Kattan. Other guests included the U.S. ambassador to Jordan and his associate from the State Department, and Jordan's distinguished cardiac surgeon, Dr. Daoud Hanania. That evening they attended a reception at the home of Dr. Hanania, who was a lieutenant general in the military, director of the Royal Medical Services of the Jordanian Armed Forces, and chief of cardiovascular surgery at the King Hussein Medical Center. Dr. Hanania and Dr. Nelson found that they had much in common as cardiac surgeons. Several other physicians also attended.
7. Nelson, personal record, 21 June 1988.
8. Ibid., 22 June 1988.
9. Ibid., 7 September 1990.

NOTES TO CHAPTER 29

1. Russell M. Nelson, personal record, 3 June 1992. Elders Merlin R. Lybbert, John K. Carmack, and Monte J. Brough were then serving in the area presidency. The mission president was Kwok Yuen Tai.
2. Ibid., 5 June 1992. The Singapore Mission was led by President Warren R. Jones and his wife, Becky.

3. Ibid., 6 June 1992.
4. Ibid., 7 June 1992.
5. Neal A. Maxwell, interview by author, 1 March 2002; Bruce C. Hafen, *A Disciple's Life: The Biography of Neal A. Maxwell* (Salt Lake City: Deseret Book, 2002), 477–78.
6. Ibid.
7. Elder Maxwell's apostolic invocation has redounded as a continued blessing upon the people of Thailand.
8. Maxwell, interview; Nelson, personal record, 10 June 1992.
9. Nelson, personal record, 11 June 1992.
10. Ibid., 12 June 1992.
11. Ibid., 13 June 1992.
12. Ibid., 14 June 1992.
13. Ibid., 15 June 1992.
14. Ibid., 16 June 1992.
15. Ibid., 17 June 1992.
16. Ibid., 17 June 1992.
17. Ibid., 19 June 1992.
18. Ibid., 20 June 1992.
19. Ibid., 21 June 1992.
20. Ibid., 22 June 1992.

NOTES TO CHAPTER 30

1. Russell M. Nelson, personal record, 18 August 1992.
2. Ibid., 19 August 1992. Zambia, part of the Zimbabwe Harare Mission, was led by President Vern L. Marble and his wife, Mary.
3. *Hymns,* 301.
4. Russell M. Nelson, "Dedicatory Prayer for the Nation of Zambia," 20 August 1992.
5. Nelson, personal record, 20 August 1992.
6. Richard G. Scott, "Dedication of Botswana, Africa," 21 August 1992. Elder Scott had previously dedicated the West African country of Sierra Leone, on 18 May 1989.
7. Nelson, personal record, 21 August 1992.
8. Ibid., 22 August 1992.
9. *Hymns,* 30.
10. Nelson, personal record, 24 August 1992.
11. Richard G. Scott, "Dedicatory Prayer of the Republic of Congo," 24 August 1992; "Prayers of Dedication Offered on Four Nations in Central, Southern Africa," *Deseret News,* 26 September 1992, 3–4.
12. Nelson, personal record, 27 August 1992.
13. Ibid., 28 August 1992.
14. Ibid., 29 August 1992.
15. Ibid., 30 August 1992.
16. Ibid.
17. Ibid., 16 November 2001; "Elder Nelson Meets Ghanaian President, Breaks Temple Ground," *Ensign,* February 2002, 76.
18. Nelson, personal record, 16 November 2001.
19. George Q. Cannon, *Millennial Star* 39 (17 September 1877): 743.
20. Nelson, personal record, 16 November 2001.
21. Ibid.; "Elder Nelson Meets Ghanaian President," 76.

NOTES TO CHAPTER 31

1. Russell M. Nelson, personal record, 18–19 January 1997.
2. "An Outpouring of Love for Prophet," *Church News,* 1 February 1997, 3.
3. Nelson, personal record, 20 January 1997.
4. "An Outpouring," 3.
5. *Hymns,* 152.

6. Nelson, personal record, 20 January 1997.
7. "An Outpouring," 8.
8. Nelson, personal record, 21 January 1997.
9. Ibid.
10. "An Outpouring," 9.
11. Ibid., 12.
12. Nelson, personal record, 23 January 1997.
13. "An Outpouring," 12.
14. Nelson, personal record, 25–26 January 1997.
15. Ibid., 12 August 1997.
16. Ibid., 25 April 1999.
17. Ibid.; Rodolfo Acevedo, "Largest LDS Gathering: Chilean Members Eagerly Greet President Hinckley with Tears," *Church News,* 8 May 1999, 3, 11.
18. Nelson, personal record, 25 April 1999.
19. Ibid.
20. Ibid., 26 April 1999.

NOTES TO CHAPTER 32

1. Russell M. Nelson, "Dedicatory Prayer for the Country of Honduras" (English translation), 1 June 1991; "Land of Honduras Is Dedicated," *Church News,* 29 June 1991, 6.
2. Russell M. Nelson, personal record, 19 October 1991.
3. Ibid., 7–9 February 1997.
4. Ibid., 1–2 August 1999.
5. James P. Bell, *In the Strength of the Lord: The Life and Teachings of James E. Faust* (Salt Lake City: Deseret Book, 1999), 41.
6. Nelson, personal record, 15–18 May 1997. Speakers at the dedicatory services included the area presidency—Elders Dallas N. Archibald, W. Craig Zwick, and Claudio R. M. Costa—and Elder

Harold Hillam, representing the Presidency of the Seventy.
7. The conferences were held June 5–6 in Campinas, Brazil, with Elders W. Craig Zwick and Jairo Mazzagardi; June 12–13 in Manaus, Brazil, with Elders Claudio R. M. Costa and Irajá B. Soáres; August 21–22 in Belo Horizonte, Brazil, with Elders Athos M. Amorim and Silvio Geschwandtner; and August 27–29 in Aracajú, Brazil, with Elders Robert S. Wood and Paulo R. Grahl.
8. Nelson, personal record, 22 February 1998.

NOTES TO CHAPTER 33

1. Isaiah 11:11; 42:4; 51:5.
2. Russell M. Nelson, personal record, 5 May 1994.
3. Russell M. Nelson, "Dedicatory Prayer for French Polynesia," 8 May 1994.
4. Nelson, personal record, 9 May 1994.
5. Ibid., 10 May 1994.
6. Ibid., 11 May 1994.
7. Ibid., 16 August 1991.
8. Ibid., 17 August 1991; *Deseret News 2001–2002 Church Almanac* (Salt Lake City: Deseret News, 2000), 405–6.
9. Ibid., 18 August 1991.
10. Ibid., 19 August 1991.
11. Ibid., 23 August 1991; "Other Faiths Support LDS in Celebrating Tongan Centennial," *Church News,* 7 September 1991, 5.
12. Ibid., 24 August 1991.
13. Ibid., 26 August 1991.
14. Ibid., 15 May 1992.
15. Ibid., 17 May 1992.
16. Russell M. Nelson, "Dedicatory

Prayer for New Zealand," 6
November 1993.

17. Russell M. Nelson, "Dedicatory
Prayer for Australia," 13
November 1993.

18. Nelson, personal record, 14
January 1996.

19. Ibid., 19–21 January 1996.

20. Ibid., 19 January 2001.

21. Ibid., 20–21 January 2001.

NOTES TO CHAPTER 34

1. James B. Allen, Ronald K. Esplin,
and David J. Whittaker, *Men with
a Mission 1837–1841: The
Quorum of the Twelve Apostles in
the British Isles* (Salt Lake City:
Deseret Book, 1992), 24–33.

2. Russell M. Nelson, personal record, 24 July 1987.

3. "A Century and a Half of Shared
Dedication," Solihull, England:
U.K./Ireland/Africa Area Office of
Public Affairs, 24 July 1987.

4. Nelson, personal record, 24 July
1987.

5. Matthias Cowley, *Wilford
Woodruff: History of His Life and
Labors* (Salt Lake City: Bookcraft,
1964), 116–19.

6. Nelson, personal record, 25 July
1987.

7. Ibid.

8. Russell M. Nelson, "Keys of the
Priesthood," *Ensign,* November
1987, 39.

9. Nelson, personal record, 26 July
1987.

10. Ibid., 27 July 1987.

11. Ibid.

12. Ibid., 29 July 1987.

13. Ibid., 30 July 1987.

14. *Encyclopedia Britannica
Micropaedia,* 15th ed., s.v.
"William Shakespeare."

15. Allen et al., *Men With a Mission,*
35.

16. Sheri L. Dew, *Go Forward with
Faith: The Biography of Gordon B.
Hinckley* (Salt Lake City: Deseret
Book, 1996), 64.

17. Russell M. Nelson Jr., interview
by author, 2 January 2002.

18. Nelson, personal record, 9 June
1997.

19. Ibid., 10 June 1997.

20. Ibid., 11–12 June 1997.

21. Ibid., 13 June 1997.

NOTES TO CHAPTER 35

1. *The Wordsworth Dictionary of
Quotations,* ed. Connie Robertson
(Hertfordshire, England:
Wordsworth Editions, 1997), 232.

2. Russell M. Nelson, "A Call to
Serve," address at the University of
Utah Salt Lake Institute of
Religion, 1 March 1985.

3. *Deseret News 1999–2000 Church
Almanac* (Salt Lake City: Deseret
News, 1998), 441–42.

4. Howard W. Hunter, "Exceeding
Great and Precious Promises,"
Ensign, November 1994, 8.

5. Gordon B. Hinckley, "Some
Thoughts on Temples, Retention
of Converts, and Missionary
Service," *Ensign,* November 1997,
49.

6. *Deseret News 2003 Church
Almanac* (Salt Lake City: Deseret
News, 2003), 473–75.

7. Robert Reeve, interview by author,
24 May 2002.

8. Russell M. Nelson, "Prepare for
the Blessings of the Temple,"
Ensign, March 2002, 17–23.

9. Monte J. Brough, interview by
author, 23 May 2002.

10. Ibid.

11. Ibid.

12. Ibid.

13. Thomas S. Monson, interview by author, 8 June 2002.

14. R. Scott Lloyd, "Today We Are Taking a Historic Step," *Church News,* 29 May 1999, 3, 8–10.

15. Jason Swensen, "Freedman's Bank: Boosting Research for African-Americans," *Deseret News,* 3 March 2001, 3; *Encyclopedia Britannica Micropaedia,* 15th ed., s.v. "Freedman's Bureau."

16. Marie Taylor, interview by author, 24 May 2002; Swensen, "Freedman's Bank," 3.

17. John L. Hart, "Freedman's Bank Project Left an Impact on Inmates," *Church News,* 24 March 2001, 5.

18. Russell M. Nelson, personal record, 16–17 April 2001.

19. Ibid.; John L. Hart, "Story of Ellis Island Is a Family Story," *Church News,* 21 April 2001, 5.

20. Russell M. Nelson, "The Spirit of Elijah," *Ensign,* November 1994, 84, 85, 86.

21. Russell M. Nelson, "A New Harvest Time," *Ensign,* May 1998, 34, 36.

22. Nelson, "The Spirit of Elijah," 86.

NOTES TO CHAPTER 36

1. Russell M. Nelson, *From Heart to Heart* (Salt Lake City: Russell M. Nelson, 1979), 275.

2. Ibid., 307.

3. Kathy Cracoft, "U Founders Day Highlight," *Salt Lake Tribune,* 1 March 1967, C3.

4. "Doctor's Affiliation with Group A 'First,'" *Deseret News,* 28 April 1969, A11.

5. Steve Hale, "Utah Medics View Problems Teens Face," *Deseret News,* 11 September 1969, B1.

6. "Heart Facility Staff Named," *Deseret News,* 12 May 1970, B5.

7. "Thoracic Unit Names Utahn," *Deseret News,* 19 January 1971, A9.

8. "S. L. Surgeon Elected," *Deseret News,* 19 October 1973, B1; "Chicago: Thoracic Surgeons Chairman," *Church News,* 27 October 1973, 11.

9. Benson B. Roe, *Maverick among the Moguls: The Adventurous Career of a Pioneer Cardiac Surgeon* (Berkeley, Calif.: Creative Arts Book, 2002) 151, 153–54, 204.

10. Nelson, *From Heart to Heart,* 307, 339.

11. "Vascular Surgeons Elect S. L. Physician President," *Deseret News,* 20 June 1974, B1.

12. "Surgeon Honored at Meet," *Deseret News,* 28 September 1974, A10.

13. "Heart Surgeon Russell Nelson Wins Kiwanis Service Honor," *Deseret News,* 12 December 1974, B2.

14. "Heart Surgeon to Give Report," *Deseret News,* 8 September 1975, B2.

15. "AHA Honors Utah Surgeon," *Deseret News,* 17 November 1976, B9.

16. Russell M. Nelson, personal record, 22–24 March 1979.

17. "Academy Honors S. L. Heart Surgeon," *Church News,* 22 June 1979, B1; "Physician, Businessman, Win Honor from Academy," *Church News,* 30 June 1979, 7.

18. "LDS Hospital Picks New Board Officer," *Deseret News,* 1 February 1980, D2.

19. "New Apostle Reminisces," *Church News,* 24 June 1984, 10.

20. "Chinese Physicians to Honor

Elder Nelson," *Deseret News,* 23 September 1985, B1.

21. "Elder Nelson Is Honorary Professor," *Deseret News,* 28 September 1985, B3.

22. "Elder Nelson Is Named Honorary Professor by Chinese Medical College," *Church News,* 29 September 1985, 6.

23. Nelson, personal record, 24–27 January 1985.

24. Ibid., 22 March 1985.

25. Julie A. Dockstader, "Elder Nelson Honored as Deserving, Talented Leader, Teacher, Surgeon," *Church News,* 1 May 1993, 13.

26. Ibid.

27. Ibid.

28. Ibid.

29. Russell M. Nelson, *The Power Within Us* (Salt Lake City: Deseret Book, 1976), viii.

30. Donald B. Doty, in "Heart of Gold: Russell M. Nelson," produced by Bonneville International Corporation, KSL, and Freebairn Entertainment, 2002, videocassette.

31. Russell M. Nelson, remarks at the Heart of Gold award ceremony, 13 April 2002.

32. James E. Faust, interview by author, 2 May 2002.

33. Nelson, personal record, 6 January 1997.

34. Ibid., 1–2 July; 8 October 1997.

35. Ibid., 23 January 1998; 15–16 September 1998; 4 November 1998.

36. Ibid., 17 May 1999.

37. Sarah Jane Weaver, "LDS Lawyer Fights for Religious Rights of Others," *Church News,* 3 November 2001, 7.

NOTES TO CHAPTER 37

1. Russell M. Nelson, personal record, 1997.

2. Ibid., 1992

3. Rudyard Kipling, "If—," in *The Golden Treasury of Poetry,* ed. Louis Untermeyer (New York: Golden Press, 1959), 314.

4. Nelson, personal record, 2–4 January 1999.

5. Ibid., 3 September 1999.

6. W. Craig Zwick, interview by author, 7 November 2001.

7. Russell M. Nelson, interview by author.

8. Russell M. Nelson, "Begin With the End in Mind," *Brigham Young University 1984–85 Devotional and Fireside Speeches* (Provo, Utah: University Publications, 1985), 13–17.

9. Nelson, personal record, 23 July 1999.

10. Ibid., 26 February 1994.

11. *Hymns,* 216.

12. Nelson, interview.

13. Conrad B. Jenson, interview by author, 21 May 2002.

14. Helen Hillier, interview by author, 15 January 2002.

15. Bonnie Marchant, interview by author, 31 January 2002.

16. Ibid.

17. Russell M. Nelson, "Teach Us Tolerance and Love," *Ensign,* May 1994, 71.

18. Jenson, interview.

19. F. Melvin Hammond, interview by author, 4 February 2002.

20. D. Todd Christofferson, interview by author, 30 May 2002.

21. Russell M. Nelson, *The Power Within Us* (Salt Lake City: Deseret Book, 1976), 45.

22. Russell M. Nelson, "Children of

the Covenant," *Ensign,* May 1995, 34.

23. Nelson, interview.

24. Joseph Smith, *Teachings of the Prophet Joseph Smith,* sel. Joseph Fielding Smith (Salt Lake City: Deseret Book, 1976), 174.

25. Brad Wittwer, interview by author, 14 January 2002.

26. Julie Wittwer, interview by author, 14 January 2002.

NOTES TO CHAPTER 38

1. Russell M. Nelson, "Identity, Priority, and Blessings," *Ensign,* August 2001, 6–12.

2. Russell M. Nelson, "Children of the Covenant," *Ensign,* May 1995, 34; Romans 2:15; Jeremiah 31:33; Mosiah 13:11.

3. John A. Widtsoe, *Evidences and Reconciliations,* 3 vols. in one (Salt Lake City: Bookcraft, 1960), 258.

4. Joseph Smith, *Teachings of the Prophet Joseph Smith,* sel. Joseph Fielding Smith (Salt Lake City: Deseret Book, 1976), 121.

5. Russell M. Nelson, "The Atonement," *Ensign,* November 1996, 33.

6. Ibid.

7. Ibid.

8. Ibid., 34, 35.

9. Russell M. Nelson, "I'll Go, I'll Do, I'll Be: Three Steps Toward a Monumental Life," *Brigham Young University 1986–87 Devotional and Fireside Speeches* (Provo, Utah: University Publications, 1987), 2–3, 4.

10. Russell M. Nelson, "We Are Children of God," *Ensign,* November 1998, 85.

11. Russell M. Nelson, "The Magnificence of Man," *Brigham Young University 1986–87*

Devotional and Fireside Speeches (Provo, Utah: University Publications, 1987), 128, 129–30, 130–31, 135.

12. Russell M. Nelson, "Self-Mastery," *Ensign,* November 1985, 32.

13. Nelson, "The Magnificence of Man," 135.

14. Nelson, "We Are Children of God," 86, 87.

15. Russell M. Nelson, "Choices," *Ensign,* November 1990, 74, 75.

16. Russell M. Nelson, "Addiction or Freedom," *Ensign,* November 1988, 7.

17. Nelson, "I'll Go, I'll Do, I'll Be," 9–10, 12.

18. Russell M. Nelson, "First Connect—Then Convert," address at Missionary Training Center, Provo, Utah, 15 June 1999.

19. Russell M. Nelson, "Missionaries and Motion," address at Missionary Training Center, 24 February 1987.

20. Russell M. Nelson, "With God Nothing Shall Be Impossible," *Ensign,* May 1988, 33–35.

21. Russell M. Nelson, "Standards of Standard-Bearers of the Lord," *Brigham Young University 1990–91 Devotional and Fireside Speeches* (Provo, Utah: University Publications, 1991), 54.

22. Nelson, "Missionaries and Motion."

23. Russell M. Nelson, "Honoring the Priesthood," *Ensign,* May 1993, 38, 39, 40, 41.

24. Russell M. Nelson, "Keys of the Priesthood," *Ensign,* November 1987, 37, 38.

25. Russell M. Nelson, "Our Sacred Duty to Honor Women," *Ensign,* May 1999, 38.

26. Russell M. Nelson, "Woman—of

Infinite Worth," *Ensign*,
November 1989, 20.

27. Russell M. Nelson, "Lessons from Eve," *Ensign*, November 1987, 87.

28. Russell M. Nelson, *Motherhood* (Salt Lake City: Deseret Book, 1987), 1–2.

29. Russell M. Nelson, "Where Is Wisdom?" *Ensign*, November 1992, 6, 8.

30. Russell M. Nelson, "Begin with the End in Mind," *Brigham Young University 1984–85 Devotional and Fireside Speeches* (Provo, Utah: University Publications, 1985), 15–16.

31. Russell M. Nelson, "Listen to Learn," *Ensign*, May 1991, 22, 23, 24.

32. Russell M. Nelson, "Living by Scriptural Guidance," *Ensign*, November 2000, 17.

33. Russell M. Nelson, "A Testimony of the Book of Mormon," *Ensign*, November 1999, 69, 70, 71.

34. Russell M. Nelson, "Integrity of Heart," *Ensign*, August 1995, 19–23.

Notes to Chapter 39

1. Russell M. Nelson, "Jesus the Christ: Our Master and More," *Ensign*, April 2000, 4.

2. Ibid., 4–5, 6, 7–8.
3. Ibid., 9.
4. Ibid.
5. Ibid., 11.
6. Ibid., 11.
7. Ibid., 11–13.
8. Ibid., 14.
9. Ibid., 14–17.
10. Ibid., 17.
11. Russell M. Nelson, "Gratitude for the Mission and Ministry of Jesus Christ," *Brigham Young University 1997–98 Devotional and Fireside Speeches* (Provo, Utah: University Publications, 1998), 346, 348, 349, 350.

12. Russell M. Nelson, "Thou Shalt Have No Other Gods," *Ensign*, May 1996, 14, 16.

13. Russell M. Nelson, "Life after Life," *Ensign,* May 1987, 10.

Notes to Epilogue

1. John L. Hart, "Elder Nelson, Pioneer Heart Surgeon, Honored," *Church News,* 20 April 2002, 4.

2. Joseph Smith, *Teachings of the Prophet Joseph Smith,* sel. Joseph Fielding Smith (Salt Lake City: Deseret Book, 1976), 255–56.

3. Thomas S. Monson, interview by author, 15 June 2002.

BIBLIOGRAPHY

The following sources were used extensively in preparing this biography. The first section contains references to Elder Russell M. Nelson's Church publications and scientific publications. Subsequent sections contain articles about Elder Nelson as well as publications referred to throughout this work. Works by Elder Nelson and about his life appear chronologically rather than alphabetically.

WORKS BY RUSSELL M. NELSON

Articles and Talks

"Place Our Homes in Order." *Improvement Era,* December 1968, 86–88.

"Four Lessons from One Life." *Speeches of the Year: BYU Devotional and Ten-Stake Fireside Addresses—1974.* Provo, Utah: Brigham Young University Press, 1975, 125–33.

"I Have a Question: 'Is it Necessary to Take the Sacrament with One's Right Hand? Does it Really Make Any Difference Which Hand Is Used?'" *Ensign,* March 1983, 68.

"Call to the Holy Apostleship." *Ensign,* May 1984, 52–53.

"Protect Spiritual Power Line." *Ensign,* November 1984, 30–32.

Durham, G. H., Q. Harris, R. M. Nelson, and C. O. Samuelson. "Parenthood, Priesthood, and Practice." *J. Collegium Aesculapium* 2 (1984): 5–13.

"Begin with the End in Mind." *Brigham Young University 1984–85 Devotional and Fireside Speeches.* Provo, Utah: University Press, 1985, 13–17.

"Daughters of Zion." *New Era: Young Women Special Issue,* November 1985, 4–9.

"Reverence for Life." *Ensign,* May 1985, 11–14.

"Self-Mastery." *Ensign,* November 1985, 30–32.

"Spencer W. Kimball: Man of Faith." *Ensign,* December 1985, 39–41.

"Truth and More." *Ensign,* January 1986, 69–73.

"Forces in Life." *New Era,* May 1986, 4–7.

"In the Lord's Own Way." *Ensign,* May 1986, 25–27.

"Joy Cometh in the Morning." *Ensign,* November 1986, 67–70.

"I'll Go, I'll Do, I'll Be: Three Steps Toward a Monumental Life." *Brigham Young University 1986–87 Devotional and Fireside Speeches.* Provo, Utah: University Press, 1987, 1–12.

"Love Thy Neighbor." *Ensign,* January 1987, 70–72.

"Life after Life." *Ensign,* May 1987, 8–10.

"The Magnificence of Man." *New Era,* October 1987, 44–50.

"Keys of the Priesthood." *Ensign,* November 1987, 36–39.

"Lessons from Eve." *Ensign,* November 1987, 86–89.

"The Magnificence of Man." *Ensign,* January 1988, 64–69.

"The Magnificence of Man." *Brigham Young University 1987–88 Devotional and Fireside Speeches.* Provo: University Press, 1988, 126–135.

"With God Nothing Shall Be Impossible." *Ensign,* May 1988, 33–35.

"Addiction or Freedom." *Ensign,* November 1988, 6–9.

"Protect the Spiritual Power Line." *Friend,* November 1988, inside front cover.

"We Add Our Witness: Living Prophets Share Their Feelings about the Book of Mormon." *Ensign,* March 1989, 5–9.

"The Canker of Contention." *Ensign,* May 1989, 68–71.

"Addiction or Freedom." *New Era,* September 1989, 4–7.

"Thanks for the Covenant." *Brigham Young University 1988–89 Devotional and Fireside Speeches.* Provo, Utah: University Press, 1989, 53–61.

"Woman—of Infinite Worth." *Ensign,* November 1989, 20–22.

"Why This Holy Land?" *Ensign,* December 1989, 12–19.

"'Thus Shall My Church Be Called.'" *Ensign,* May 1990, 16–18.

"Choices." *Ensign,* November 1990, 73–75.

"Reflection and Resolution." *Brigham Young University 1989–90 Devotional and Fireside Speeches.* Provo, Utah: University Press, 1990, 59–67.

"Listen to Learn." *Ensign,* May 1991, 22–25.

"Standards of the Lord's Standard-Bearers." *Ensign,* August 1991, 5–11.

"'These . . . Were Our Examples.'" *Ensign,* November 1991, 59–61.

"Drama on the European Stage." *Ensign,* December 1991, 6–17.

"Standards of Standard-Bearers." *Brigham Young University 1990–91 Devotional and Fireside Speeches,* Provo, Utah: University Press, 1991, 51–59.

"Doors of Death." *Ensign,* May 1992, 72–74.

"Jesus the Christ: Our Master and More." *Brigham Young University 1991–92 Devotional and Fireside Speeches.* Provo, Utah: University Press, 1992, 57–66.

"Where Is Wisdom?" *Ensign,* November 1992, 6–8.

"Honoring the Priesthood." *Ensign,* May 1993, 38–41.

"A Treasured Testimony." *Ensign,* July 1993, 61–65.

"Combating Spiritual Drift—Our Global Pandemic." *Ensign,* November 1993, 102–8.

"Constancy Amid Change." *Ensign,* November 1993, 33–35.

"Integrity of Heart." *Brigham Young University 1992–93 Devotional and Fireside Speeches.* Provo, Utah: University Press, 1993, 75–82.

"'Teach Us Tolerance and Love.'" *Ensign,* May 1994, 69–71.

"Shepherds, Lambs, and Home Teachers." *Ensign,* August 1994, 14–19.

"The Spirit of Elijah." *Ensign,* November 1994, 14–16.

"A More Excellent Hope." *Brigham Young University 1994–95 Devotional and Fireside Speeches.* Provo, Utah: University Press, 1995, 73–82.

"Children of the Covenant." *Ensign,* May 1995, 32–35.

"Integrity of Heart." *Ensign,* August 1995, 18–23.

"Perfection Pending." *Ensign,* November 1995, 86–88.

"'Thou Shalt Have No Other Gods.'" *Ensign,* May 1996, 14–16.

"The Atonement." *Ensign,* November 1996, 33–36.

"Endure and Be Lifted Up." *Ensign,* May 1997, 70–73.

"Spiritual Capacity." *Ensign,* November 1997, 14–16.

"A New Harvest Time." *Ensign,* May 1998, 34–36.

"The Exodus Repeated." *Brigham Young University 1997–98 Devotional and Fireside Speeches.* Provo, Utah: University Press, 1998, 1–8.

"We Are Children of God." *Ensign,* November 1998, 85–87.

"Gratitude for the Mission and Ministry of Jesus Christ." *Brigham Young University 1998–99 Devotional and Fireside Speeches.* Provo, Utah: University Press, 1999, 345–50.

"Our Sacred Duty to Honor Women." *Ensign,* May 1999, 38–40.

"The Exodus Repeated." *Ensign,* July 1999, 6–13.

"A Testimony of the Book of Mormon." *Ensign,* November 1999, 69–71.

"Jesus the Christ: Our Master and More." *Ensign,* April 2000, 4–17.

"The Creation." *Ensign,* May 2000, 84–86.

"Living by Scriptural Guidance." *Ensign,* November 2000, 16–18.

"Called to Serve and to Save." *Journal of Collegium Aesculapium* (Spring 2001): 6–11.

"Personal Preparation for Temple Blessings." *Ensign,* May 2001, 32–34.

"A Gift from God." *New Era,* August 2001, 4–7.

"Identity, Priority, and Blessings." *Brigham Young University 2000–2001 Devotional and Fireside Speeches.* Provo, Utah: University Press, 2001, 87–93.

"Identity, Priority, Blessings." *Ensign,* August 2001, 6–12.

"Set in Order Thy House." *Ensign,* November 2001, 69–71.

"Prepare for Blessings of the Temple." *Ensign,* March 2002, 16–23.

Books and Book Chapters

"Addiction or Freedom." In *Morality.* Salt Lake City: Bookcraft, 1977, 40–47.

"Reverence for Life." In *Morality.* Salt Lake City: Bookcraft, 1977, 110–16.

From Heart to Heart. Salt Lake City: Russell M. Nelson, 1979.

Motherhood. Salt Lake City: Deseret Book, 1987.

The Power Within Us. Salt Lake City: Deseret Book, 1988.

"Addiction or Freedom." In *Speaking Out on Moral Issues.* Salt Lake City: Bookcraft, 1992, 40–47.

"Reverence for Life." In *Speaking Out on Moral Issues.* Salt Lake City: Bookcraft, 1992, 110–15.

Lessons from Mother Eve: A Mother's Day Message. Salt Lake City: Deseret Book, 1993.

The Gateway We Call Death. Salt Lake City: Deseret Book, 1995.

"Nephi, Son of Lehi." In *Heroes from the Book of Mormon.* Salt Lake City: Bookcraft, 1995, 1–15.

"At the Heart of the Church." In *The Prophet and His Work: Essays from General Authorities on Joseph Smith and the Restoration.* Salt Lake City: Deseret Book, 1996, 50–65.

"Orson Hyde." In *Heroes of the Restoration.* Salt Lake City: Bookcraft, 1997, 35–37.

"The Canker of Contention." In *Peace: Essays of Hope and Encouragement.* Salt Lake City: Deseret Book, 1998, 85–93.

Classic Talk Series: The Magnificence of Man: Truth—and More. Salt Lake City: Deseret Book, 1998.

"Liberty, License, and Law." In *The Spirit of America.* Salt Lake City: Bookcraft, 1998, 57–67.

Perfection Pending and Other Favorite Discourses. Salt Lake City: Deseret Book, 1998.

"Fundamentals and Initiatives." In *Life in the Law: Answering God's Interrogatories.* Provo, Utah: Brigham Young University Press, 2002, 49–58.

Scientific Publications

Nelson, R. M., S. R. Friesen, and A. J. Kremen. "Refractory Alkalosis and the Potassium Ion in Surgical Patients." *Surgery* 27 (1950): 26.

Nelson, R. M., W. P. Eder, F. D. Eddy, K. E. Karlson, and C. Dennis. "Production of a Hemorrhagic State by the Infusion of Hemolyzed Blood." *Proc. Soc. Biol. and Med.* 73 (1950): 208.

Dennis, C., K. E. Karlson, R. M. Nelson, W. P. Eder, J. V. Thomas, and G. E. Nelson. "A Simple, Efficient Respirator and Anesthesia Bag for Open Chest Surgery." *Surgical Forum, Am. Coll. Surg.,* 1951, 583.

Dennis, C. D., S. Spreng Jr., G. E. Nelson, K. E. Karlson, R. M. Nelson, J. V. Thomas, W. P. Eder, and R. L. Varco. "Development of a Pump-Oxygenator to Replace the Heart and Lungs: An Apparatus Applicable to Human Patients, and Applicable to One Case." *Ann. Surg.* 134 (1951): 709.

Friesen, S. R., and R. M. Nelson. "Occurrence of Massive Generalized Wound

Bleeding During Operation: With Reference to Possible Role of Blood Transfusion in Its Etiology." *Am. Surgeon* 17 (1951): 609.

Nelson, R. M. "Discussion of Above Paper at American Surgical Association." *Ann. Surg.* 134 (1951): 741.

———. "Metabolic Effects of Canine Infusion with Paracolon Bacillus. A Contaminant of Pump-Oxygenator Perfusions." Ph.D. dissertation, University of Minnesota, 1951.

———. "Metabolic Effects of Paracolon Bacteremia." *Ann. Surg.* 134 (1951): 709.

Nelson, R. M., and C. Dennis. "Some Effects of Paracolon Bacteremia." *Proc. Soc. Exp. Biol. and Med.* 76 (1951): 737.

Dennis, C., K. E. Karlson, W. P. Eder, R. M. Nelson, F. D. Eddy, and D. Sanderson. "Pump Oxygenator to Supplant the Heart and Lungs for Brief Periods. A Method Applicable to Dogs." *Surgery* 29 (1952): 697.

Nelson, R. M. "Fluid and Electrolyte Problems of the Severely Wounded." Symposium on Treatment of Trauma in the Armed Forces. *Army Med. Serv. Grad. Sch. Bull.*, Washington, D.C., March 1952.

———. "Shock and Circulatory Homeostasis." Transactions of the First Conference, October 1951 (participant). New York: Josiah Macy Jr. Foundation, 1952.

Seeley, Brig. Gen. S. F., and 1ˢᵗ Lt. R. M. Nelson. "Intra-Arterial Transfusion: A Review of the Literature." *Surg. Gyn. and Obst.* 94 (1952): 209.

Nelson, R. M., and H. E. Noyes. "Permeability of the Intestine to Bacterial Toxins in Shock." *Surgical Forum, Am. Coll. Surg.*, 1953, 474.

Seeley, Brig. Gen. S. F., 1ˢᵗ Lt. R. M. Nelson, and 1ˢᵗ Lt. S. A. Wesolowski. "Techniques of Intra-Arterial Transfusion." *U. S. Armed Forces Med. J.* 3 (December 1952): 1801.

Nelson, R. M. "Shock and Circulatory Homeostasis." Transactions of the Second Conference, October 1952 (participant). New York: Josiah Macy Jr. Foundation, New York, 1953.

Nelson, R. M., and D. Seligson. "Studies on Blood Ammonia in Normal and Shock States." *Surgery* 34 (1953): 1.

Cohen, A., and R. M. Nelson. "A Simplified Method for Clinical Estimation of Acid-Base Balance." *Surgical Forum, Am. Coll. Surg.*, 1954, 589.

Nelson, R. M., and D. Seligson. "Blood Ammonia Studies in Shock." *Surgical Forum, Am. Coll. Surg.*, 1954, 511.

Nelson, R. M., and H. E. Noyes. "Blood Culture Studies in Normal Dogs and in Dogs in Hemorrhagic Shock." *Surgery* 35 (1954): 782.

Noyes, H. E., J. P. Sanford, and R. M. Nelson. "The Effect of Chlorpromazine and Dibenzyline on Bacterial Toxins." *Proc. Soc. Exp. Biol. and Med.* 92 (July 1956): 617.

Nelson, R. M., H. H. Hecht, R. W. Hardy, D. G. McQuarrie, and J. Burge.

"Extra-corporeal Circulation for Open Heart Surgery." *J. Thor. Surg.* 32 (November 1956): 638.

Nelson, R. M. "Current Concepts in the Pathophysiology of Shock." *Am. J. Surg.* 93 (1957): 644.

Nelson, R. M., J. G. Maxwell, J. O. Mason, J. H. Nelson, and J. M. Peters. "Right Atrial Pressure Measurements with Changes in Total Blood Volume." Presented before the Western Surgical Association, 22 November 1957.

Nelson, R. M. "Studies on Cardioplegic Agents," in *Extracorporeal Circulation.* Springfield, Ill.: Charles C. Thomas, 1958, 487.

Nelson, R. M., H. H. Hecht, and R. P. Carlisle. "The Determination of the End-Diastolic Gradient Across the Mitral Valve at the Time of Commissurotomy." *AMA Arch. Surg.* 76 (1958): 830.

Nelson, R. M., J. H. Nelson, J. O. Mason, J. G. Maxwell, and J. M. Peters. "Electrocardiographic Patterns Associated with Cardioplegic Drugs." *Clin. Res.* 6 (1958): 82.

———. "Heparin-Diphenhydramine Antagonism." *Clin. Res.* 6 (1958): 78.

Nelson, R. M. "The Correlation of Tobacco Smoking with Lung Cancer." *The Instructor*, November 1959, 362.

———. "'Tranquilization' of the Heart with the Ataractic Drugs." *J. Thor. Surg.* 38 (November 1959): 610.

Nelson, R. M., and J. H. Lyman. "Non-Penetrating Injury to the Heart." Presented before the American Association for the Surgery of Trauma, September 1959.

Nelson, R. M., C. G. Frank, and J. O. Mason. "The Anti-Heparin Properties of the Antihistamines, Tranquilizers, and Certain Antibiotics." *Surgical Forum, Am. Coll. Surg.* 10 (1959): 525.

Nelson, R. M., J. W. Henry, C. G. Frank, D. W. Christensen, and J. M. Peters. "The Anti-Arrhythmia Properties of the Tranquilizer Drugs." *Surgical Forum, Am. Coll. Surg.* 10 (1959): 525.

Englert, E., Jr., R. M. Nelson, H. Brown, T. W. Nielsen, S. N. Chou. "Effects of Changing Hepatic Blood Flow on 17-Hydroxycortico-Steroid Metabolism in Dogs." *Surgery* 47 (1960): 982.

Christensen, F. K., and R. M. Nelson. "Similar Congenital Heart Disease in Siblings." Presented before the Western Society for Clinical Research, 26 January 1961. *Clin. Res.* 9 (1961): 84.

Nelson, R. M., J. W. Henry, and C. G. Frank. "Critical Evaluation of the Effects of Procaine Amide on Ventricular Fibrillation Threshold." *Circulation* 24 (1961): 1004.

Nelson, R. M., J. W. Henry, and J. H. Lyman. "Influence of 1-Norepinephrine on Renal Blood Flow, Renal Vascular Resistance, and Urine Flow in Hemorrhagic Shock." Presented before the Society of University Surgeons, 10 February 1961. *Surgery* 50 (1961): 115.

Pearse, H. D., and R. M. Nelson. "Serum Lipase Studies after Median Sternotomy." *Clin. Res.* 9 (1961): 101.

Nelson, R. M. "A Device for Holding Surgical Tubing to the Drapes." *Surgery* 51 (1962): 797.

———. "Technique of Removal, Carotid Body Tumors." *Surg. Gyn. and Obst.* 115 (1962): 115.

Nelson, R. M., and J. H. Lyman. "Renal Effects of Tris (Hydroxymethyl) Aminomethane (THAM) in Experimental Hemorrhagic Shock." *Clin. Res.* 10 (1962): 109.

Nelson, R. M., J. W. Henry, and G. M. Winn. "Diuretic, Renal Hemodynamic, and Metabolic Effects of Amine Buffers in Oligemic Hypotension." *Circulation* 26 (1962): 767.

Pearse, H. D., and R. M. Nelson. "Studies on Fibrinolysin in Experimentally Produced Hemothorax." *Clin. Res.* 10 (1962): 109.

Trautwein, W., D. G. Kassebaum, R. M. Nelson, and H. H. Hecht. "Electrophysiologic Study of Human Heart Muscle. *Circ. Res.* 10 (1962): 306.

Nelson, R. M. "Renal Problems in Aortic Surgery with and without a Pump Oxygenator." Postgraduate Course on Pre- and Post-Operative Care, 49th Annual Clinical Congress, American College of Surgeons, 28 October–1 November 1963, 59.

Nelson, R. M., and A. M. Poulson. "Further Studies on Tris (Hydroxymethyl) Aminomethane (THAM) in Experimental Hemorrhagic Shock." *Clin. Res.* 11 (1963): 98.

Nelson, R. M., and F. K. Christensen. "Similar Congenital Heart Disease in Siblings." *J. Thor. and Cardiovasc. Surg.* 45 (1963): 592.

Nelson, R. M., J. H. Lyman, A. M. Poulson, and J. W. Henry. "Evaluation of Tris (Hydroxymethyl) Aminomethane (THAM) in Hemorrhagic Shock." *Surgery* 54 (1963): 86.

Nelson, R. M., W. E. Hess, and J. H. Lyman. "Venous Obstruction with Hypertrophy of Upper Extremity Due to Osteochondroma." *Surgery* 54 (1963): 871.

Nelson, R. M., and B. C. Sanders. "Carbodissection of Perivascular Tissue." *J. Thor. and Cardiovasc. Surg.* 48 (1964): 964.

Pearse, H. D., and R. M. Nelson. "Study of Fibrinolysin in Clotted Hemothorax." *J. Thor. and Cardiovasc. Surg.* 48 (1964): 272.

Nelson, R. M., C. B. Jenson, C. A. Peterson, and B. C. Sanders. "Effective Use of Prophylactic Antibiotics in Open Heart Surgery." *Arch. Surg.* 90 (1965): 731.

Goldschmied, F. R., A. G. Prakouras, and R. M. Nelson. "Experimental Investigation of Fluidic and Peristaltic Heart Pumps." *Proc. Am. Inst. Aeronautics and Astronautics*, Boston, Massachusetts, 29 November–2 December, 1966.

Nelson, R. M. "Current Status of Tumors of the Thymus (Thymomas)." *Prog. in Clin. Cancer* 2 (1966): 284.

Horsley, B. L., and R. M. Nelson. "Metabolic Acidosis in the Ischemic Limb During Open Heart Surgery." *Ann. Thor. Surg.* 4 (1967): 474.

Jenson, C. B., and R. M. Nelson. "Tracheal Stenosis Due to Aberrant Left Pulmonary Artery." *Rocky Mtn. Med. J.* 64 (1967): 97.

Nelson, J. C., and R. M. Nelson. "The Incidence of Hospital Wound Infection in Thoracotomies." *J. Thor. and Cardiovasc. Surg.* 54 (1967): 586.

Nelson, R. M., and C. B. Jenson. "Plotocostotomy for Thoracic Outlet Obstruction Syndrome. *Circulation* 36, supp. no. 2 (1967): 198.

Nelson, R. M., C. B. Jenson, and B. L. Horsley. "Idiopathic Retroperitoneal Fibrosis Producing Distal Esophageal Obstruction." *J. Thor. and Cardiovasc. Surg.* 55 (1968): 216.

Nelson, R. M., C. B. Jenson, and K. W. Jones. "Aortic Valve Replacement." *Ann. Thor. Surg.* 6 (1968): 343.

Nelson, R. M., C. B. Jenson, and R. W. Davis. "Differential Atrial Arrhythmias in Cardiac Surgical Patients." *Circulation* 38, supp. no. 6 (1968): 147.

Nelson, R. M., H. R. Warner, R. E. Gardner, and J D Mortensen. "Computer-Based Monitoring of Patients Following Cardiac Surgery." *Israel J. Med. Sci.* 5 (1969): 926; Proceedings of Fourth Asian-Pacific Congress of Cardiology, 1–7 September 1968, 484.

Nelson, R. M., C. B. Jenson, R. W. Davis. "Differential Atrial Arrhythmias in Cardiac Surgical Patients." *J. Thor. and Cardio-vasc. Surg.* 58 (1969): 581.

Nelson, R. M., C. B. Jenson, and W. M. Smoot III. "Pericardial Tamponade Following Open Heart Surgery." *J. Thor. and Cardiovasc. Surg.* 58, no. 4 (1969): 510.

Nelson, R. M., and C. G. Vaughn. "Double Valve Replacement in Marfan's Syndrome." *J. Thor. and Cardiovasc. Surg.* 57 (1969): 732.

Nelson, R. M., and R. W. Davis. "Thoracic Outlet Compression Syndrome." *Ann. Thor. Surg.* 8 (1969) 437.

Tikoff, G., T. B. Keith, R. M. Nelson, and H. Kuida. "Clinical and Hemo-dynamic Observations after Surgical Closure of Large Atrial Septal Defect Complicated by Heart Failure." *Am. J. Cardiol.* 23 (1969): 810.

Nelson, R. M., and C. B. Jenson. "Anterior Approach for Excision of the First Rib." *Ann Thor. Surg.* 9 (1970): 30.

Vaughn, C. C., H. R. Warner, and R. M. Nelson. "Cardiovascular Effects of Glucagon Following Cardiac Surgery." *Surgery* 67 (1970): 204.

Lindsay, A. E., R. M. Nelson, J. A. Abildskov, and R. Wyatt. "Attempted Surgical Division of the Pre-excitation Pathway in the Wolff-Parkinson-White Syndrome." *Am. J. Cardiol.* 28 (1971): 581.

Nelson, R. M. "Sovereigns and Servants." *Rocky Mtn. Med. J.* 68 (1971): 9.

Nelson, R. M., and A. G. Osborn. "Systemic Heparinization for Percutaneous Catheter Arteriography." *Circulation* 44, supp. no. 2 (1971): 205.

Nelson, R. M., C. B. Jenson, and G. K. Sethi. "Isolated Aortic Valve Replacements in Patients Over Sixty." Proceedings of the International Society of Surgery, Moscow, Russia, 24 August 1971.

Saksena, D. S., B. L. Tucker, G. C. Lindesmith, R. M. Nelson, Q. R. Stiles, and B. W. Meyer. "The Superior Approach to the Mitral Valve: A Review of Clinical Experience." *Ann. Thor. Surg.* 12 (1971): 146.

Hauser, R. G., R. M. Nelson, H. Javid, S. J. Blatt, A. F. Toronto, C. G. Frank, M. L. Long, and H. C. Peacock. "Clinical Evaluation of the Dow Hollow Fiber Membrane Oxygenator." *Circulation* 46, supp. no. 4 (1972): 3.

Nelson, R. M., C. B. Jenson, and G. K. Sethi. "Isolated Aortic Valve Replacement in Patients Over Sixty." *Bulletin de la Societe Internationale de Chirurgie* 32 (1973): 42.

———. "Use of the Hollow Fiber Membrane Oxygenator in Open Heart Surgery." *Bulletin de la Societe Internationale de Chirurgie* 32 (1973): 568.

Sethi, G. K., R. M. Nelson, and C. B. Jenson. "Surgical Management of Acute Pericarditis." Presented at the 24th Annual Meeting of the Southwestern Surgical Congress, 1–4 May 1972, Albuquerque, New Mexico; *Chest* 63 (1973): 732–35.

Nelson, R. M., and A. F. Toronto. "Use of the Hollow Fiber Membrane Oxygenator in Open Heart Surgery: Clinical Experience." *Bulletin de la Societe Internationale de Chirurgie* 33 (1974): 285.

Nelson, R. M., and M. Wertheimer. "Reoperation for Replacement of Prosthetic Aortic Valve." Edited by J. Wada and S. Komatsu. Proceedings of the Second Asian Congress on Thoracic and Cardiovascular Surgery, Sapporo, Japan, 1974, 216.

Nelson, R. M. "Current Surgical Management for Disorders of the Mitral Valve." *Clinical Congress of the American College of Surgeons,* Postgraduate Course on Cardiac Surgery, October 1975, Syllabus 41.

———. "Era of Extracorporeal Respiration." Presidential address, Society for Vascular Surgery; *Surgery* 78 (1975): 685.

Nelson, R. M., C. B. Jenson, and C. S. Kim. "Ten Year Follow-up of Isolated Aortic Valve Replacement." *Bulletin de la Societe Internationale de Chirurgie* 34 (1975): 522.

Nelson, R. M. "Prophylactic Antibiotics in Open Heart Surgery." *Contemp. Surg.* 8 (1976): 75.

Sethi, G. K., and R. M. Nelson. "Gastroduodenal Arterial Aneurysm: Report of a Case and Review of the Literature." *Surgery* 79 (1976): 233.

Nelson, R. M. "Extracorporeal Circulation." In *Christopher's Textbook of Surgery.* Edited by Sabiston. 11th ed. Philadelphia: W. B. Saunders, 1977, 2436.

Nelson, R. M. "The Selection of a Cardiac Valve Substitute." *Ann. Thor. Surg.* 26 (1978): 291.

Prian, G. W., and R. M. Nelson. "Infection Control and Antibiotic Use in Cardiovascular Thoracic Surgery." *J. Surg. Prac.* 7 (1978): 41.

Nelson, R. M. "Complications of Cardiac Surgery." In *The Complications of*

Thoracic and Cardiac Surgery. Edited by Cordell and Ellison. Boston: Little, Brown and Co., 1979, 101–14.

———. "Cardiovascular Surgery." In *The American Heart Association Heartbook.* New York: E. P. Dutton, 1980, 288–301.

———. "Extracorporeal Circulation." In *Davis-Christopher's Textbook of Surgery.* Edited by Sabiston. 12ᵗʰ ed. Philadelphia: W. B. Saunders, 1981, 2450.

Nelson, R. M., E. J. Neil, S. F. Mohammad, R. R. Williams, and R. G. Mason. "Timed Sequential Endothelial Ultrastructural Changes in Human and Canine Saphenous Veins." Federation Proceedings 40, no. 3 (1981): 3322.

Prian, G. W., and R. M. Nelson. "Infection Control and Antibiotic Use in Cardiovascular-Thoracic Surgery." In *Surgical Infections: Selective Antibiotic Therapy.* Edited by Condon and Gorbach. Baltimore: The Williams & Wilkins Co., 1981, 119–24.

Joyce, L. D., and R. M. Nelson. "Comparison of Bjork-Shiley and Porcine Valve Replacement—A Seven and One-Half Year Experience." Presented at Prosthetic Valve Symposium, Pebble Beach, California, 30 August 1982.

Joyce, L. D., and R. M. Nelson. "Comparison of Porcine Valve Xenografts with Mechanical Prosthesis: A 7–Year Experience." *J. Thorac. Cardiovasc. Surg.* 88 (1984): 102–113.

Anderson, J. L., S. A. Battistessa, P. D. Clayton, C. Y. Cannon, J. C. Askins, and R. M. Nelson. "Coronary Bypass Surgery Early after Thrombolytic Therapy for Acute Myocardial Infarction." *Ann. Thor. Surg.* 41 (1986): 176–83.

Doty, D. B., and R. M. Nelson. "Aortic Valve Replacement: Continuous-Suture Technique." *J. Cardiac Surg.* 1 (1986): 379–82.

Nelson, R. M., and D. J. Dries. "The Economic Implications of Infection in Cardiac Surgery." *Ann. Thor. Surg.* 42 (September 1986): 240–46.

Dries, D., S. F. Mohammad, S. C. Woodward, and R. M. Nelson. "The Influence of Harvesting Technique on Endothelial Preservation in Saphenous Veins." *J. of Surg. Res.* 52 (1992): 219–25.

WORKS BY OTHER AUTHORS

Articles about Russell M. Nelson

"Boys Made Happy With Gift of Second Lieutenant Bars." *Salt Lake Tribune,* 18 June 1933, 18.

Patrick, William C. "Complex Machine Adds New S. L. Medical Stride." *Salt Lake Tribune,* 7 April 1956, 19–20.

Walker, Rhonda. "Utah Scientific Session: Rapid Strides Told in Surgery of Heart." *Deseret News,* 7 April 1956, 3.

"Doctor Gains S. L. Jaycees' Award of '56." *Salt Lake Tribune,* 25 January 1957, B1.

"U. Medic Named 'Man of Year' by S. L. Jaycees." *Deseret News*, 25 January 1957, B2.

"Utah Jaycees Honor 4 Young Men of State." *Deseret News*, 18 February 1957, B1.

"The Power of Example." *Deseret News*, 19 February 1957, A18.

"Professor at University Wins Prize Medical Scholarship." *Salt Lake Tribune*, 8 March 1957, C15.

"S. L. Surgeon to Address Cancer Parley." *Deseret News*, 5 November 1957, B13.

"U. Doctor Finds Complication from Wonder Drugs, 'Happy Pills.'" *Deseret News and Telegram*, 8 October 1958, B7.

"Research Grants Awarded 3 Doctors in Utah." *Deseret News*, 25 May 1959, A12.

"Heart Grants Awarded." *Deseret News*, 18 January 1961, C6.

"Funds Given Utahns for Heart Research." *Deseret News*, 6 December 1961, 2B.

"Surgeon Takes Utah Helm in Heart Group." *Deseret News*, 27 May 1964, F2.

"Bonneville Stake Sustains Leaders." *Church News*, 12 December 1964, 4.

"'Make Time' for Church, Doctor Says." *Salt Lake Tribune*, 12 December 1964, 16.

"Bonneville Stake Sustains New Leaders at Conference." *Church News*, 12 December 1964, 4.

"Another Girl; That Makes 9." *Deseret News*, 26 October 1965, B1.

"U. of U. Medical College, Alumni Pay Honors to 7." *Deseret News*, 4 June 1966, B5.

Patrick, William C. "Medic Tells of Optimism on Kidney Transplants." *Salt Lake Tribune*, 15 January 1967, 4C.

Cracroft, Kathy. "U. Founder's Day Highlight." *Salt Lake Tribune*, 1 March 1967, C3.

"Doctor's Affiliation with Group a 'First.'" *Deseret News*, 28 April 1969, A11.

"Dad Is an Extra-Special Person." *Deseret News*, 14 June 1969, B16.

"Utah Medics View Problems Teens Face." *Deseret News*, 11 September 1969, B1.

"Heart Facility Staff Named." *Deseret News*, 12 May 1970, B5.

"Thoracic Unit Names Utahn." *Deseret News*, 19 January 1971, A9.

"The Fruit of Faith." *Deseret News*, 28 June 1971, 12A.

"Sunday School Superintendency Is Reorganized." *Church News*, 3 July 1971, 3.

"God's Greatest Creation." *Church News*, 26 May 1973, 4.

"S. L. Surgeon Elected." *Deseret News*, 19 October 1973, B1.

"Chicago: Thoracic Surgeons Chairman." *Church News*, 27 October 1973, 11.

"Vascular Surgeons Elect S. L. Physician President." *Deseret News*, 20 June 1974, B1.

"Surgeon Honored at Meet." *Deseret News*, 23 September 1974, A10.

"Heart Surgeon Russell Nelson Wins Kiwanis Service Honor." *Deseret News*, 12 December 1974, 2.

"Heart Surgeon to Give Report." *Deseret News,* 8 September 1975, B2.

"AHA Honors Utah Surgeon." *Deseret News,* 17 November 1976, B9.

"A Utahn's View: Why Health Care Costs Keep Rising." *Deseret News,* 3 February 1979, S6.

"LDS Achievers Selected for National Honors." *Church News,* 16 February 1979, 13.

"Academy Honors S. L. Heart Surgeon." *Deseret News,* 22 June 1979, B9.

"Physician, Businessman, Win Honor from Academy." *Church News,* 30 June 1979, 7.

"LDS Hospital Picks New Board Officer." *Deseret News,* 1 February 1980, D2.

"Utahn's Life Gets Bonus from Heart Surgery: 25 Extra Years to Love, Learn, Live." *Deseret News,* 15 December 1980, B8.

Johnson, Lane. "Russell M. Nelson: A Study in Obedience." *Ensign,* August 1982, 18–24.

"2 Named to Council of Twelve." *Deseret News,* 8 April 1984, A1.

"Surgeon, Jurist Called to Council of Twelve." *Church News,* 15 April 1984, 3, 16.

"Elder Russell M. Nelson of the Quorum of the Twelve Apostles." *Ensign,* May 1984, 87–88.

"Called to Serve: Quorum of the Twelve." *New Era,* June 1984, 8–9.

Gardner, Marvin K. "Elder Russell M. Nelson: Applying Divine Laws." *Ensign,* June 1984, 8–13.

"The Council of the Twelve: Special Witnesses." *Church News,* 24 June 1984, 9.

"New Apostle Reminisces." *Church News,* 24 June 1984, 10.

"LDS Physicians Must Be Artful Jugglers as Well." *Deseret News,* 26 July 1984, B6.

Avant, Gerry. "Looking at Medicine from LDS Standpoint." *Church News,* 5 August 1984, 6.

"Chinese Physicians to Honor Elder Nelson." *Deseret News,* 23 September 1985, B1.

"Elder Nelson Is Honorary Professor." *Deseret News,* 28 September 1985, B3.

"Elder Nelson Is Named Honorary Professor by Chinese Medical College." *Church News,* 29 September 1985, 6.

"Elder Russell M. Nelson of the Council of the Twelve Has Been Named an Honorary Professor by Shandong Medical College." *Ensign,* November 1985, 112.

Peterson, Janet. "Friend to Friend." *Friend,* January 1986, 4–5.

"Elder Nelson: Husband, Father Are Highest Titles." *Church News,* 16 February 1986, 4–5.

Wie, Zhao. "Actor Gives Heart to Keeping Tradition Alive." *China Daily,* 15 July 1986, 5.

"Computerized Scriptures Now Available: A Conversation with Elder Boyd K. Packer and Elder Russell M. Nelson." *Ensign,* April 1988, 72–75.

"Hungary Recognizes Mormon Church." *Salt Lake Tribune,* 6 July 1988, A14.

"LDS Leaders Meet with E. Germans." *Salt Lake Tribune,* 29 October 1988, A1.

"Meetinghouse Dedicated in Hungary." *Church News,* 11 November 1989, 3–4.

Avant, Gerry. "Russia Recognizes LDS Church." *Deseret News,* 25 June 1991, 1.

Rolly, Paul. "Russia Recognizes LDS Faith." *Salt Lake Tribune,* 25 June 1991, 1.

Avant, Gerry, and Matthew Brown. "Church Is Recognized by Russia Republic." *Church News,* 29 June 1991, 11–12.

"Land of Honduras Is Dedicated." *Church News,* 29 June 1991, 6.

"Other Faiths Support LDS in Celebrating Tongan Centennial." *Church News,* 7 September 1991, 5.

"90 on Hand for Dedication of [Salvation Army] Dining Hall." *Deseret News,* 28 October 1991, B3.

"Prayers of Dedication Offered on 4 Nations in Central, Southern Africa." *Church News,* 26 September 1992, 3–4.

"Award Honors Elder Nelson for Contributions in Medicine." *Church News,* 24 April 1993, 7.

Dockstader, Julie A. "Elder Nelson Honored as Deserving, Talented Leader, Teacher, Surgeon." *Church News,* 1 May 1993, 13.

"4 European Lands Dedicated: Apostles 'Turn Keys, Unlock Doors' for Gospel in Nations of Latvia, Lithuania, Belarus, and Albania." *Church News,* 12 June 1993, 3–6.

Hart, John L. "Sesquicentennial: 'Spiritual Feast' Celebration Spans Four Island Chains, Makes LDS History in French Polynesia." *Church News,* 21 May 1994, 3–5.

Thompson, Jan. "U. Graduates Told to Teach and Serve." *Deseret News,* 22 May 1994, B6.

"Family History Given to Bolivian President." *Church News,* 5 November 1994, 3.

Schwenke, Reg. "Chinese Leader Enjoys Hawaiian Visit: Vice Premier of China Tours Polynesian Center." *Church News,* 26 November 1994, 6.

Nakoryakov, Michael. "Russian Diplomat Makes Another Visit to Utah." *Salt Lake Tribune,* 13 October 1995, A18.

Taylor, Rebecca M. "Friend to Friend." *Friend,* March 1997, 6–7.

"Church Leaders Meet with Hong Kong Official." *Ensign,* July 1997, 78.

Carter, Edward L. "Annual BYU Education Week Emphasizes Divine Learning." *Deseret News,* 19 August 1998, B2.

"Remember Mission, Ministry of Christ." *Church News,* 22 August 1998, 3–4.

Hart, John L. "Ellis Island Project Is a Bridge between Families, Countries." *Church News,* 21 April 2001, 3.

"Elder Nelson Meets Ghanaian President, Breaks Temple Ground." *Ensign,* February 2002, 76.

"Elder Russell M. Nelson Is Given American Heart Association Award." *Ensign,* July 2002, 76.

Books

Allen, James B., Ronald K. Esplin, and David J. Whittaker. *Men with a Mission 1837–41: The Quorum of the Twelve Apostles in the British Isles.* Salt Lake City: Deseret Book, 1992.

Bell, James P. *In the Strength of the Lord: The Life and Teachings of James E. Faust.* Salt Lake City: Deseret Book, 1999.

Benson, Ezra Taft. *A Labor of Love: The 1946 European Mission of Ezra Taft Benson.* Salt Lake City: Deseret Book, 1989.

Browning, Gary. *Russia and the Restored Gospel.* Salt Lake City: Deseret Book, 1997.

Browning, Robert. "Paracelsus." In *The Poetical Works of Robert Browning.* 2 vols. London: Smith, Elder & Co., 1902, 16–76.

Cowley, Matthias. *Wilford Woodruff: History of His Life and Labors.* Salt Lake City: Deseret News, 1909.

Deseret News 1999–2000 Church Almanac. Salt Lake City: Deseret News, 1998.

Deseret News 2001–2002 Church Almanac. Salt Lake City: Deseret News, 2000.

Deseret News 2003 Church Almanac. Salt Lake City: Deseret News, 2003.

Dew, Sheri L. *Go Forward with Faith: The Biography of Gordon B. Hinckley.* Salt Lake City: Deseret Book, 1996.

Eliot, T. S. *T. S. Eliot: Collected Poems 1909–1962.* London: Faber and Faber, 1963.

Gray, Thomas. "Elegy Written in a Country Church Yard." In *The Poem: An Anthology.* Edited by Stanley B. Greenfield and A. Kingsley Weatherhead. New York: Appleton-Crofts, 1968.

Hafen, Bruce C. *A Disciple's Life: The Biography of Neal A. Maxwell.* Salt Lake City: Deseret Book, 2002.

Hickman, Martin Berkeley. *David Matthew Kennedy: Banker, Statesman, Churchman.* Salt Lake City: Deseret Book, 1987.

Höglund, Inger, and Caj-Aage Johansson. *Stegitro: Jesu Kristi Kyrka av Sista Dagars Heliga i Sverige 1850–2000.* Stockholm: Informationstjästen, 2000.

Hymns of The Church of Jesus Christ of Latter-day Saints. Salt Lake City: The Church of Jesus Christ of Latter-day Saints, 1985.

Jenson, Andrew. *History of the Scandinavian Mission.* New York: Arno Press, 1979.

Kipling, Rudyard. "If—." In *The Golden Treasury of Poetry.* Edited by Louis Untermeyer. New York: Golden Press, 1959.

Lee, Harold B. *The Teachings of Harold B. Lee.* Edited by Clyde Williams. Salt Lake City: Deseret Book, 1996.

Our Yesterdays: A History of Ephraim, Utah, 1854–1979. Edited by the Centennial Book Committee. Ephraim, Utah, Centennial Book Committee, 1979.

Pratt, Parley P. *Key to the Science of Theology.* Salt Lake City: Deseret Book, 1978.

Roe, Benson B. *Maverick among the Moguls: The Adventurous Career of a Pioneer Cardiac Surgeon.* Berkeley, Calif.: Creative Arts Book, 2002.

Smith, Joseph. *Teachings of the Prophet Joseph Smith.* Edited by Joseph Fielding Smith. Salt Lake City: Deseret Book, 1976.

The Wordsworth Dictionary of Quotations. Edited by Connie Robertson. Hertfordshire, England: Wordsworth Editions Ltd., 1997.

Widtsoe, John A. *Evidences and Reconciliations.* 3 vols. in one. Salt Lake City: Bookcraft, 1960.

Other Works Cited

"A Century and a Half of Shared Dedication." Solihull, England: United Kingdom/Ireland/Africa Area Public Affairs Office. 24 July 1987.

Cannon, George Q. *Millennial Star* 39 (17 September 1877): 743.

"Church Will Help Armenian Homeless." *Church News,* 19 August 1989, 3–4.

Gibbs, Josiah F. "Black Hawk's Last Raid—1866." *Utah Historical Quarterly* 4 (1931): 108.

Haslam, Gerald. "The Norwegian Experience with Mormonism, 1842–1920." Ph.D. dissertation, Brigham Young University, 1981.

Hinckley, Gordon B. "Some Thoughts on Temples, Retention of Converts, and Missionary Service." *Ensign,* November 1997, 49.

Hunsaker, Keith A. "The Life and Educational Contributions of Superintendent A. C. Nelson." Master's thesis, University of Utah, 1941.

Hunter, Howard W. "Exceeding Great and Precious Promises." *Ensign,* November 1994, 8.

Johnson, Anna S. D. "The Seventh Handcart Company." *The Relief Society Magazine* 35 (1948): 449–51, 501.

The Journal History of The Church of Jesus Christ of Latter-day Saints. LDS Historical Department Library.

Kimball, Spencer W. "Fundamental Principles to Ponder and Live." *Ensign,* November 1978, 43–44.

Lloyd, R. Scott, "Today We Are Taking a Historic Step." *Church News,* 29 May 1999, 3, 8–10.

Matthews, Thomas. "The Secret History of the War." *Newsweek,* 18 March 1991, 28–32, 36–39.

Metcalf, Warren. "A Precarious Balance: The Northern Utes and the Black Hawk War." *Utah Historical Quarterly* 57 (1989), 24–25.

Monson, Thomas S. "Thanks Be to God." *Ensign,* May 1989, 50–53.

Mormon Immigration Index Family History Resource File. Salt Lake City: The Church of Jesus Christ of Latter-day Saints, CD-Rom Library, 2000.

Packer, Boyd K. "Covenants." *Ensign,* May 1987, 24.

Spencer, Deloy J. "The Utah Black Hawk War, 1865–1871." Master's thesis, Utah State University, 1969.

Stevenson, Ford. "Church Marks 150 Years in Scandinavia." *Church News,* 15 July 2002, 8–10.

Stowe, Dorothy. "Film Makers Satisfy Europe's Curiosity." *Church News,* 11 November 1984, 10.

Swensen, Jason. "Freedman's Bank: Boosting Research for African-Americans." *Deseret News,* 3 March 2001, 3.

Todd, Jay M. "An Encore of the Spirit." *Ensign,* October 1991, 42–44.

INDEX

taking children on trips, 98–99; *Nelson News,* 99–101

Heart surgeon
Returns to Salt Lake City, 129; accepts position on faculty of University of Utah College of Medicine, 129–30; works as general surgeon, 130; continues research into development of pump-oxygenator, 130–31; performs first human open-heart surgery using oxygenator, 131–32; passes American Board of Thoracic Surgery examination, 132–33; receives local awards for pioneering contributions to open-heart surgery, 133; fails in efforts to save two children from same family, 133–34; receives Markle Foundation research grant, 134–35; resigns from University of Utah College of Medicine faculty, 134–35, 190; affiliates with LDS Hospital and Salt Lake Clinic, 135; receives Utah Heart Association and other research grants, 135; accepts Conrad B. Jenson as clinic associate, 135–36; leaves Salt Lake Clinic and forms partnership with Conrad B. Jenson, 136–37; serves as catalyst for development of LDS Hospital-University of Utah thoracic surgical residency program, 137–40; accepts Kent W. Jones into practice, 140; philosophy on role of doctor, 140; surgical mortality rate drops as promised in priesthood blessing, 146–47, 150–51; declines offer of faculty position at University of Chicago, 148–50; receives inspiration while performing surgery, 151; performs heart surgery on Spencer W. Kimball, 153–56; attends Spencer W.

Kimball during convalescence and upon deaths of Joseph Fielding Smith and Harold B. Lee, 156–58; writes letter to Spencer W. Kimball assuring him of good health, 158; attends international surgical and cardiovascular society meetings in Russia, 164–66; serves as visiting professor in Mexico City, Mexico, and Santiago, Chile, 177; serves as visiting professor in Montevideo, Uruguay, 179; *Ensign* assistant editor writes narrative of surgical procedure, 179–82; performs coronary bypass surgery on James E. Faust, 189–90; performs last open-heart operation in America, 190; makes presentation at American College of Surgeons conference, 193; role in saving life of David B. Haight, 204–5; attendance at surgery of M. Russell Ballard, 208; service to Ann Wirthlin Farnsworth, 208–9; attendance at surgery of Robert D. Hales, 210; meets Wu Yingkai, exchanges visiting medical professorships, 215–16; meets Zhang Zhengxiang, lectures and performs surgeries in China, 216–18; professional honors received, 353–61; letter of commendation from Spencer W. Kimball, 356

Photographs
With Dantzel in churchyard in Gørding, Denmark, *2;* in Sweden, *15;* with father Marion and son Russell Jr., *27;* at age two, *32;* at age twelve, *33;* family portrait 1935, *36;* with Dantzel at the University of Utah 1942, *45;* wedding portrait, *47;* with Dantzel just prior to engagement, *53;* family portrait 1982, *91;*

death of Spencer W. Kimball,
196–97; assigned to speak at
funeral of Spencer W. Kimball,
197; participates in reorganization
of First Presidency and Quorum of
the Twelve, 198; assigned as first
contact for Europe and Africa,
198–99; participates in Athens,
Greece district conference, 199;
speaks at Richard P. Condie
funeral, 199; serves as visiting
professor of surgery in China, 218;
journeys to China to perform
surgery on opera singer Fang
Rongxiang, 218–21; offers
apostolic prayer in China, meets
with Chinese leaders, 221–23;
organizes Beijing and Xi'an China
branches, 223; travels to China
with Dallin H. Oaks, meets with
Chinese government and religious
leaders, 223–26; baptizes and seals
Zhang Zhenxiang and Zhou
Quingguo, 226–27; hosts Chinese
officials at Polynesian Cultural
Center, 227–28; travels to China
with Neal A. Maxwell, meets with
Chinese leaders to learn how
Church can assist in China,
228–31; attends Hong Kong
regional conference with James E.
Faust, receives assurances of
religious freedom in Hong Kong,
231–32; dual ministry with Hans
B. Ringger in Eastern Europe,
245–46, 258; meets with Polish
government officials, 249;
dedicates chapel in Warsaw,
Poland, 250; meets with faithful
Saints in Czechoslovakia, 250;
meets with Miroslav Houstecky,
expresses Church's desire for
recognition in Czechoslovakia,
251; travels to Czechoslovakia to
meet with government and Church
leaders, 251, 252; presents Church

materials to government leaders in
Czechoslovakia, 252; travels to
Czechoslovakia, learns of official
Church recognition, offers
apostolic prayer, 252–54; meets
with East German leaders, receives
approval for missionaries, 256–57;
assists in realignment of mission
and stake boundaries in unified
Germany, 257–58; assigned as first
contact for Pacific Islands, 258;
travels to Hungary, offers
dedicatory prayer, and secures
cooperation of government officials
in establishing Church presence,
259–60; hosts Washington, D.C.,
reception for Hungarian officials,
261; travels to Hungary, learns of
official Church recognition, 261;
visits Hungary with Thomas S.
Monson, participates in television
interview, 261–62; visits
Yugoslavia, obtains cooperation of
government officials on key
concerns, 262–64; meets
Yugoslavian ambassador at
Washington, D.C., dinner, 265;
visits Moscow, meets with
government officials to discuss
legal recognition for Church,
268–69; travels to Moscow, signs
document pledging Church
support for program to aid
homeless in Armenia, 270–71;
hosts Washington, D.C., luncheon
for Yuri Dubinin, 271; meets with
mission presidents, announces
Church's decision to take gospel to
Russia and Baltic Republics, 272;
travels to Estonia, participates in
television interview, and dedicates
Estonia for preaching of the gospel,
272–74; visits Leningrad,
rededicates Russia for preaching of
the gospel, and holds fireside,
274–76; learns of official Church

recognition in Leningrad and Vyborg, 277; meets with Soviet officials visiting Salt Lake City, 277; holds fireside in Minsk, dedicates Belarus for preaching of the gospel, 277–78; performs sealing for Russian couple, 278–79; discusses gospel with Mikhail Gorbachev at Salt Lake City reception, 279; conducts series of priesthood leadership meetings in Eastern Europe, 280–81; hosts Salt Lake City luncheon for Russian dignitaries, 281; hosts Los Angeles breakfast for Ivan S. Silaev, 283–84; accompanies Tabernacle Choir on European tour, 283–88; hosts Washington, D.C., luncheon for Viktor G. Komplektov, 284; meets in Salt Lake Temple with Tabernacle Choir members, 284; meets with mayor of Friedrichsdorf, Germany, 285; presents fireside in Zürich, Switzerland, 285; assists Dallin H. Oaks in dedicating Armenia for preaching of the gospel, 286; attends ribbon-cutting ceremony, accepts gift of land for Church in Yerevan, Armenia, 286; visits Moscow, learns of official Church recognition throughout Republic of Russia, and transfers working relationship to Dallin H. Oaks, 287; travels to Romania, meets with government leaders, 289–90; visits Romania, pledges humanitarian aid in meetings with government leaders, 290–92; dedicates Romania for preaching of the gospel, 292; meets with Romanian leaders to discuss official Church recognition, 292; observes plight of Romanian orphans, organizes relief efforts, 292–93;

hosts Salt Lake City luncheon for Romanian dignitaries, 293–94; travels to Bulgaria, meets with government official, 294–95; visits Bulgaria, offers dedicatory prayer, meets with government and education leaders, and gives interview to local media, 295–96; attends Washington, D.C., dinner with Velichko Velichkov, 296; travels to Turkey, meets with government officials, 297–98; meets with head of Turkish State Archives to discuss Church's assistance with genealogical records, 298–99; visits Jordan, meets with government leaders, 299–300; meets with members and missionaries in Hong Kong and Malaysia, 301; meets with members in Thailand, pronounces blessing on nation, 301–2; meets with members and missionaries in India and Pakistan, 303; meets with University of Jordan officials, visits Mohammed Kamal, and travels to Mount Nebo, 303–5; visits Garden Tomb and Mount Tabor, meets with members in Jerusalem, 305–6; travels to Kenya with Richard G. Scott, meets with members and missionaries, 307; visits Zambia, meets with government leaders, and offers dedicatory prayer, 307–8; dedicates Namibia for preaching of the gospel, 308–9; travels to Republic of Congo with Richard G. Scott, assists in dedication, 309; visits Ivory Coast with Richard G. Scott, meets with government officials and members, 309–10; travels to Ghana with Richard G. Scott, meets with members and missionaries, 310–11; dedicates Accra Ghana Temple site, meets